Creating Web Portals with BEA WebLogic

HOWARD BLOCK, ROB CASTLE, AND DAVID HRITZ

Creating Web Portals with BEA WebLogic

ISBN (pbk): 1-59059-069-4

Printed and bound in the United States of America 12345678910

Technical Reviewer: Gregory Smith
Editorial Directors: Dan Appleman, Gary Cornell, Jason Gilmore, Simon Hayes, Martin Streicher, Karen Watterson, John Zukowski
Managing Editor: Grace Wong
Project Manager and Development Editor: Tracy Brown Collins
Copy Editor: Ami Knox
Compositor: Susan Glinert
Artist and Cover Designer: Kurt Krames
Indexer: Valerie Robbins
Production Manager: Kari Brooks
Manufacturing Manager: Tom Debolski

Distributed to the book trade in the United States by Springer-Verlag New York, Inc., 175 Fifth Avenue, New York, NY, 10010 and outside the United States by Springer-Verlag GmbH & Co. KG, Tiergartenstr. 17, 69112 Heidelberg, Germany.

In the United States, phone 1-800-SPRINGER, email orders@springer-ny.com, or visit http://www.springer-ny.com.

Outside the United States, fax +49 6221 345229, email orders@springer.de, or visit http://www.springer.de.

For information on translations, please contact Apress directly at 2560 9th Street, Suite 219, Berkeley, CA 94710. Phone 510-549-5930, fax: 510-549-5939, email info@apress.com, or visit http://www.apress.com.

The source code for this book is available to readers at http://www.apress.com in the Downloads section.

I would like to dedicate this book to several people. First to my love, best friend, and soul mate, Marsha, I want to thank for all the love and support you have given me. You have really made a difference in my life.

To my son, Scott, I want to thank for putting a smile to my face every time I see you.

To my parents, Larry and Charlotte, my brother, Michael, my business partner, Mark, and my many friends, I want to thank for all the support you have given me over the last two years. They weren't the easiest and it was nice having all of your support.

—Howard Block

I would like to dedicate this book to my family. To my lovely wife Rita, whose support in this effort was invaluable, thank you for allowing me the time to work on this book. And to my boys Chad, Joshua, and Drew, I couldn't ask for better children. Thank you all for being patient through all the nights and weekends of writing and never-ending revisions.

—Rob Castle

A most sincere thank you to my fiancée, Stephanie, whose love, thoughtfulness, and support made this possible. I eagerly anticipate our marriage and our life together. I also wish to thank my parents, George and Teresa, for all they have taught me in life. Your generosity, compassion, and wisdom are gifts that I carry close to my heart.

—David Hritz

Contents at a Glance

Contents

Foreword

PORTAL SOFTWARE CONTINUES to mature and become a more strategic part of the common enterprise application infrastructure. Just as application servers have become an accepted way for most enterprises to make their applications and content available to the Web, many companies are now coming to the conclusion that portal servers are an excellent way to provide a common and secure user interface to an enterprise.

The increased adoption of portal software along with technology advances has provided increased requirements from customers for portal solutions. These factors have combined to drive the fast-paced evolution of the portal market from first generation, prepackaged, content-centric "mysites" to next-generation solutions that provided dynamic and secure provisioning of applications, content, and business processes to multiple audiences.

Technology trends also favor the continued adoption of portal solutions that complement enterprise application infrastructure. These trends include improvements in Web services, XML- and J2EE-based standards that increase the flexibility for creating enterprise applications. All of these mechanisms will provide improved ways for developers to build loosely coupled standards-based applications that can communicate with users or other applications internal or external to the enterprise.

It is also important to understand that portal solutions, at their best, are meant to drive development and maintenance costs down. An enterprise portal solution should provide returns on investments by allowing a company to consolidate and leverage the many applications it already owns as well as develop new applications. Today, many companies have been able to use portal software to solve their 10, 20, or 100 Web site problems by consolidating these silos of information into a common portal framework. Consolidation can allow a company to reduce its overall total cost of ownership for maintaining these multiple corporate Web sites by providing developers a common portal framework and extensible portal services for building applications and portals as well as application components that can be reused across audience-specific portals.

BEA WebLogic Portal is built on the market leading J2EE-based application server, BEA WebLogic Server. WebLogic Portal provides an enterprise portal solution that includes a flexible portal framework, extensible portal service, portal and Web service development tools, and portal administration tools. This combination of features combined with a highly scalable architecture provides a flexible solution for quickly implementing a portal solution. Also, because of its standards-based and open design, WebLogic Portal provides the developer increased flexibility to deliver the optimal solution as your application and portal needs in change with your business requirements.

The acceptance of BEA WebLogic Portal in providing just this type of solution is evident from the many customer successes using the product and from being recognized by several industry awards, including

- *Java Pro* Readers' Choice, Best Java Enterprise Portal Server, 2002

- *Transform Magazine,* Product of the Year, Enterprise Content & Collaboration Technologies, 2002

- *InfoWorld*'s Portal Technology of the Year, 2001

- Software Industry and Information Association Best Enterprise Portal, 2001

In my own career I have had the opportunity to work in many areas of the software development life cycle. These roles have included implementing software, providing development consulting, and developing enterprise software at several companies. The common error made across all of these projects is that development teams do not take the time to fully understand the project or business requirements. This lack of initial investment generally means that developers are not able to fully maximize the use of the chosen software solution's capabilities.

This book provides the developer an overview of the features and concepts needed to successfully leverage the capabilities of BEA WebLogic Portal 7.0. The introductory chapters lay the foundation for understanding the architecture and services that are available to the portal development team. After learning about the portal services available, developers can explore detailed explanations to gain deeper understanding of how these features can be used to best meet their requirements.

Shane Pearson
Director of Product Management
BEA WebLogic Portal

About the Authors

Howard Block is a founder and principal of NuWave Solutions. During his 18 plus years in the computer consulting industry, Howard has played many roles including office leader, technical director, project manager, and system architect. He has coauthored technology books and is a frequent speaker at major computer conferences. Howard oversees the system architecture design for customer projects and teaches Java and application server technology classes. Howard has a masters degree in computer science from Johns Hopkins University and a B.S. degree in information systems management from the University of Maryland, Baltimore County.

Rob Castle is a principal at NuWave Solutions. He has over 16 years of experience in the computer industry including stints as program manager, project management, system architect, and lead developer for many large application development efforts. At NuWave Solutions, Rob's leadership responsibilities include strategic planning, sales, and recruiting. Additionally, Rob has program management and system architecture responsibilities for strategic customer engagements and is a certified trainer. He also codeveloped and maintains a cross-platform J2EE framework that greatly enhances the development process, and is used on several projects at NuWave Solutions. Prior to NuWave Solutions, Rob has lead major development efforts at Metamor Technologies, Per-Se Technologies, and AON Consulting. Rob graduated summa cum laude from Elon College with a B.A. degree in mathematics.

David Hritz is an Architect at NuWave Solutions. He has 5 years of experience in the software industry where he has played the role of developer, lead developer, technical lead, and architect. At NuWave Solutions, David dictates coding standards and design for each project. He also codeveloped and maintains a cross-platform J2EE framework that greatly enhances the development process, and is used on several projects at NuWave Solutions. David graduated cum laude from Indiana University of Pennsylvania with a B.S. degree in computer science.

About the Technical Reviewer

Gregory P. Smith is a lead software engineer at BEA Systems, Inc. on the BEA WebLogic Portal team. Having been a technical lead on the original BEA WebLogic Personalization Server, he personally developed the Content services in the product and guided the direction of the personalization advisor. He then led the design and development of the BEA Campaign Manager for WebLogic, which became the Portal Campaign services. He is involved in the general architecture of the BEA WebLogic Portal, and is currently focusing on the portal developer experience.

Prior to working at BEA, Greg was a lead consultant at Avitek, LLC, an Authorized Java Center software consulting company that was purchased by BEA in 1999, where he led development teams for custom Java solutions. Before Avitek, Greg worked at BDM Technologies, which became the TRW Commercial Technologies Internet/Intranet Group when TRW purchased BDM. At TRW, Greg developed custom software solutions with distributed computing technologies (CORBA and CGI).

Greg graduated from the University of Colorado at Boulder with a B.S. in applied mathematics (emphasis in computer science).

Acknowledgments

THE AUTHORS OF THIS BOOK would like to send special thanks to the following people who helped to make this effort happen:

To Mark Keyser, his support in this project has been invaluable. To John Zukowski for making this effort a reality. To Mary Reeping for her editorial advice and feedback. To Greg Smith for the incredible job in reviewing the book for technical correctness. His valuable feedback helped make the book more informative. To the Apress team of Tracy Brown, Ami Knox, and Kari Brooks for their excellent guidance throughout the writing process. Their counsel helped make this book a success.

Introduction

THE TERM *PORTAL* means different things to different people. If you asked ten people what a portal was, you would probably get ten different answers because portal terminology has become very generic and abused. The portal concept and technology is rapidly emerging and changing, making it increasingly important to understand and focus on the various types of portals and their appropriate roles and applications.

What Is a Portal?

Portals can be classified into the following types:

- Internet public or mega portals

- Intranet corporate or enterprise portals

- Extranet e-business portals

These different portal types are described next.

Internet Public or Mega Portals

These types of portals are focused on building large online audiences with large demographics or professional orientation. Examples of these types of portals are Yahoo, MSN, AOL, etc. These types of portals provide changing content, collaboration, and a user community for a targeted group.

Intranet Corporate or Enterprise Portals

These portals are usually designed around business processes, activities, and communities to improve the access, processing, and sharing of structured and unstructured information within and across the enterprise. These portals also incorporate roles, processes, workflow, collaboration, content management, data warehousing and marts, enterprise applications, and business intelligence. Corporate or enterprise (intranet) portals enable companies to access internally stored information, and provide users with a single gateway to corporate information and knowledge to make informed business decisions.

Extranet e-Business Portals

These types of portals are focused on the ability to tie an enterprise to its customers. An example of this type of portal is a business-to-consumer (B2C) portal, which extends the enterprise to its customers for the purpose of ordering, billing, customer service, self-service, etc. Another example of this portal is a business-to-business (B2B) portal, which extends the enterprise to its suppliers and partners. B2B portals are transforming the supplier and value chain process and relationships.

Evolving Portal Technology

Several years ago when a company wanted to build any type of portal, that company had to build it from scratch. The authors of this book built PlanetGov.com several years ago, a portal for the federal government that contained functionality similar to Yahoo but focused on the government. When this site was built, portal software was just starting to become reality. A proprietary portal framework was used to build PlanetGov.com. This framework contained some of the services any portal architecture should provide such as

- Personalization services

- Security services

- Content management services

- Caching services

- Data access services

Many companies built their own portal frameworks similar to the framework used by PlanetGov.com to support their portals. As time evolved, vendors saw that there was a need for portal frameworks that enabled companies to build portals without having to first create their own portal frameworks. Vendors have taken two approaches when building a portal framework. The first approach is to build a portal framework that is supported across several application servers. Companies such as PlumTree, BroadVision, and SilverStream have built portal frameworks that fall into this category. In addition, many of these products include libraries of prebuilt code that are available for free or for an additional charge. The second approach is for application server vendors to build their own portal frameworks. The BEA WebLogic Portal is an example of this type of approach. These vendors typically build their portal frameworks around their application servers, meaning that they take advantage of the internals of their application server technology.

Additional benefits are that new releases of a portal framework typically occur faster because the same company supports both products. One negative about the first approach is that anytime there is a new release of an application server, there might be a delay in a new release of the portal framework.

Which approach is best? That is a hard answer that should be based on the individual requirements of the organization looking to build a portal. If the organization supports several application servers and cannot standardize on one, the first approach might be the best. On the other hand, if your organization is standardized on one application server, the second approach might be the best, because as new versions of the application server are released, new releases of the portal framework will be available in a timelier manner. Additionally, vendors like BEA have started to make it easy to integrate other portals such as a WebSphere portal using the Portlet Web Services Wizard to bring that functionality into a WebLogic Portal.

Services Provided in a Portal

Any portal solution should provide many of the services needed to support the development and implementation of a portal. By providing services, organizations can concentrate on meeting the requirements of the portal they are building and not on building the underlying services. Any portal solution should support some of the services detailed next.

Presentation Services

This layer of a portal framework deals with the presentation of the portal components/portlets to the end users and serves as the Web interface. Components/portlets are executed and return HTML that is organized by the Presentation service into an HTML page for display to the end user in a browser.

Infrastructure Services

Infrastructure services provide basic services such as load balancing, caching, high availability, and performance that are provided by the Web server environment, as well as the underlying security infrastructure.

Security Services

Security services provide authentication services (user name/password management, LDAP synchronization, single sign-on, groups, etc.). This also consists of authorization services, which map the roles and privileges of end users to individual security policies and to domains of content within the portal. While the infrastructure for managing authorizations is provided at this level, end users typically set up the security for individual components/portlets via the Administration/Management services.

Administration/Management Services

Administration/Management services are necessary for the portal to be easily administered and supported, allowing administrators to configure the portal framework and configure, manage, and support the environment. Administration services are offered through a Web interface in many portals, and in some cases there is a separate client/server program that makes administration easy. These services might include user management, configuration management, role management, registration of modules, and information services.

Access and Integration Services

Many portals need access to back-end databases and applications. Services that are seamless and easy to use are needed to provide this support. This functionality is offered to the portal, and even to individual components/portlets. This layer may tie into existing applications to get access to certain back-end adapters or APIs.

Content Management Services

Content management is an important part of most portals built. Content management services deal with the management of unstructured data within the portal. This can include a full text indexing engine so that content and its metadata can be searched, a set of crawlers that are capable of navigating and indexing existing content, a metadata repository, and a content management system to allow for the submittal and approval of content into the portal.

Collaboration Services

Collaboration services allow end users of the portal to work together more effectively by establishing shared workspaces, shared document repositories, interaction in real-time, and shared discussion forums. Collaboration services also allow for the definition and execution of workflow across the enterprise and outside the enterprise to different content sources and back-end systems.

Development Services

Development services form an environment that allows for the development of custom portals, custom portal modules, or components/portlets. Many times these components/portlets are written using JSPs. Development services also include the supporting tools and methodologies.

Personalization Services

Personalization services allow for the portal to target specific content to particular users. For example, you might have content in your portal about a sale for a particular store on or before the date of the sale. Or you might wish to display an advertisement for new products to a visitor who has previously purchased products that were similar to the ones being advertised. The use of personalization services greatly reduces the effort needed to maintain a personalized site because these services will help you maintain the necessary information needed to personalize it.

The BEA WebLogic Portal

The BEA WebLogic Portal is a robust portal architecture that gives any organization the ability to build robust portals. It supports many of the services just described. The BEA WebLogic Portal classifies those services as the following:

- *Portal services:* A single solution for creating, deploying, and managing enterprise portals

- *Campaign services:* Provide the ability to target advertising, e-mail, and product discounts within a portal

- *Commerce services:* Support e-commerce functions such as shopping carts, product catalogs, transaction management, and order fulfillment

- *Personalization services:* Deliver dynamic and personalized content

By using these services, you will be able to build very robust applications that will support all your organization's needs. We have developed several large portals using the BEA WebLogic Portal. This book focuses on the learning experiences and wisdom we have gained deploying these portals. When you have finished reading this book, you should have a good understanding of everything you need to develop a functional portal using the BEA WebLogic Portal. This book is geared toward developers who are looking for a book that provides all the necessary information needed to build a portal using the BEA WebLogic Portal. It is written from a developer's perspective and will help you understand everything that is necessary to build a portal from scratch using the BEA WebLogic Portal. We hope you enjoy reading this book and gain all the knowledge you are seeking.

About This Book

This book goes into details on the BEA WebLogic Portal. Some of the topics this book covers are the following:

- *Introduction to the BEA WebLogic Portal:* Our opening chapter covers how the BEA WebLogic Portal is architected as well as basic portal concepts such as a portal page, a layout, skins, and portlets. Finally, we introduce you to the E-Business Control Console (EBCC).

- *Building a portal from scratch:* We discuss the file structure of a BEA WebLogic Portal, the database tables used for metadata, and steps for creating a portal from scratch.

- *Basic Java concepts:* Here you can find the basic concepts of Servlets, JSPs, and JavaBeans.

- *Introduction to portlets and portal pages:* We discuss what a portlet is, how to build a basic portlet, extending the JSP, using taglibs within a portlet, and finally what a portal page is. We also show you how to begin building an application using the BEA WebLogic Portal.

- *How to customize the look and feel of a portal:* We show you the flow of JSPs, the different JSPs in the framework directory, skins, layouts, and modifying the different JSPs to customize their look and feel.

- *Content management:* We discuss when to use BEA Content Manager, database tables and file directories for content, displaying content using content taglibs, and content selectors.

- *Webflow:* We explain the details of Webflow, including Input Processors and Pipeline Components, and demonstrate its implementation in examples for portlet navigation and input processing.

- *Front Controllers:* As an alternative to using Webflow, we explain how to implement a Front Controller strategy as a standardized methodology for application processing.

- *EJBs within the portal:* We show you how to build an EJB within the portal, how to register an EJB, and implementation within a portlet.

- *Security:* We cover what security roles are, users and user groups, portal permissions, managing security, implementing security.

- *Deployment:* You learn about the deployment process, establishing deployment environments, and how to deploy a BEA WebLogic Portal.

- *Personalization:* We discuss how you can use the BEA WebLogic Portal for personalization.

- *Campaign Services:* We show you what a campaign is and how you can set up a campaign.

- *Miscellaneous Topics:* We include a few topics that don't warrant an entire chapter of their own but are important nonetheless in putting together a solid corporate portal. These topics include content management configuration, JSP configuration, using connection pools, and configuring e-mail.

- *Debugging:* We walk through the process of instrumenting Java code for debugging, demonstrate the process of debugging your code via a traditional debugger while it is running inside of the portal, and explore the logging mechanism of BEA WebLogic Portal.

- *Best Practices:* We discuss many best practices for every stage of portal development.

Intended Audience

This book was written for application developers. Whether you have just started using the BEA WebLogic Portal or have been using the product for a while, this book should give you a good foundation for building portal applications using the BEA WebLogic Portal. You will find examples included in this book to guide you through the many facets of BEA WebLogic Portal.

CHAPTER 1

Introduction to BEA WebLogic Portal

THE **BEA WEBLOGIC PORTAL** simplifies development of Web portal applications, enables personalization, supports the creation of business processes, and allows for easy access to information. BEA, as a vendor, has chosen to build its own portal framework using the BEA WebLogic application server. As we discuss in more detail a little later in this chapter, it has many of the basic services that any robust portal should have, such as the following:

- Presentation services

- Infrastructure services

- Security services

- Administration/Management services

- Access and Integration services

- Content Management services

- Development services

The BEA WebLogic Portal supports these basic services by providing a robust portal framework. This framework can be broken down into four categories:

- Portal services

- Campaign services

- Commerce services

- Personalization services

Together these different services offer any portal developer the ability to build very sophisticated portal applications.

This chapter gives you a high-level understanding of all the different pieces that together form the BEA WebLogic Portal. We discuss the BEA WebLogic architecture first. Next, we explain some basic concepts that you need to know when building a portal such as portal pages, portlets, skins, and layouts. Finally, we cover in depth some of the portal tools such as the BEA E-Business Control Center (EBCC), Administration Tools, and the BEA WebLogic Console. These tools are important when developing portal applications using BEA WebLogic Portal.

High-Level Architecture

The BEA WebLogic Portal sits on top of the BEA WebLogic Server and comprises four different services. As mentioned, these services are

- *Portal services:* Services that allow for the creation, deployment, and management of a portal. This includes User Interface and Presentation services.

- *Campaign services:* Services that provide the ability to target advertising, e-mail, and product discounts within a portal.

- *Commerce services:* Services that support e-commerce functions such as shopping carts, product catalogs, transaction management, and order fulfillment.

- *Personalization services:* Services that help deliver dynamic and personalized content. This includes Content Management and User/Group Management services.

A WebLogic Domain sits on top of the BEA WebLogic Portal framework, as shown in Figure 1-1. A *domain* is a grouping of applications, application components, JDBC connection pools, servers, other objects, and the administration tools needed to manage the portal applications.

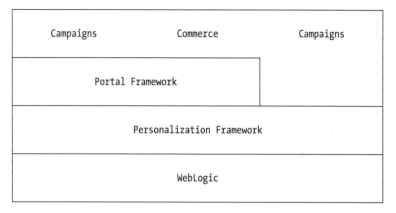

Figure 1-1. BEA WebLogic Portal services

The architecture of the BEA WebLogic Portal is designed so that the developer builds or uses the following:

- Java Server Pages (JSPs, used in portlets)

- Enterprise JavaBeans (EJBs)

- Java classes/tag libraries

- Content

- Security

- Data

Later chapters of this book explain how to use JSPs, EJBs, Java classes/tag libraries, content, and security to build portal applications using the BEA WebLogic Portal.

The WebLogic Portal uses metadata stored in a database to support the functionality of the portal framework. When you install the BEA WebLogic Portal, a default portal database is installed.

NOTE   *Please see the BEA WebLogic Portal installation procedures for further instructions on how to install it.*

The default database is a PointBase database.

 NOTE *To install a portal database that you can use with another database program such as Oracle, please see the BEA WebLogic Portal setup documentation.*

Table 1-1 lists some examples of the tables that compose the portal database.

Table 1-1. Sample Tables in Portal Database

PORTAL SERVICE	TABLE
Portal	PORTLET
	SKIN
	LAYOUT
Campaign	DISCOUNT
	MAIL_ADDRESS
Commerce	WLCS_PRODUCT
	WLCS_PRODUCT_CATEGORY
Personalization	PORTAL_P13N
	PORTAL_P13N_LAYOUT
	PORTAL_P13N_SKIN_POOL
	USER_SECURITY
	USER_PROFILE

Later chapters further explain how many of these tables are used within the BEA WebLogic Portal and its services.

Portal Concepts

In order to develop an application that uses the BEA WebLogic Portal, you first need to understand some basic concepts. This section is meant to give you a high-level understanding of these concepts. Later chapters go into these concepts in more detail.

Group Portal

A *group portal* is a collection of resources designed for use by a specific group of visitors. Any given portal Web application can support multiple group portals, each of which is an instantiation of a larger, single portal. An example of this is a portal that provides information for a specific company. Three types of groups are needed for this portal:

- External company users

- Internal company users

- Company administrators

Within the portal, you can maintain one collection of resources, yet provide the different groups access to different sets of resources. You set up these groups in the Administration Tools. Figure 1-2 shows an example of managing a group.

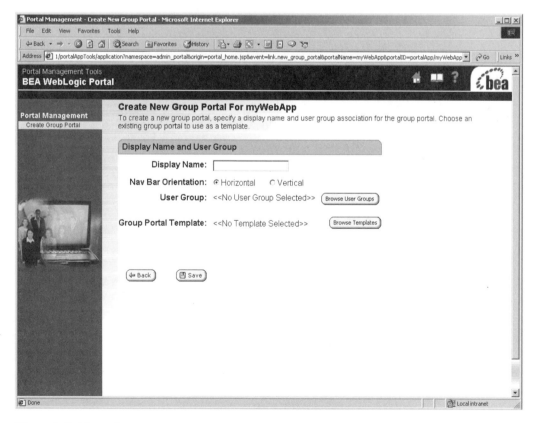

Figure 1-2. Managing a group

Portal Page

A *portal page* is a portal construct for creating Web pages for your application. You use the EBCC to indicate the portlets that you want to display on a portal page. This information is then saved as metadata in the portal database. Figure 1-3 shows an example of how you use the EBCC to define what portlets will be available for a portal page.

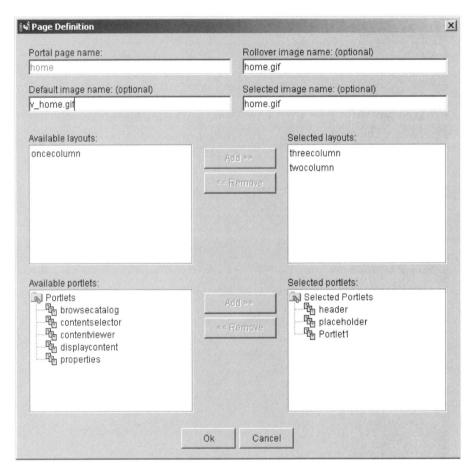

Figure 1-3. Setting up a portal page in the EBCC

When you enter a URL such as http://www.nuwavesolutions.com/nuportal/application?pageid="aboutus" in your browser, you are asking the portal to display the portal page aboutus (see Figure 1-4).

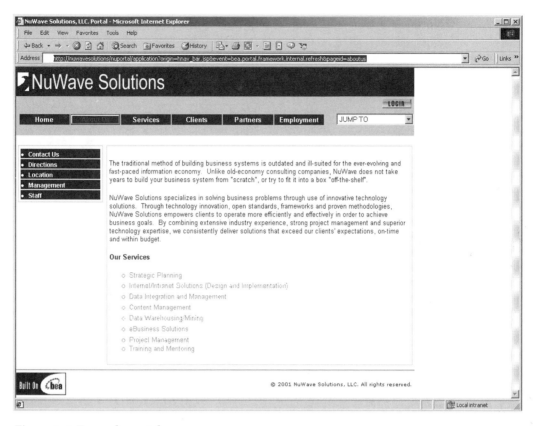

Figure 1-4. Example portal page

The BEA WebLogic Portal has a Presentation service that is driven by Webflow (all processors and presentation nodes for the portal itself can be found in the portal.wf Webflow file) and is accessed by a servlet, PortalWebflowServlet, with the name "application".

NOTE   *Actually, "application" is the default. You can define any
name in the web.xml file as follows:*

```
<!-- Portal webflow servlet -->
<servlet>
     <servlet-name>portalwebflow</servlet-name>
     <servlet-class>com.bea.portal.appflow.servlets.internal.
PortalWebflowServlet
     </servlet-class>
</servlet>
<servlet-mapping>
     <servlet-name>portalwebflow</servlet-name>
     <url-pattern>/application/*</url-pattern>
</servlet-mapping>
```

When you pass a query parameter of pageid=aboutus, you are telling
the Presentation service servlet to look in the portal metadata stored in the
PORTAL_PAGE and PORTAL_PAGE_P13N tables in the portal database for information on the page such as portlets, skins, and styles. The Presentation service
will use this information to form the page requested and display it in the user's
browser.

Layouts

A *layout* is the predefined setup for the portal page to be displayed. A set of
portlets can be arranged on a given layout in one page, and reused or reshuffled
on the same or a different layout for a different page. You set up the different layouts based on the design of the different pages you want to display. Through the
EBCC, you can assign all the layouts that can be used by a portal page and specify
which is the default layout. Figure 1-5 shows how you can use the Administration
Tools to set up a layout and indicate where each portlet will be placed in that
layout.

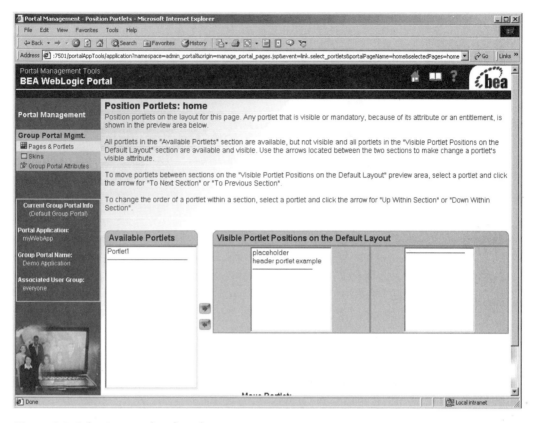

Figure 1-5. Selecting portlets for a layout

The layout used in this example is named twocolumn and was selected as the default, as shown earlier in Figure 1-3.

Portlets

A *portlet* is the component within a portal that gives the portal its functionality. In its simplest form, a portlet is a JSP and some metadata that determines how the portlet will be positioned and formatted within a portal page (JSP). Think of a portlet as component or self-contained container that is used to perform some unit of work. Once a portlet has been written (the details of which are discussed later in this book), the EBCC is used to register the portlet with the portal. Figure 1-6 shows an example of a portlet within the EBCC.

NOTE *Chapter 3 goes into details of Java Server Pages (JSPs).*

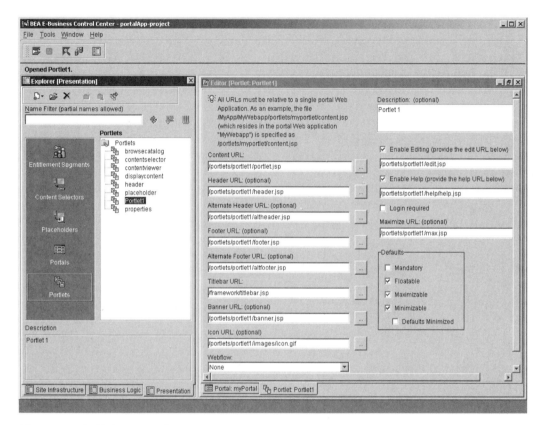

Figure 1-6. Defining a portlet

As you can see, you are asked to enter information about the portlet. The meta information for a portal and portlet are stored in XML files (*.portal and *.portlet, respectively). These files are then "data synched' using the EBCC, and the relationships between portal, portal pages, and portlets are stored in the portal database along with the XML reference. The tables used to store this metadata are PORTLET, PORTLET_P13N, and PORTLET_PLACEHOLDER.

A portlet can be designated as a separate JSP page. You can define the following for each portlet:

- *Header:* Displays a header for the portlet

- *Footer:* Displays a footer for the portlet

- *Titlebar:* Defines a titlebar for the portlet

- *Banner:* Defines the banner for the portlet

- *Icon:* Associates an icon if you are using a titlebar

- *Content:* Indicates the actual JSP that will perform some task

You can also define which Webflow (if any) should control the portlet's behavior. The portlet Webflow includes the ability to respond to requests to minimize, maximize, edit, and refresh the portlet.

An example portlet showing all of the aforementioned attributes is shown in Figure 1-7. Please note that creating a header, footer, titlebar, banner, icon, and content is discussed in greater detail in Chapters 5 and 6.

Figure 1-7. Portlet example

Portlets can also have the following properties that allow them to possess special characteristics:

- *Editable:* User can edit and save the content of the body page.

- *Floatable:* Portlet can be displayed outside the portal container in a separate browser window.

- *Minimizable:* The user can minimize the portlet.

- *Helpable:* The user can open online help from within the portlet.

Figure 1-8 shows a portlet that has maximize and minimize icons.

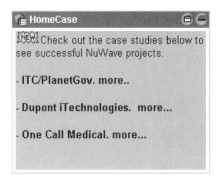

Figure 1-8. Portlet example with maximize and minimize icons

If a user clicks the maximize icon, then the portlet is maximized as shown in Figure 1-9.

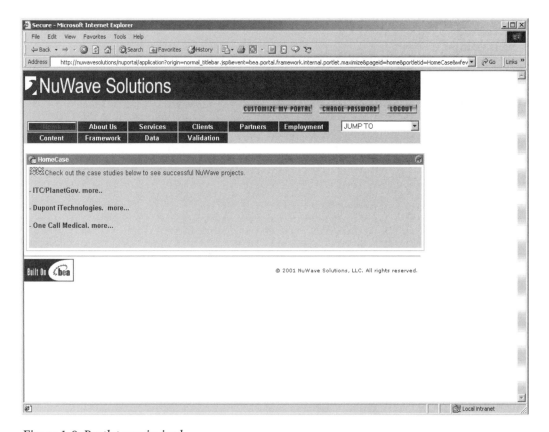

Figure 1-9. Portlet maximized

Portal Tools

The BEA WebLogic Portal comes with several portal tools that help set up, manage, and deploy any portal. We cover the following portal tools at a high level in the next sections so you understand all the different things you can do with these tools:

- The BEA E-Business Control Center

- Administration Tools

- The BEA WebLogic Console

We discuss these tools in greater detail throughout the remainder of this book.

The BEA E-Business Control Center

The BEA E-Business Control Center, or EBCC, is a tool designed to simplify the tasks that are necessary to create and maintain a portal. You can access this tool by selecting Start ➤ Programs ➤ BEA WebLogic Platform 7.0 ➤ WebLogic Portal 7.0 ➤ E-Business Control Center. You can also locate the file ebccw.exe in the bea70\weblogic700\ebcc\bin directory.

The EBCC has three tabs at the bottom (see Figure 1-10):

- Site Infrastructure

- Business Logic

- Presentation

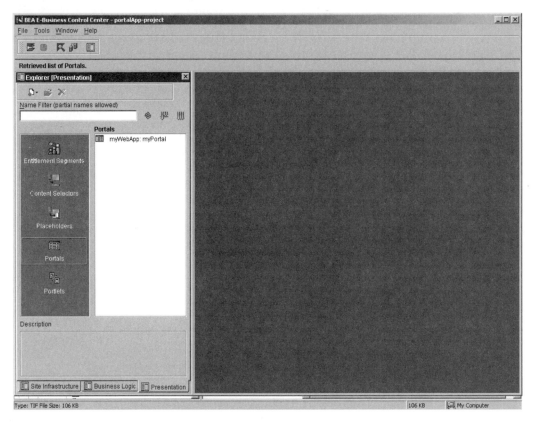

Figure 1-10. E-Business Control Center

In the following sections, we take a look at the properties these tabs control.

Site Infrastructure

The following can be maintained in the Site Infrastructure tab:

- *User Profiles:* This is where you define name/value pairs (a property set) that apply to a user and group profiles.

- *HTTP Requests:* Here you define name/value pairs (a property set) that apply to HTTP requests.

- *HTTP Sessions:* This is where you define name/value pairs (a property set) that apply to HTTP sessions.

- *Catalog Structure:* Here you define name/value pairs (a property set) that specify custom attributes for product items and product categories in the Commerce services catalog. These custom attributes can be used in addition to the default attributes provided by Commerce services in the catalog database tables.

NOTE *During the registration of any property set, you specify the property set's name, description, and one or more properties. Each property has a range, type of permissible value, and default value.*

- *Events:* Here you define name/value pairs (a property set) needed to register a custom event. For the purpose of registering an event, you can consider an event property as a name-value pair.

NOTE *We discuss details on property sets and how they are used in later chapters of the book.*

- *Webflow:* This is where you define mechanisms designed to help you build Web applications that maintain a separation between presentation logic and the underlying business processes. It is optional for a portlet to use a Webflow.

Business Logic

The following can be maintained in the Business Logic tab:

- *Campaigns:* A campaign is a set of circumstances under which certain actions are taken such as placing an ad in a placeholder, sending an e-mail after a user registers, or offering a discount based on the number of products bought. This is where you set up the business rules to react to events that occur based on certain circumstances.

- *Discounts:* This area of the Business Logic tab allows for the setup of discounts that can be used independently or in a campaign. An example of a discount that could be used would be a 20 percent discount for anyone buying an order that totals $100.00.

- *Segments:* Use segments to classify users according to values of properties in their user profiles.

Presentation

The following can be maintained in the Presentation tab:

- *Entitlement Segments:* This tool lets you determine which users or groups see specific portal content.

- *Content Selectors:* Using content selectors, you can specify conditions under which the WebLogic Portal or WebLogic Personalization Server retrieves one or more documents from your content management system.

- *Placeholders:* These are targets for content searches. Many times a placeholder is employed for ads that are displayed to users.

- *Portals:* When you create a new portal definition, you associate metadata for elements such as skins, portlets, pages, layouts, and Webflow mechanisms.

- *Portlets:* When you create a new portlet definition, you associate metadata for elements such as title bars, headers, and Webflow mechanisms.

Administration Tools

The Administration Tools allow you to perform user management, catalog management, order management, payment management, and portal management. Figure 1-11 shows the entry point for the initial Administration Tools Web page.

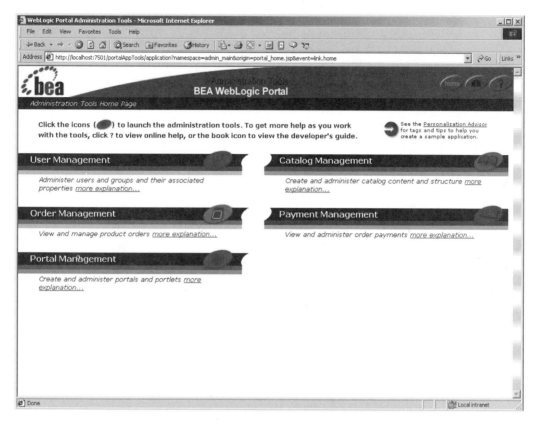

Figure 1-11. Administration Tools

You can access this tool by going into your browser and entering
http://*hostname*:*port*/portalAppTools, where *hostname* is the DNS name or IP
address of the Administration Server and *port* is the address of the port on which
the Administration Server is listening for requests. If you are running locally, your
server would be localhost and your port defaults to 7501.

NOTE   *The user ID and password for this tool defaults to "adminis-*
trator" and "password", respectively.

Next, we give you a quick tour of the different features available through the Administration Tools.

User Management

Figure 1-12 shows the User Management page. This tool allows you to do three things:

- Edit users

- Edit groups

- Clean up realms

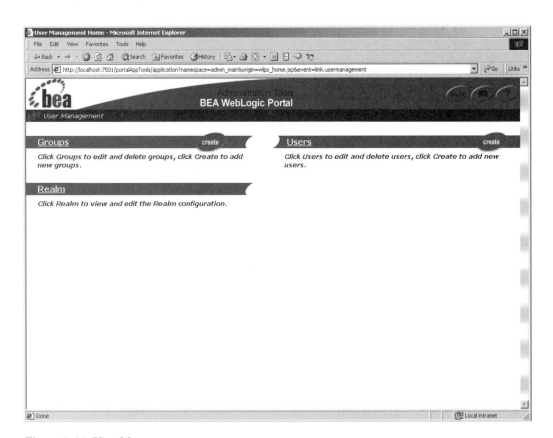

Figure 1-12. User Management page

Catalog Management

Figure 1-13 shows the Catalog Management page. This tool allows you to do the following:

- Create, edit, and remove categories

- Create, edit, and remove product items

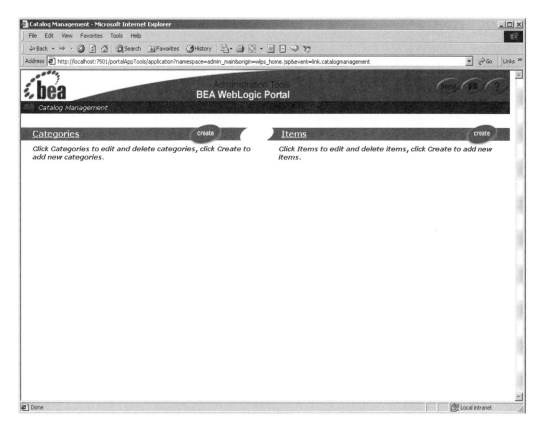

Figure 1-13. Catalog Management page

The categories and products you maintain in this tool are used by the Commerce services of the BEA WebLogic Portal as shown in Figures 1-14 and 1-15.

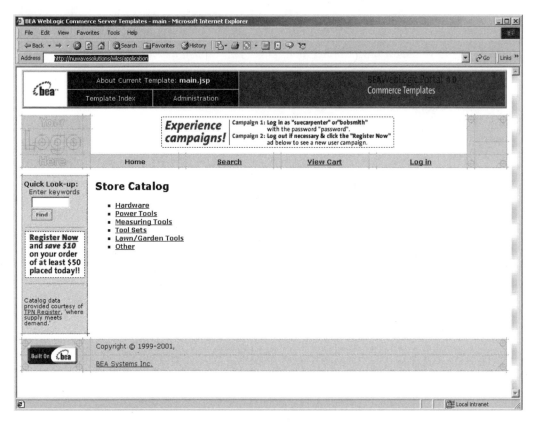

Figure 1-14. Maintain categories displayed through the Catalog Management page

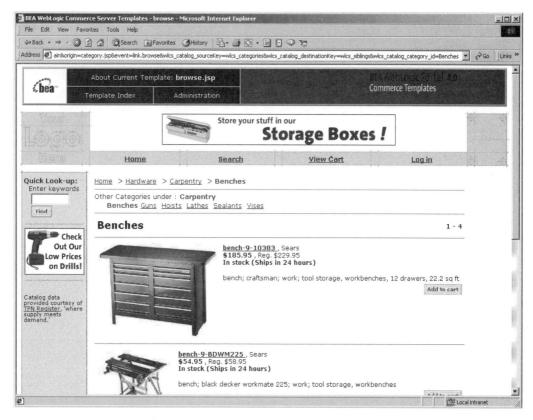

Figure 1-15. Maintain products displayed through the Catalog Management page

Order Management

Figure 1-16 shows the Order Management page. This tool allows you to search orders three ways:

- Search by customer

- Search by order identifier

- Search by date range

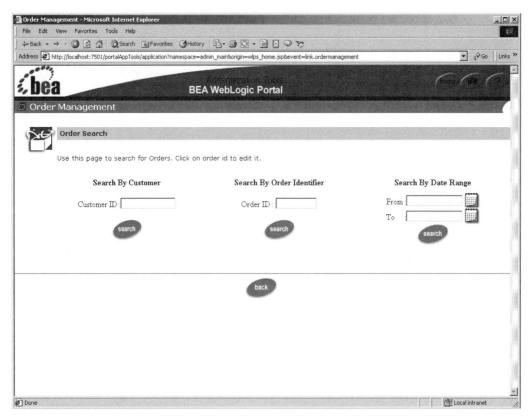

Figure 1-16. Order Management page

Payment Management

Figure 1-17 shows the Payment Management page.

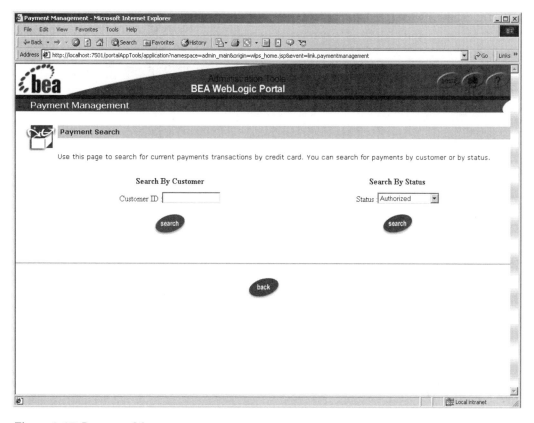

Figure 1-17. Payment Management page

This tool allows you to search payments two ways:

- Search by customer

- Search by status

Portal Management

Figure 1-18 shows the Portal Management page.

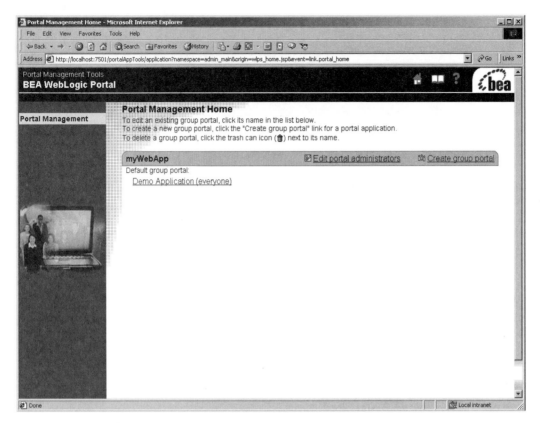

Figure 1-18. Portal Management page

This tool allows you to manage the portals you have deployed. With this tool, you can handle such things as skins, pages, layouts, portlets, user management, and group management for the specified portal.

The BEA WebLogic Console

The BEA WebLogic Console is a Web browser-based graphical user interface for managing WebLogic Servers. This console allows you to manage one or more domains containing multiple WebLogic Server instances and applications with a single domain being the active domain. Its management capabilities include configuration, stopping and starting servers, monitoring server performance, monitoring application performance, viewing server logs, and editing application deployment descriptors.

If you want to run the BEA WebLogic Console, go to your browser and enter the URL http://*hostname*:*port*/console, where *hostname* is the DNS name or IP address of the Administration Server and *port* is the address of the port on which the Administration Server is listening for requests. If you are running locally, your server would be localhost and your port defaults to 7501. You will then be prompted to enter a user name and password.

Once you enter your user name and password, you are presented with the Web page that is shown in Figure 1-19.

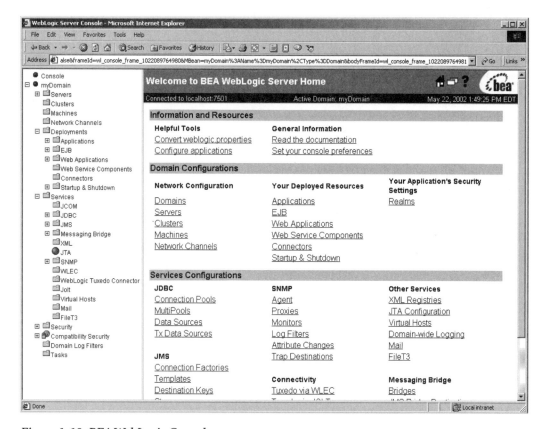

Figure 1-19. BEA WebLogic Console

In this figure, the active domain for the portal is myDomain. Listed under portalDomain are the following:

- Servers

- Deployments

- Services

- Security

We take a closer look at these areas of the WebLogic Console in the next sections.

Servers

You can configure servers, clusters, and machines here. Figure 1-20 shows the different items that can be configured for the server myServer.

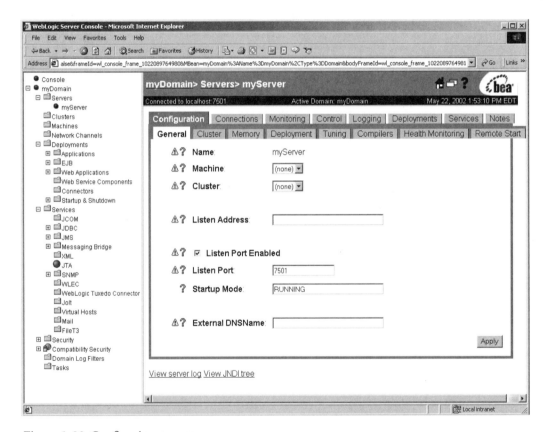

Figure 1-20. Configuring a server

Deployments

Under Deployments, notice the items Applications, EJB, Web Applications,
Connectors, and Startup & Shutdown. Clicking Applications displays all Web
applications and EJBs together. You can configure both application types here. If
you click EJB in the left pane of the Web page, you can then install or configure
a new EJB. Figure 1-21 shows an example of configuring an EJB.

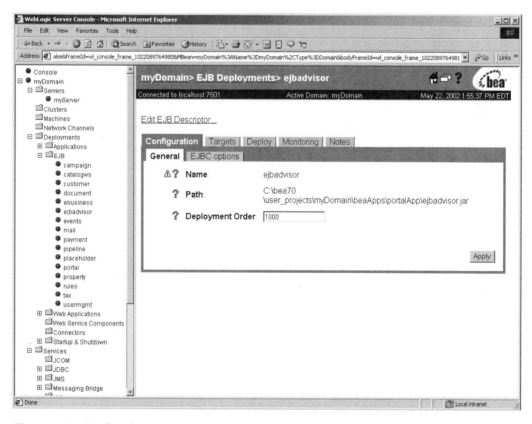

Figure 1-21. Configuring an EJB

If you click Web Applications in the left pane of the Web page, you can then install or configure a new Web application. Figure 1-22 shows an example of configuring a Web application. Chapter 2 shows you detailed steps on how to install a new Web application.

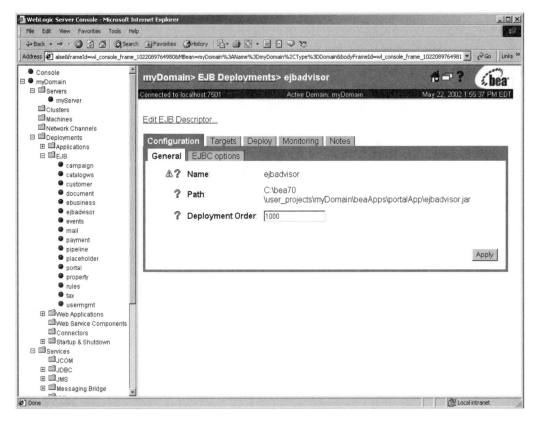

Figure 1-22. Configuring a Web application

Services

Under Services, you can configure the following: JDBC, JMS, XML, SNMP, WLEC, Jolt, Virtual Hosts, Mail, FileT3. For example, if you click JDBC in the left pane of the Web page, you will see that you can configure connection pools, data sources, and transactional data sources. Figure 1-23 shows an example of the different JDBC connection pools that can be configured.

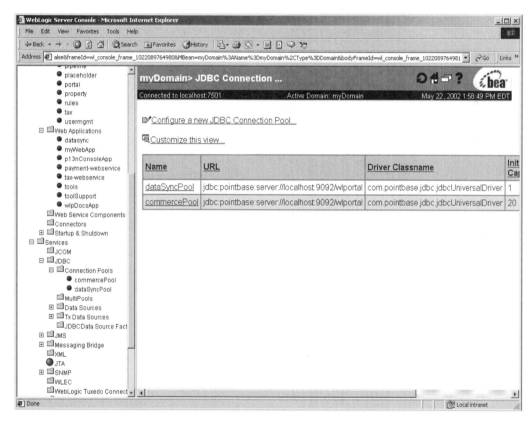

Figure 1-23. JDBC connection pools

Security

Under Security, you can configure realms. Figure 1-24 shows an example of how realms can be configured.

Figure 1-24. Configuring realms

Summary

This chapter gave an overview of all the different elements that together form the BEA WebLogic Portal. Now that you have a general understanding of all the elements in the BEA WebLogic Portal, you are ready to begin learning how to build a portal application. The remainder of this book will help guide you through the process of building a portal application. When you are finished reading this book, you should have enough information to build, deploy, and maintain robust portal applications using the BEA WebLogic Portal.

CHAPTER 2

Building a Portal from Scratch

"**WHAT IS AN ENTERPRISE APPLICATION?** What is a portal? How do I build all the configuration files that are required for enterprise applications? How do I put all the pieces together?" These may be some of the questions that you are asking yourself. If so, rest assured—WebLogic has gone a long way to make this process easier and more manageable.

This chapter is the starting point for putting it all together. By the end of this chapter, you will have a working enterprise application running in the WebLogic Portal Server. Although this application will be an admittedly simple one, it will feature many of the common components that your Web applications require.

This chapter is meant to give you the big picture. Here we explain the architecture of WebLogic Portal applications. We review key portal concepts and the physical implementation of these concepts including directory structures and configuration files used in a WebLogic Portal application. We also discuss the steps to creating a portal application.

WebLogic Portal Architecture

In this section, we discuss several key concepts that will enable you to understand the context in which a WebLogic Portal application will run. Each portal Web application may have one or more components used to implement the functionality for the portal. These components may include portlets, Java classes, Enterprise JavaBeans (EJBs), etc.

An enterprise application is the highest-level component that can be contained within a portal domain. A portal Web application must be deployed within an enterprise application. One or more portal Web applications may be deployed in the context of an enterprise application. In turn, one or more enterprise applications may be deployed in a portal domain.

As we mentioned in the previous chapter, a *portlet* is the component of a portal Web application that is used to build functionality into your application. In this chapter, we show you how to build your first portlet and deploy it in the sample portal application.

Figure 2-1 illustrates the relationships between portal domains, enterprise applications, portal Web applications, and application components.

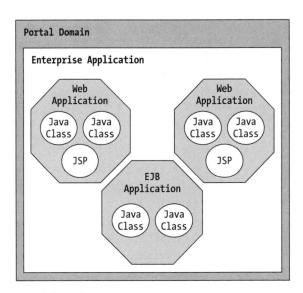

Figure 2-1. The portal domain

WebLogic Domains

Any discussion of the architecture of a WebLogic Portal must include the concept of domains. A *portal domain* is one implementation of a WebLogic Domain. A *WebLogic Domain* is a grouping of applications, application components, JDBC connection pools, servers, and other objects. What items or objects are placed under the umbrella of a portal domain is a matter to be determined by the portal architect; however, certain items must be considered when designing a domain implementation:

- If an application is deployed within a certain domain, all objects or components used by that application must also be deployed in the same domain.

- If you configure a cluster within a portal domain, all servers in the cluster must be configured as a part of the portal domain.

WebLogic Domain configurations are managed and monitored using a *WebLogic Administration Server.* You may run your applications on the Administration Server, and for the purposes of the examples in this book that is what we will do. For production environments, however, it is recommended that you run your Administration Server on a separate machine. WebLogic Administration Servers are the central point for managing and monitoring a WebLogic Domain configuration.

The physical implementation of a WebLogic Portal Domain is constructed in the following way.

WebLogic Portal Domain configuration information and other required files are stored in the root directory for the portal domain on the Administration Server.

Table 2-1 shows the required files for a WebLogic Portal Domain.

Table 2-1. Required Files for a WebLogic Portal Domain

FILE OR DIRECTORY	COMMENT
portal domain root/config.xml	The config.xml file is the persistent configuration repository for the domain. When the Administration Server starts up, it reads the configuration information for the domain from the config.xml file. When a managed server within the domain starts up, it retrieves the domain configuration information from the Administration Server for the domain.
portal domain root/fileRealm.properties	This file stores the security information for the default security realm, as well as storing users, passwords, groups, and Access Control List (ACL) information for the file realm. In particular, this file stores information about the system user, which is the user required to boot the server.
portal domain root/SerializedSystemIni.dat	This file is used in conjunction with the fileRealm.properties file by the file realm. If you copy the fileRealm.properties file from one of the "reference" domains to create a new domain, the SerializedSystemIni.dat file should be copied along with it.
portal domain root/logs directory	This directory is used to output portal server log files, such as weblogic.log, which is a log of server activity.

Enterprise Application

An *enterprise application,* which is a Java 2 Platform, Enterprise Edition (J2EE) concept, consists of a grouping of Web applications and EJBs. In a WebLogic Portal Server, an enterprise application may be deployed in its expanded form or as a J2EE enterprise application archive (.ear file). The expanded directory structure for an enterprise application mimics exactly the structure of an .ear file. We recommend that during development you deploy your applications in expanded form, and when you are ready to go to production, deploy your application as an .ear file.

Multiple enterprise applications may be deployed within a WebLogic Portal Domain. While enterprise applications may be placed anywhere in your server's directory structure by default, enterprise applications that you create are deployed in the BEA_HOME/user_projects directory. Figure 2-2 illustrates the default installation along with the sample applications that are installed by the WebLogic Portal installation.

Figure 2-2. Default enterprise application installation

Notice that each enterprise application directory contains a META-INF directory. This directory contains the enterprise application deployment descriptor files, application.xml and application-config.xml. The application.xml enterprise application deployment descriptor specifies the Web applications and EJB applications that are deployed within the enterprise application and defines security roles for the enterprise application. The application-config.xml enterprise application deployment descriptor file specifies general configuration information for the enterprise application that is used by the Administration Server. Most of the settings in these files can be configured through the server console, therefore it is not recommended that you edit these files manually. However, an understanding of these files will give you better comprehension of how an enterprise application is deployed and configured.

Listing 2-1 shows the default application.xml configuration when WebLogic Portal is installed.

Listing 2-1. Default application.xml Configuration

```xml
<?xml version="1.0"  encoding="UTF-8"?>

<!DOCTYPE application PUBLIC
'-//Sun Microsystems, Inc.//DTD J2EE Application 1.3//EN'
'http://java.sun.com/dtd/application_1_3.dtd'>

<application>
  <display-name>Sample Portal</display-name>
  <description>BEA Sample Portal Application</description>

  <module>
    <web>
      <web-uri>defaultWebApp</web-uri>
      <context-root>defaultWebApp</context-root>
    </web>
  </module>

  <!-- Portals -->
  <module>
    <web>
      <web-uri>sampleportal</web-uri>
      <context-root>sampleportal</context-root>
    </web>
  </module>

  <!-- Tool Stuff -->
  <module>
    <web>
      <web-uri>tools</web-uri>
      <context-root>sampleportalTools</context-root>
    </web>
  </module>
  <module>
```

```
<web>
  <web-uri>datasync</web-uri>
  <context-root>sampleportalDataSync</context-root>
</web>
</module>
<module>
  <web>
    <web-uri>toolSupport</web-uri>
    <context-root>sampleportalTool</context-root>
  </web>
</module>

<!-- P13N Modules -->
<module>
  <ejb>document.jar</ejb>
</module>
<module>
  <ejb>ejbadvisor.jar</ejb>
</module>
<module>
  <ejb>events.jar</ejb>
</module>
<module>
  <ejb>mail.jar</ejb>
</module>
<module>
  <ejb>pipeline.jar</ejb>
</module>
<module>
  <ejb>placeholder.jar</ejb>
</module>
<module>
  <ejb>property.jar</ejb>
</module>
<module>
  <ejb>rules.jar</ejb>
</module>
<module>
  <ejb>usermgmt.jar</ejb>
</module>
```

```
<!-- Commerce Modules -->
<module>
  <ejb>catalogws.jar</ejb>
</module>
<module>
  <ejb>customer.jar</ejb>
</module>
<module>
  <ejb>ebusiness.jar</ejb>
</module>

<!-- Campaign Modules -->
<module>
  <ejb>campaign.jar</ejb>
</module>

<!-- Portal Modules -->
<module>
  <ejb>portal.jar</ejb>
</module>

<!-- Modules used by portals -->
<module>
  <ejb>sampleportal.jar</ejb>
</module>
<module>
  <connector>BlackBoxNoTx.rar</connector>
</module>


<!-- wlcs and ebusiness -->
<security-role>
  <description>Registered customers with role CustomerRole</description>
  <role-name>CustomerRole</role-name>
</security-role>

<!-- tools -->
<security-role>
  <description>Portal Administrators</description>
  <role-name>SystemAdminRole</role-name>
</security-role>
```

```
<security-role>
  <description>Portal Administrators</description>
  <role-name>DelegatedAdminRole</role-name>
</security-role>

<!-- ebusiness -->
<security-role>
  <description>Anonymous access</description>
  <role-name>AnonymousRole</role-name>
</security-role>

<security-role>
  <description>Administrative role for ebusiness</description>
  <role-name>AdministrativeRole</role-name>
</security-role>


</application>
```

Four types of modules can be specified under the application element: <web>, <ejb>, <connector>, and <java>.

The <connector> descriptor element specifies a J2EE Connector Architecture (JCA) component within the enterprise application. JCA is a J2EE 1.3 standard for allowing enterprise information systems to be integrated into a J2EE environment. The <java> descriptor element specifies a Java client application. The <web> descriptor element specifies a Web application component. The <ejb> descriptor element specifies an Enterprise JavaBean component. For our purposes, we will focus on the Web and EJB enterprise application components.

Module descriptions for an enterprise application require <web-uri> and <context-root> elements to describe them. The <web-uri> element specifies the location of the module relative to the enterprise application root within the server's directory structure. The <context-root> describes the base URL path that the server will accept to access the functionality of the deployed Web application. For example, <context-root>myportal</context-root > would correspond to a URL of http://<server>:<port>/myportal/... .

 NOTE *In the sample application.xml, the Web modules are described with a <web-uri> of a directory (see <web-uri>sampleportal</web-uri>). As with enterprise applications, WebLogic allows you to deploy enterprise application modules in either exploded form or archived form. To deploy a Web module in archived form, simply specify the archive name for the <context-root> node.*

The <security-role> element defines security roles that are applicable to the enterprise application. Security roles defined here are WebLogic users or groups that are required for authorization in the enterprise application.

Enterprise Java Bean

Enterprise JavaBeans are a J2EE standard for deploying distributed business functionality. Notice the entry for describing EJB modules in the deployment descriptor in the previous section:

```
<module>
  <ejb>document.jar</ejb>
</module>
```

Coding an EJB and creating an EJB jar is a bit involved. For that reason we discuss EJBs further in Chapter 10; however, describing and deploying an EJB that is already built is as easy as deploying any other enterprise application module. For now, it is important to know that an EJB is another module that may be deployed within an enterprise application.

Portal Web Application

A *portal Web application* is what could be considered a child application to an enterprise application. Each enterprise application may have many portal Web applications. A portal Web application is a grouping of related business functionality. The WebLogic Portal provides several supporting Web applications that you can deploy in your enterprise application along with your portal Web application to provide enhanced functionality to your application. We discuss these applications and the functionality that they provide later.

A WebLogic Portal application has a deployment structure that follows the structure identified by the J2EE specification. Like an enterprise application, a WebLogic Portal Web application may be deployed in either exploded form or in archived form. An archive for a Web application is called a Web application archive, or .war file.

Each Web application, whether in exploded form or in archived form, has a WEB-INF directory as shown in Figure 2-3.

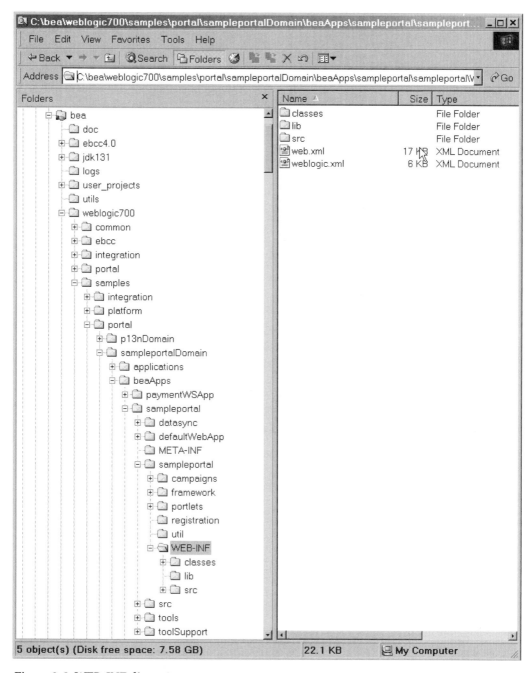

Figure 2-3. WEB-INF directory

The following four directories appear under the WEB-INF directory (these are covered in more detail in the upcoming sections):

- _tmp_war...

- classes

- lib

- src

In addition, WEB-INF contains the application descriptor files.

_tmp_war... Directory

Remember that we said a Web application could be deployed in either exploded format or in archived format. However, when WebLogic runs the Web application, it employs this directory to format and store temporary application files in a structure that it uses for running applications.

classes Directory

The WEB-INF directory also includes a classes directory containing classes required for the Web application. The classes directory is where the compiled Java classes for the Web application are deployed. The class files under this directory must be deployed in a directory structure that corresponds to the package structure for the class.

For example, say your application uses class Foo, as illustrated here:

```
package com.mycompany.myportal;
public class Foo{

    .

    .

}
```

The compiled class file for the Foo class should be deployed in the WEB-INF directory, as illustrated by the following:

```
- WEB-INF
     -  classes
           - com
               - mycompany
                  - myportal
                        - Foo.class
```

lib Directory

The WEB-INF directory also may have a lib directory. In the lib directory, you can place jar files to be used by the Web application. For example, any tag library jars that are used in your Web application should be placed in this directory.

src Directory

The WEB-INF directory also may have a src directory. In the src directory, you can place your Java source code that you compile to classes that are located in the classes directory.

Application Descriptor Files

The WEB-INF directory also contains the web.xml or Web application descriptor file and a WebLogic-specific descriptor file, weblogic.xml.

The following is an empty Web application descriptor file from the WebLogic sampleportal Web application. Notice that as with the enterprise application descriptor file, a Web application descriptor file also has <display-name> and <description> elements.

```xml
<?xml version="1.0" encoding="UTF-8"?>
<!DOCTYPE web-app PUBLIC
"-//Sun Microsystems, Inc.//DTD Web Application 2.3//EN"
"http://java.sun.com/dtd/web-app_2_3.dtd">

<web-app>

    <display-name>sampleportal</display-name>
    <description>Sample Portal WebApp</description>
```

`<servlet-mapping>`

The <servlet-mapping> node allows you to map a servlet described under the <servlet> node with a URL that may be used to access the servlet after deployment. Following is an example <servlet-mapping> descriptor for the ShowDoc servlet. The <url-pattern> node specifies the URL relative to the root of the Web application for the servlet being described.

```
<servlet-mapping>
  <servlet-name>ShowDocServlet</servlet-name>
  <url-pattern>/ShowDoc/*</url-pattern>
</servlet-mapping>
```

`<taglib>`

The <taglib> node describes any Java Server Page (JSP) tag libraries that will be used in the deployed Web application. Following is an example <taglib> descriptor. The <taglib-uri> node specifies the filename for the tag library that is being described. The <taglib-location> node describes the location of the tag library relative to the root of the Web application.

```
<taglib>
  <taglib-uri>dam.tld</taglib-uri>
  <taglib-location>/WEB-INF/lib/dam_taglib.jar</taglib-location>
</taglib>
```

`<ejb-ref>`

The <ejb-ref> element describes Enterprise JavaBeans that the Web application references, and is demonstrated here:

```
<ejb-ref>
  <description>
    The EjbAdvisor for this webapp
  </description>
  <ejb-ref-name>ejb/EjbAdvisor</ejb-ref-name>
  <ejb-ref-type>Session</ejb-ref-type>
  <home>com.bea.p13n.advisor.EjbAdvisorHome</home>
  <remote>com.bea.p13n.advisor.EjbAdvisor</remote>
</ejb-ref>
```

`<context-parm>`

The <context-parm> element allows you to define parameters that are available throughout the Web application. These parameters can be accessed via the following methods:

```
javax.servlet.ServletContext.getInitParameter()
javax.servlet.ServletContext.getInitParameterNames()
```

Class Loaders and Scoping

It is important to understand how class loaders work with enterprise applications. A *class loader* is a Java mechanism that turns a class that is referenced in a Java application into an instantiated class in the Java virtual machine. The relationships between class loaders that operate in enterprise applications indicate the visibility among classes and modules in enterprise applications.

All classes, including the enterprise application classes, the Web application classes, and utility classes that the Web applications use, could be loaded from the class path at server startup using the server's class loader. However, this would mean that there would be no ability to load and unload classes without restarting the server.

The WebLogic Server uses a separate class loader to load each enterprise application. The enterprise application class loader also loads any EJBs within the enterprise application. Each Web application within the enterprise application is loaded by a child class loader of the enterprise application class loader. Figure 2-4 illustrates these relationships between class loaders. Using a separate class loader for different modules or components within the server allows the server to control the loading and unloading of classes within the server.

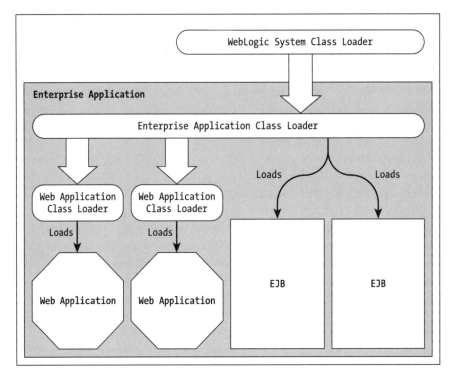

Figure 2-4. Class loader relationships

Though the relationships between class loaders are not class inheritance relationships but more like conceptual parent-child relationships between class loaders, they do indicate visibility among classes loaded by each class loader.

A class will have visibility to other classes loaded by its class loader or its class loader's parent class loader. For example, a Web application will have visibility to any classes loaded by the enterprise application. If you have defined a Web application A and an EJB application B in the enterprise application descriptor, classes running in Web application A will be able to see all EJB classes, home interfaces, and utility classes defined in EJB application B that are loaded by the enterprise application class loader.

In fact, this is a good way to make utility classes that are required by multiple Web applications available to all Web applications within an enterprise application. Even if you don't have any EJBs, you can create a dummy EJB and load it as an EJB application within the enterprise application. All Web applications within the enterprise application will then have access to the utility classes within this dummy EJB application.

Portal Metadata

The WebLogic Portal Server uses metadata stored in a database to support the functionality of the portal framework. The portal metadata stores the definition of portal pages, portlets, and other portal objects and the relationships between these objects. This allows the portal framework to put these objects together dynamically at run time instead of hard coding application data, like application content and navigation.

Though at run time the metadata is stored in the metadata database, this data is initially configured using files in the native file system. Once the metadata is configured and ready for deployment, it is then transferred to the metadata database via a process called *synchronization*.

The WebLogic Portal includes an application called the E-Business Control Center (EBCC) for configuring metadata. We discuss the E-Business Control Center more thoroughly in later chapters. In this section, we simply describe the underlying files used by the E-Business Control Center. Figure 2-5 illustrates the directory and file structure provided by the default installation of the WebLogic Portal.

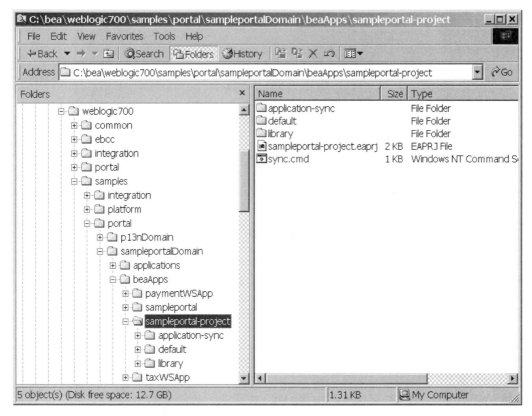

Figure 2-5. WebLogic Portal directory and file structure

As illustrated in Figure 2-5, the EBCC application is installed in the BEA_HOME/weblogic700/ebcc directory. By default, the metadata information for each enterprise application is stored in *domain root directory*\beaApps*application name*-project/application-sync. The EBCC stores all of the metadata configured for the enterprise application in XML files in this directory.

For example, the portlets directory stores metadata for portlets defined for the enterprise application. Listing 2-2 is the XML from the Dictionary.portlet file, which is a sample portlet installed with the WebLogic Portal.

Listing 2-2. Dictionary.portlet File XML

```xml
<?xml version="1.0" encoding="UTF-8"?>
<portlet
xmlns= http://www.bea.com/servers/portal/xsd/portlet/1.0.1
xmlns:xsi="http://www.w3.org/2001/XMLSchema-instance"
xsi:schemaLocation=
"http://www.bea.com/servers/portal/xsd/portlet/1.0.1 portlet-1_0_1.xsd">
    <portlet-name>Dictionary</portlet-name>
    <is-complete>true</is-complete>
    <description>A Dictionary portlet</description>
    <content-url>/portlets/dictionary/dictionary.jsp</content-url>
    <header-url/>
    <alternate-header-url/>
    <footer-url/>
    <alternate-footer-url/>
    <titlebar-url>/framework/titlebar.jsp</titlebar-url>
    <banner-url/>
    <editable>false</editable>
    <edit-url/>
    <helpable>false</helpable>
    <help-url/>
    <icon-url>/portlets/dictionary/images/pt_dictionary.gif</icon-url>
    <minimizable>true</minimizable>
    <maximizable>true</maximizable>
    <maximize-url/>
    <mandatory>false</mandatory>
    <movable>true</movable>
    <floatable>false</floatable>
    <default-minimized>false</default-minimized>
    <login-required>false</login-required>
</portlet>
```

Portlets are one of many metadata items that can be configured via the EBCC. Once the metadata for the object is modified on the native file system and synchronized, this configuration change is, in most cases, immediately visible in the deployed application. This powerful feature of the WebLogic Portal allows you to make high-level changes to applications without code changes.

Creating a New Portal Application

The BEA WebLogic Portal provides several reference or sample enterprise applications that may be used as a starting point for new applications. You should review these sample applications to determine which application most closely represents the type of application that you want to create. Once you have determined which reference application you would like to use as a starting point for your new enterprise application, you can begin the process of creating your own application.

The BEA WebLogic Portal provides a large amount of functionality out of the box, from e-commerce functionality to content management to basic portal necessities. In the text that follows, we walk you through starting and modifying a sample portal application as a quick start. This section outlines the process of starting the sample portal and creating a new page and a new portlet as a means of building a new application.

Review/Modify Server Startup Files

You could create a new domain to run your portal enterprise application and your new portal Web application. However, here you learn how to use the sample portal, which already has an enterprise application; this enterprise application is already deployed by default in the sampleportalDomain. You will use the sampleportalDomain configuration and startup files to deploy and run a new Web application.

Earlier in this chapter we discussed WebLogic domains. Now let's look specifically at the sampleportalDomain's files and directory structure. Figure 2-6 shows the sampleportalDomain directory structure that is installed by default with the BEA WebLogic Portal.

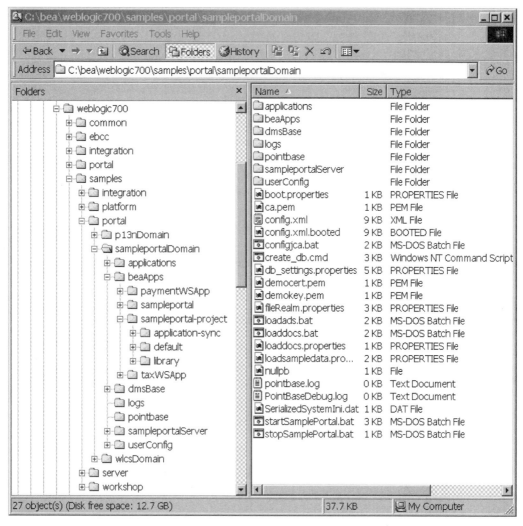

Figure 2-6. The sampleportalDomain directory structure

startSamplePortal.bat

We've already discussed many of the files that reside under the domain directory. Now we want to look at the startPortal.bat file. This file is the main batch file that is used to start the WebLogic Portal Server. Listing 2-3 shows the default sampleportalDomain startSamplePortal.bat file. We have included comments in this listing to point out several items that you may need to modify for your application.

Listing 2-3. Default sampleportalDomain startSamplePortal.bat File

```
@ECHO OFF
SETLOCAL


REM ######################################################################
REM (c) 2002 BEA SYSTEMS INC. All rights reserved
REM
REM BEA WebLogic Portal Server startup script.
REM This script can also install/uninstall a Portal Window Service. Use the
REM -installService or -uninstallService command-line arguments.
REM ######################################################################


REM ######################################################################
REM The WLP installation directory
REM ######################################################################
SET WLP_HOME=C:\bea\weblogic700\portal


REM ######################################################################
REM Set the WebLogic server name
REM ######################################################################
REM This line sets the name of the server that we are starting:
SET SERVER_NAME=sampleportalServer


REM ######################################################################
REM Set the database type
REM Valid values are: POINTBASE, ORACLE_THIN, MSSQL, SYBASE_JCONNECT, DB2_TYPE2
REM Set set-environment.bat for more details
REM ######################################################################
SET DATABASE=POINTBASE
REM Try to get it from the db_settings.properties file
IF not exist .\db_settings.properties goto _setenv
SET DB_SETTINGS=.\db_settings.properties
FOR /F "eol=# tokens=1,2 delims==" %%i in (%DB_SETTINGS%) do  (
    if %%i == database SET DATABASE=%%j
)
:_setenv


REM ######################################################################
REM Set the environment
REM See set-environment.bat for more details on the available parameters
REM ######################################################################
REM Notice the call to set-environment .bat--this file sets environment variables
```

```
REM that are used to set the class path for the server and used by the start
server
REM command. You modify this file to set JDBC drivers and other items that are
REM required at server startup.
CALL "%WLP_HOME%\bin\win32\set-environment.bat"


REM #######################################################################
REM Set any additional CLASSPATH information
REM #######################################################################
REM If you introduced new environment variables in the set-environment.bat file
REM that need to be added to the class path, these variables should be appended
REM to this line:
SET CLASSPATH=%CLASSPATH%;%P13N_DIR%\lib\commerce_system.jar;
%P13N_DIR%\lib\campaign_system.jar
REM #######################################################################
REM Start WebLogic with the above parameters.
REM See startWebLogic.cmd for more details on the available parameters.
REM #######################################################################
set MEM_ARGS=-Xms128m -Xmx128m -XX:MaxPermSize=128m
set JAVA_OPTIONS=-Dcommerce.properties="%WLP_HOME%/weblogiccommerce.properties"

if "%1" == "-installService" goto _installService
if "%1" == "-uninstallService" goto _uninstallService

:_startWebLogic
call "%P13N_DIR%\bin\win32\startWebLogic.cmd"
goto _the_end

:_installService
call "%P13N_DIR%\bin\win32\installWebLogicService.cmd"
goto _the_end

:_uninstallService
call "%P13N_DIR%\bin\win32\uninstallWebLogicService.cmd"
goto _the_end

:_the_end
ENDLOCAL
```

Set-environment.bat

Carefully review the set-environment.bat file shown in Listing 2-4. In the Windows environment this file is located in the PORTAL_HOME/bin/win32 directory. The main item that you need to modify is the specification of the database that will be used for your application. Notice in this file that the commands already exist to specify Cloudscape, Oracle, or Sybase as the database server. It is just a matter of commenting and uncommenting the appropriate lines to set up this file for your application.

However, if you need to use a JDBC driver other than the ones that are already set up in this file (e.g., Oracle thin driver), you must modify this file with commands that set up the class path and other items required for your driver.

Listing 2-4. set-environment.bat

```
@ECHO OFF
REM ##############################################################################
REM #\      (c) 2001-2002 BEA SYSTEMS INC. All rights reserved
REM #
REM #\      BEA Portal Server variable setup script.
REM #
REM ##############################################################################


REM ----------- Set the following variables appropriately -----------
REM ----------- or define them as environment variables   -----------
REM ----------- in your system properties and comment out -----------
REM ----------- the next 4 lines.                          -----------
SET PORTAL_HOME=C:\bea\weblogic700\portal
SET WL_COMMERCE_HOME=C:\bea\weblogic700\portal
SET PORTAL_LIB=%PORTAL_HOME%\lib


SET JDK_HOME=C:\bea\jdk131
SET WLCS_ORACLE_HOME=
SET SYBASE_HOME=not set
SET SYBASE_OCS=@SYBASE_OCS@
SET DB2_HOME=@DB2_HOME_BACK_SLASH@
SET BEA_HOME=C:\bea
SET WEBLOGIC_HOME=C:\bea\weblogic700\server
SET OI_HOME=not set
```

```
REM Location of the P13N platform
SET P13N_DIR=C:\bea\weblogic700\portal

REM ----------- Specify which Database Driver to use -----------
REM Valid values are: POINTBASE, ORACLE_THIN, MSSQL, SYBASE_JCONNECT,
REM DB2_TYPE2
IF "%DATABASE%" == "" SET DATABASE=POINTBASE

REM -- Add WebLogic bin directories to the path --
SET PATH=%WEBLOGIC_HOME%\bin;%JDK_HOME%\bin;%PATH%

if %DATABASE% == POINTBASE GOTO POINTBASE
if %DATABASE% == ORACLE_THIN GOTO ORACLE_THIN
if %DATABASE% == MSSQL GOTO MSSQL
if %DATABASE% == SYBASE_JCONNECT GOTO SYBASE_JCONNECT
if %DATABASE% == DB2_TYPE2 GOTO DB2_TYPE2


:POINTBASE

REM ----------- POINTBASE classes -----------

REM ---------
REM NOTE: POINTBASE_HOME should be set to BEA_HOME when we move to WLS 7.0
REM ---------
SET DB_CLASSPATH=C:\bea\weblogic700\samples\server\eval\pointbase\
lib\pbserver42ECF172.jar
SET DB_CLASSPATH=%DB_CLASSPATH%;
C:\bea\weblogic700\samples\server\eval\pointbase\lib\pbclient42ECF172.jar
SET DB_CLASSPATH=%DB_CLASSPATH%;
C:\bea\weblogic700\samples\server\eval\pointbase\lib\pbtools42ECF172.jar

GOTO continue

:ORACLE_THIN

REM
REM version 8.1.7 of the Oracle thin driver (classes12.zip) in the manifest for
REM weblogic.jar.  weblogic.jar is added to the CLASSPATH below.
REM

GOTO continue
```

```
:SYBASE_JCONNECT

REM
REM The Sybase jConnect driver is a type 4 driver that is supplied with WLS and
REM included in the manifest for weblogic.jar.
REM weblogic.jar is added to the CLASSPATH below.
REM

GOTO continue

:DB2_TYPE2
call @DB2_HOME_BACK_SLASH@\java12\usejdbc2.bat
SET DB_CLASSPATH=%DB2_HOME%\java\db2java.zip
SET PATH=%DB2_HOME%\bin;%PATH%

GOTO continue

:MSSQL

REM
REM The Microsoft SQL Server driver (Weblogic jDriver for SQL Server) is a type 4
REM driver that is supplied with WLS and included in the manifest for weblogic.jar.
REM weblogic.jar is added to the CLASSPATH below.
REM

:continue

REM ----------- JDK classes and executables -----------
SET JDK_TOOLS=%JDK_HOME%\lib\tools.jar
SET JAVA_CLASSPATH=%JDK_TOOLS%

SET WLS_CLASSPATH=%WEBLOGIC_HOME%\lib\weblogic.jar;
%WEBLOGIC_HOME%\lib\webservices.jar

REM ----------- BEA WebLogic Personalization Server classes ------------

SET WLPS_CLASSPATH=%P13N_DIR%\lib\p13n_system.jar;
%PORTAL_LIB%\portal_system.jar;
%P13N_DIR%\lib\ext\jdom.jar;
%P13N_DIR%\lib\ext\HTTPClient.jar;
%P13N_DIR%\lib\ext\wlcsparsers.jar
```

```
REM ----------- WebLogic CLASSPATH -----------
SET CLASSPATH=%WLS_CLASSPATH%;
%WLPS_CLASSPATH%;
%JAVA_CLASSPATH%;
%DB_CLASSPATh%
```

startWebLogic.cmd

Listing 2-5 shows the startWebLogic.cmd batch file. Notice that the environment variables in this file are ones that have been set by the scripts discussed previously.

Listing 2-5. startWebLogic.cmd Batch File

```
@rem ****************************************************************************
@rem This script is used to start WebLogic Server
@rem
@rem To create your own start script for your domain, all you need to set is
@rem SERVER_NAME, then call this script from the domain
@rem directory.
@rem If you set DOMAIN_NAME, then this will assume WLS6.1 compability -- it
@rem pass in -Dweblogic.domain and you should invoke it from the parent
@rem directory of config\%DOMAIN_NAME%
@rem
@rem Other variables that startWebLogic takes are:
@rem
@rem DB_SETTINGS   - the db_settings.properties to use pass to
@rem                   startPBServer.bat, if DATABASE==POINTBASE
@rem WLS_USER      - admin username for server startup
@rem WLS_PW        - cleartext password for server startup
@rem ADMIN_URL     - if this variable is set, the server started will be a
@rem                   managed server, and will look to the url specified (i.e.
@rem                   http://localhost:7001) as the admin server.
@rem WLS_PROD_MODE- set to true for production mode servers, false for
@rem                   development mode
@rem WLS_MGMT_DISC- set to true for production mode servers, false for
@rem                   development mode
@rem JAVA_OPTIONS - Java command-line options for running the server. (These
@rem                   will be tagged on to the end of the JAVA_VM and MEM_ARGS)
@rem JAVA_VM       - The java arg specifying the VM to run.  (i.e. -server,
@rem                   -client, etc.)
@rem MEM_ARGS      - The variable to override the standard memory arguments
@rem                   passed to java
```

```
@rem JAVA_SEC_POLICY - The Java Security policy file to use (defaults to
@rem                   weblogic.policy)
@rem
@rem This assumes that your PATH and CLASSPATH are configured for
@rem the various native libraries and system classes required by the server.
@rem This also supports starting up a Pointbase server
@rem
@rem ***************************************************************************


@echo off
setlocal

@rem Invoke set-environment.bat if we haven't already
if "%WL_COMMERCE_HOME%"==""
call "C:\bea\weblogic700\portal\bin\win32\set-environment.bat"

@rem Now BEA_HOME, WEBLOGIC_HOME, WL_COMMERCE_HOME, and JDK_HOME should be set

@rem Check that the WebLogic classes are where we expect them to be
:checkWLS
if exist "%WEBLOGIC_HOME%\lib\weblogic.jar" goto checkJava
echo The WebLogic Server wasn't found in directory %WEBLOGIC_HOME%.
echo Please edit your set-environment script so that the WEBLOGIC_HOME variable
echo points to the WebLogic Server installation directory.
goto finish

@rem Check that java is where we expect it to be
:checkJava
if exist "%JDK_HOME%\bin\java.exe" goto runWebLogic
echo The JDK wasn't found in directory %JDK_HOME%.
echo Please edit your set-environment script so that the JDK_HOME variable
echo points to the location of your JDK.
goto finish

:runWebLogic

@rem set defaults for these, if they weren't set in either the invoker or
@rem set-environment

@rem By default the server will start with the Java hotspot setting turned on.
@rem If you have code that will not run correctly using the Java hotspot, you
@rem may want to change this by setting JAVA_VM to something different
@rem in the server's start script; however, in most cases you should use the
@rem hotspot engine to enhance the performance of the server.
```

```
if "%JAVA_VM%"=="" set JAVA_VM=-hotspot
if "%MEM_ARGS%"=="" set MEM_ARGS=-Xms200m -Xmx200m
if "%WLS_PROD_MODE%"=="" set WLS_PROD_MODE=true
if "%WLS_MGMT_DISC%"=="" set WLS_MGMT_DISC=false
if "%JAVA_SEC_POLICY%"=="" set JAVA_SEC_POLICY=%WEBLOGIC_HOME%\lib\weblogic.policy

if not "%DOMAIN_NAME%"=="" set JAVA_OPTIONS=%JAVA_OPTIONS% -
Dweblogic.Domain=%DOMAIN_NAME%

set SAVED_CLASSPATH=%CLASSPATH%
set CLASSPATH=%CLASSPATH%;%WL_COMMERCE_HOME%\lib\p13n\ejb\p13n_util.jar

@rem Start PointBase, if needed
set PBOWNER=
if not "%DATABASE%"=="POINTBASE" goto NOT_PB1

set PB_HOST=localhost
set PB_PORT=9092
set PB_DB=wlportal

@rem Get the PointBase host, port, and database name from db_settings.properties
if "%DB_SETTINGS%"=="" goto _NO_DB_SETTINGS
FOR /F "eol=# tokens=1,2 delims==" %%i in (%DB_SETTINGS%) do  (
    if %%i == host SET PB_HOST=%%j
)
FOR /F "eol=# tokens=1,2 delims==" %%i in (%DB_SETTINGS%) do  (
    if %%i == port SET PB_PORT=%%j
)
FOR /F "eol=# tokens=1,2 delims==" %%i in (%DB_SETTINGS%) do  (
    if %%i == db_name SET PB_DB=%%j
)

:_NO_DB_SETTINGS
@rem Check if PointBase is up (sets errorlevel)
"%JDK_HOME%\bin\java"
com.bea.p13n.db.internal.PointBasePing
-host %PB_HOST%
-port %PB_PORT%
-database %PB_DB%

@rem PointBase already running
IF NOT ERRORLEVEL 1 GOTO NOT_PB1
```

```
IF "%DB_SETTINGS%"=="" START /I /B "PointBase Server"
"%WL_COMMERCE_HOME%\bin\win32\startPBServer.bat"
IF NOT "%DB_SETTINGS%"=="" START /I /B "PointBase Server"
"%WL_COMMERCE_HOME%\bin\win32\startPBServer.bat"
%DB_SETTINGS%

@rem set PBOWNER so that we will shutdown down PB at the end
set PBOWNER=THIS_SCRIPT

@rem  if not using PointBase or already started, continue on...
:NOT_PB1

set CLASSPATH=%SAVED_CLASSPATH%

@rem Start Server

echo ***************************************************
echo *  To start WebLogic Server, use a username and   *
echo *  password assigned to an admin-level user.  By  *
echo *  default, this is user: weblogic                *
echo *  and password: weblogic                         *
echo *  These should both be changed using the         *
echo *  WebLogic Server console at                     *
echo *       http://[hostname]:[port]/console          *
echo ***************************************************
@rem This is the line of the file that actually starts the WebLogic Portal Server.
@rem Notice that based on the disposition of the ADMIN_URL environment
@rem variable the server will either start as an Administration Server or a
@rem Managed Server.

@rem If you are restarting an Administration Server and you already have Managed
@rem Servers running, set the -Dweblogic.management.discover argument to true by
@rem setting the WLS_MGMT_DISC environment variable to true in the server's start
@rem script. The default startup mode for the server, if this parameter is not
@rem set, is to automatically try to discover Managed Servers that are running.
@rem So if you only have one server in your domain or if you are starting
@rem a Managed Server, you should explicitly set this argument to false to
@rem improve startup speed.
```

```
echo on
@if "%ADMIN_URL%" == "" goto runAdmin
"%JDK_HOME%\bin\java"
%JAVA_VM% %MEM_ARGS% %JAVA_OPTIONS%
-Dweblogic.Name=%SERVER_NAME%
-Dbea.home="%BEA_HOME%"
-Dweblogic.management.username=%WLS_USER%
-Dweblogic.management.password=%WLS_PW%
-Dweblogic.management.server=%ADMIN_URL%
-Dweblogic.ProductionModeEnabled=%WLS_PROD_MODE%
  -Djava.security.policy=="%JAVA_SEC_POLICY%" weblogic.Server
@goto finish

@:runAdmin
"%JDK_HOME%\bin\java"
%JAVA_VM% %MEM_ARGS% %JAVA_OPTIONS%
-Dweblogic.Name=%SERVER_NAME%
-Dbea.home="%BEA_HOME%"
-Dweblogic.management.username=%WLS_USER%
-Dweblogic.management.password=%WLS_PW%
-Dweblogic.ProductionModeEnabled=%WLS_PROD_MODE%
-Dweblogic.management.discover=%WLS_MGMT_DISC%
-Djava.security.policy=="%JAVA_SEC_POLICY%" weblogic.Server
@goto finish

:finish

@echo off
@rem #####################################################################
@rem if PointBase was launched by this script then shut it down
@rem #####################################################################
if not "%PBOWNER%"=="THIS_SCRIPT" goto _the_end

if "%DB_SETTINGS%"=="" call
"%WL_COMMERCE_HOME%\bin\win32\stopPBServer.bat"
if not "%DB_SETTINGS%"=="" call
"%WL_COMMERCE_HOME%\bin\win32\stopPBServer.bat"
%DB_SETTINGS%

:_the_end
endlocal
```

Start the Sample Portal

To start the sample portal, click Start ➤ Programs ➤ BEA WebLogic Platform 7.0 ➤ WebLogic Portal 7.0 ➤ Portal Examples ➤ Portal Example ➤ Launch Portal Server.

The server will start in a command window. Figure 2-7 shows the messages you will see as the server is starting. You will know that the server has finished the startup process when you see the following message:

```
<Server started in RUNNING mode>
```

Figure 2-7. Server console

Open the Sample Portal Project

You are now ready to create and deploy the metadata for your Web application and run a test. To do this you use the E-Business Control Center. We go into more detail about the EBCC in a later chapter. For now, we walk you through some simple steps that allow you to deploy some very simple metadata for your application.

1. Open the EBCC by clicking Start ➢ Programs ➢ BEA WebLogic Platform 7.0 ➢ WebLogic Portal 7.0 ➢ E-Business Control Center.

2. Open the sample portal project by clicking File ➢ Open Project (see Figure 2-8).

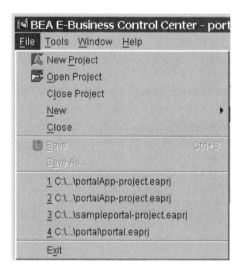

Figure 2-8. Selecting the Open Project menu item

3. Using the Open Project dialog box (see Figure 2-9), navigate to the sample portal project file (sampleportal-project.eaprj), located at BEA_HOME\weblogic700\samples\portal\sampleportalDomain\ beaApps\sampleportal-project.

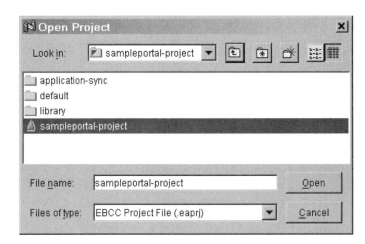

Figure 2-9. Open Project dialog box

Create the Portlet Functionality

The following steps show how to create the functionality for your portlet:

1. Create a new portlet directory called helloworld in the sample portal (see Figure 2-10).

2. Create a new JSP file in the helloworld directory that you just created.

3. Enter the following code into the helloworld.jsp file:

```
<table>
<tr>
<td class=contentheading>
Hello World this is my first portlet!
</td>
</tr>
</table>
```

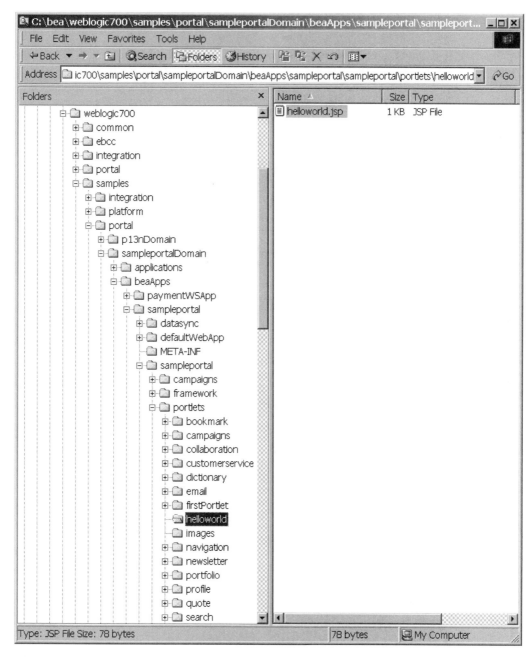

Figure 2-10. Creating the helloworld portlet directory

Create the Portlet Definition (Metadata)

The following steps show how to create the portal definition or metadata for your portlet:

1. Select the Portlet menu item in the toolbar as shown in Figure 2-11.

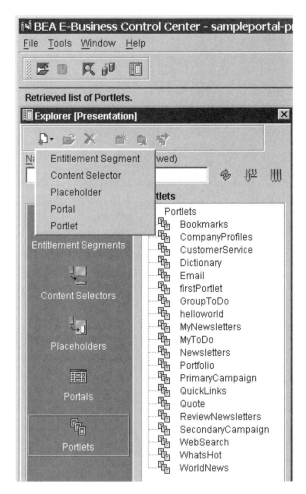

Figure 2-11. Selecting the Portlet menu item

2. Choose the "Use the Portlet Editor to create a new portlet with existing resources" radio button option in the New Portlet dialog box (see Figure 2-12).

Figure 2-12. New Portlet dialog box

3. Enter the following items in the Portlet Editor (see Figure 2-13):

   Description: Hello World

   Content URL: /portlets/helloworld/helloworld.jsp

   Icon URL: (blank)

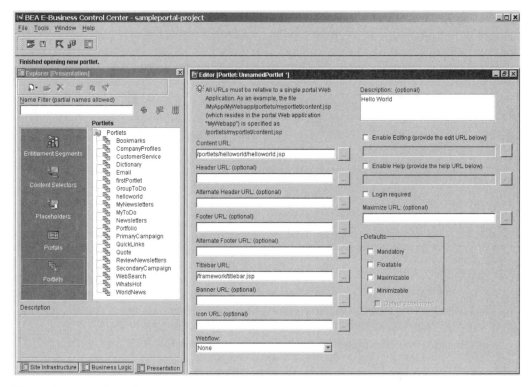

Figure 2-13. Portlet Editor

NOTE *The Icon URL is initially populated with a value of "/portlets/images". Remove this value and leave this field blank.*

4. Save the new portlet definition by clicking the File ➤ Save menu item.

5. Enter helloworld in the File name field in the Save dialog box (see Figure 2-14).

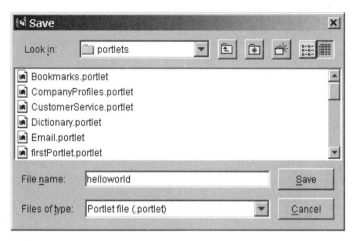

Figure 2-14. Saving your new portlet

6. Select the Portals icon from the EBCC explorer panel.

7. Double-click sampleportal in the list of portals. The Portal Editor will display in the right panel.

8. Open the General section of the Portal Editor.

9. From the Portlets tab in the Portal Editor, add the helloworld portlet to the selected portlets for this portal (see Figure 2-15).

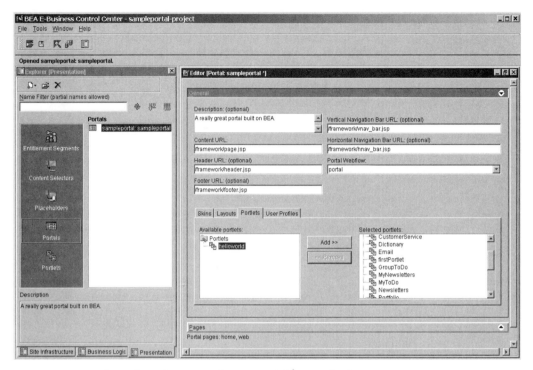

Figure 2-15. Portlets tab in the General section of the Portal Editor

10. Open the Pages section of the Portal Editor.

11. Select the home page from the list and click the Edit button.

12. Add the helloworld portlet to the Selected portlets list in the Page defi-
    nition dialog box, and then click the OK button to close the dialog box
    (see Figure 2-16).

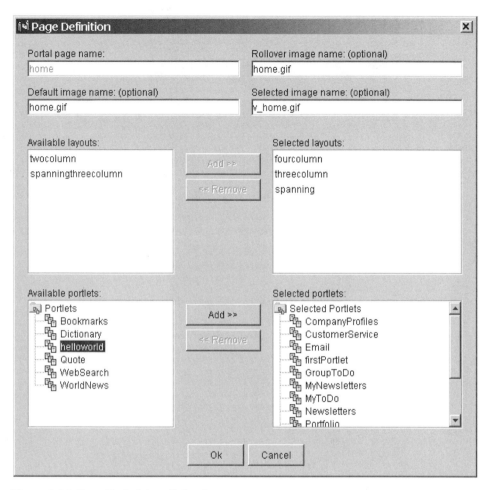

Figure 2-16. Page Definition dialog box

13. Save the portal definition by choosing Save from the File menu.

14. Select Tools ➤ Synchronize. When the synchronization process is completed, close the dialog box (see Figure 2-17). In the password dialog box, enter a valid datasync user name/password combo; from a fresh installation, the valid combos are system/weblogic, weblogic/weblogic, administrator/password.

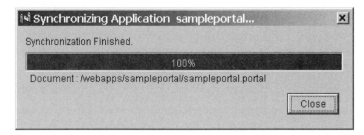

Figure 2-17. Synchronizing the sampleportal application

15. Click Cancel to close the Reset Campaigns State dialog box, which appears after the synchronization process is complete.

Make the New Portlet Available to the Home Page

Follow these steps to make your new portlet accessible from the home page:

1. Open the Portal Tools application in your browser by navigating to the following URL: http://*server*:*port*/sampleportalTools/index.jsp. Log in using administrator/password as the user/password combination.

2. Click the Portal Management link as shown in Figure 2-18.

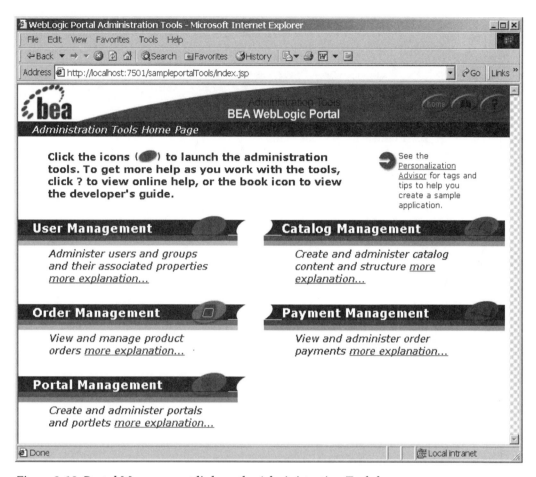

Figure 2-18. Portal Management link on the Administration Tools home page

3. Click the Avitek Portal link from the Portal Management window (see Figure 2-19).

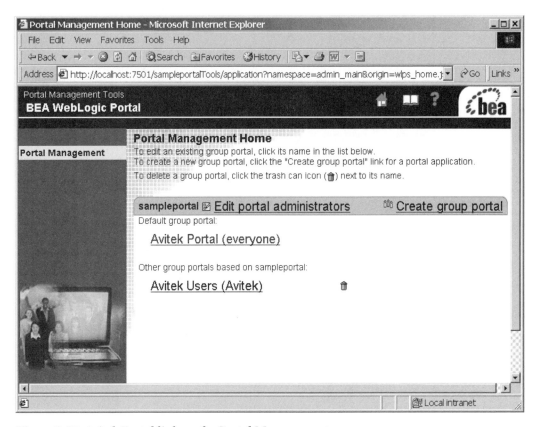

Figure 2-19. Avitek Portal link on the Portal Management page

4. Click the Manage Pages and Portlets link from the Group Portal Management page as shown in Figure 2-20.

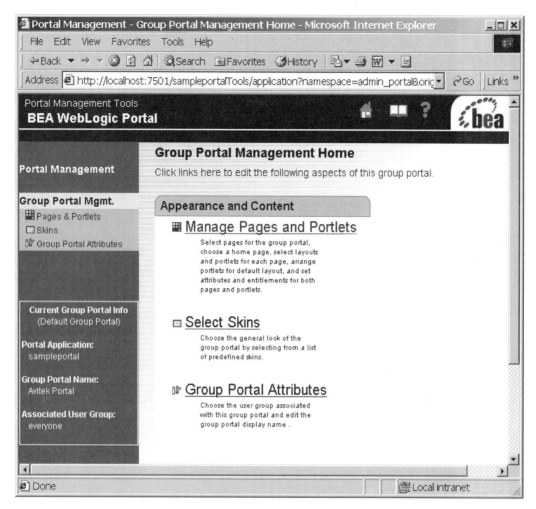

Figure 2-20. Manage Pages and Portlets link on the Group Portal Management page

5. Click the Edit Portlets button next to the home page on the Pages and Portlets page as shown in Figure 2-21.

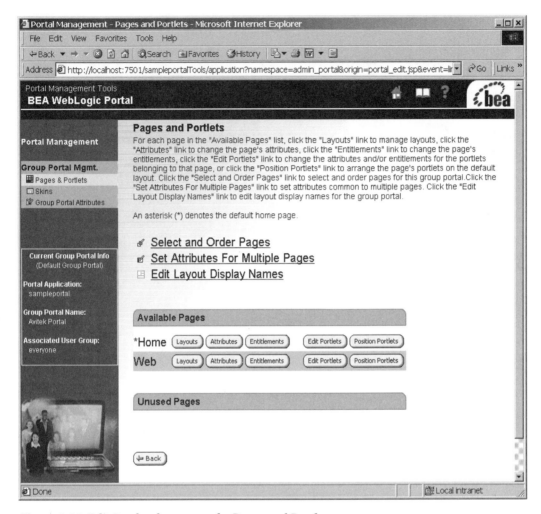

Figure 2-21. Edit Portlets button on the Pages and Portlets page

6. Select the helloworld portlet and click Set Attributes.

7. Select the Available and Visible check boxes and click the Save button as shown in Figure 2-22.

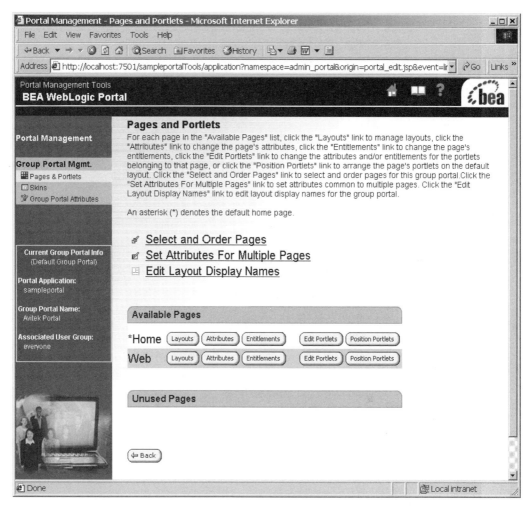

Figure 2-22. Setting portlet attributes

Test the New Functionality

You have now completed the steps required to add new functionality to
the sample portal. You can test your application by browsing to
http://*server:port*/sampleportal in your Web browser as shown in Figure 2-23.
You should now have a very simple working portal Web application.

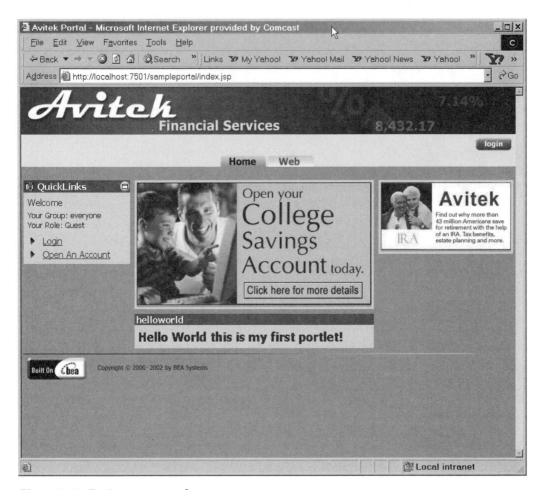

Figure 2-23. Testing your portal

Summary

This chapter explained some important portal concepts that you need to understand before moving forward. It also gave you step-by-step instructions for creating a new portal application based on the existing sample portal application supplied by the WebLogic Portal. We cover creating portal applications in more detail in later chapters, but you should now have a foundation on which you can build. At this point you should have created your own sample portal functionality following the instructions in this chapter. You now have the base knowledge that is required to create more advanced functionality and build your own portal application from scratch.

Basic Java Concepts

SERVLETS, AND JSPS, AND JAVABEANS, OH MY! Java is nothing to be scared about, although it is not uncommon for beginners to feel lost in the woods. This is very understandable considering the polymorphic lingo, inherited from senior-level developers, that encapsulates a beginning Java developer's daily life.

This chapter introduces you to three types of objects that are crucial in the development of an enterprise portal: servlets, JSPs, and JavaBeans. These objects provide a multitude of functionality alone, but a Web Developer realizes the true value of these objects when he or she combines all three. After reading this chapter, you will be ready to start work on the most complex of portals.

When building an enterprise portal using the BEA WebLogic Portal, knowledge of servlets, Java Server Pages (JSPs), and JavaBeans is fundamental. A *servlet* is one of the basic building blocks of a Web application and is used in communication between the client and Web server. *JSPs* are used heavily in a BEA WebLogic Portal. All portals are comprised of componentized modules of functionality. These modules are JSPs or a collection of JSPs, and they manage the content generation for the client browser. The BEA WebLogic Portal refers to these modules as *portlets*, and we cover these in more detail in Chapter 4. *JavaBeans* are specialized, self-contained Java classes that can be used easily throughout the JSP. They support content generation by providing additional functionality within the JSP.

Servlets

A servlet is the Java version of a CGI script. The Common Gateway Interface (CGI) was traditionally the methodology used to add functionality to a Web application. A separate instance of a CGI process was executed to fulfill each HTTP request. This required the use of more system memory and resulted in the overhead of creating a new process for every single request.

Servlets are Java classes that run in a Web application server. Each request for a servlet is handled by a single instance of the Java class. Servlets commonly process or store data submitted by an HTML form, to provide content or to manage state information.

In a Web application that uses the BEA WebLogic Portal, a portlet may need to communicate with the Web server. For example, it may need to request some additional content to be displayed, or it may have collected information that needs to be sent to the Web server. This communication is most commonly handled with servlets.

For the purposes of this book, servlet will refer to an object of type javax.servlet.http.HttpServlet. This object has a base class of javax.servlet.GenericServlet, which implements the javax.servlet.Servlet interface. This is a generic object and not the object of choice for use in Web applications. HttpServlet is an abstract class that provides much functionality to servlet developers.

The following sections describe the methods within the HttpServlet class and provide a servlet example demonstrating the use of some of these methods.

Methods of HttpServlet

Several methods can be overridden in a subclass of HttpServlet. These methods provide a variety of functionality including initialization and destruction of the servlet, and handling of servlet requests and servlet responses, as well as accessing configuration information for the servlet itself.

init(ServletConfig config)

The init method is called at servlet initialization. You are guaranteed that execution of this method will be complete before the servlet handles any request. The init method sets up any system resources or connections that may be necessary during the processing of a request. An input parameter of type javax.servlet.ServletConfig provides access to initialization parameters that the init method can make use of. The init method is called once for the lifetime of the servlet, and it will not run again until the servlet is reloaded.

NOTE *When overriding this method, it is necessary to call super.init(config). This allows initialization to proceed as normal in the base class.*

init()

If the intended functionality of the overridden init(ServletConfig config) method does not include special treatment of the ServletConfig object, it may be acceptable to override the init() method instead. This method is called at the end of the init(ServletConfig config) method and can also be used to set up resources needed during servlet execution. Since this method is called from within the init(ServletConfig config) method, it is executed only once for the lifetime of the servlet.

destroy()

The destroy() method executes prior to the garbage collection of the object. This is your last chance to clean up resources other than memory or to close any connections that may have remained open during execution.

CAUTION *This method is automatically invoked after the processing of the last request or after a specific period of time has elapsed regardless of the status of the current request. Therefore, you must be extremely careful when cleaning up resources that may still be in use.*

service(ServletRequest req, ServletResponse res)

The service method handles the client's request. This method, inherited from javax.servlet.Servlet, is overridden in HttpServlet to provide added functionality. Basically, the entire purpose of the service method is to read a client's request and produce an appropriate response.

HTTP, or Hypertext Transfer Protocol, is composed of many different HTTP methods. Each HTTP method is a type of message that requests a certain type of response. HTTP defines several methods, including GET, POST, HEAD, PUT, and DELETE. The HttpServlet implementation of the service method dispatches requests of each type to their respective special methods. For instance, for the HTTP method GET, HttpServlet defines doGet. Of the many methods defined in HttpServlet, the doGet and doPost methods are used most often.

doGet(HttpServletRequest req, HttpServletResponse res)

An HTTP GET method is the result of a client requesting information from the server. Requests of this type are automatically routed through the service method to the doGet method. Here the request parameters can be read, the information retrieved, and the response set for the client.

doPost(HttpServletRequest req, HttpServletResponse res)

An HTTP POST method is generated when an HTML form or a large amount of data is submitted to the server. As opposed to the GET method, the POST method is expected to update data on the server. Since many client requests can be sent simultaneously, it is important to safeguard these updates.

getServletConfig()

This method returns a javax.servlet.ServletConfig object. This is the same object that is passed to the init() method during instantiation. The ServletConfig object provides access to initialization parameters and configuration information.

Example Servlet

The following example demonstrates a simple servlet that displays content on the client's browser. This example uses the doGet method mentioned earlier. The doPost method and form processing are more complicated tasks, and as such we discuss them more thoroughly in Chapters 8 and 9.

This servlet acts as a content dispatcher for a site and uses many of the methods mentioned previously. The task for this servlet is to serve static content for an entire site. All content is located on the file system. An HTTP GET is issued to acquire page content by name.

The init() method uses the ServletConfig parameter to get an initialization parameter. In this case, the parameter is a file path where all the static content is located for the site. This way only a filename is necessary to be passed along the query string. No reference is kept to the ServletConfig, since it won't need to be used later in the servlet. If it were needed, a reference would have to be made here.

The doGet method is implemented in this servlet because the client machine is requesting the resources. A parameter containing the content filename to display is passed along the request. In order to pass a parameter into the servlet, it needs to be appended to the request URL, preceded by a "?" character. You can pass in multiple parameters by preceding each additional parameter with a "&" character. In the case of this servlet, the request URL would end with "?CONTENT=filename".

The content filename and file path, acquired at initialization, are used to create a java.io.File object. A java.io.FileReader is created with the file object as long as the requested file exists, and the content is retrieved. In the case of no parameter being passed via the request query string, or the requested document not existing, an appropriate error message is displayed.

The response object provides a reference to a java.io.PrintWriter object. This object prints the lines of HTML to the response output stream.

This servlet does not need to utilize the destroy() method. At destruction time, there are no resources that the servlet need regain. If the file system were used to store temporary files, this would be a good place to ensure that those files were deleted prior to destroying the servlet object.

Listing 3-1 shows the complete servlet code.

Listing 3-1. Example Servlet

```
import javax.servlet.*;
import javax.servlet.http.*;
import java.io.*;
import java.util.*;

public class ContentServlet extends HttpServlet {
  private static final String CONTENT_TYPE = "text/html";
  private static final String PARAM_CONTENT_DIRECTORY = "CONTENT_DIRECTORY";
  private static final String PARAM_CONTENT = "CONTENT";
  private static final String ERROR_NO_CONTENT_FOUND =
    "The document you requested no longer exists.";
  private static final String ERROR_NO_PARAM = "Please specifiy a content file.";
  private static final String ERROR_READ_FAIL =
    "Error: Failed reading the content file.";

  private String contentDirectory;

  public void init(ServletConfig config) throws ServletException {

    contentDirectory = config.getInitParameter(PARAM_CONTENT_DIRECTORY);

  }
```

```java
protected void doGet(HttpServletRequest request, HttpServletResponse response)
    throws ServletException, IOException {

  response.setContentType(CONTENT_TYPE);
  PrintWriter out = response.getWriter();
  String html = "";

  String content = request.getParameter(PARAM_CONTENT);

  if ((content != null) && (!content.equals(""))) {
    File contentFile = new File(contentDirectory, content);

    if (contentFile.exists()) {
      FileReader reader = new FileReader(contentFile);

      try {
        char[] data = new char[(int)contentFile.length()];
        reader.read(data);
        html = new String(data);
      }
      catch (IOException ioe) {
        System.out.println(ERROR_READ_FAIL);
        html = ERROR_NO_CONTENT_FOUND;
      }

    }
    else {
      html = ERROR_NO_CONTENT_FOUND;
    }
  }
  else {
    html = ERROR_NO_PARAM;
  }

  out.println("<html>");
  out.println("<head><title>DescriptionServlet</title></head>");
  out.println("<body>");
  out.println("<p>");
  out.println(html);
  out.println("</p>");
  out.println("</body></html>");
}
}
```

Java Server Pages

A Java Server Page, or JSP, is a normal HTML file with the addition of specialized tags. These tags contain Java source code that allow for simplified generation of dynamic content. The JSP is the view of the portal, and the job of the view is to interpret information and present it to the end user in a clear and concise manner. JSPs provide a clear separation of page logic from its presentation, allowing development chores to be divided between Web designers and Java developers. JSPs can utilize other technologies such as JavaBeans and EJBs to provide a highly scalable architecture for Web applications.

A JSP is compiled into a basic servlet within a JSP servlet engine on the Web server. This compilation usually takes place the first time the JSP is requested. All page content, static HTML as well as dynamically created, is output via the servlet OutputStream within the service method.

The BEA WebLogic Portal uses a framework of JSPs that display generic portal entities such as a header, footer, and navigation panes. The framework JSPs also control the structure and layout of the portal itself. Additionally, any portlet created in BEA WebLogic Portal could be comprised of a JSP. Other child JSPs may be included in a parent JSP.

Template Text

The major portion of a JSP is regular HTML. In the world of JSPs, this static HTML portion is referred to as *template text*. Since there is nothing special about this HTML, it can be created in any development environment the Web designer feels comfortable with. This makes JSPs easy to develop and maintain. JSP tags, much like HTML tags, can be added to the static portion to provide the dynamic content.

JSP Constructs

The dynamic portion of JSPs is made up of many special tags that enable you to create dynamic content for a Web application. Three main types of tags are found within a JSP: scripts, directives, and actions. *Scripts* allow for the inclusion of Java source code, which then becomes part of the servlet. *Directives* control and modify the overall structure of the servlet. *Actions* provide the ability to utilize predefined Java components and control the flow of the servlet.

Scripting Elements

Scripting elements allow the developer to insert standard Java source code directly into the JSP. This construct is made up of three types of elements: expressions, scriptlets, and declarations. The following sections describe these elements in more detail.

Scriptlets

Scriptlets have the following syntax:

```
<% source %>
```

The source code placed between the special JSP beginning and ending tags, <% and %>, is added to the servlet's service method. Scriptlets give the developer more flexibility than expressions can provide. Any type and amount of Java source code can be placed within the scriptlet tags, giving the developer full control over the presentation of the JSP.

In Listing 3-2, the name of each parameter contained within the servlet's request will be displayed on the page.

Listing 3-2. Sample Scriptlet

```
<%
    for(Enumeration e = request.getParameterNames(); e.hasMoreElements();) {
      out.println(e.nextElement());
    }
%>
```

NOTE *It is important to remember that the scriptlet code can be placed anywhere within the JSP. It may be surrounded by template text. The static HTML is converted to println() statements within the servlet, and the exact location of the scriptlet is retained.*

Scriptlets need not contain entire code blocks of Java source code. It is possible to leave statements open-ended to add an additional dynamic level to the page.

Listing 3-3 expands on the previous listing. It includes template text used to format the list of parameters. The for loop has been broken apart, or left open-ended so that template text for a table row definition can be inserted. The for loop is ended after this definition.

Listing 3-3. Scriptlet with Embedded Template Text

```
<TABLE BORDER="1">
<%
    for(Enumeration e = request.getParameterNames(); e.hasMoreElements();) {
%>
    <TR>
        <TD>
            <% out.println(e.nextElement()); %>
        </TD>
    </TR>
<%
    }
%>
</TABLE>
```

Expressions

Following is the syntax for expressions:

```
<%= expression%>
```

An expression can take on many forms as long as the resulting object can be converted to a java.lang.String object. This conversion takes place at request time, and the resulting string replaces the expression at its current location in the JSP. Much like scriptlets, expressions can be placed anywhere throughout the JSP.

A JSP expression can contain a class instantiation.

```
<%= new java.util.Date() %>
```

JSP expressions can also contain variables defined in a scriptlet.

```
<%
String firstName = "John";
String lastName = "Doe";
%>
The Name is: <%= lastName %>, <%= firstName %>
```

Method calls can also be used within a expression tag.

```
Milliseconds: <%= System.currentTimeMillis() %>
```

Declarations

Declarations have the following syntax:

```
<%! source %>
```

A JSP declaration is a complete Java declarative statement. These statements can be used to declare variables or even methods. Although some of the preceding code samples have illustrated the ability to create declarative statements in scriptlets, there are major differences between declarations and scriptlets: the location of the code within the resulting servlet and the initialization of this code.

As mentioned previously, when compiled, all scriptlets as well as expressions are placed within the servlet service method. Declarations, on the other hand, are placed outside of the service method, making them accessible from everywhere within the servlet and possibly the entire application, depending on scope.

JSP scriptlets and expressions, being situated within the service method, are local variables and thus initialized with each request. A JSP declaration belongs to the servlet as a whole and therefore is initialized only once, when the JSP is initialized.

Following is an example declaration of two variables:

```
<%! java.util.Random rand = new java.util.Random() %>
<%! int number = rand.nextInt() %>
```

A method could be created to return this variable as follows:

```
<%! private int getNumber() {return number;} %>
```

Finally, the getNumber method can be used in an expression as shown here:

```
Random Number: <%= getNumber() %>
```

The result of the preceding code examples does indeed produce a random number that is displayed to the user. However, each time this page is reloaded, the same number will appear, since the number is initialized only once for the lifetime of the server.

NOTE   *Variables declared using the <%! %> tags in turn are class variables of the compiled servlet. For this reason, it is necessary for these values to be thread-safe.*

Comments

JSPs have several different commenting mechanisms. It is necessary to have separate methodologies since JSPs are comprised of separate parts, static and dynamic. Placing a comment in template text requires the use of the standard HTML comment style, as shown here:

```
<!--Comment in Template Text -->
```

There are several ways to place comments in scripting elements. For instance, you can use the following JSP comment tag:

```
<%-- Comment --%>
```

The JSP engine will ignore all text or code within the preceding tags and can enclose anything except a %> tag.

Regular Java-style comments can also appear within declaration and scriptlet statements. These comments can either be a single line:

```
// Comment
```

or a block:

```
/* Comments */
```

Directives

Following is the syntax for directives:

```
<%@ directive attribute="value" %>
```

A directive is a JSP tag that affects the structure of the JSP as a whole.

The page Directive

Attributes of the page directive directly affect the compilation of the JSP. Developers can use the page directives discussed in this section, alone or in combination, to provide information at the page level.

In the previous code samples, all class declarations have been fully qualified. This can be avoided by importing these packages. Of the many attributes associated with the page directive, only the import attribute may be used multiple times. Multiple imports may be placed within a single directive.

```
<%@ page import="java.util.* " %>
<%@ page import="java.util.*, java.io.* " %>
```

When the JSP is compiled into a servlet, a parent class may be specified by using the extends attribute.

```
<%@ page extends="parentClass" %>
```

In order to provide a productive error-handling methodology, a JSP can dictate that it is an error page. By default, this attribute is set to false.

```
<%@ page isErrorPage="true|false" %>
```

In order to use a JSP error page, a relative URL to the error-handling page must be specified.

```
<%@ page errorPage="relativeURL" %>
```

Most often a JSP is used to display HTML, so by default its MIME type is set as "text/html". However, it is possible to specify other MIME types that may be more appropriate.

```
<%@ page contentType="MIMEType" %>
```

HTML content is sent to the client as an output stream. By default the stream is buffered, and its default size is 8K. The size of the buffer can be specified otherwise.

```
<%@ page buffer="size|none" %>
```

This buffer is flushed automatically unless the autoFlush attribute is used. If the buffer is not set to be flushed automatically and the buffer happens to over-flow, an exception is thrown.

```
<%@ page autoFlush="true|false" %>
```

Information about the JSP can be made available via the getServletInfo method.

```
<%@ page info="text message" %>
```

By default, a JSP has access to the session object. By setting the session attribute to false, it is possible to revoke this access. When set to false, any attempt to access the session via the JSP results in errors.

```
<%@ page session="true|false" %>
```

By default, JSPs are thread-safe, and use a multiple-thread model. There is only one instance of the servlet, and it handles multiple requests simultaneously. This assumes that the JSP developer takes all the necessary precautions to ensure that the JSP is synchronized properly. This may not always be the case, and the resulting servlet could be unable to handle multiple requests simultaneously. A single-thread approach can be used by specifying the isThreadSafe attribute. Each request would be handled by the one instance, but only serially, or there may be multiple instances of the servlet to resolve any thread safety issues.

```
<%@ page isThreadSafe="true|false" %>
```

Finally, the language attribute specifies the scripting language to be used within the JSP. Currently, "java" is the only available language that can be used.

```
<%@ page language="language" %>
```

The include Directive

This directive provides the ability to insert additional HTML files or JSPs when the JSP is initialized. Within the include directive, the file attribute specifies the relative URL of the file to include.

```
<%@ include file="relativeURL" %>
```

It is important to remember that since the included file is inserted at initialization, if this file were to change, any JSP that has included the file must be reinitialized.

The taglib Directive

It is possible to create custom JSP tags for use within a JSP. These custom sets of tags are known as *tag libraries*. BEA has created a multitude of these libraries to aid the developer in construction on a BEA WebLogic Portal. BEA's libraries provide functionality ranging from static content inclusion to custom business logic flow management. We discuss tag libraries in detail elsewhere throughout this book, but we mention the existence of the taglib directive here to illustrate its use.

To specify that a tag library be available to a page, a URI uniquely names the library, and a prefix is chosen that will be used throughout the page in accessing custom tags.

```
<%@ taglib uri="libraryURI" prefix="prefix" %>
```

Once a library has been included, all classes and methods of that library are available in the JSP. One of the many taglibs BEA provides is a portal utility library full of utility methods, saving developers from having to develop their own. This taglib's URI is es.tld. The following example illustrates using the taglib directive with this library:

```
<%@ taglib uri="es.tld" prefix="es" %>
```

NOTE *The specified prefix is "es". This could be any prefix the developer chooses, as long as it is not already in use by another included taglib. The prefix appears later in the JSP code to access methods within the library.*

One of the methods in the portal utility library is convertSpecialChars. This method takes a string as a parameter and translates any special characters within the string to their HTML entity equivalent for proper display within an HTML page. The next example shows a call to this method using the prefix and passing the string argument. In this example, the string argument contains two double quote characters. The double quote character does not display properly in the value attribute of an HTML input box; it must be encoded.

```
<% String someString = "\"What's going on?\""; %>
<input type="text" name="X"
    value="<es:convertSpecialChars string="<%= someString%>"/>"/>
```

Actions

JSP actions provide extra functionality to the JSP. Much like directives, they affect the JSP as a whole during translation by modifying the compilation of the servlet. Each JSP action tag is explained in the following sections.

The param Action

The param action syntax is as follows:

```
<jsp:param name="name" value="value"/>
```

The param action is not used alone. Instead, it functions as a subaction for the actions to follow. The param action holds a name/value pair that will be associated with the parent action.

The include Action

Following is the include action syntax:

```
<jsp:include page="relativeURL" flush="true"/>
```

Not to be confused with the include directive, the include action includes an HTML file or JSP at request time rather than at initialization. This means that you can modify the included file on the fly, and changes will be immediately applied. Currently, the only valid Boolean value for the flush attribute is true; this field is mandatory nonetheless.

When including a JSP, the param action can pass parameters to the included JSP. These parameters are accessible via the servlet request.

The forward Action

The forward action syntax looks like this:

```
<jsp:forward page="relativeURL"/>
```

The forward action forwards the request to another JSP or servlet. The param action can also be used with this action. Like the include action, the parameters can be accessed via the request.

The plugin Action

The plugin action syntax is as follows:

```
<jsp:plugin type="pluginType" code="classFile" codebase="relativeURL"/>
```

This action enables the use of a Java component, applet, or the download of a plug-in. The plugin action inserts the appropriate browser-specific <EMBED> or <OBJECT> tags in place of the <jsp:plugin> tag. Presentation information is specified with the attributes of this action.

The plugin action has many attributes that can be associated with it. Most attributes are optional, but three are mandatory: type, code, and codebase. The type attribute specifies the type of plug-in that is being included. The code attribute is the class file of the plug-in, whereas the codebase attribute is the directory where the class file resides.

The plugin action also supports the param action. However, in the case of plug-ins, an enclosing <jsp:params> tag encompasses these param action tags.

```
<jsp:params>
    <jsp:param name="parameterName" value="parameterValue"/>
</jsp:params>
```

Another special action that the plugin action supports is the fallback action. In the case of a plug-in not being supported by the client, the fallback action provides content that will be displayed in its place.

```
<jsp:fallback>
    HTML Content
</jsp:fallback>
```

Other Actions

JSP has three other actions for the inclusion and utilization of JavaBeans. These actions are useBean, getProperty, and setProperty, and they help to integrate the usage of JavaBeans into JSPs. The "JavaBeans" section of this chapter discusses these action tags as well as JavaBeans.

Implicit Objects

Before deeply delving into the JSP constructs, it is important to know that certain implicit objects are available within all JSPs. These objects are predefined values that give the developer access to underlying objects associated with the servlet. We discuss these variables—specifically, request, response, out, page, session, application, config, and pageContext—in the next sections.

The request Object

The request variable is a reference to the javax.servlet.http.HttpServletRequest object that is passed to the service method of the servlet. This object gives you access to HTTP header information. The request object most commonly accesses parameter names and values passed. Client browsers pass parameters to the Web server to request information or to notify the server of information. For the example that follows, the parameter USERID is expected to be passed in the request. The request object obtains this parameter value and then displays a generic welcome message.

```
<%! private static final String PARAM = "USERID"; %>

<html>
   <body>
       <h3>Welcome <%= request.getParameter(PARAM) %></h3>
   </body>
</html>
```

The response Variable

The response variable is a reference to the javax.servlet.http.HttpServletResponse object within the service method of the servlet. This variable allows you to modify HTTP header information and to set information returned to the client. Although a common use of this object within servlets is to return data to the client via the servlet PrintWriter object or its OutputStream object, it is not used in this fashion in JSPs since a reference to a Writer object is also provided as another implicit object, out.

The out Object

The out object, as mentioned previously, is an object referencing a JSPWriter object, a subclass of Writer. This object allows the developer to print or write data directly to the servlet OutputStream object. This information will be displayed within the client's browser.

```
<html>
   <body>
       <%
           for(Enumeration e = request.getParameterNames(); e.hasMoreElements();) {
           String name = (String)e.nextElement();
```

```
            out.println(name);
            out.println(" = ");
            out.println(request.getParameter(name));
            out.println("<br>");
            }
        %>
    </body>
</html>
```

The session Variable

The session variable is a reference to the javax.servlet.http.HttpSession object associated with the servlet request. The session provides a relationship between a client and the Web application, and can store objects between requests. These objects are stored as key/value pairs, and persist for the lifetime of the Web session.

```
<%! private static final String ATTRIB_PAGE_COUNT = "PAGE_COUNT"; %>

<% Integer pageCount = (Integer) session.getAttribute(ATTRIB_PAGE_COUNT);
    StringBuffer sb = new StringBuffer();
    int count = 0;

    if (pageCount != null) {
        count = pageCount.intValue();
    }

    ++count;

    sb.append("This page has been accessed ");
    sb.append(count);
    sb.append(" times during your current session.");

    session.setAttribute(ATTRIB_PAGE_COUNT, new Integer(count));

%>

<html>
    <body>
        <b><%= sb%></b>
    </body>
</html>
```

The application Variable

A reference to javax.servlet.ServletContext is present in the application variable. The application variable is provided at initialization; therefore, this object persists for the lifetime of the application. Developers can use this object to access certain environment information, log events, and store attributes much like the session object, only with a greater longevity.

```
<%@ page import="java.util.*" %>

<%! private static final String ATTRIB_DATE = "DATE"; %>

<% Date lastAccess = (Date)application.getAttribute(ATTRIB_DATE);
   String dateString = "";

   if (lastAccess == null) {
      dateString = "This application has not been accessed.";
   }
   else {
      dateString = "This application was last accessed " + lastAccess.toString();
   }

   application.setAttribute(ATTRIB_DATE, new Date());

%>

<html>
   <body>
      <b><%= dateString%></b>
   </body>
</html>
```

The exception Object

The exception object is only available on pages defined as error pages. This object is of type javax.servlet.jsp.jspException. When the error page is invoked, the exception that caused the invocation becomes available in this object. The JSP error page would then display a user-friendly message to the client, and the application would be saved from possibly terminating a session less than gracefully.

```
<%@ page isErrorPage="true" %>

<html>
    <body>
        <b>Exception:</b> <% exception.getMessage(); %>
    </body>
</html>
```

The page Variable

The page variable is one of the least useful JSP variables; page is a reference to the JSP itself, otherwise known as "this". It accesses the current instance of the servlet.

```
<html>
    <body>
        <b>JSP Class = <% out.println(page.getClass()); %></b>
    </body>
</html>
```

The config Variable

The config variable, much as its name implies, is a reference to javax.servlet.ServletConfig. This variable gives access to initialization parameters of the servlet as well as a method for acquiring a reference to javax.servlet.ServletContext. As mentioned, ServletContext is already available via the application variable. Therefore, the config object does not appear often in JSPs.

The pageContext Object

The pageContext object references a javax.servlet.jsp.PageContext object. This object has many uses, which include accessing all scoped namespaces, storing attributes at the JSP level, forwarding the request and response objects, including files, and error handling. While these methods are used extensively by the generated servlet, this object doesn't provide much functionality at the JSP level, except when using custom tags.

JavaBeans

JavaBeans are self-contained, reusable software components that can be manipulated visually by various builder tools. A JavaBean, simply referred to as a *bean*, is written the same way as any other Java class, but follows a certain specification that separates it from other classes. All bean functionality is contained within the class and can be easily integrated into any application. This is Java's answer to the ActiveX component, and you can use it in integrated development environments the very same way.

JavaBeans can also be nonvisual components. This is more related to how JavaBeans are used in correlation with JSPs. These entities can encapsulate a set of information and the functionality needed to support this data. JavaBeans make it possible for multiple JSPs to reuse the same business logic. With business logic separated from presentation logic, the quality of the JSPs is increased, the page logic is easier to maintain, and the Web application is made more robust by encapsulating logic in one place. Using the dynamic powers of Java, a bean can expose its properties, which in turn takes away some of your programming chores and allows Java itself to take over.

JavaBean Concepts

Each class instantiated is very knowledgeable about itself. It knows information about its type, the methods it contains, and the types of its instance variables. An object has the ability to gather this information from any object it has a reference to. With this information, objects can be instantiated and method calls can be invoked almost automatically.

The ability for obtaining this information from objects is referred to as *introspection*. Introspection and object manipulation classes and interfaces are located in one of the core APIs in the JDK, the Reflection API. JavaBeans provide a much higher implementation of the Reflection API's general objects with the Introspector class. Developers normally do not use this class, but JSPs use it often to obtain important characteristics of beans.

JavaBean Design

JavaBeans are just normal Java classes that follow a prescribed design methodology to allow for reflection and introspection. In this design methodology, JavaBeans must

- Provide a public empty constructor.

- Implement java.io.Serializable.

- Follow a design pattern for access methods.

In order for a bean to be instantiated, it must provide a no-argument constructor. Eventually, when this bean is integrated into a JSP, this instantiation will be done by Java, not the developer. The empty constructor makes it easy for Java to perform its task. Preserving the state of a JavaBean can only be accomplished by storing this information. Serializing the object saves the entire state of the bean. The access methods must follow a predicated pattern for naming, return value, and signature. This pattern allows for the automatic acquisition of variables.

Listing 3-4 shows a very simple JavaBean that fulfills all of the requirements necessary and is ready to be used in a JSP.

Listing 3-4. Sample JavaBean

```
import java.io.Serializable;

public class SimpleBean implements Serializable{

  private int age;

  public SimpleBean() {
  }

  public int getAge() {
    return age;
  }

  public void setAge(int value) {
    this.age = value;
  }
}
```

JavaBean Properties

A bean's property is any public attribute of the bean. These attributes are made accessible via methods that follow a prescribed pattern—each attribute is associated with two methods that share the name of the attribute. One method, prefixed with "get", retrieves the attribute. The other method, prefixed with "set", modifies the attribute.

The following is the syntax for using properties:

```
private type X;
public type getX() {}
public void setX(type value) {}
```

The following applies the property syntax:

```
private String name;
public String getName() {
    return name;
}
public void setName(String name) {
    this.name = name;
}
```

This is the syntax for defining a simple property, name. This property of type String is defined with private access. The Introspector class knows that in order to access the name attribute, it must use the access methods. Therefore, getName() and setName() are also defined. This is how the methods and attributes are tied together, and represents the standard way to define properties of a bean. More than likely this will suffice for all of a developer's needs.

Alternate methods exist for defining properties within a bean. Properties may be indexed if necessary, and these are known as *indexed properties*. This type of property can be useful when it is necessary to include attributes that can have multiple values.

The following is the syntax for using indexed properties:

```
private type[] X;
public void setX(int index, type value);
public type getX(int index);
public void setX(type values[]);
public type[] getX();
```

The following applies the indexed property syntax:

```
private String[] filenames;
public void setFileNames(int index, String value) {
    filenames[index] = value;
}
public String getFileNames (int index) {
    return filenames[index];
}
public void setFileNames(String values[]) {
    filenames = values;
}
public String[] getFileNames() {
    return filenames;
}
```

Using JavaBeans with JSPs

JSP defines three additional action tags that support JSP development with
JavaBeans: <jsp:useBean>, <jsp:getProperty>, and <jsp:setProperty>. By employ-
ing these tags, a developer can literally drop a JavaBean onto a JSP and
immediately begin to use it with ease.

The useBean Action

The syntax for the useBean action is as follows:

```
<jsp:useBean id="beanName"scope="beanName" class="beanClass" />
```

The <jsp:useBean> tag is JSP's handle to using a bean by simply specifying
a class name and an ID to reference the bean. Beans can be instantiated under
several different scopes, which determine the lifetime of the bean. The useBean
tag first attempts to find the bean with the given ID, in the scope specified. If not
found, the bean is automatically instantiated, a reference is given to the ID specified, and the object is stored in the given scope.

The useBean action has several attributes, the most common of which are id,
scope, and class. The id attribute specifies the variable name of the bean that is
used throughout the JSP to reference the instantiated object. The class attribute

is the fully qualified class name of the bean. Again, the scope attribute specifies the lifetime of the bean. There are four available scopes that a bean can use:

- *Page:* This scope, which is the default, is the shortest lifetime available for a bean. A bean defined with page scope is only accessible within the page in which it is created. A reference to a bean with page scope is released when the response is sent to the client or the request is forwarded to a different resource. The pageContext object stores a reference to a bean of page scope.

- *Request:* A bean declared with request scope follows the request as long as it lives. If the request is forwarded to another JSP, the bean reference is kept alive. The object reference is released once the request is fully processed. References to request scope beans are kept within the request itself.

- *Session:* A session scope bean is active for the entire session in which the bean is created. A bean cannot be created with a scope of session if the JSP has the session attribute of the page directive set to false. The session object is in charge of storing references to session scope beans.

- *Application:* Beans that have application-level scope are alive for the lifetime of the application. This is the longest lifetime that a bean can have. References to application scope beans can be reached regardless of the session attribute for the page. The JSP's application object stores these references.

The getProperty Action

Following is the syntax for the getProperty action:

```
<jsp:getProperty name="beanName" property="propertyName" />
```

Now that a bean has been instantiated or referenced, the properties of this bean can be accessed. The getProperty action retrieves a property from the bean for display in a JSP or for further processing.

Only two attributes are associated with the getProperty action. The name attribute is the reference name declared in the useBean action, and the property attribute is the name of the property to be retrieved.

A limitation of the getProperty action is that it can only retrieve simple properties. Notice that there is no additional attribute that can be used to specify a certain index to acquire an index property.

The setProperty Action

The setProperty action has the following syntax:

```
<jsp:setProperty name="beanName" property="*"/>
<jsp:setProperty name="beanName" property="propertyName" param="paramName"/>
<jsp:setProperty name="beanName" property="propertyName" value="text|expression"/>
```

Only a few attributes exist for the setProperty action, but these few attributes supply several ways to set the properties of a bean. The name attribute, once again, is the reference name declared in the useBean action, and the property attribute is the name of the property to be set. Properties are set with the param or value attributes.

It is possible for a property to be set from parameters associated with the request. All properties can be set at once by specifying "*" as the property attribute value. All properties matching request parameters will be set. Also, bean properties can be set singly by specifying the name of the property as the property attribute value. The param attribute can be used if the request parameter name does not match that of the property. If the parameter is null or is empty, the corresponding bean property will not be set.

A property value does not have to be set by a request parameter. The value attribute allows the developer to set the property value with a string or a JSP expression. The value attribute cannot be used along with the param attribute.

A JSP/JavaBean Example

The example shown in Listing 3-5 encompasses everything we outlined within the prior section. The first step is to create a JavaBean. This bean has several simple properties that are accessed via the get and set methods in numerous ways. The example uses the UserBean class.

Listing 3-5. Simple UserBean

```java
import java.io.*;

public class UserBean implements Serializable{

    private String firstName;
    private String lastName;
    private int age;
```

```
public UserBean() {
}

public String getFirstName() {
  return firstName;
}

public void setFirstName(String value) {
  this.firstName = value;
}

public String getLastName() {
  return lastName;
}

public void setLastName(String value) {
  this.lastName = value;
}

public int getAge() {
  return age;
}

public void setAge(int value) {
  this.age = value;
}
}
```

NOTE   *In order to use this class as a JavaBean within a JSP, it must fulfill the minimum requirements, which it does. First, it has an empty constructor, UserBean(). Secondly, this class implements the Serializable interface. Lastly, the properties firstName, lastName, and age each have access methods that follow the proper pattern. This class functions as a JavaBean and is ready for use within a JSP.*

Now that a bean has been created, a JSP can utilize its functionality. In Listing 3-6, the JSP uses the "*" property attribute value to automatically set all properties within the bean. The properties are then displayed on the page. This JSP is accessed with a URL similar to this one:

`http://host/page.jsp?firstName=John&lastName=Doe&age=25`. Notice that each of the properties is located on the request.

*Listing 3-6. Simple User JSP Using **

```
<jsp:useBean id="user" scope="request" class="com.nws.samples.UserBean" />

<jsp:setProperty name="user" property="*" />

<html>
    <body>
        <b>Last Name:</b> <jsp:getProperty name="user" property="lastName" />
        <br>
        <b>First Name:</b> <jsp:getProperty name="user" property="firstName" />
        <br>
        <b>Age:</b> <jsp:getProperty name="user" property="age" />
    </body>
</html>
```

This JSP displays on the page the following output:

```
Last Name: Doe
First Name: John
Age: 25
```

Since the parameter names located on the request are exact matches of the properties of the bean, introspection takes over and sets these values for the developer. Not always will the developer have the luxury of parameter names being exact matches. In these cases, the parameters need to be mapped to their associated properties. Listing 3-7 uses the same UserBean class, but in this case the JSP is accessed with a different URL:
`http://host/page.jsp?A=John&B=Doe&C=25`.

Listing 3-7. Simple User JSP Matching Parameters

```
<jsp:useBean id="user" scope="request" class="com.nws.samples.UserBean" />

<jsp:setProperty name="user" property="firstName" param="A" />
<jsp:setProperty name="user" property="lastName" param="B" />
<jsp:setProperty name="user" property="age" param="C" />
```

```
<html>
    <body>
        <b>Last Name:</b> <jsp:getProperty name="user" property="lastName" />
        <br>
        <b>First Name:</b> <jsp:getProperty name="user" property="firstName" />
        <br>
        <b>Age:</b> <jsp:getProperty name="user" property="age" />
    </body>
</html>
```

The request parameters A, B, and C are mapped using the setProperty action to their respective properties within the bean. This JSP displays a result exactly the same as the JSP in the prior example, as shown here:

```
Last Name: Doe
First Name: John
Age: 25
```

Although a bean seems like an object that is different from other classes in a developer's bag of tricks, it is still just a normal Java class and can be used as such within a JSP scriptlet. Listing 3-8 illustrates this functionality. The same URL used in the last example is used again:
`http://host/page.jsp?A=John&B=Doe&C=25`.

Listing 3-8. Simple User JSP Using Bean Accessor Methods

```
<jsp:useBean id="user" scope="request" class="com.nws.samples.UserBean" />

<jsp:setProperty name="user" property="firstName" param="A" />
<jsp:setProperty name="user" property="lastName" param="B" />
<jsp:setProperty name="user" property="age" param="C" />

<%

StringBuffer info = new StringBuffer();

info.append(user.getFirstName());
info.append(" ");
info.append(user.getLastName());
info.append(" is ");
info.append(user.getAge());
info.append(" years old.");
%>
```

```
<html>
   <body>
      <p><%= info.toString() %></p>
   </body>
</html>
```

The UserBean class is used just as a normal class would be. This allows the developer to apply any special processing on bean properties prior to display. In this case, the properties are included in an information string about the current user. This JSP displays a result similar to this:

```
John Doe is 25 years old.
```

The last JSP example demonstrates using the setProperty action with both a static string and a JSP expression. This method of setting properties can be used when none or some of the property values exist within the request object. In this example, a flag property has been added to UserBean. This property, "type", contains a static string value that could be later used in the application to dictate that a record should be inserted or updated. This example uses a URL similar to the following: `http://host/page.jsp?lastName=Doe&firstName=John`.

The updated UserBean class is shown in Listing 3-9.

Listing 3-9. Modified UserBean

```
import java.io.*;

public class UserBean implements Serializable{

   private String firstName;
   private String lastName;
   private int age;
   private String type;

   public UserBean() {
   }

   public String getFirstName() {
      return firstName;
   }

   public void setFirstName(String value) {
      this.firstName = value;
   }
```

```java
  public String getLastName() {
    return lastName;
  }

  public void setLastName(String value) {
    this.lastName = value;
  }

  public int getAge() {
    return age;
  }

  public void setAge(int value) {
    this.age = value;
  }

  public String getType() {
    return type;
  }

  public void setType(String value) {
    this.type = value;
  }
}
```

Listing 3-10 shows the sample JSP setting bean properties with a static string and expression.

Listing 3-10. User JSP Setting Record Type

```jsp
<jsp:useBean id="user" scope="request" class="com.nws.samples.UserBean" />

<jsp:setProperty name="user" property="*" />

<jsp:setProperty name="user" property="type" value="INSERT"/>

<% int defaultAge = 0; %>

<jsp:setProperty name="user" property="age" value=<%= defaultAge %> />
```

```
<html>
    <body>
        <b>Last Name:</b> <jsp:getProperty name="user" property="firstName" />
        <br>
        <b>First Name:</b> <jsp:getProperty name="user" property="lastName" />
        <br>
        <b>Age:</b> <jsp:getProperty name="user" property="age" />
        <br>
        <b>Record Type:</b> <jsp:getProperty name="user" property="type" />
    </body>
</html>
```

In this example the age property is not expected on the request. A default age has been set to 0 by using a JSP expression. Also, for the sake of the example, this page is known to be in charge of inserting user information. The type property has been set by the static string "INSERT". This JSP produces output similar to the following:

```
Last Name: Doe
First Name: John
Age: 0
Record Type: INSERT
```

Summary

This chapter quickly covers all of the basic information about servlets, JSPs, and JavaBeans that you need to begin building a portal. It is quite understandable if you are feeling a little overwhelmed at this point; this chapter introduced many new classes, interfaces, and methodologies. In later chapters, we reinforce these concepts, as all of the information discussed here will be focused towards building Web applications using the BEA WebLogic Portal.

CHAPTER 4

Portals, Pages, and Portlets

I N C HAPTER 2, WE SHOWED YOU how portal Web applications fit into the architecture of WebLogic Domains and enterprise applications. In this chapter, we discuss the architecture of the WebLogic Portal. We also cover in detail the how to create and deploy the basic components of a WebLogic Portal.

What Is a Portal?

A portal is a Web application that brings many different functional modules together in a common forum. The term *portal* has been used to describe many different types of Web applications, and everyone seems to have their own view of what a portal is. However, since the WebLogic Portal framework can be used to define and construct almost any type of Web application, it will probably accommodate your requirements, whatever your definition of a portal might be.

In simplest terms, a WebLogic Portal is a Web application that ties together pages and portlets and logic. Constructing a WebLogic Portal application involves two distinct processes:

- Building the code required to perform the functionality within the application

- Building the portal definition

You build the code for a portal Web application using JSPs and Java classes deployed as a J2EE application within the WebLogic server. Figure 4-1 shows the sample portal application deployed as a Web application in exploded format. The JSPs are deployed under the portlets directory. The Java classes are deployed in the WEB-INF/classes directory.

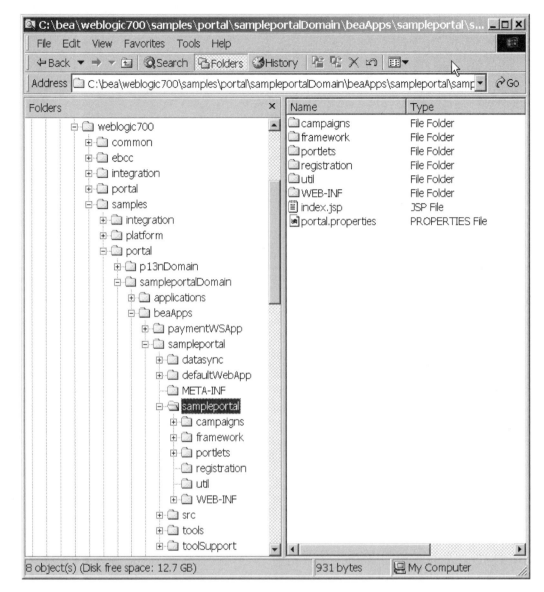

Figure 4-1. Sample portal directory

The portal definition, which defines all the pages within the application and how those pages will function and interact, is constructed using the EBCC and deployed using the synchronization process.

As illustrated by Figure 4-2, the portal definition is stored in XML format for use by the EBCC. When the portal definition is synchronized with the server, it is transferred to the relational database for access by the portal server at run time.

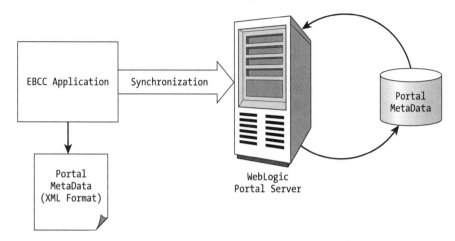

Figure 4-2. Portal architecture

This distinction of portal code and portal definition provides for a separation between the functionality and the user interface. It also provides portal administrators the ability to plug in previously coded functionality, as desired.

What Is a Portal Page?

A portal page is a view to one or more functional modules within the portal. In the WebLogic Portal environment, a portal page is constructed in the portal definition using the EBCC, not by using portal code. Figure 4-3 shows a portal page from the example portal application that comes with WebLogic Portal. Notice that this page has a header and footer and several functional modules with title bars. This page and all its components are dynamically generated at run time based on the portal framework and the portal definition or portal metadata.

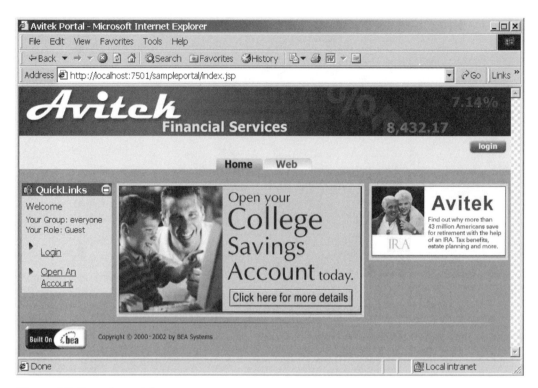

Figure 4-3. Sample portal page

Overview of Portal Page Components

By definition, a portal page is made up of several components. A layout, a skin, and one or more portlets will be coded and defined for each portal page in a portal application. In the following sections, we define and discuss each these components.

What Is a Portlet?

As you may recall from Chapter 1, a portlet is the component within a portal that performs the functionality. In its simplest form, a portlet is a JSP and some metadata that determines how the portlet will be positioned and formatted within a portal page.

What Is a Layout?

Earlier in this book, we defined a layout as something that specifies how portlets can be positioned on a page. In Figure 4-3 you can see portlets positioned on a page in a three-column layout. Several layouts come installed with the portal framework; however, you may also create custom layouts. Within the deployed application, the layouts are stored in the framework\layouts directory. Figure 4-4 shows the directory location of the two-column layout within the example portal application.

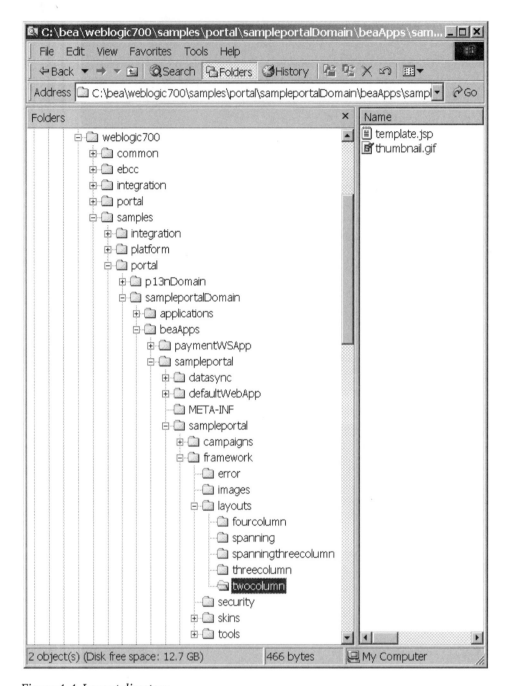

Figure 4-4. Layout directory

Notice that the layout component consists of a JSP and a GIF file. These files must be called template.jsp and thumbnail.gif respectively. We discuss creating a custom layout in detail in Chapter 5. However, to give you a sense of how layouts work, we've included the code for the JSP of the two-column layout from the example portal application here:

```
<%@ taglib uri='ren.tld' prefix='layout' %>
<layout:placePortletsinPlaceholder placeholders="left,right" />

<table width="100%" border="0" cellspacing="0" cellpadding="0">
  <tr>
    <td valign="top">
        <layout:render section='left'/>
    </td>
    <td valign="top">
        <layout:render section='right'/>
    </td>
  </tr>
</table>
```

NOTE *Notice that the layout is basically just an HTML table layout with some portal-specific JSP tags that tell the portal where to position portlets.*

What Is a Skin?

A skin determines the look and feel of a portal page by dictating such characteristics as the images that will be used for common buttons and icons and the font face and point size for text used in the portal. This component consists of a cascading style sheet and a collection of images.

In a deployed application, you will find the skins for the application in the framework\skins directory. Each skin has its own css directory and images directory. The css directory contains a cascading style sheet named main.css. Figure 4-5 shows the directory structure for the brightlight skin in the example portal application.

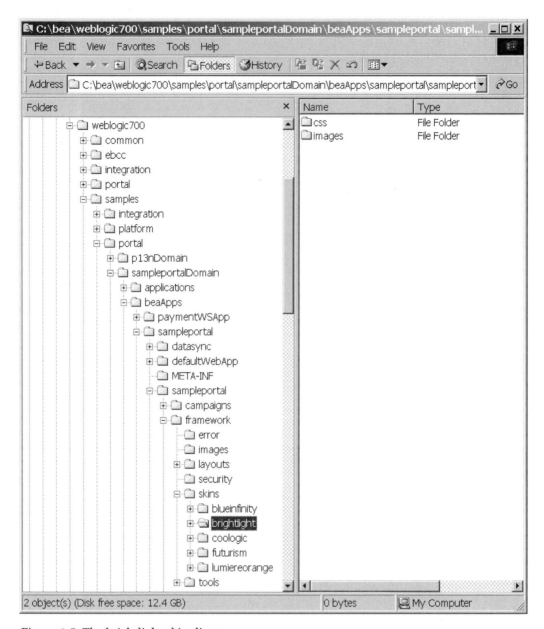

Figure 4-5. The brightlight skin directory

What follows is the code for the cascading style sheet of the brightlight skin in the stock portal application. The styles defined in this style sheet for the skin specify the font faces, colors, and other style elements that can be changed by an administrator or by a user, without code, simply by altering the metadata for a page or group of pages within a portal.

NOTE *Notice each of the styles defined here for the brightlight skin. It is fairly easy to make simple changes to the look and feel of your portal by simply modifying the styles in the style sheets that are defined in your portal. For instance, to change the color of the header background for each page that uses the brightlight skin, simply change the color number for the headerBgColor style.*

```
/* ================= Brightlight ======================= */

BODY{
        background-color: #FFFFFF;
        font-family:Arial,Tahoma,Helvetica,Verdana,sans-serif;
        font-size:9pt;
        margin:0px;
        background-repeat: no-repeat;
}

A:LINK{
        color: #026F93;
        text-decoration:none;
        font-family:Arial,Tahoma,Helvetica,Verdana,sans-serif;
        }

A:VISITED{
        color: #0099CC;
        text-decoration:none;
        font-family:Arial,Tahoma,Helvetica,Verdana,sans-serif;
        }

TD{font-family:Arial,Tahoma,Helvetica,Verdana,sans-serif; }

UL{ list-style-type: circle; color: #FC6C04; }

/* === Portal Styles === */
```

```
/* Use for the background color of portal page header sections */
.headerBgColor {   background-color: #FFFFFF}

/* Tab background color */
.titlebar{ background-color: #CCCCCC; }

/* Used when tabs are being displayed as text vs GIFs */
.tabselected{
     background-color: #026F93;
     font-family:Arial,Tahoma,Helvetica,Verdana,sans-serif;
     font-size:9pt;
     font-weight: bold;
     color: white;
     text-decoration:none;
     VERTICAL-ALIGN: middle;
}
.tabunselected{
     background-color: white;
     font-family:Arial,Tahoma,Helvetica,Verdana,sans-serif;
     font-size:9pt;
     font-weight: bold;
     color: #026F93;
     text-decoration:none;
     VERTICAL-ALIGN: middle;
}


.homebackground { background-color: #FFFFFF; }
.contentbgcolor { background-color: #FFFFFF; }

/* === Portlet Styles ==== */

.portletcontainer {
     border : 1px solid #CCCCCC;
     background-color: #FFFFFF;
    font-family:Arial,Tahoma,Helvetica,Verdana,sans-serif;
}
.portletcontainerBlended {
     background-color: #FFFFFF;
    font-family:Arial,Tahoma,Helvetica,Verdana,sans-serif;
}
```

```
.portlettitlebar{
     background-color: #0099CC;
     color: #FFFFFF;
     font-family:Arial,Tahoma,Helvetica,Verdana,sans-serif;
     font-size:9pt;
     line-height: 14px;
     font-weight: bold;
}
/* exact duplicate of .portlettitlebar until we convert
completely to .portlettitlebar */
.portletheading{
     background-color: #0099CC;
     color: #FFFFFF;
     font-family:Arial,Tahoma,Helvetica,Verdana,sans-serif;
     font-size:9pt;
     line-height: 14px;
     font-weight: bold;
}

.portletbanner{
     color: #0099CC;
     FONT-SIZE:12pt;
     font-weight: bold;
}
.portletheader{
     color: #0099CC;
     font-weight: bold;
}
.portletcontent {
     font-size:9pt;
}

.portletfooter{
     font-size:8pt;
     background-color: #eeeeee;
}

/* ================= Content ====================== */
```

```css
/* style used for content/page heading */
.pageheader{
  FONT-FAMILY:Arial,Helvetica,Tahoma,Verdana,sans-serif;
  COLOR:#000000;
  LINE-HEIGHT: 18pt;
  FONT-SIZE:14pt;
  FONT-WEIGHT:bold;
}

/* use for any instructional text */
.instructions{
  FONT-FAMILY:Arial,Helvetica,Tahoma,Verdana,sans-serif;
  COLOR:#000000;
  FONT-SIZE:9pt;
}

.contentheading{
    color: #0099CC;
    FONT-SIZE:12pt;
    font-weight: bold;
}
.contentsubheading{
    color: #0099CC;
    font-weight: bold;
}
.minortext{
    font-size:8pt;
}
.headerlink{
    FONT-SIZE:12pt;
    font-weight: bold;
}

/* use for any error message text */
.errorMessage{
  FONT-FAMILY:Arial,Helvetica,Tahoma,Verdana,sans-serif;
  COLOR:red;
}

/* use for any success message text */
.successMessage{
  FONT-FAMILY:Arial,Helvetica,Tahoma,Verdana,sans-serif;
  COLOR:green;
}
```

```css
/* Use for lists where we want the row colors to be the same each row. */
.row {
  BACKGROUND-COLOR: white;
}
/* Use for multi-column lists where we want the row
colors to be different each row. */
.row1 {
  BACKGROUND-COLOR: white;
}
/* Use for multi-column lists where we want the row
colors to be different each row. */
.row2 {
  BACKGROUND-COLOR: lightgrey;
}


/* Use for adding space at end of line items list. */
.spacerRow {
  BACKGROUND-COLOR: white;
  HEIGHT: 10px;
}


/* Use for adding space at end of line items list. */
.emptyRow {
  HEIGHT: 15px;
}



form {  margin-top: 0px; margin-right: 0px; margin-bottom: 0px; margin-left: 0px}



/* Use for all labels that are associated with some sort of input field. */
.fieldlabel{
  FONT-WEIGHT:bold;
  align: right;
}

.priorityLow {
  color:blue;
  FONT-WEIGHT:bold;
}
.priorityMedium {
  color:goldenrod;
  FONT-WEIGHT:bold;
}
```

```
.priorityHigh {
  color:red;
  FONT-WEIGHT:bold;
}
```

Creating a Portal Domain

To create a new portal, you must first create a portal domain. In Chapter 2, we discussed the architecture of portal domains. The BEA Domain Configuration Wizard allows you to easily create a new domain for a variety of purposes. With the configuration wizard, you can create many types of domains including WLPortal Domains and WLServer Domains. In this section, we discuss the steps required to create a new portal domain using the WebLogic Domain Configuration Wizard.

To start this wizard, select Start ➤ Programs ➤ BEA WebLogic Platform 7.0 ➤ Domain Configuration Wizard. The following steps show how to create a new domain once you have the started the wizard:

1. To create a portal domain, choose the WLP Domain template in the first wizard step. Change the domain name to portalDomain.

2. In the second wizard step, choose the server type that is appropriate for your environment. For this demonstration, choose the Single Server (Standalone Server) option.

3. The third wizard step allows you to choose the directory location for the new domain. For the domain location, choose the standard directory that your organization has established. In this case, choose the default directory that the wizard offers.

4. In the fourth wizard step, enter the server name and ports for this installation. For this example, accept the default options that the wizard offers.

5. In the fifth wizard step, enter a user name and password for the administrative user for the domain. You will use this user to start the server. Specify "weblogic" as the user and "weblogic" as the password for this example.

6. In the sixth step of the wizard, make sure that the Yes option is selected so that you can start the server from the start menu.

7. The next step of the wizard displays a summary of the information that you entered. This information is used to create the new domain. The summary step allows you to review your choices prior to creating the domain. Click the Create button to create the domain according to the options you have specified.

8. In the next wizard step, choose End Configuration Wizard and click the Done button to close the Domain Configuration Wizard.

You've just created a domain to support your Web application and portal. Next we discuss how to create the portal.

Building a Portal

The Domain Configuration Wizard automatically created an enterprise application called portalApp as it was establishing your new domain. Figure 4-6 shows the directory structure for the new domain and enterprise application created by this wizard.

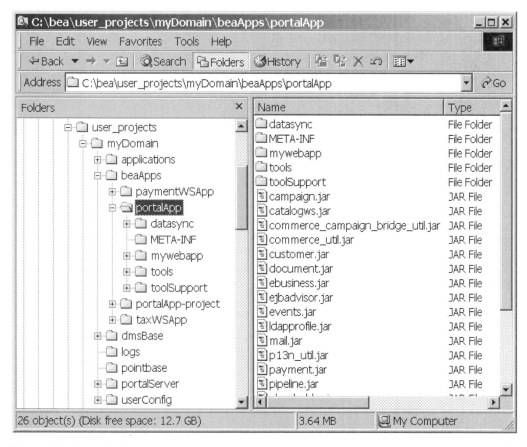

Figure 4-6. Domain directory structure

Each portal within the WebLogic Portal architecture is required to have a Web application to support it. Now that you have a domain and an enterprise application, you can use the EBCC to create your new Web application and portal.

1. Start the server for the new domain you just created. Click Start ➢ Programs ➢ BEA WebLogic Platform 7.0 ➢ User Projects ➢ *domain name* ➢ Start Portal Server. Use the domain name that you specified in the Domain Configuration Wizard. If you followed our example, the domain name is myDomain.

2. To start the server, you must enter the user name and password that you specified in the Domain Configuration Wizard.

3. Now start the EBCC. Click Start ➢ Programs ➢ BEA WebLogic Platform 7.0 ➢ WebLogic Portal 7.0 ➢ E-Business Control Center.

4. When the Domain Configuration Wizard created the enterprise application for the new domain, it also created an EBCC project. This project is named portalApp-project.eaprj and can be found at \bea\user_projects*domain name*\beaApps\portalApp-project. Select File ➢ Open menu to open this project, as shown in Figure 4-7.

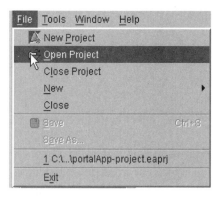

Figure 4-7. Opening a project through the File menu

5. Now generate the new Web application that is required to support the portal you will create. Select the Portal menu item from the drop-down menu as shown in Figure 4-8.

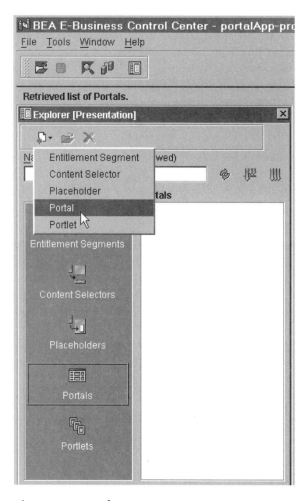

Figure 4-8. Creating a new portal

6. Select the first option from the dialog box that appears to create a portal with some default settings including a default home page. With these default settings you will be able to run your empty portal to test it as soon as you create and deploy it.

7. In the Portal Name step of the wizard that appears, enter the name of the portal and the name of the Web application that will support the portal. For this example, use "mywebapp" and "myportal" respectively.

8. In the Portal Templates step of the wizard, choose the baseportal option.

9. Next is the Resource Files Location step of the wizard. Enter the parent directory for the Web application that will be created—in this case, accept the default location provided.

10. Step 4 of the wizard is the Summary step, which displays a summary of the resources that have been created for the Web application and the portal.

11. Step 5 of the wizard allows you to choose whether to "hot deploy" now or to manually deploy the portal at a later time. If you choose the hot deploy option, the Web application and portal will be deployed automatically to the server when you click the Deploy button. Choose the hot deploy option for this example.

    During the hot deploy process you will be asked for a user name and password. Enter the user name and password that you entered in the Domain Configuration Wizard when you created the domain. For this example, that would be "weblogic" for the user name and "weblogic" for the password.

12. Finally the status screen indicates when the deploy process is completed.

You should now be able to view your empty portal by going to the following URL in your browser: `http://localhost:7501/web application name/index.jsp`. Figure 4-9 shows the page from the new portal application that you will see in your browser.

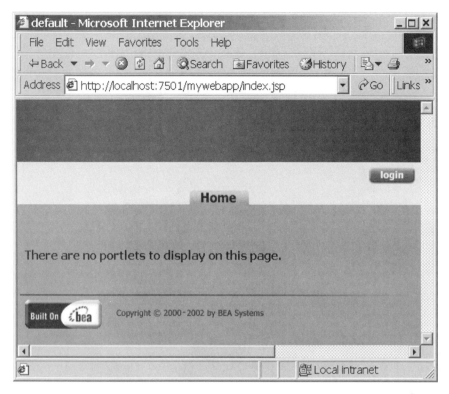

Figure 4-9. Portal page for your newly created portal

NOTE *Because this is the first time that your portal page has been accessed, the server must first compile the portal JSPs that are used to display the page. As a result, pages within the portal will take a minute to display the first time you access them.*

Next we discuss how to make manage the new portal and its components using the portal management tools.

Portal Management Tools

WebLogic has provided three utilities for developing and managing portals. Following is a description of these tools and their purpose.

E-Business Control Center

The E-Business Control Center (EBCC) is mainly a developer tool. Power users can also use the EBCC to modify properties of the portal definition for a portal. This tool lets you create and modify almost every component within a portal. For instance, through the EBCC you can create new portal applications, new portlets, and portal Webflow logic.

portalAppTools

The portalAppTools utility allows portal administrators to modify portal attributes. It can be used to modify the skins for a portal, modify the availability and visibility of portlets, and manage portal users among other things.

Server Console

Portal system administrators administer the deployed portal environment through the server console. This tool can be used to deploy and undeploy a portal and other components of a Web application. It lets you manage the portal server or cluster as well as other server and domain configuration parameters.

Building a Basic Portlet

The following sections describe how to build a basic portlet. We discuss the steps required to create a new portlet definition and how to add functionality to it.

Creating an Empty Portlet

Here we demonstrate how to create a new portlet using the EBCC and portalAppTools. The portlet you create with these steps will be an empty one with no functionality associated with it. However, once you create the portlet, you will be able to modify it to add the functionality required for your application.

1. As shown in Figure 4-10, in the EBCC, select the Portlet menu item.

2. Select the first option in the dialog box that displays to bring up a wizard for creating your new portlet.

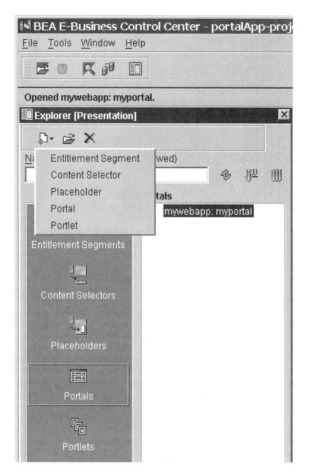

Figure 4-10. Creating a new portlet

3. In the Portlet Name step of the wizard, enter the name of the portlet that you want to create. For this example, name your portlet firstPortlet.

4. In the Portlet Pages step of the wizard, select the portlet home page created by default with the Portal Creation Wizard. Selecting the home page causes the new portlet to be available for display on the home page.

5. In the Portlet Components step of the wizard, select all the available options. This allows you to see components that the wizard will generate for you. When creating your own portlets, you would choose the options that are necessary based on the design of your portal.

6. In the Content Types step of the wizard, select the Basic (no Webflow) option. (We discuss Webflow and Web services in later chapters.)

7. In the Resource Files Location step of the wizard, accept the default location provided by the wizard.

8. The Summary step of the wizard gives you a list of the items that the wizard creates for you when you click the Create button. Click the Create button to complete the portlet creation process.

9. The Next Steps step of the wizard gives you the option of opening an edit window within the EBCC for the portlet you have just created. If you select this option, you will also open the portal edit window within the EBCC. For this example, accept the default and open the portlet edit window.

10. As specified in the last step of the wizard, the portlet edit window automatically opens for you in the EBCC. Note the configuration options that were automatically set for you by the wizard. Do not change any of these options at this time.

11. Now select Tools ➤ Synchronize in the EBCC. This synchronizes the new portlet definition with the portal server. When the synchronize process is finished, click the Close button.

12. When you see the Reset Campaign States dialog box, click the Cancel button.

13. Now the definition has been created for your new portlet and synchronized with the server. The wizard has also created template code for your new portlet in the form of several JSPs. In order to force the new portlet to show up on the home page of portal, you need to use the portalAppTools utility to modify the Visible and Available attributes of the new portlet that you created.

    To start the portalAppTools utility, go to the following URL in your browser: `http://server name:7501/portalAppTools/index.jsp`.

14. You will need to log in to the portalAppTools utility (see Figure 4-11) using the following user name and password:

    User name: administrator

    Password: password

Figure 4-11. portalAppTools login dialog box

15. Select the Portal Management link within the portalAppTools utility (see Figure 4-12).

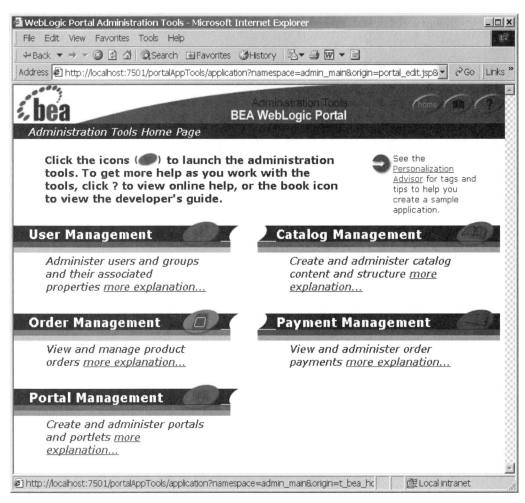

Figure 4-12. Click the Portal Management link.

16. Click the default (everyone) group portal link on the Portal Management Home page (see Figure 4-13).

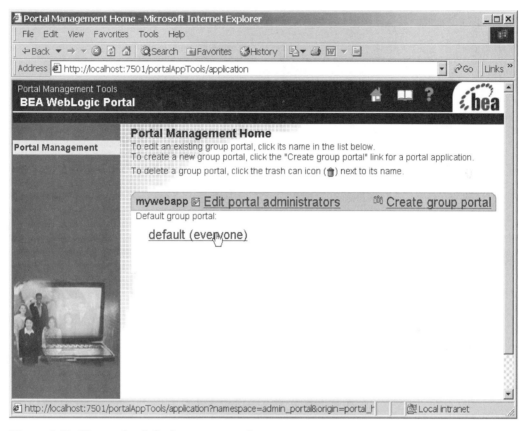

Figure 4-13. Choose the default group portal.

17. Click the Manage Pages and Portlets link on the Group Portal Management Home page (see Figure 4-14).

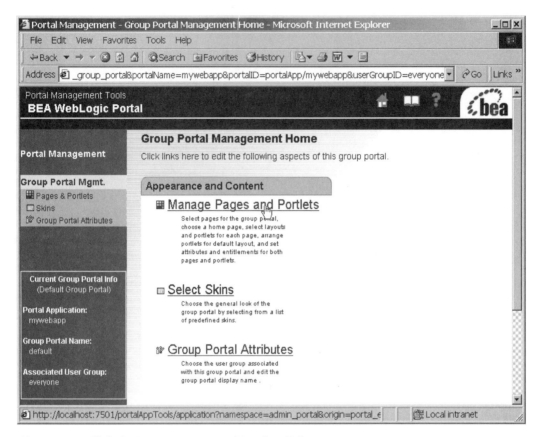

Figure 4-14. Click the Manage Pages and Portlets link.

18. Click the Edit Portlets button on the Pages and Portlets page (see Figure 4-15).

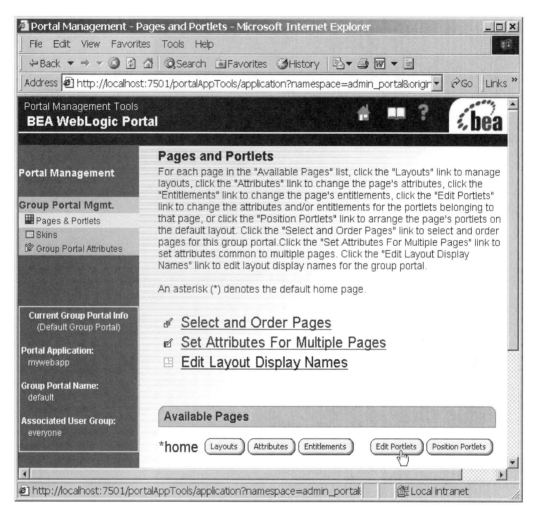

Figure 4-15. Click the Edit Portlets button.

19. Select the portlet you created in the wizard and click the Set Attributes button on the Edit Portlet Entitlements and Attributes page (see Figure 4-16).

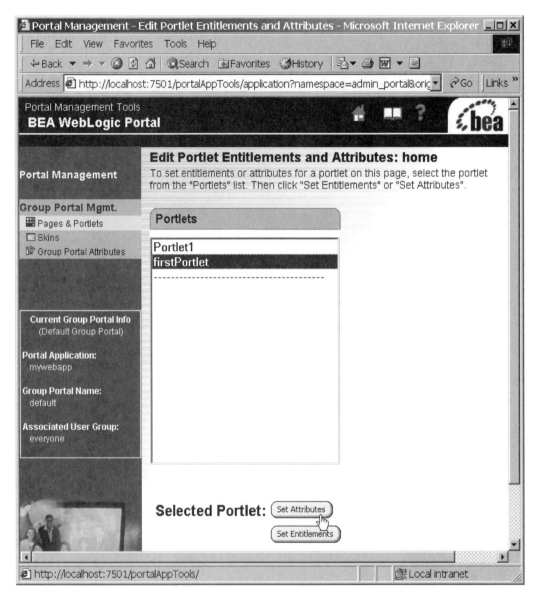

Figure 4-16. Click the Set Attributes button.

20. Select the Available and Visible check boxes and click the Save button on the Set home Portlet Attributes page (see Figure 4-17). After the save is complete, the browser returns you to the Select Portlet page. Click the Back button to go back to the Pages and Portlets page.

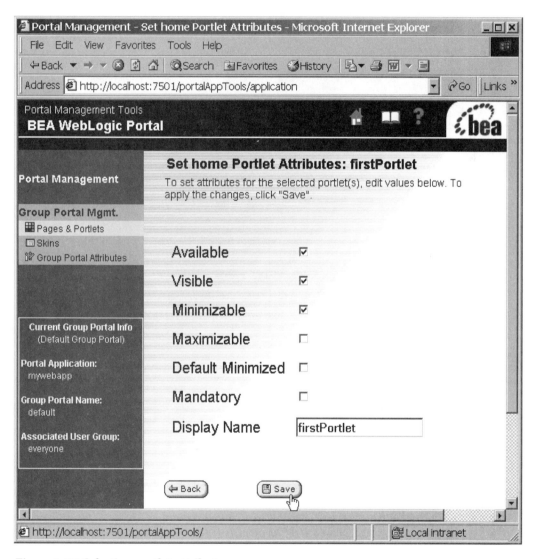

Figure 4-17. Selecting portlet attributes

21. Click the Position Portlets button (see Figure 4-18).

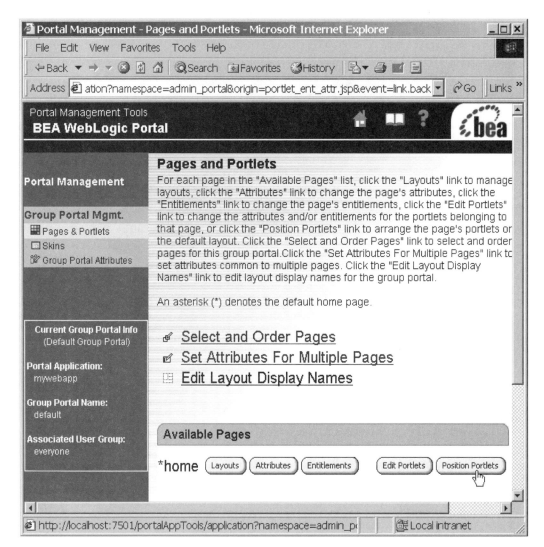

Figure 4-18. Click the Position Portlets button.

22. Your portlet should already be positioned in the first column of the lay-out (see Figure 4-19). If it is not, move it to the first column of the layout. Click the Save button.

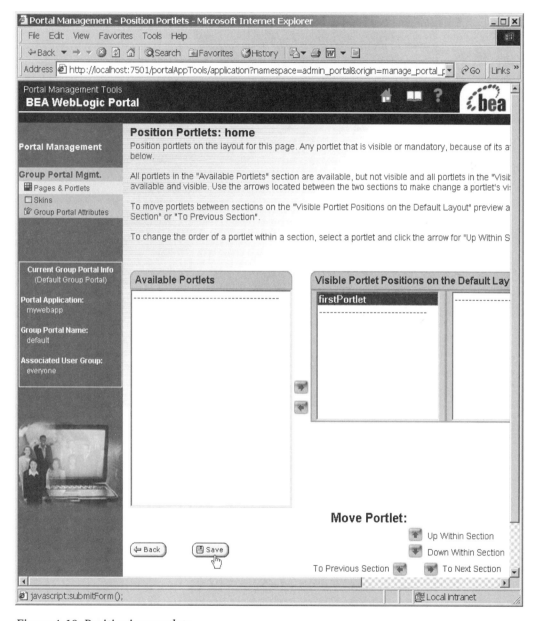

Figure 4-19. Positioning portlets

23. You should now be able to view your new portlet in the portal that you created previously by going to the following URL in your browser: http://*server name*:7501/*web application name*/index.jsp (see Figure 4-20).

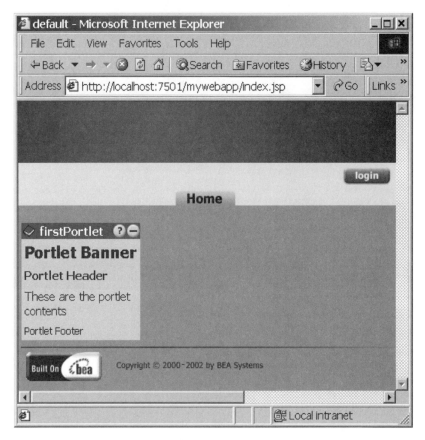

Figure 4-20. The newly created portlet appears on the portal page.

Adding Functionality to a Portlet

Up to now, we have walked you through creating an empty portal, an empty page, and a portlet with no functionality. Now we discuss how to add functionality to the portlet that you created.

Notice in Figure 4-21 the JSPs that were automatically generated for you by the portlet wizard. You can see that banner.jsp, header.jsp, footer.jsp, and help.jsp correspond to the options that you chose when you were creating the portlet in the wizard. These JSPs allow you to modify the look and feel of your portlet and provide help content for the user.

Also notice that the portlet wizard created a content.jsp file. This is the default JSP, and it enables you to provide content or functionality for your portlet. In fact, you can use any JSP for this purpose simply by placing the JSP in this directory and modifying the portlet definition in the EBCC. For this example, you will modify the content.jsp to provide functionality for your portlet.

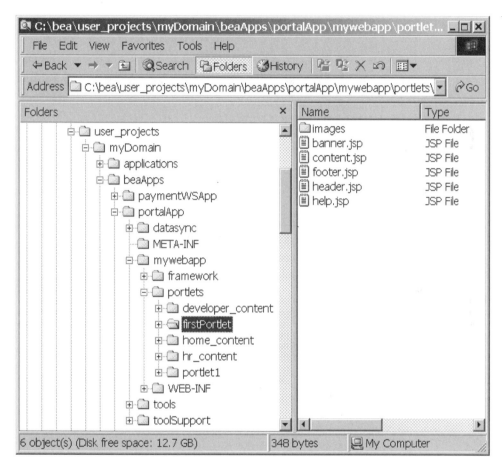

Figure 4-21. New portal functionality

We are going to show you how to make your new portlet read a list of American presidents from a file and generate a table listing with links to a biography page for each president. Before we do that, modify the banner, header, and footer display content appropriate for your portlet.

1. Modify the banner.jsp file so that the code appears as follows:

```
<!-- put the contents of your banner here -->
American Presidents
```

2. Modify the header.jsp file so that the code looks like this:

```
<!-- put the contents of your header here -->
Biography
```

3. Modify the footer.jsp file so that the code appears as follows:

```
<!-- put the contents of your footer here -->
American Presidents &copy; bogus copyright 2002
```

Notice that you didn't use any HTML to modify the style of the text for these components. The skin associated with this page will determine the style of the text for these components.

Next, modify the skin associated with the home page. To do this, you first need to use the EBCC to make a new skin available for your portal. Then you use the portalAppTools utility to change the default skin for your portal.

Make the coologic skin available to the portal:

1. Open the EBCC utility.

2. Click the portals icon to display your portal.

3. Double-click your portal—myportal in this example. This displays the editor for the portal in the right pane.

4. Click the General separator bar to display the general properties for your portal in the Portal Editor.

5. Select the Skins tab in the Portal Editor.

6. Move the coologic skin from the Available skins list to the Selected skins list as shown in Figure 4-22.

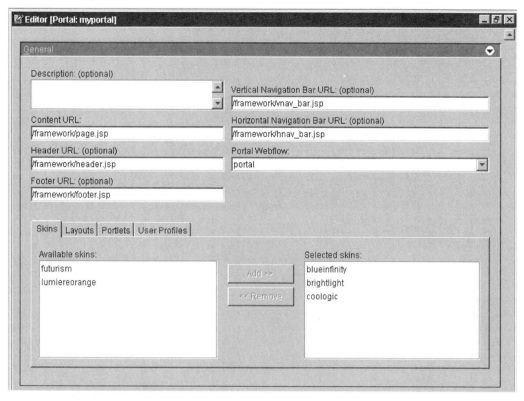

Figure 4-22. Selecting from available skins

7. Select File ➤ Save to save the new portal definition.

8. Select Tools ➤ Synchronize in the EBCC.

9. Cancel the Reset Campaign State dialog box.

Modify the default skin for the home page:

1. Log in to the portalAppTools utility.

2. Select the default (everyone) group portal.

3. Click the Select Skins link.

4. Move the coologic skin from the Unused list to the Available skins list.

5. Select the coologic skin item from the Available skins list and click the Set as default button (see Figure 4-23).

6. Click the Save button.

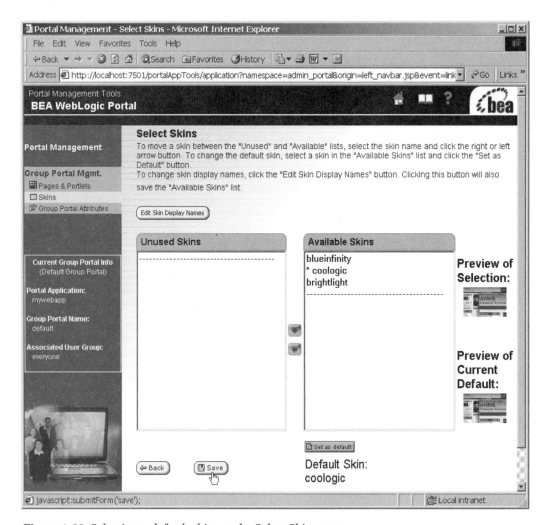

Figure 4-23. Selecting a default skin on the Select Skins page

To modify the titlebar text, you also use the portalAppTools utility:

1. Select Pages and Portlets from the Group Portal Mgmt. menu in the left menu bar.

2. Click the Edit Portlets button in the right pane.

3. Select the firstPortlet item from the Portlets list.

4. Click the Set Attributes button.

5. Modify the Display Name field as shown in Figure 4-24 and click the Save button.

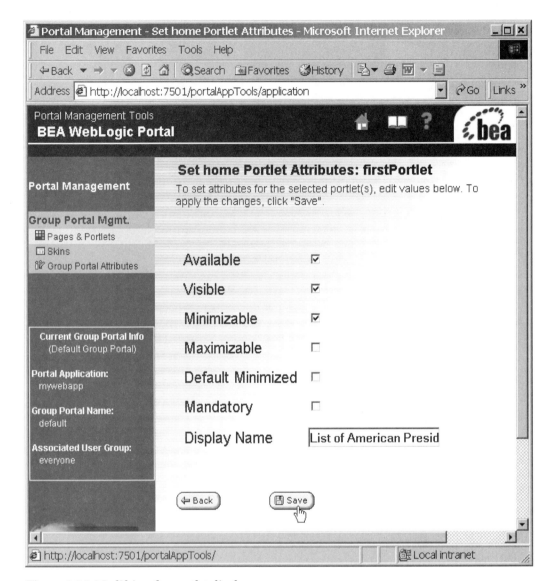

Figure 4-24. Modifying the portlet display name

Figure 4-25 shows the portlet with the changes you have made so far.
You can view the portlet by browsing to the following URL:
`http://server:7501/web app name/index.jsp.`

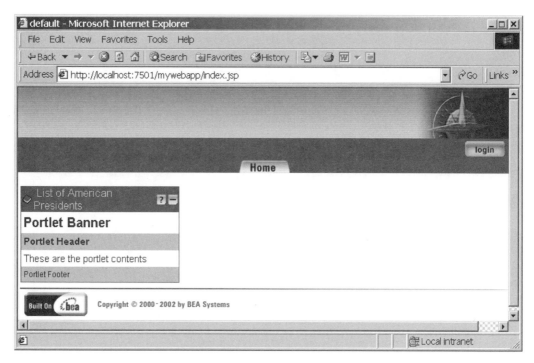

Figure 4-25. Portal page with modified portlet

You now know how to modify the look and feel of your portlet. As you can see, it is fairly simple to make some pretty powerful changes to the look and feel of your portal and portlets. In the next chapter, we discuss how to modify the portlets even further.

Next, you want to add some real functionality to your portlet. Figure 4-26 shows the rendered portlet with the new functionality that you will add.

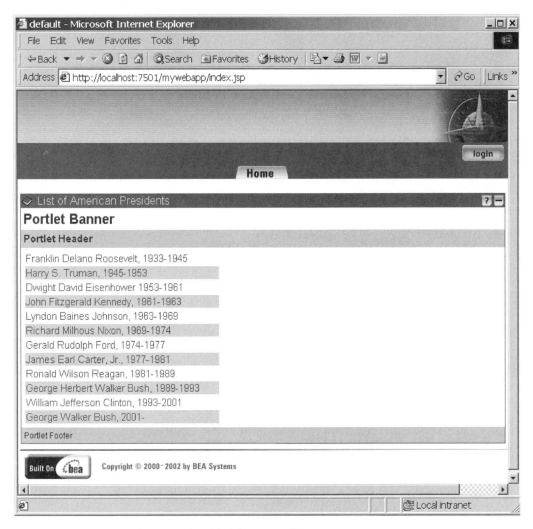

Figure 4-26. New portal page with added functionality

Here is the JSP code for content.jsp that adds the functionality to your portlet:

```
<%@ page import="java.util.*"%>
<%@ page import="java.io.*"%>

<%
```

The following ArrayList holds the items that you read from the file. Notice the scriptlet open tag preceding this paragraph. Scriptlets were discussed in Chapter 3. The code between the scriptlet open tag and the scriptlet close tag can contain any valid Java code.

```
ArrayList names = new ArrayList();

String item = null;
String rowclass = "row1";

// Retrieve name list
  String record = null;

  BufferedReader br = null;
  try {
```

The presidents.txt file holds a list presidents' names formatted with anchor tags and hrefs. The following code reads this file from the firstPortlet directory in your portal directory structure. The items in the file are separated by a carriage return line feed and is read in a line at a time and placed into the ArrayList.

```
        InputStreamReader fr = new InputStreamReader(
application.getResourceAsStream("/portlets/firstPortlet/presidents.txt"), "ASCII");
        br = new BufferedReader(fr);

        while ((record = br.readLine()) != null) {
            names.add(record);
        }
    } catch (IOException e) {
        // catch possible io errors from readLine()
        System.out.println("IOException error!");
        e.printStackTrace();
    }
    finally
    {
        try { if (br != null) br.close(); } catch (IOException ignore) { }
    }
%>
```

Outside of the scriptlets you place valid HTML. It is important to note that malformed HTML can cause your portlet to function improperly or not to function at all. Make sure that all HTML in your JSPs is well formed. Next, you begin the HTML table.

```
<table width=100%>
<%
```

The following code loops through the ArrayList, formatting the items as HTML table rows:

```
Iterator i = names.iterator();
while (i.hasNext()) {
        item = (String)i.next();
%>
```

Here you format the items in HTML rows. Notice that you use a JSP expression to specify the class for each row. Using the scriptlet code that follows, you alternate the row class so that the background color for the row will alternate. The class names that you use for the rows are default class names specified in each skin. Using these class names allows the look and feel of the portal and portlets to change based on the skin you choose.

```
<tr class='<%=rowclass%>'><td><%= item %></td></tr>
<%
            // Alternate row class
            if(rowclass.equals("row1")){
                            rowclass = "row2";
            }
            else{
                            rowclass = "row1";               }
```

Here you end the preceding for loop. Notice that we have you close this code block in a different scriptlet than the one you used to open it:

```
}
%>
</table>
```

The following steps show how to add this new functionality to your portal:

1. Place the preceding code in the content.jsp within the firstPortlet directory in your portal directory structure.

2. Place the presidents.txt text file in the same directory.

3. Browse to the portal server console at the following url:
   `http://server:7501/console`.

4. Log in to the console using the user name and password you set up when
   you ran the Domain Configuration Wizard.

5. Navigate to myDomain ➤ Deployments ➤ Applications ➤ portalApp
   ➤ mywebapp and select the Deploy tab as shown in Figure 4-27.

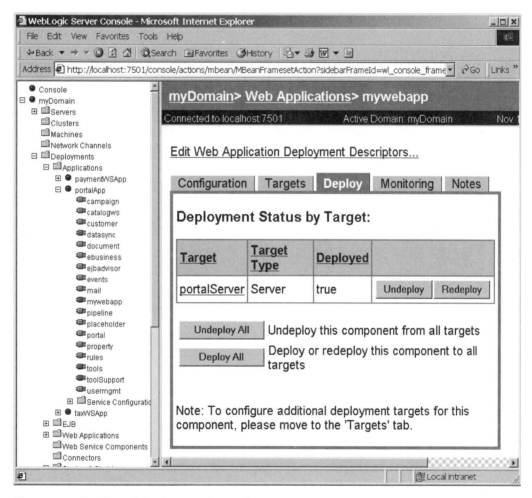

Figure 4-27. Deploy tab in the portal console

6. Click the Undeploy All button.

7. When the undeploy process is finished, click the Deploy All button.

Now you should be able to browse to your portlet and test it again.

Summary

In this chapter, we have shown how to create a new domain, a new portal, and a new portlet. We have also shown some of the ways you can modify the look and feel of the portal. Finally we have added real functionality to the portal using the components provided by the portal framework. You should now have a good foundation in your understanding of BEA WebLogic Portal basics. In the next chapters, you will build on this foundation as you learn how to modify the portal framework and use other components of the WebLogic Portal Server to accommodate your specific requirements.

CHAPTER 5

How to Customize the Look and Feel of a Portal

THE PREVIOUS CHAPTER talked about how you can use portlets, portal pages, skins, and layouts to build a portal. You will likely want to change the look and feel of the portal that you installed using the New Portal Wizard in the EBCC. Figure 5-1 shows an example of a portal that has been customized.

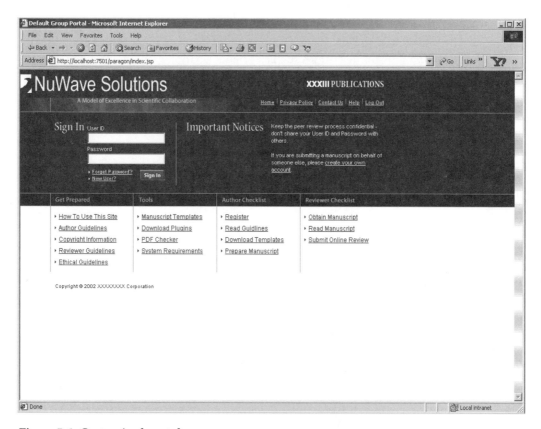

Figure 5-1. Customized portal

As you can see, the look and feel is entirely different from the base portal you installed. In this chapter, you learn the details of how you can customize the portal you created in the previous chapter to produce portals such as the one shown in Figure 5-1. We show you how to customize the following items:

- Framework JSPs

- Portlets

- Portal pages

- Skins

- Layouts

Let's begin with framework JSPs.

Framework JSPs

The BEA WebLogic Portal uses a framework of JSPs and include files (.inc) that display generic portal entities such as a header, a footer, and navigation panes. Preexisting JSPs serve as portal defaults. The framework JSPs are located in the user_projects\myDomain\beaApps\portalApp\myWebApp\framework directory, which is shown in Figure 5-2.

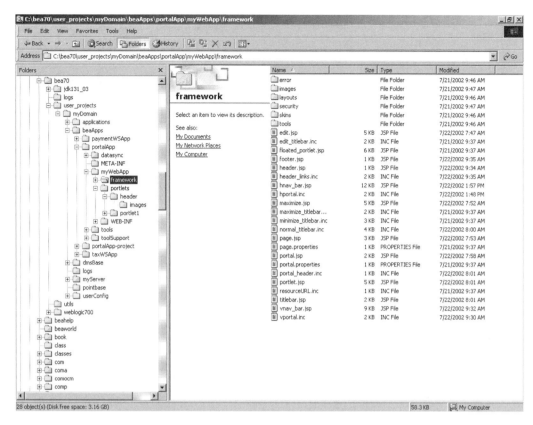

Figure 5-2. Framework JSPs and directory

You can change many of the JSPs that the portal employs in its framework.
For example, you define some of these JSPs in the EBCC under the General tab of
the Portal Editor, as shown in Figure 5-3.

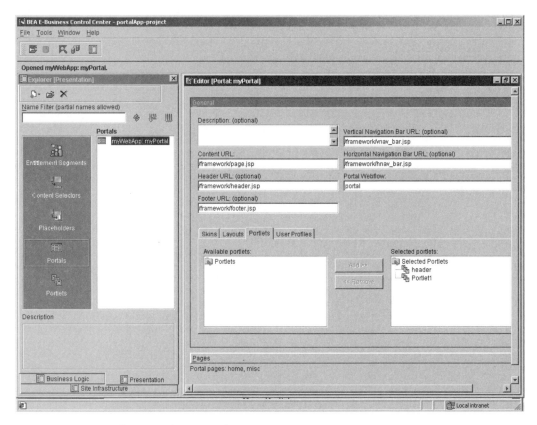

Figure 5-3. Setting framework JSPs in the EBCC

If you want to change the way any of these JSPs execute, you can write your own JSPs and define them in the General tab of the EBCC. Table 5-1 lists the definable framework JSPs.

Table 5-1. Framework JSPs

JSP	DESCRIPTION
page.jsp	Calls each portlet defined on a page. This file determines what portal attributes have been set.
header.jsp	Specifies the header that is displayed in the portal.
footer.jsp	Specifies the footer that is displayed in the portal.
hnav_bar	Represents the horizontal navigation bar. Use this JSP to create the horizontal tabs that are displayed in the portal.
vnav_bar.jsp	Represents the vertical navigation bar. Use this JSP to create the vertical tabs that are displayed in the portal.

Defining Additional Framework JSPs and Include Files

In addition to the JSPs just mentioned, there are other JSPs and include files that you should know about. It is important to understand all the JSPs and include files in the framework directory, because a slight modification to one of these files could be all you need to get the look and feel you desire. Also, many of these files are used internally by the BEA WebLogic Portal and should not be modified unless you really know what you are doing.

The portal.jsp is called first by the BEA WebLogic presentation manager. The purpose of this JSP is twofold:

- Establish the style sheet (.css file) based on the skin selected.

- Render the body of the portal. Essentially there two modes for this: Horizontal or Vertical. The mode is set in the Group Portal Attributes page of the Administration Tools. Figure 5-4 shows the default setting for the Nav Bar Orientation option, Horizontal. If the setting is Horizontal, then the JSP includes the hportal.inc file. If the setting is Vertical, it calls the vportal.inc file.

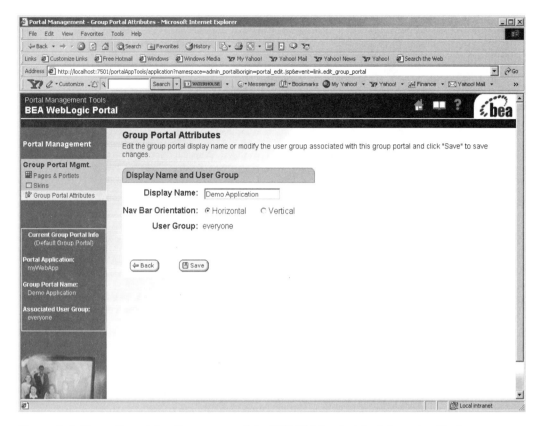

Figure 5-4. Group Portal Attributes page of the BEA WebLogic Administration Tools

The vportal.inc and hportal.inc files come with portal.jsp. These include files do the following:

- Include the portal_header.inc file that builds the header. The portal_header.inc file includes the header.jsp. This is set in the EBCC, and we discuss this process more fully later in the chapter. The portal_header.inc file also includes the header_links.inc file, which builds the links in the header such as the login button shown in the default portal you built in Chapter 2.

NOTE   *If you do not want the login button to be displayed (see Figure 5-1 for an example of a portal without tabs), you can modify portal_header.inc so that it does not call the header_links.inc file. To do so, comment out the following line in the JSP:*
`<%@ include file="header_links.inc"%>`*.*

- Include the vertical navigation bar or horizontal navigation bar depending on the Nav Bar Orientation option setting (see Figure 5-3). We discuss this option, which is set in the EBCC, later in the chapter. In the EBCC, the default for this is hnav_bar.jsp or vnav_bar.jsp.

- Include the content JSP that formats each portlet. In the EBCC, the default for this is page.jsp.

- Include the footer JSP. This is set in the EBCC, as we discuss later in the chapter. In the EBCC, the default for this is footer.jsp.

NOTE   *If you do not want tabs to be displayed (see Figure 5-1 for an example of a portal without tabs), you can modify vportal.inc or hportl.inc so that it does not call the vertical or horizontal nav_bar, respectively. To do so, comment out the following line in the JSP:* `<jsp:include page="<%= navbar %>"/>`.

Portal Pages

As defined earlier, a portal page is a view to one or more functional modules within the portal. You define the desired attributes for your pages in the EBCC. Once you have defined these attributes, you go to the WebLogic Portal Administration Tools to select and order the pages and specify which of the attributes you want applied to the page.

Defining Page Attributes

To define page attributes, you must go into the EBCC and select the page you want to define attributes for. To see how this is done, create a new page called misc. Figure 5-5 shows all the attributes you need to define for the misc page.

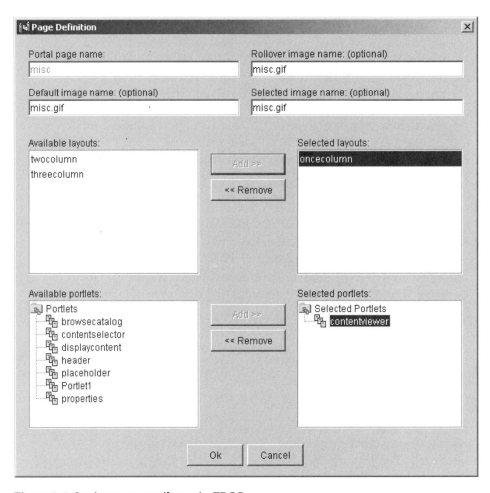

Figure 5-5. Setting page attributes in EBCC

As you can see, various attributes are available for defining your page. Table 5-2 describes all the different attributes you can define for pages.

Table 5-2. EBCC Attributes for Pages

ATTRIBUTE	DESCRIPTION
Default image name	Path for tab image that appears as a default for the page. If you do not define an image, the portal will build the tab based on text. Note that the path for these images is relative to the skin's directory. This means that you need an image in each skin's directory.
Rollover image name	Path for tab rollover image for the page.
Selected image name	Path for tab image that is displayed if the page is selected. If you do not select an image, the portal will build the tab based on text.
Available layouts	List of layouts available for a page.
Available portlets	List of portlets available for a page.

You can enter all the attributes you want defined for the page you selected, after which you need to save the changes and synchronize the EBCC to have the newly entered page attributes available to the portal.

Selecting and Ordering Pages

After assigning page attributes in the EBCC, you can select the pages you want available to the portal through the Select and Order Pages page in the Administration Tools. Select the misc page from the Unused Pages list and moved it to the Available Pages list as shown in Figure 5-6.

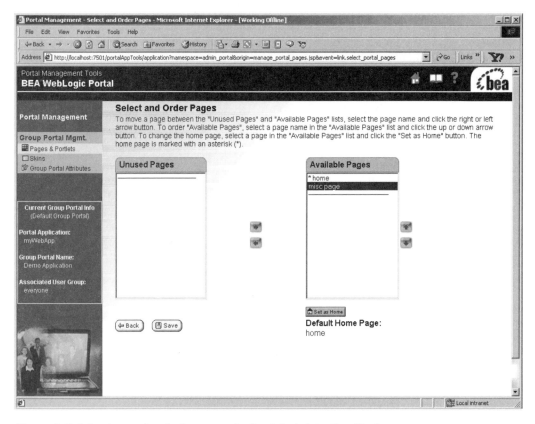

Figure 5-6. Selecting and ordering pages in the Administration Tools

This page also lets you specify a default home page by selecting an available page and clicking the Set as Home button.

Selecting Page Attributes

Next, you use the Administration Tools to set additional attributes for the pages you made available. Table 5-3 explains all the attributes you can set.

Table 5-3. Administration Tools Attributes for Pages

ATTRIBUTE	DESCRIPTION
Visible	This attribute makes a page visible to users. Note that this attribute is disabled for the default home page you defined.
Mandatory	Users always see the page with this attribute set. They cannot remove it from their personalized portals. Note that this attribute is disabled for the default home page you defined.
Display Name	The display name for the page. Also serves as the text display on the tab if you decide not to enter a default image.
Visitor Editable Name	If this option is checked, users can modify the page name when they personalize their portals.
Use Image	If this option is checked, a specified image displays the page name. If it is not selected, the text specified for the Display Name attribute is used.

Figure 5-7 shows how to set the page attributes for the example page you created, misc.

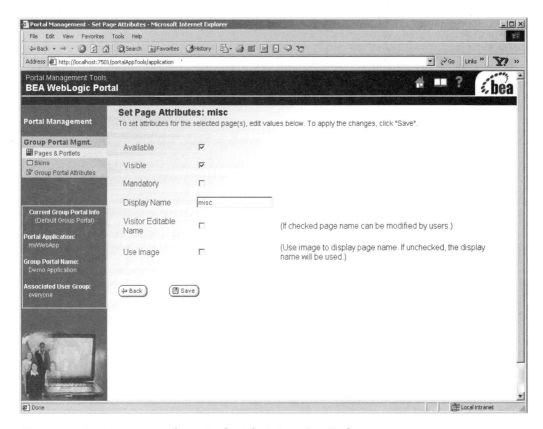

Figure 5-7. Setting page attributes in the Administration Tool

After you have made a page available to the portal and set its portal attributes, display your page to see how your selections take effect. Figure 5-8 shows how the misc page looks with the page attributes from Figure 5-7. Note that the misc tab was built using text because you did not specify images in the EBCC for those attributes.

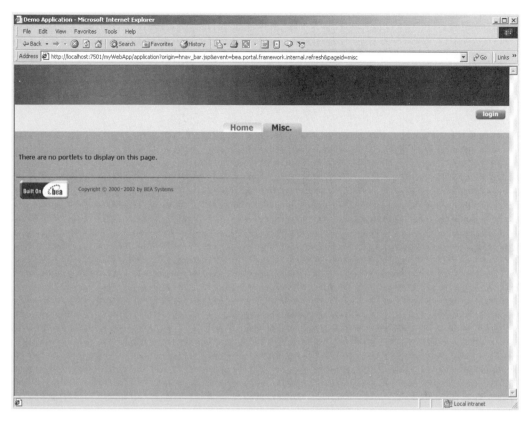

Figure 5-8. Misc. page with portal attributes set

NOTE *As you can see, no portlets are displayed for the misc page. Selecting portlets to display on the page is explained when we discuss layouts later in this chapter.*

Portlets

As you know, a portlet is the component within a portal that gives it its functionality. In its simplest form, a portlet is a JSP and some metadata that determines how the portlet will be positioned and formatted within a portal page. Portlet attributes, such as displayed headers and footers, are the visual and behavioral aspects that a visitor experiences when accessing a portlet. As with portal pages, you use the EBCC to define the desired attributes for your portlets. Once you have defined these attributes, you select the attributes you want for each portlet in the Administration Tools.

Defining Portlet Attributes

To define portlet attributes, you must go into the EBCC and select the portlet you want to define attributes for. To see how this is done, create a portlet called header. Figure 5-9 shows all the attributes you define for the header portlet.

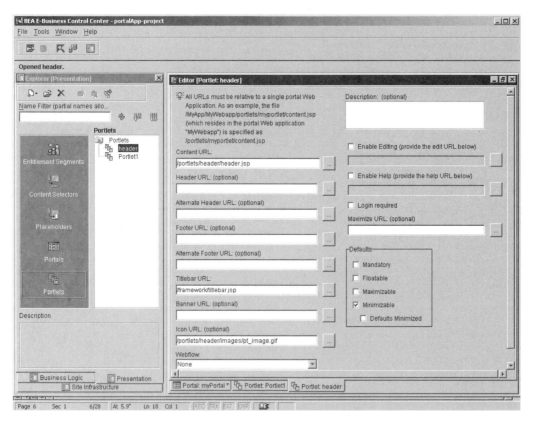

Figure 5-9. Setting portlet attributes in the EBCC

As you can see, portlets have many attributes that can be defined. Table 5-4 describes all these different portlet attributes. The last column in the table indicates whether the attribute in question is populated when a portlet is created using the Portlet Wizard.

Table 5-4. EBCC Attributes for Portlets

ATTRIBUTE	DESCRIPTION	POPULATED?
Description	Describes what the portlet does.	No
Content URL	Indicates location of the actual portlet. For the header portlet, the location is /portlets/header/header.jsp.	Yes
Header URL	Indicates location of the default header JSP that can appear at the top of the portlet.	No
Alternate Header URL	Specifies default location of the header when the portlet is maximized.	No
Footer URL	Indicates location of the default footer JSP.	No
Alternate Footer URL	Specifies location of the footer when the portlet is maximized.	No
Titlebar URL	Indicates location of the default titlebar.	Yes
Banner URL	Indicates location of the banner JSP.	No
Icon URL Header	Indicates location of the image displayed when a header is used for a portlet.	Yes (if check box has been selected in the Portlet Wizard)
Enable Editing	Displays an edit icon in the portlet that allows users to go to the edit JSP defined in the Edit URL attribute.	No
Edit URL	Specifies location of the Portlet Editor JSP that is displayed if editing is enabled.	No
Enable Help	Displays a help icon in the portlet that allows users to go to the help JSP defined in the Help URL attribute.	No
Help URL	Indicates location of the portlet help JSP that is displayed if help is enabled.	No
Maximize URL	Indicates location of the maximized body JSP.	No
Webflow	Defaults to None but can be changed to specify portlet Webflow if desired.	Yes
Login Required	Indicates whether the portlet should not be displayed in the default group portal.	No

(Continued)

Table 5-4. EBCC Attributes for Portlets (Continued)

ATTRIBUTE	DESCRIPTION	POPULATED?
Mandatory	Determines if the portlet must be included in the user experience, in which case it cannot be removed by the visitor. This is used in conjunction with personalization. You can allow users to modify what they display on a page.	No
Maximizable	Determines whether the portlet can be maximized by users.	No
Floatable	Determines whether the portlet can be opened as a floating widow.	No
Minimizable	Determines whether the portlet can be minimized by users.	Yes
Defaults Minimized	Determines whether the portlet appears minimized by default when the portlet is displayed.	No

You can specify all the attributes you want defined for any portlet you create, after which you need to save the changes and synchronize the EBCC to have the newly entered portlet attributes available to the portal. Figure 5-10 shows how the header portlet you created looks with the default settings retained. As you can see, the header portlet features content, a titlebar, titlebar icon, and minimize icon.

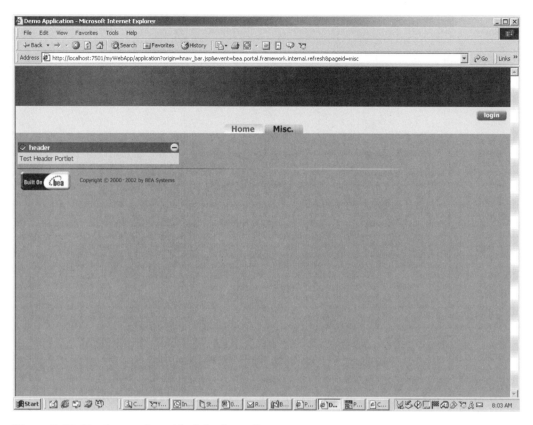

Figure 5-10. Header portlet with default attributes

> **NOTE** *Remember, if you don't like the way the default titlebar works, you can create your own titlebar. Note that you will not be able to view the portlet that you have created until some additional steps have been completed, which we discuss in the next section.*

Next, try setting some of the attributes for the header portlet: Specify a header and footer for the header portlet and enable help, as shown in Figure 5-11.

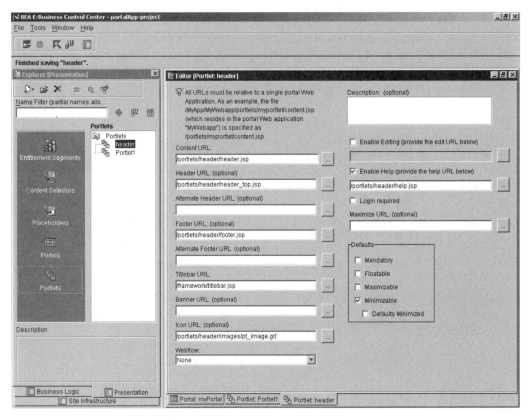

Figure 5-11. Setting portlet attributes in EBCC

 TIP   *Remember to save your changes and synchronize the EBCC after you define your portlet's attributes.*

Selecting Portlet Attributes

After you create a portlet and set some of its attributes, you need to set the specific Administration Tools portlet attributes in the BEA WebLogic Administration Tools. Table 5-5 explains all the portlet attributes available in the Administration Tools.

Table 5-5. Administration Tools Portlet Attributes

ATTRIBUTE	DESCRIPTION
Available	Determines if you will be able to add this portlet to a page.
Visible	Determines whether this portlet is visible to users. This is useful if you want a portlet to execute on a page but not have anything displayed to users.
Minimizable	Determines whether the portlet can be minimized by users.
Maximizable	Determines whether the portlet can be maximized by users.
Mandatory	Determines whether users always sees the portlet.
Display Name	Indicates the display name for the portlet that users will see in the titlebar.

To see how the attributes here work, specify that your portlet be available, visible, and minimizable, and change the display name, as demonstrated in Figure 5-12.

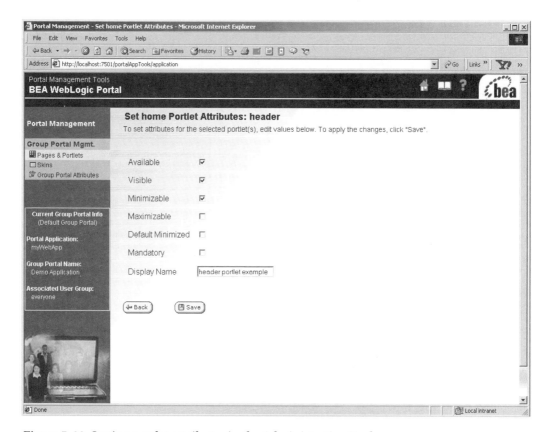

Figure 5-12. Setting portlet attributes in the Administration Tool

Figure 5-13 shows how the portlet looks after you have set all the attributes. As you can see, a new display name, a header, footer, and help icon appear on the portlet.

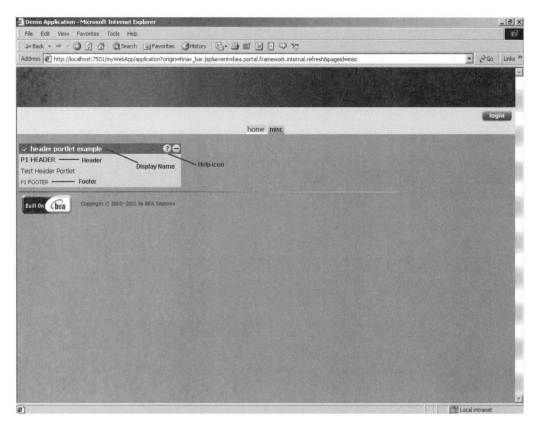

Figure 5-13. Header portlet after setting attributes

Skins

As you learned in Chapter 1, a skin determines the look and feel of a portal page. It establishes the images for common buttons and icons. It also determines the font face and point size for text appearing in the portal. A skin component consists of a cascading style sheet (CSS) and a collection of images. In the following sections, we first discuss how to change the default skin used by the portal, and then we show you how to build your own skin.

Changing the Skin of a Page

In the Select Skins page of the Administration Tools, you can select the skin you want to use for the portal you have built. Figure 5-14 shows this page. Notice that when the portal is installed, you are only given blueinfinity as a skin choice.

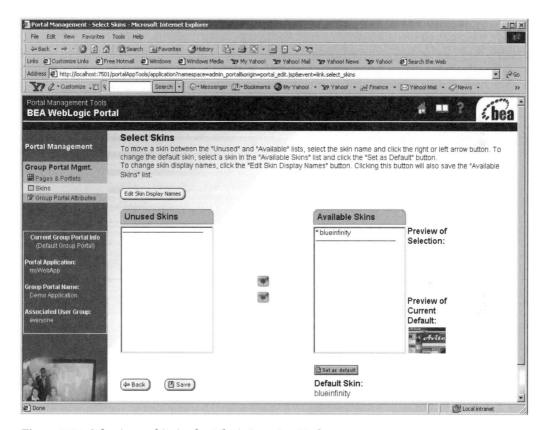

Figure 5-14. Selecting a skin in the Administration Tools

Although you only see one skin choice in the Administration tools, five skins appear in the EBCC: brightlight, coologic, futurism, lumierorange, and, of course, blueinfinity. To make one of the other four skins available for selection as the default skin for your portal, you first need to go into the EBCC. In the General section, you select one or more of the skins shown under Available skins and click Add. This moves your chosen skin or skins to the Selected skins list. For this example, make the brightlight skin available as shown in Figure 5-15.

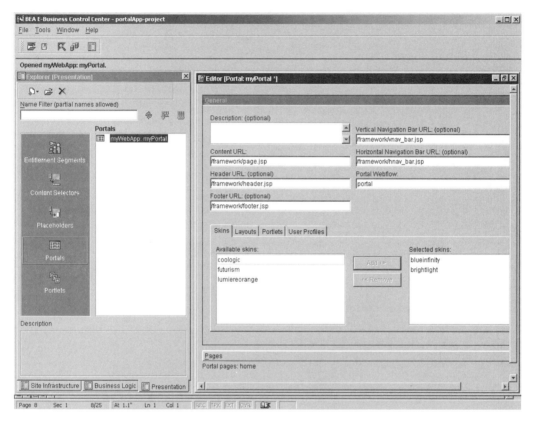

Figure 5-15. Selecting skins in the EBCC

Next, save the changes and synchronize the EBCC so that the newly selected skin becomes available for the portal. Figure 5-16 shows the Administration Tools with the newly selected skin now the default skin for the portal.

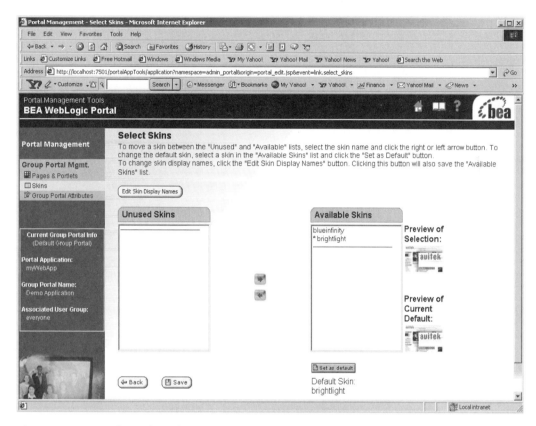

Figure 5-16. New skin selected in the Administration Tools

Figure 5-17 shows how the misc page looks with the brightlight skin selected as the default skin.

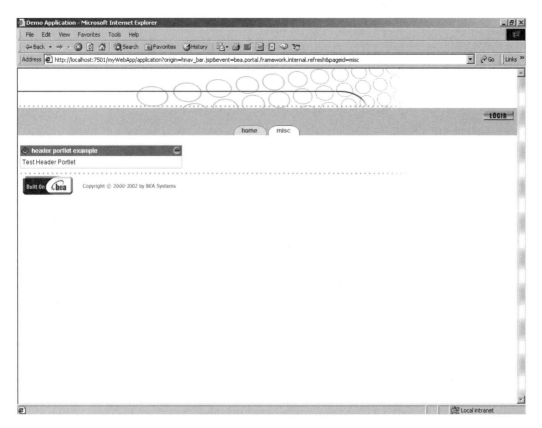

Figure 5-17. Portal with brightlight skin selected

Adding New Skins

Each skin consists of a css directory and an images directory. The css directory contains the cascading style sheet named main.css. Figure 5-18 shows the directory structure for the brightlight skin of the myWebApp portal application.

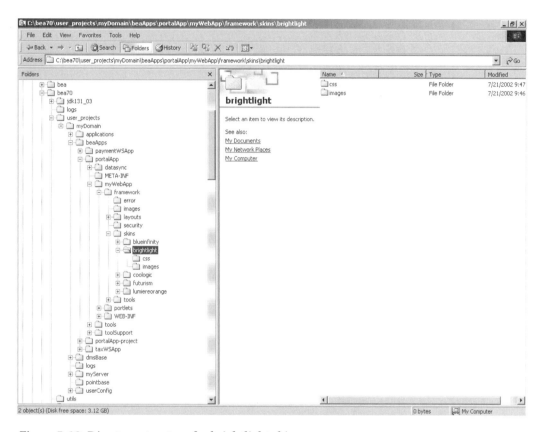

Figure 5-18. Directory structure for brightlight skin

To add a new skin, you must create a new folder for it under the skins directory. Let's go through the steps for adding a new skin called "dull" to the skin directory. First, you create a dull directory within the skins directory. Next, go to one of the other skin directories, copy the folders css and images, and place the copies of these folders in the newly created skin directory dull. This gives you the ability to change the images that are in the image directory and the style sheet in the css directory.

Now the skin needs to be made available for display in the EBCC. Do this by creating a new directory called "dull" in the portalApp-project\library\portal\skins\ directory. The portalApp_project directory was the portal project you created in the EBCC in Chapter 2. Place a GIF image that has the name of your skin in this directory. You can copy any of the GIF images in any of the other skin directories and modify this copy. This image is displayed in the Administration Tools. Figure 5-19 shows the structure for the dull directory.

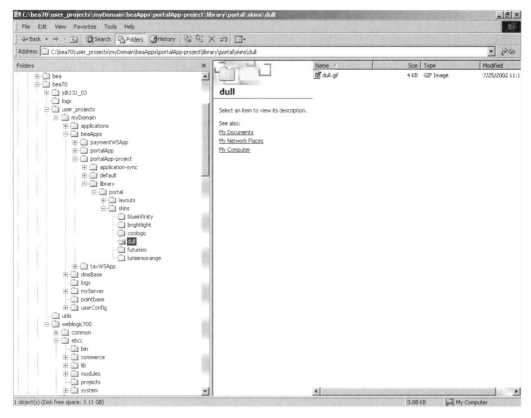

Figure 5-19. Directory structure for dull skin for use by the EBCC

Now you are ready to make the newly created skin available to the portal using the EBCC. Select the newly created skin, dull, under Available skins and click Add. This moves your chosen skin to the Selected skin list as shown in Figure 5-20.

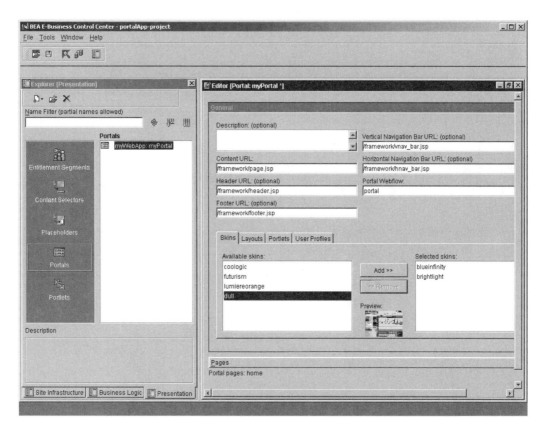

Figure 5-20. Selecting the dull skin in the EBCC

Save your changes and synchronize the EBCC to have the newly created skin available for selection as a skin in the portal. Figure 5-21 shows the Administration Tools with the new skin now available for selection.

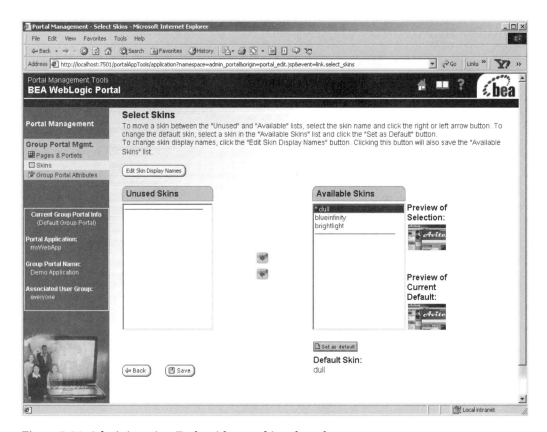

Figure 5-21. Administration Tools with new skin selected

Now you have everything set up so that the portal can use your newly created skin. Next, we show you how to alter the style sheet and images to see changes when you are in the portal.

Changing the Style Sheet

Style sheets are very powerful in that they make it easy to change the look and feel of many things in your portal. By defining different style sheets, you can change the appearance of a portal without doing much work. Let's take the style sheet copied into the skins/dull/css directory of the dull skin and modify the tab background color so you see the effects.

Listing 5-1 shows only the top portion of the style sheet that demonstrates the tab background color change.

Listing 5-1. Style Sheet Change for the Dull Skin Example

```
/* ================= Dull ======================= */
BODY{
    background-color: #D7DFF6
    font-family:Tahoma,Helvetica,Verdana,Arial,sans-serif;
    font-size:9pt;
    margin:0px;
    background-repeat: no-repeat;
}

A:LINK{
    font-family:Tahoma,Helvetica,Verdana,Arial,sans-serif;
}

A:VISITED{
    font-family:Tahoma,Helvetica,Verdana,Arial,sans-serif;
}

TD{
    font-family:Tahoma,Helvetica,Verdana,Arial,sans-serif;
    font-size:9pt;
}

UL, LI { list-style-type: circle; color: #0863D8; }

/* === Portal Styles === */

/* Use for the background color of the portal header */
.headerBgColor {  background-color: #0C136B}

/* Tab background color */
.titlebar{ background-color: #C0C0C0; }
```

Changing the Images

Here we show you how to go about changing any of the images that are in the skins/dull/image directory. Note that there are images in each skin directory with the same name. When a particular skin is specified for a portal, the portal will use the images from the chosen skin's directory. If you want an image in your portal to change based on the skin selected, you create an image for each skin you have in your portal. To see how images are used with skins, modify the v_home.gif and portal_header.gif files to have gray in them, and then use the v_home.gif image as the default image name. You also need to go into the Administration Tools and check the Use Image attribute for each page if you want images to appear in the tabs that are created.

You might wonder how the portal is able to use different images for the different skins. Many of the JSPs such as the hnav_bar.jsp in the framework directory contain the following line of code at the top of them:

```
<%@ include file="/framework/resourceURL.inc"%>
```

In the resourceURL.inc file, there is a line of code that gets the directory path for the selected skin:

```
imagesPath  = "/framework/skins/" + skinId.getName() + "/images/";
```

Any reference to an image that you want to be selected from a skin's directory needs to include the imagesPath variable. An example of this appears in the hnav_bar.jsp file:

```
<img src="<wf:createResourceURL resource='<%=imagesPath +
page_name_right_selected.gif"  %>' />" border="0">
```

When you are creating your own JSPs, keep this in mind so you can have images that change based on the skin selected. Remember to add the preceding code to get this to work correctly. Figure 5-22 shows how your page looks with the dull skin selected as the default skin and the misc tab selected.

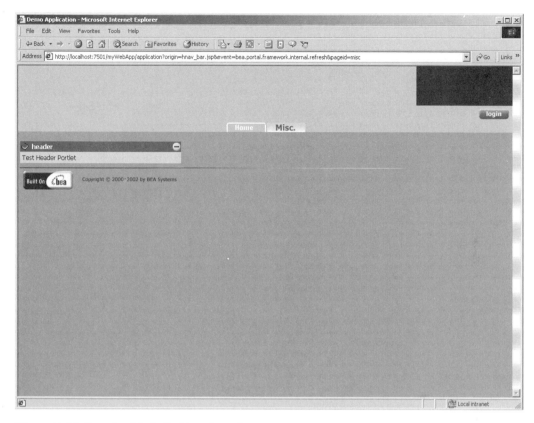

Figure 5-22. Portal with dull skin selected

Notice that the background of the tabs and the header and tab images have changed based on modifications you made to the images for the dull skin.

Layouts

As you know by now, a layout defines how portlets can be positioned on a page. We first discuss how to change the layout of a page in the following sections, and then we show you how to build your own layout.

Changing the Layout of a Page

You use the Administration Tools to select a layout for displaying portlets as well as specify how portlets are displayed within a selected layout. Figure 5-23 shows where in the Administration Tools you accomplish this. The Pages and Portlets page displays a list of pages that have been created for the portal. For each page listed, you can modify the layout used and the positioning of the portlets in that layout. In Figure 5-23, the pages home and misc can be selected. If you were to click the Layouts button for the home page, you could select the layout you wanted to use for that particular page.

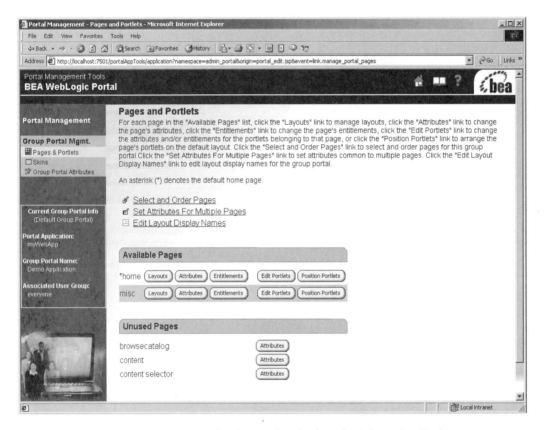

Figure 5-23. Selecting a page to position its portlets in the Administration Tool

Figure 5-24 shows how you can select the layout you want for a specific page. In this example, only one layout is available to select: threecolumn.

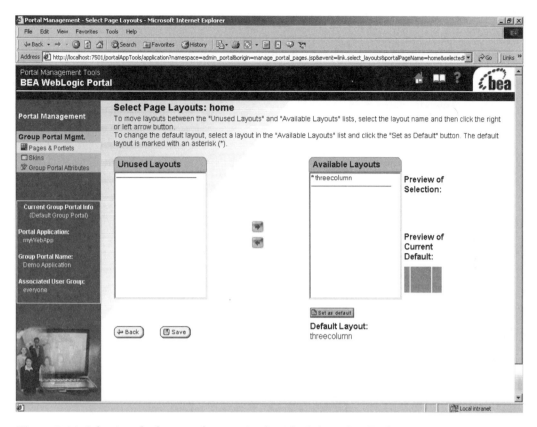

Figure 5-24. Selecting the layout of a page in the Administration Tool

To make more layouts available for selection, you go to the EBCC and do two things:

1. Select the layouts you want to make available for the portal.

2. Select the layouts you want available for a particular page.

When you install the portal, five layouts appear in the EBCC: twocolumn, threecolumn, fourcolumn, spanning, and spanningthreecolumn. Figure 5-25 shows how you make any of the other layouts available for the portal. Under the General section, you select one of the layouts shown in the Available layouts list and click Add. This moves your chosen layout to the Selected layouts list as shown in Figure 5-25.

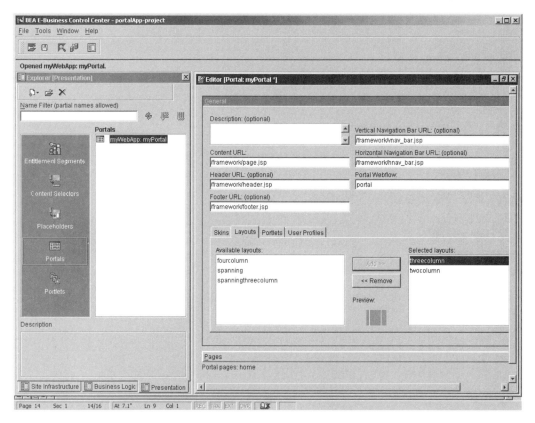

Figure 5-25. Selecting additional layouts for the portal using the EBCC

Once you have made a layout available to the portal, you can now select it for use on a particular page you have created. Figure 5-26 shows how you can make a layout available to a page.

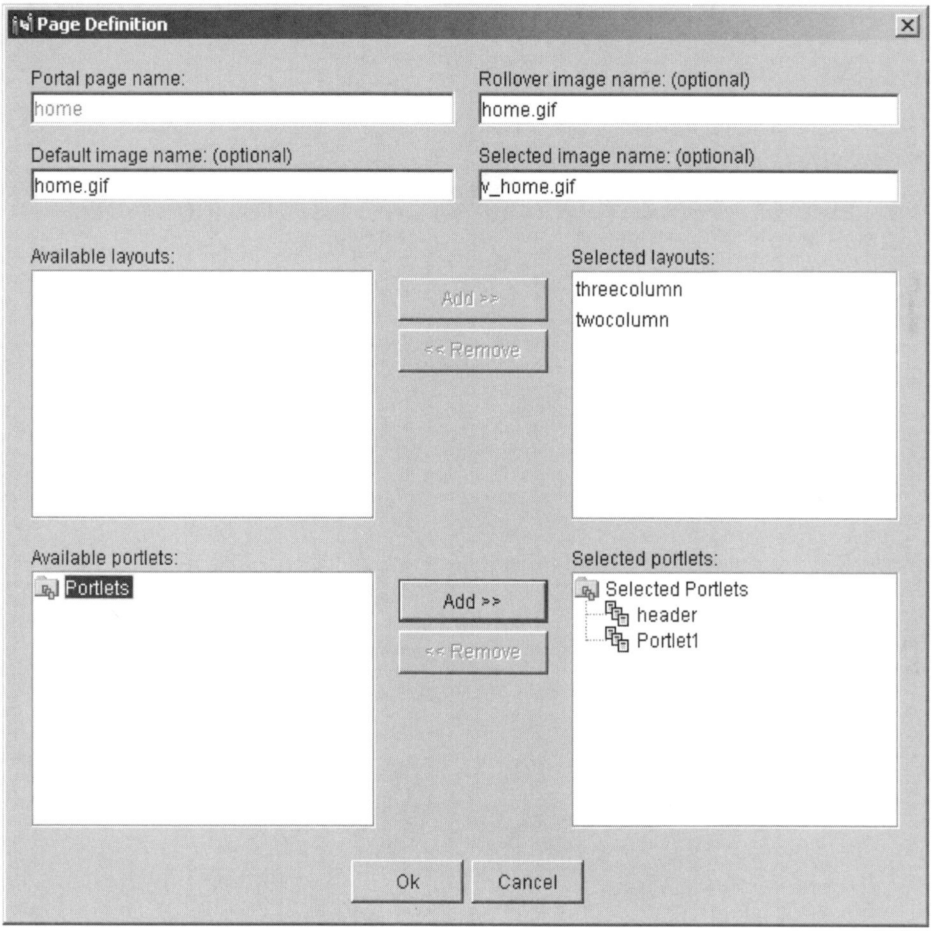

Figure 5-26. Making a layout available to a page in the EBCC

You then save your changes and synchronize the EBCC to have the newly selected layout available for your page. Figure 5-27 shows the Administration Tools with the newly selected layout now ready to be made available.

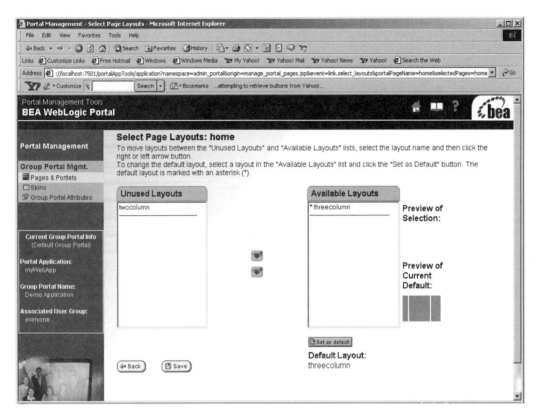

Figure 5-27. Selecting page layouts in the Administration Tools

You can now select the layout, twocolumn in this example, from the Unused Layouts list and make it available to the page. Once you have done this, you have the option of choosing the layout twocolumn to make it the default for that page. Once you do so, you can then position the portlets on the newly selected layout for a page by clicking the Position Portlets button. The Position Portlets page shown in Figure 5-28 allows you to position the portlets you have made available for a specific page.

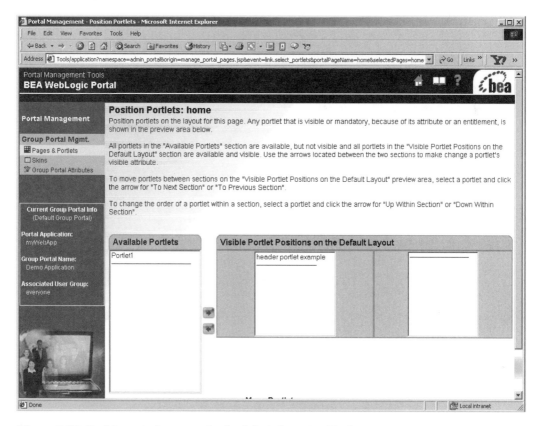

Figure 5-28. Position portlets page in the Administration Tools

Figure 5-29 shows how the home page might look after you have positioned portlets the way you want them to be displayed in your new layout.

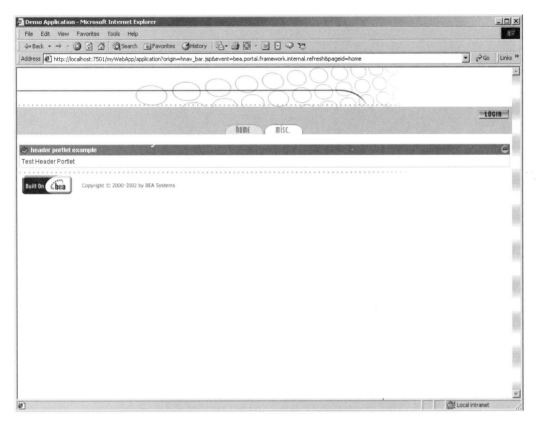

Figure 5-29. Portal page with new layout

Adding New Layouts

So far we have shown you how to use existing layouts when you create a portal. What happens if none of these layouts match what you want for your portal? Here we go into the details of creating a new layout. In order to create a new layout, you must first know where layouts are stored. Within the deployed application, layouts are stored in the framework\layouts directory. Figure 5-30 shows the directory location of different layouts within the myWebApp portal application.

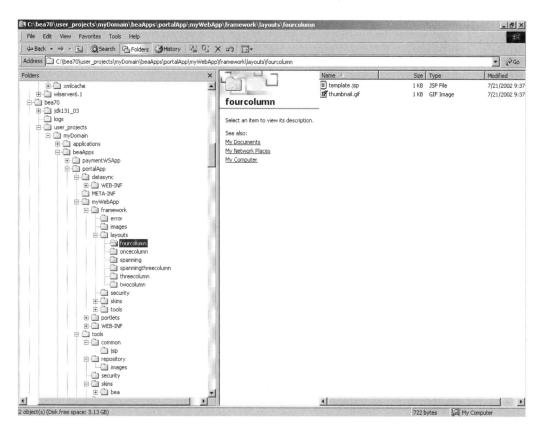

Figure 5-30. Layouts directory

If you look in any one of the directories such as fourcolumn (shown in Figure 5-30), you will notice that there are two files, a JSP and a GIF file. These files must be called template.jsp and thumbnail.gif, respectively.

Now we walk you through the steps for creating a new layout called onecolumn. Start by creating a new directory called onecolumn in the framework\layouts directory (shown is Figure 5-30). You then copy the template.jsp and thumbnail.gif files from one of the other layouts into this directory. Once you have done this, you want to modify the thumbnail.gif file so it looks like the layout you are creating. Next, you have to modify the template.jsp file. Listing 5-2 shows you how.

Listing 5-2. Template JSP

```
<%@ taglib uri='ren.tld' prefix='layout' %>
<layout:placePortletsinPlaceholder placeholders="left" />
<table width="100%" border="0" cellspacing="0" cellpadding="0">
  <TR>
    <TD WIDTH="100%" VALIGN="TOP">
      <layout:render section='left'/>
    </TD>
  </TR>
</TABLE>
```

Notice that this is basically just an HTML table layout with some portal-specific JSP tags that tell the portal where to position portlets. You should also modify the thumbnail.gif image to show a quick preview of what the layout should look like. After you modify the template.jsp file, you need to make the new layout available to the EBCC for selection. This is done by copying the onecolumn directory you created and placing it in the EBCC project directory you are working with.

For this example, move the onecolumn directory to the portalApp-project\library\portal\layouts directory as shown in Figure 5-31. You also need to rename thumbnail.gif to *layout-name*.gif (e.g., onecolumn.gif) in the project/library/portal/layouts directory. This enables the WBCC to display the image to users when they select the layout in the Portal Editor.

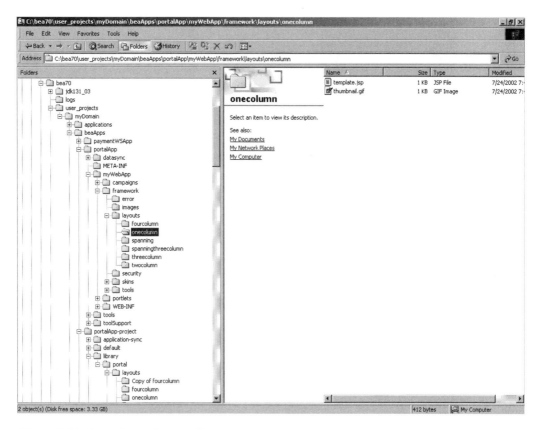

Figure 5-31. Onecolumn layout directory

You can now use your newly created layout. If you look at the EBCC, you will see that onecolumn is now available for selection as shown in Figure 5-32.

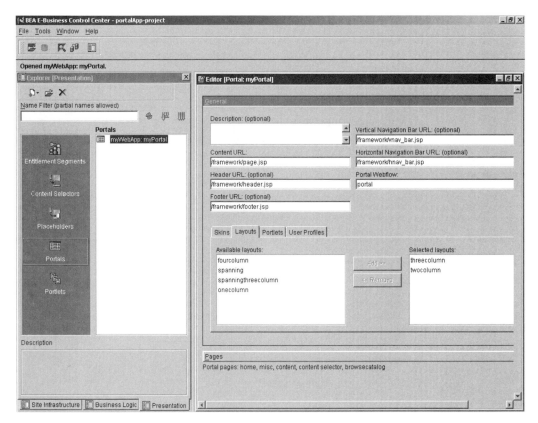

Figure 5-32. Making a new layout available to the portal in the EBCC

At this point, you can go through the process of selecting onecolumn as a layout, as described previously, and then go into the Administration Tools to specify it as the default layout for the home page. Figure 5-33 shows how the onecolumn layout is selected as the default layout for the home page.

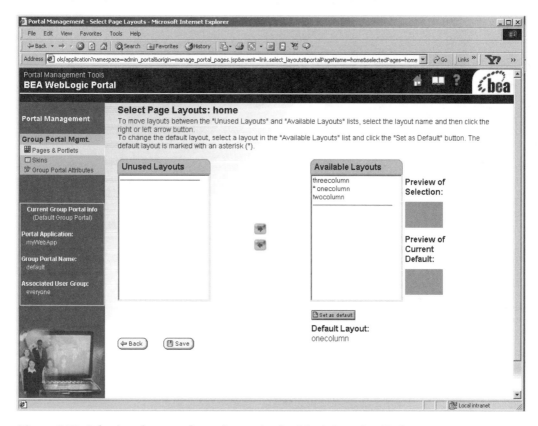

Figure 5-33. Selecting the onecolumn layout in the Administration Tools

Notice how the image displayed for Preview of Selection and Preview of Current Default shown in Figure 5-33 reflects the images you created for this new layout. Now that you have selected the layout you want to use for a page, you must define the position of the portlets on the page that uses the layout you just created. You do this by selecting the Position Portlets button for the desired page in the Pages and Portlets page in the Administration Tools. The Position Portlets page will be displayed for the page you selected. This is where you can position the portlets defined for this page. Figure 5-34 shows how to position portlets for the home page.

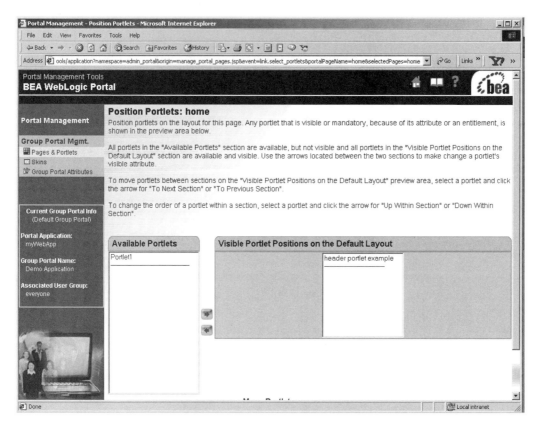

Figure 5-34. Positioning portlets using the Administration Tools

Summary

This chapter gave an overview of different ways you can modify the look and feel of a portal. We discussed the overall JSPs and include files in the framework directory. We then went into the details of setting the different page and portlet attributes. Finally, we showed you how to use and create skins and layouts.

Using Content

A KEY COMPONENT of any portal is content. Managing and displaying the content in a portal can be a large task. Over the last few years, third-party vendors have created many content management systems to manage and display content.

A *content management system* (CMS) is a tool that enables a variety of technical (centralized) and nontechnical (decentralized) staff to create, edit, manage, and finally publish a variety of content (such as text, graphics, video, etc.) while being constrained by a centralized set of rules, processes, and workflows that ensure a coherent, validated Web site appearance.

The following are some basic features of any content management solution:

- Database content storage

- Capability to add metadata to content

- Check-out/check-in feature

- Attachments

- Versioning

- Some type of foldering concept

- APIs to get content out of the database

The BEA WebLogic Portal provides content through the Content Manager. The Content Manager offers content and document management capabilities for use in personalization services to target users with dynamic Web content. It works with files or with content managed by third-party vendor tools, and serves as a runtime subsystem that provides access to content through tags and EJBs. When developing JSPs, the Content Manager tags allow you to receive an enumeration of content objects by querying the content database directly through search expression syntax. Note that the Content Manager does not have a GUI-based tool for edit-time customization.

The BEA WebLogic Portal has a predefined data model for storing content. If you have a small budget or low volume of content to maintain in your portal, this could be a good solution for you. If you are looking for features such as a robust interface for adding content, versioning, workflow, and check-in/check-out, you might want to integrate a third-party content management solution. Although third-party solutions can be expensive, they provide many capabilities that are necessary when managing content. Once you have entered content using the BEA WebLogic solution or a third-party content management system, you use various content-related tags that are part of the BEA WebLogic Portal to access your content.

In this chapter, we show you the following:

- The organization of the BEA content management database tables and file directories

- How to load data using the BulkLoader

- How to configure the Content Manager

- How to display content using content taglibs

- What Content Selectors are and how to use them

- How to integrate the BEA WebLogic Portal with third-party content management solutions

BEA Content Manager File Directories and Database Tables

If you want to use the BEA WebLogic Content Manager, you first need to understand how file directories and database tables work within Content Manager, and in the following sections we go into the details.

File Directories

When you use the Domain Configuration Wizard, a directory called user_projects*domain*\dmsBase is created, where *domain* is the directory that you built using the wizard. The directory dmsBase is where you keep all content to be displayed. You first create your content and place it in directories under the dmsBase directory. In order to show you how content works, we have created a file directory called examples that contains two subdirectories, NuWave and CompanyA. We will place content in these directories for use in the examples later in this chapter. To get a better understanding of the concepts we present in this chapter, you may want to follow along and do the same. Figure 6-1 shows the directory structure created for these examples under the domain myDomain.

Figure 6-1. File directory structure for content

If you need to change content remotely or want to build an interface for managing content, you need to build a portlet that can do this. Figure 6-2 shows an example of an interface that creates folders, uploads the content to the file directories, and creates the metadata (explained later in this chapter) in the database.

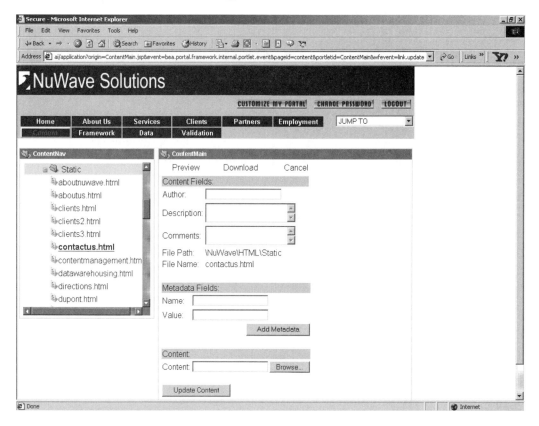

Figure 6-2. Example of a portlet created for adding content

Database Tables

The BEA WebLogic Content Manager stores information about the content you place in the dmsBase directory in two database tables: DOCUMENT and DOCUMENT_METADATA. You must insert a record into the DOCUMENT table for each piece of content in the dmsBase directory. Table 6-1 shows the columns defined for the DOCUMENT table. Note that the Content Manager does not use some of the columns in the table, but you can extend the Content Manager to use these columns.

Table 6-1. DOCUMENT Table

COLUMN NAME	REQUIRED	DESCRIPTION
ID	YES	The key for the table. This must contain the exact file directory and filename that is used in the dmsBase directory. An example is Examples/NuWave/aboutus.html.
DOCUMENT_SIZE	YES	The size of document in bytes. If the size of the document is 5000 bytes and you enter 1K, the entire document might not be displayed.
VERSION	NO	The current version of the content. Note that the Content Manager does not use this currently. You could add functionality to use this column.
AUTHOR	NO	The author of the content.
CREATION_DATE	NO	The date the content was created.
LOCKED_BY	NO	Who locked the content.
MODIFIED_DATE	NO	The modified date of the content.
MODIFIED_BY	NO	Who modified the content.
DESCRIPTION	NO	A description of the content.
COMMENTS	NO	Comments for the content.
MIME_TYPE	YES	The type of content. For HTML documents, this will be text/html.

The DOCUMENT_METADATA table is used to store metadata about the content. Table 6-2 shows the columns defined for the DOCUMENT_METADATA table.

Table 6-2. DOCUMENT_METADATA Table

COLUMN NAME	REQUIRED	DESCRIPTION
ID	YES	The key for the table. This must contain the exact file directory and filename that is used in the dmsBase directory for the file you want to have metadata for. An example is Examples/NuWave/aboutus.html.
NAME	YES	Name of the metadata. An example is company.
STATE	NO	The state of the metadata. When it is initially loaded by the BulkLoader, it's value is NEW.
VALUE	NO	The value of the metadata. An example is NuWave Solutions, LLC.

Metadata allows you to associate additional data related to a piece of content. To explain this better, let's look at an example. Say you want to display information about a company, and you created a document called aboutus.html. When you display that content, you decide you also want to display the company's name. You would add the company's name as metadata and associate it with the aboutus.html document. We discuss how to display content and metadata later in this chapter.

Loading Data

The easiest way to add content to a portal is to use the BulkLoader scripts provided by BEA. In order to do this, you must follow these directions:

1. Publish files to a directory on the file system at a specified interval. We recommend that you publish content in subdirectories under the \dmsBase directory in the appropriate domain folder. Figure 6-1, shown earlier, shows an example of a directory called NuWave where content could be published.

2. When you are done writing your content, place it in the file directory you have created.

3. Run the BulkLoader. Run loaddocs.bat to load all the files you need loaded (loaddocs.sh for UNIX users). Note that when you create your domain, this batch file is created for you under the directory \user_projects*domain*, where *domain* is the domain you created.

There are many switches that the BulkLoader can use. Look at the BEA WebLogic Portal documentation for more information on these switches. The BulkLoader takes each file in the dmsBase directory and adds the appropriate metadata to the DOCUMENT database table.

You need to define the values for the metadata using one of the following four ways to associate metadata to a document:

- Placing <META NAME="..." Content="..."> tags in HTML documents.

- Creating a *filename*.md.properties file (e.g., aboutus.html.md.properties) and putting the metadata in this file.

- Registering a LoaderFilter class when you run the BulkLoader (this is how the BulkLoader internally gets the height and width of the images).

- Placing metadata in the dir.md.properties file. The dir.md.properties file is a convenience for associating metadata with multiple files at once; all files underneath a directory that has a dir.md.properties file will have the metadata in that file (unless it's overridden by one of the other three mechanisms).

To create metadata, use the dir.md.properties file to add a value for the metadata name company. Place the value you want to associate with this metadata name in the dir.md.properties file as shown here:

```
company=NuWave Solutions, LLC
```

Once you have done this, place the file in the directory where the content you want to associate with the metadata is located. In this example, we associate the content aboutus.html with the metadata in the directory /dmsBase/examples/NuWave. This has to be done for all the metadata you wish to associate. Figure 6-3 shows the placement of the dir.md.properties file for this example.

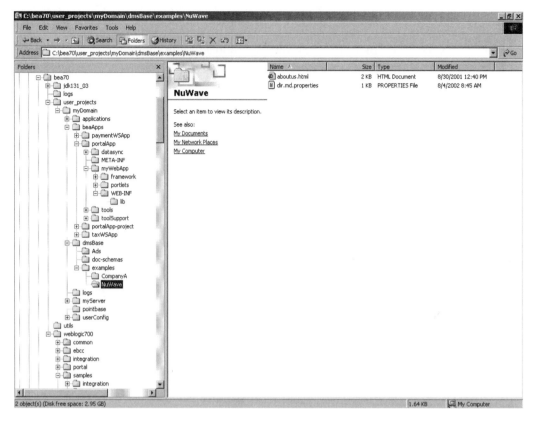

Figure 6-3. Directory structure showing placement of the dir_md_properties file

Once you have associated the metadata to the appropriate content files, you need to rerun the BulkLoader. The BulkLoader takes the metadata you created and places it in the DOCUMENT_METADATA database table.

Verifying the Configuration of the Content Manager

In order to use the Content Manager, you must make sure it has been configured properly by following these steps:

- Verify the content taglibs are configured.

- Verify the document jar file exists.

- Verify the appropriate configuration XML files have been configured to enable the Content Manager EJBs and connection pools to work.

Verifying Content Taglibs Have Been Configured

To verify the content taglibs have been configured, you must first copy the cm_taglib.jar file into the Web application's WEB-INF/lib directory. Copy this file from BEA_HOME/weblogic700/portal/lib/p13n/web, since this is the official home of the portal jars, and therefore the file is guaranteed to be updated by the service pack installers.

You must now map the cm.tld tag library to /WEB-INF/lib/cm_taglib.jar in a <taglib> entry in your Web application's WEB-INF/web.xml file. Verify the following XML is located in the web.xml file within the <web-app></web-app> tokens:

```
<taglib>
    <taglib-uri> cm.tld </taglib-uri>
    <taglib-location> WEB-INF/lib/cm_taglib.jar </taglib-location>
</taglib>
```

Verifying the Document JAR Exists

You need to make sure that the document.jar file is in the directory user_projects*domain*\beaApps\portalApp, where *domain* is the domain you created. This jar file contains the code for the Content Manager.

Verifying Appropriate XML Files Have Been Modified

Now you need to verify several XML files to make sure Content Manager EJBs and connection pools have been enabled. First define the ShowDoc servlet. You must verify the following XML is located in the web.xml file found in the WEB-INF/ directory:

```
<!-- The ShowDoc Servlet -->
<servlet>
    <servlet-name>ShowDocServlet</servlet-name>
    <servlet-class>com.bea.p13n.content.servlets.ShowDocServlet</servlet-class>
    <!-- Make showdoc always use the local ejb-ref DocumentManager -->
    <init-param>
        <param-name>contentHome</param-name>
        <param-value>java:comp/env/ejb/DocumentManager</param-value>
    </init-param>
</servlet>
```

Next, you map the ShowDoc servlet. Verify the following XML is located in the web.xml file found in the WEB-INF/ directory:

```
<servlet-mapping>
    <servlet-name>ShowDocServlet</servlet-name>
    <url-pattern>/ShowDoc/*</url-pattern>
</servlet-mapping>
```

NOTE *If you are migrating from BEA WebLogic Portal 4.0, the default servlet mapping installed was ShowDocServlet. You can add an additional entry in the XML to map this:*

```
<!-- The old mapping for backwards-compatability; please use
/ShowDoc -->
<servlet-mapping>
    <servlet-name>ShowDocServlet</servlet-name>
    <url-pattern>/ShowDocServlet/*</url-pattern>
</servlet-mapping>
```

Now you add the EJB definitions. Verify the following XML is located in the web.xml file found in the WEB-INF/ directory:

```
<ejb-ref>
    <description>
    The ContentManager for this webapp
    </description>
    <ejb-ref-name>ejb/ContentManager</ejb-ref-name>
    <ejb-ref-type>Session</ejb-ref-type>
    <home>com.bea.p13n.content.document.DocumentManagerHome</home>
    <remote>com.bea.p13n.content.document.DocumentManager</remote>
</ejb-ref>
<ejb-ref>
    <description>
    The DocumentManager for this webapp
    </description>
    <ejb-ref-name>ejb/DocumentManager</ejb-ref-name>
    <ejb-ref-type>Session</ejb-ref-type>
    <home>com.bea.p13n.content.document.DocumentManagerHome</home>
    <remote>com.bea.p13n.content.document.DocumentManager</remote>
</ejb-ref>
```

Next, verify the EJBs have been configured between the
tokens in the weblogic.xml
file found in the WEB-INF/ directory:

```
<ejb-reference-description>
    <ejb-ref-name>ejb/ContentManager</ejb-ref-name>
    <jndi-name>
    ${APPNAME}.BEA_personalization.DocumentManager
    </jndi-name>
</ejb-reference-description>
<ejb-reference-description>
    <ejb-ref-name>ejb/DocumentManager</ejb-ref-name>
    <jndi-name>
    ${APPNAME}.BEA_personalization.DocumentManager
    </jndi-name>
</ejb-reference-description>
```

You must also define the document connection pool and document manager
cache. These are already defined if you create the domain using wizards. The
application-config.xml file contains the definitions, and they can be found in the
META-INF directory of the application for the domain you created. The following
are the XML entries that should have been added:

```
<DocumentConnectionPool CapacityIncrement="0"
DriverName="com.bea.p13n.content.document.jdbc.Driver" InitialCapacity="20"
LoginTimeout="0"
MaxCapacity="20" Name="default"
Properties="schemaXML=C:\bea70\user_projects\myDomain\dmsBase/doc-schemas;
URL="jdbc:beasys:docmgmt:com.bea.p13n.content.document.ref.RefDocumentProvider"/>
docBase=C:\bea70\user_projects\myDomain\dmsBase;
jdbc.dataSource=weblogic.jdbc.pool.commercePool"
ShrinkingEnabled="false"
<DocumentManager ContentCacheName="documentContentCache" ContentCaching="true"
DocumentConnectionPoolName="default" MaxCachedContentSize="32768"
MetadataCacheName="documentMetadataCache" MetadataCaching="true" Name="default"
PropertyCase="none" UserIdInCacheKey="false"/>
```

 NOTE *You can use the BEA WebLogic Console to add these entries
yourself under* domain ➢ *Deployments* ➢ *Applications* ➢ app ➢
Service Configuration, if these settings aren't there.

Testing the Content Manager

Now that you have verified and modified as necessary all these XML files, you must shut down the portal and bring it back up to reflect your changes. If you want to test the changes you made, you can use the ShowDoc servlet to do so. Bring up a browser and enter `http://localhost:7501/`*application*`/ShowDoc/`*contentid*, where *application* is the portal application you defined and *contentid* is the content ID stored in the DOCUMENT table for the content you want to display.

To demonstrate how this works, we add the content aboutus.html to the directory dmsBase/examples/NuWave/ and then run the BulkLoader. Figure 6-4 shows what is displayed when we use the ShowDoc servlet by entering `http://localhost:7501/myWebApp/ShowDoc/examples/NuWave/aboutus.html` in our browser.

Figure 6-4. Testing using ShowDoc servlet

Refer to the BEA WebLogic Portal documentation for additional information on the Content Manager EJBs, connection pools, and caching content.

Displaying Content with Content Taglibs

The Content Manager has several JSP tags. These tags allow you to include nonpersonalized content in an HTML-based page. The <cm:select> and <cm:selectById> tags support content caching for content searches. Note that none of the tags support or use a body. We discuss the tags <cm:printDoc>, <cm:selectById>, <cm:getProperty>, and <cm:select> in further detail in the following sections.

<cm:printDoc>

The <cm:printDoc> tag puts the raw bytes of a Document object into the JSP output stream. It only displays content you have added to the dmsBase directory that has corresponding metadata in the DOCUMENT table. Table 6-3, from the WebLogic Portal 7.0 documentation, lists all attributes for this tag. WebLogic Portal 7.0 documentation reprinted with permission from BEA Systems, Inc. Copyright© 2002 BEA Systems, Inc. All rights reserved.

Table 6-3. <cm:printDoc> Tag Attributes

TAG ATTRIBUTE	REQUIRED*	TYPE	DESCRIPTION	R/C**
id	No	String	The JSP script variable name which contains the Content instance from which to get the properties.	R
blockSize	No	String, int	The size of the blocks of data to read. The default is 8K. Use 0 or less to read the entire block of bytes in one operation.	R
start	No	String, int	Specifies the index in the bytes where to start reading. Defaults to 0.	R
end	No	String, int	Specifies the index in the bytes where to stop reading. The default is to read to the end of the bytes.	R
encode	No	String	Either html, url, or none: If html, then the value will be html encoded so that it appears in HTML as expected (& becomes &, < becomes <, > becomes >, and " becomes "). If url, then it is encoded to x-www-form-urlencoded format via the java.net.URLEncoder. If none or unspecified, no encoding is performed.	R
document	No	Document	Specifies the com.bea.p13n.content. document.Document to use. If this is specified and non-null, id will be ignored. Otherwise, id will be used.	R
failOnError	No	String, Boolean	This attribute can have one of two values: False (default value): Handles JSP processing errors gracefully and prints nothing if an error occurs. True: Throws an exception. You can handle the exception in the code, let the page proceed to the normal error page, or let the application server handle it less gracefully.	R
baseHref	No	String	The URL of the document's BASE HREF. This can be either an absolute URL or a relative URL.	R

* The Required column specifies if the attribute is required (yes) or optional (no).

** In the R/C column, C means that the attribute is a compile-time expression, and R means that the attribute can be either a request-time expression or a compile-time expression.

To show you how this tag is used, we display the aboutus.html content that was added by the BulkLoader. We recommend that you place the <cm:printDoc> tag within a table so that you can control the width of the content displayed by using a table width if necessary. Note that we discuss the tag <cm:selectById> later in this chapter.

We add the following code to a portlet called contentviewer:

```
<%@ taglib uri="cm.tld" prefix="cm"%>

<%
    // define the content id
    String contentId = "examples/NuWave/aboutus.html";
%>
<%  // select content based on the content id %>
<cm:selectById contentId="<%=contentId%>" id="doc" />
<table> <tr><td>
<% // display the content %>
<cm:printDoc id="doc" blockSize="1000" >
</td></tr></table>
```

We then place the portlet contentviewer on a page called content. Figure 6-5 shows the content page that displays the content, aboutus.

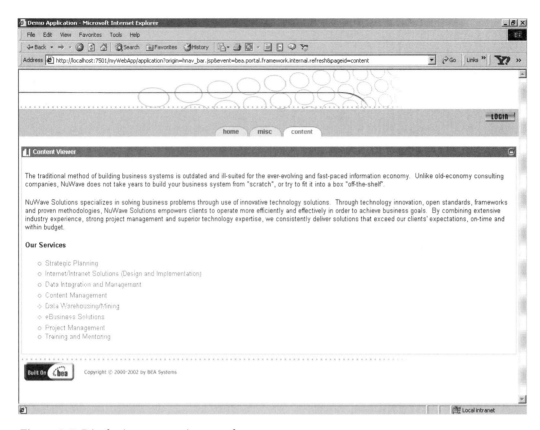

Figure 6-5. Displaying content in a portlet

There is a means of passing content dynamically so that you don't have to hard-code the content ID in the JSP as we've just shown, and we demonstrate this next. The recommended way is to pass the content ID using a query parameter so that you can have one page that displays content based on the content ID passed. To show you how this is done, we build a portlet, called displaycontent, that displays links to content. For each content link there is a query parameter, contentid. The following is the code in the JSP:

```
<p><b>Content to Display</b></p>

<p><a href="application?pageid=content&contentid=examples/NuWave/aboutus.html">
NuWave Solutions</a></p>
<p><a href="application?pageid=content&contentid=examples/CompanyA/aboutus.html">
Company A</a></p>
```

Figure 6-6 shows how this portlet looks when displayed on the page.

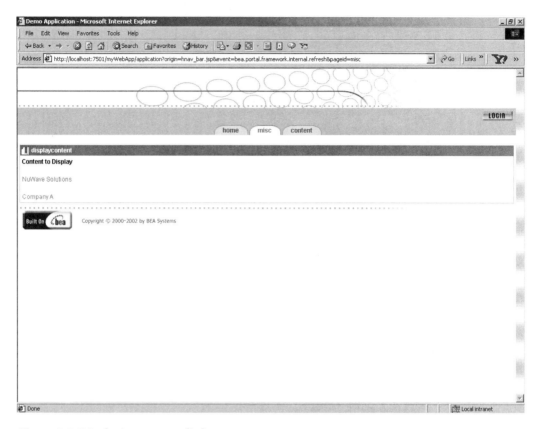

Figure 6-6. Displaying content links

We next modify the contentviewer portlet so that it can get the query parameter passed and display content based on the content ID passed by the query parameter. The modified JSP code is as follows:

```
<%@ taglib uri="cm.tld" prefix="cm"%>
<%
    // get the contentid query parameter
    String contentId = (String)request.getParameter("contentid");
%>

<% // select content based on the content id %>
<cm:selectById contentId="<%=contentId%>" id="doc" />
```

```
<table> <tr><td>
<% // display the content %>
<cm:printDoc id="doc" blockSize="1000" >
</td></tr></table>
```

Now if you've been following along up to this point, and you clicked the Company A link shown in Figure 6-6, you would be redirected to the content page and the appropriate content would be displayed, as illustrated in Figure 6-7.

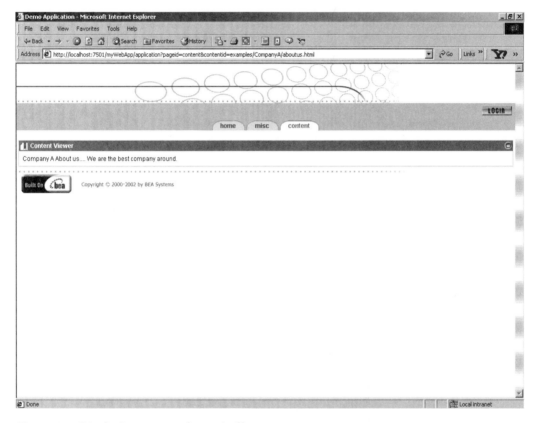

Figure 6-7. Displaying content dynamically

If you want to display an image, you first add the image to the appropriate directory under dmsBase. You then rerun the BulkLoader to add the image to the DOCUMENT table. Finally you use the showDoc servlet to display the image. The following code displays an image called logo.jpg:

```
<img src="ShowDoc/examples/NuWave/logo.jpg">
```

`<cm:selectById>`

In the code that appears in the previous section, we use the tag <cm:selectById>. This tag, which does not have a body, retrieves content using the content's unique identifier. It works against any Content object that has a string-capable primary key. Table 6-4, from the WebLogic Portal 7.0 documentation, lists all attributes for this tag. WebLogic Portal 7.0 documentation reprinted with permission from BEA Systems, Inc. Copyright© 2002 BEA Systems, Inc. All rights reserved.

Table 6-4. <cm:selectById> Tag Attributes

TAG ATTRIBUTE	REQUIRED*	TYPE	DESCRIPTION	R/C**
contentHome	No	String	The JNDI name of the ContentManager EJB Home to use to find content. The object in JNDI at this name must implement a create method which returns an object that implements the ContentManager interface. If not specified, the system searches the default content home.	R
contentId	Yes	String	The string identifier of the piece of content.	R
onNotFound	No	String	If the content object specified by contentId cannot be found, this controls the behavior. If this is set, then an Exception will be thrown with the value as the message; if this is not set, the tag will return null.	R
failOnError	No	String, Boolean	This attribute can have one of two values: False (default value): Handles JSP processing errors gracefully and returns null if an error occurs. True: Throws an exception that causes the JSP page to stop. You can handle the exception in the code, let the page proceed to the normal error page, or let the application server handle it less gracefully.	R
id	Yes	String	The JSP script variable name that contains the Content object after this tag finishes. If the Content object with the specified identifier does not exist, it contains null.	C

(Continued)

Table 6-4. <cm:selectById> Tag Attributes (Continued)

TAG ATTRIBUTE	REQUIRED*	TYPE	DESCRIPTION	R/C**
useCache	No	String, Boolean	Determines whether Content is cached. This attribute can have one of two values: False (default value): ContentCache is not used. If false (not specified), the cacheId, cacheScope and cacheTimeout settings are ignored. True: ContentCache is used.	R
cacheId	No	String	The identifier name used to cache the Content. Internally, the cache is implemented as a map; this will become the key. If not specified, the id attribute of the tag is used.	R
cacheTimeout	No	String, long	The time, in milliseconds, for which the cached Content is valid. If more than this amount of time has passed since the Content was cached, the cached Content will be cleared, retrieved, and placed back into the cache. Use -1 for no-timeout (always use the cached Content). Default = -1.	R
cacheScope	No	String	Specifies the lifecycle scope of the content cache. Similar to <jsp:useBean>. Possible values: application session (the default) page request	R
contextParams	No	String or java.util.Map	Additional search parameters to pass to the ContentManager. Some ContentManager implementations may support this.	R
readOnly	Ignored		This attribute is deprecated and no longer used. When found, it is ignored.	

* The Required column specifies if the attribute is required (yes) or optional (no).

** In the R/C column, C means that the attribute is a compile-time expression, and R means that the attribute can be either a request-time expression or a compile-time expression.

<cm:getProperty>

The <cm:getProperty> tag, which does not have a body, retrieves the value of the specified content metadata property and places it into a variable specified by resultId. If resultId is not specified, the value is inlined into the page, similar to the <cm:printProperty> tag. The data that this tag retrieves is located in the DOCUMENT_METADATA table. Table 6-5, from the WebLogic Portal 7.0 documentation, lists all attributes for this tag. WebLogic Portal 7.0 documentation reprinted with permission from BEA Systems, Inc. Copyright© 2002 BEA Systems, Inc. All rights reserved.

Table 6-5. <cm:getProperty> Tag Attributes

TAG ATTRIBUTE	REQUIRED*	TYPE	DESCRIPTION	R/C**
id	No	String	The JSP script variable name which contains the Content instance from which to get the properties.	R
entity	No	ConfigurableEntity	Specifies the com.beasys.commerce.foundation. ConfigurableEntity object from which to get the property. If this is specified and non-null, id is ignored. Otherwise, id will be used.	R
name	Yes	String	The name of the property to print.	R
scope	No	String	The scope name for the property to get. If not specified, null is passed in, which is what Document objects expect.	R
resultId	No	String	The name of the JSP script variable which will be populated with the value of the property. If this is not specified, then the value of the property will be inlined into the body of the JSP. If this is specified, then encode, default, maxLength, dateFormat, and numFormat are ignored.	C
resultType	No	String	The Java type of the property. If this is not specified, then java.lang.Object is used.	C

(Continued)

Table 6-5. <cm:getProperty> Tag Attributes (Continued)

TAG ATTRIBUTE	REQUIRED*	TYPE	DESCRIPTION	R/C**
encode	No	String	Either html, url, or none: If html, then the value will be html encoded so that it appears in HTML as expected (& becomes &, < becomes <, > becomes >, and " becomes "). If *url,* then it is encoded to x-www-form-urlencoded format via the java.net.URLEncoder. If *none* or unspecified, no encoding is performed.	R
default	No	String	The value to print if the property is not found or has a null value. If this is not specified and the property value is null, nothing is printed.	R
maxLength	No	String, int	The maximum length of the property's value to print. If specified, values longer than this will be truncated.	R
failOnError	No	String, Boolean	This attribute can have one of two values: False (default value): Handles JSP processing errors gracefully and prints nothing if an error occurs. True: Throws an exception. You can handle the exception in the code, let the page proceed to the normal error page, or let the application server handle it less gracefully.	R
dateFormat	No	String	The java.text.SimpleDateFormat string to use to print the property, if it is a java.util.Date. If the property is not a Date, this is ignored. If this is not set, the Date's default toString method is used.	R
numFormat	No	String	The java.text.DecimalFormat string to use to print the property, if it is a java.lang.Number. If the property is not a Number, this is ignored. If this is not set, the Number's default toString method is used.	R

* The Required column specifies if the attribute is required (yes) or optional (no).

** In the R/C column, C means that the attribute is a compile-time expression, and R means that the attribute can be either a request-time expression or a compile-time expression.

To show you how this tag works, we modify the contentviewer JSP to display the company property that was loaded when the BulkLoader was used previously. The following code displays the company and then the content:

```
<%@ taglib uri="cm.tld" prefix="cm"%>

<%
    // get the content id from the query parameter passed
    String contentId = (String)request.getParameter("contentid");
%>

<%  // select content based on the content id %>
<cm:selectById contentId="<%=contentId%>" id="doc" />

<% // get the property company and then display it %>
<cm:getProperty id="doc" name="company" resultId="company"
resultType="java.lang.String"/>

<b>company:</b> <%=company%>
<BR><BR

<table> <tr><td>
<% // display the content %>
<cm:printDoc id="doc" blockSize="1000" >
</td></tr></table>
```

Now if you've been following along up to this point, and you clicked the Company A link shown in Figure 6-6, you would be redirected to the content page, and the appropriate property and content would be displayed, as illustrated in Figure 6-8.

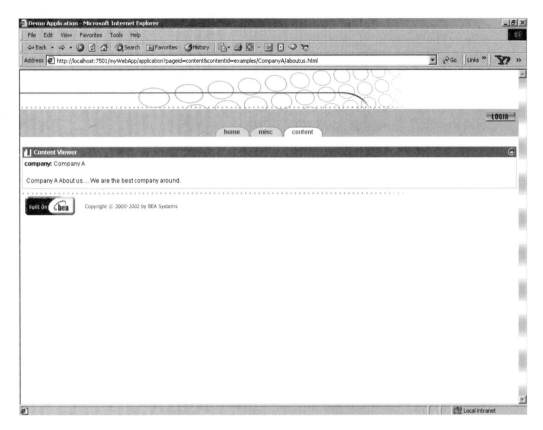

Figure 6-8. Displaying properties and content dynamically

`<cm:select>`

The <cm:select> tag, which does not support or use a body, employs only the search expression query syntax to select content. Once you have content, you can use the <es:forEachInArray> tag to loop through the array of content that is returned from the <cm:select tag>. Table 6-6, from the WebLogic Portal 7.0 documentation, lists all attributes for this tag. WebLogic Portal 7.0 documentation reprinted with permission from BEA Systems, Inc. Copyright© 2002 BEA Systems, Inc. All rights reserved.

Table 6-6. <cm:select> Tag Attributes

TAG ATTRIBUTE	REQUIRED*	TYPE	DESCRIPTION	R/C**
contentHome	No	String	The JNDI name of the ContentManager EJB Home to use to find content. The object in JNDI at this name must implement a create method which returns an object which implements the ContentManager interface. If not specified, the system searches the default content home.	R
max	No	String, long	Limits the maximum number of content items returned. If not present, or zero or less, it returns all of the content items found.	R
sortBy	No	String	A list of document attributes by which to sort the content. The syntax follows the SQL *order by* clause. The sort specification is limited to a list of the metadata attribute names and the keywords ASC and DESC. Examples: sortBy="creationDate" sortBy="creationDate ASC, title DESC".	R
failOnError	No	String, Boolean	This attribute can have one of two values: False (default value): Handles JSP processing errors gracefully and returns an empty array if an error occurs. True: Throws an exception that causes the JSP page to stop. You can handle the exception in the code, let the page proceed to the normal error page, or let the application server handle it less gracefully.	R
id	Yes	String	The JSP script variable name that will contain the array of Content objects after this tag finishes.	C
query	No	String	A content query string used to search for content. Example: query="mimetype contains 'text' && author='Proulx'".	R
expression	No	Expression	The com.beasys.commerce.foundation. expression.Expression object to use to search for content. If this is null or not specified, then query must be specified. Otherwise, query is ignored.	R

(Continued)

Table 6-6. <cm:select> Tag Attributes (Continued)

TAG ATTRIBUTE	REQUIRED*	TYPE	DESCRIPTION	R/C**
useCache	No	String, Boolean	Determines whether content is cached. This attribute can have one of two values: False (default value): ContentCache is not used. If false (not specified), the cacheId, cacheScope, and cacheTimeout settings are ignored. True: ContentCache is used.	R
cacheId	No	String	The identifier name used to cache the content. Internally, the cache is implemented as a map; this will become the key. If not specified, the id attribute of the tag is used.	R
cacheTimeout	No	String, long	The time, in milliseconds, for which the cached content is valid. If more than this amount of time has passed since the content was cached, the cached content will be cleared, retrieved, and placed back into the cache. Use -1 for no-timeout (always use the cached content). Default = -1.	R
cacheScope	No	String	Specifies the lifecycle scope of the content cache. Similar to <jsp:useBean>. Possible values: application session (the default) page request	R
contextParams	No	String or java.util.Map	Additional search parameters to pass to the Content Manager. Some Content Manager implementations may support this.	R
readOnly	Ignored		This attribute is deprecated and no longer used. When found, it is ignored.	

* The Required column specifies if the attribute is required (yes) or optional (no).

** In the R/C column, C means that the attribute is a compile-time expression, and R means that the attribute can be either a request-time expression or a compile-time expression.

To demonstrate how the <cm:select> tag works, we add several more content documents to the examples/NuWave directory and then rerun the BulkLoader. All content documents that were in the examples/NuWave directory had the metadata company = NuWave Solutions, LLC associated with it. We write a portlet that uses the <cm:select tag> with a query of company = NuWave Solutions, LLC. The tag <es:forEachInArray> is then used to loop through each array element returned from <cm:select>. Within the loop the content name is displayed. The code for the portlet is shown here:

```
<%@ taglib uri="cm.tld" prefix="cm"%>
<%@ taglib uri="es.tld" prefix="es" %>
<%@ page import="com.bea.p13n.content.document.Document" %>

<%
    // define the query string
    String queryStr = "company = 'NuWave Solutions, LLC'";
%>

<cm:select query="<%=queryStr%>" id="contentList"/>

<es:forEachInArray id="content" array="<%=contentList%>"
type="com.bea.p13n.content.Content">

    <cm:getProperty resultId="contentName" resultType="String"
    id="content" name="name" encode="html" />

    <br>
    <%= contentName %>
<%
    }
%>
</es:forEachInArray>
```

The results of this portlet are shown in Figure 6-9.

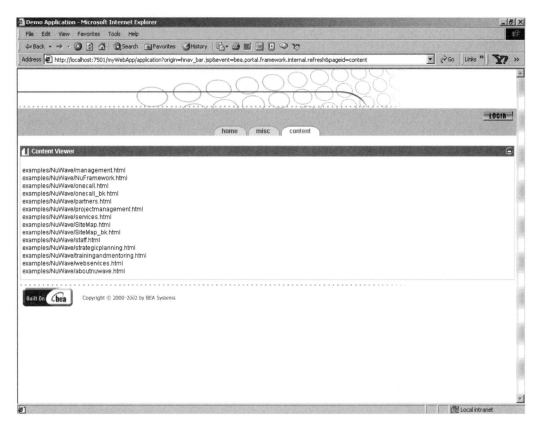

Figure 6-9. Displaying results using the <cm:Select> tag

Content Selectors

Content Selectors are another way of retrieving documents from a content management system. By using Content Selectors, you can personalize a portal or portlet by specifying conditions under which WebLogic Portal retrieves one or more documents. Content Selectors are part of the WebLogic Portal Advisor, which provides Personalization services including personalized content, user segmentation, and the underlying rules engine. The Advisor can deliver content to a personalized application based on a set of rules and user profile information. It can also retrieve any type of content from a document management system and display it in a JSP. The Advisor includes an Advisor EJB and a JSP tag library for accessing the content selected.

An example of when you might want to use a Content Selector would be if you needed to display a certain piece of content after August 5, 2002. You can then use Content Selector tags in a portlet to display the specific Content Selector you have created if the conditions you set are met. Creating a Content Selector involves the following:

- Verifying the Advisor is configured

- Creating the Content Selector in the EBCC

- Using Content Selector tags in a portlet

Verifying the Advisor Is Configured

In order to use the Personalization services, you must verify that the personalization taglibs have been configured and that certain XML files have been configured properly.

Verify Personalization Taglibs

First, you have to make sure that the pz_taglib.jar file is in the Web application's WEB-INF/lib directory. Copy this file from BEA_HOME/weblogic700/portal/lib/p13n/web, since that's the official home of the portal jars, and therefore the file is guaranteed to be updated by the service pack installers.

Next, you must verify the mapping of the pz.tld tag library to /WEB-INF/lib/pz_taglib.jar in a <taglib> entry in your Web application's WEB-INF/web.xml file. Verify the following XML has been placed in the web.xml file within the <web-app></web-app> tokens:

```
<taglib>
    <taglib-uri> pz.tld </taglib-uri>
    <taglib-location> WEB-INF/lib/pz_taglib.jar </taglib-location>
</taglib>
```

Verify the Appropriate XML Files

You need to ensure that the Advisor EJB has been configured. This is done by verifying the following XML has been placed in the web.xml file:

```
<ejb-ref>
    <description>The EjbAdvisor for this webapp
    </description>
    <ejb-ref-name>ejb/EjbAdvisor</ejb-ref-name>
    <ejb-ref-type>Session</ejb-ref-type>
    <home>com.bea.p13n.advisor.EjbAdvisorHome</home>
    <remote>com.bea.p13n.advisor.EjbAdvisor</remote>
</ejb-ref>
```

Next, verify the following XML appears in weblogic.xml (within the <reference-descriptor></reference-descriptor> tags):

```
<ejb-reference-description>
    <ejb-ref-name>ejb/EjbAdvisor</ejb-ref-name>
    <jndi-name>${APPNAME}.BEA_personalization.EjbAdvisor</jndi-name>
</ejb-reference-description>
```

Finally, verify that this line appears in config.xml:

```
<EJBComponent Name="ejbadvisor" Targets="p13nServer" URI="ejbadvisor.jar"/>
```

Creating the Content Selector in the EBCC

In the EBCC, select **New** to display the New menu and select **Content Selector**. The Content Selector Editor is now displayed as shown in Figure 6-10. Note that in this chapter we show you how to create a Content Selector. In Chapter 13, you will learn how to personalize a Content Selector based on a user's profile.

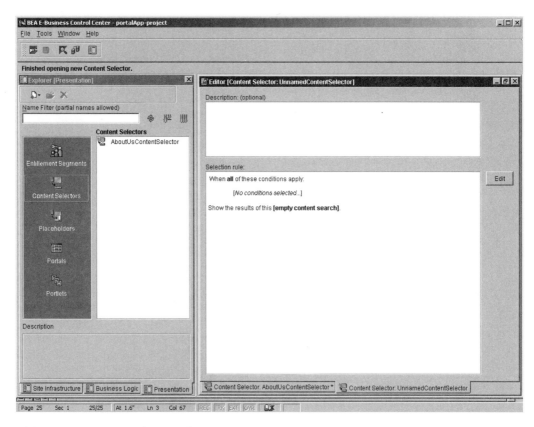

Figure 6-10. Content Selector Editor

Next, click the Edit button to create the rules for this Content Selector. The Selection Rule dialog box appears. This dialog box is divided into two sections: Conditions and Action. There are ten different conditions that you can select. When you select a condition, a corresponding action is displayed in the Action section of the dialog box. Figure 6-11 shows the action that appears when you check the condition "It is after a given date."

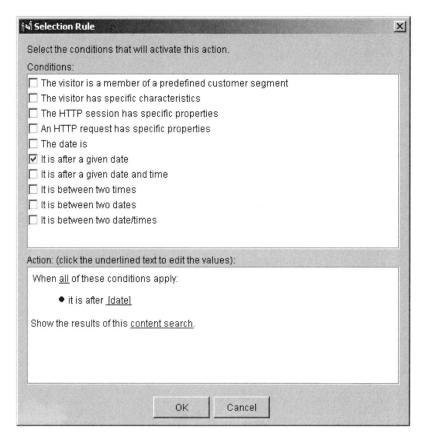

Figure 6-11. Selection Rule dialog box

To finish the selection rule for this particular condition, you need to click the [date] link displayed in the Action portion of the screen and enter the date you want the content to be displayed after. For our example, August 02, 2002 was entered. Next, you define the content by clicking the [empty content search] link displayed in the Action portion of the dialog box. The Content Search dialog box shown in Figure 6-12 appears.

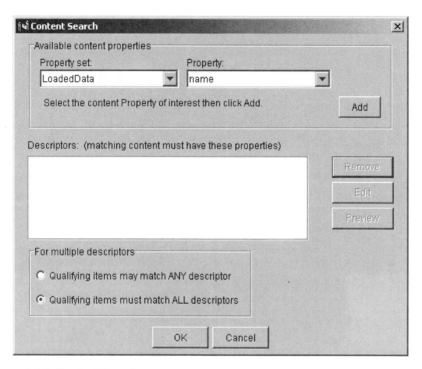

Figure 6-12. Content Search screen

To add search values, click the Add button. The Content Search Values dialog box is then displayed. Enter the value you want the content to search on. In our example, we enter the value examples/NuWave/aboutus.html (see Figure 6-13) and click the Add button.

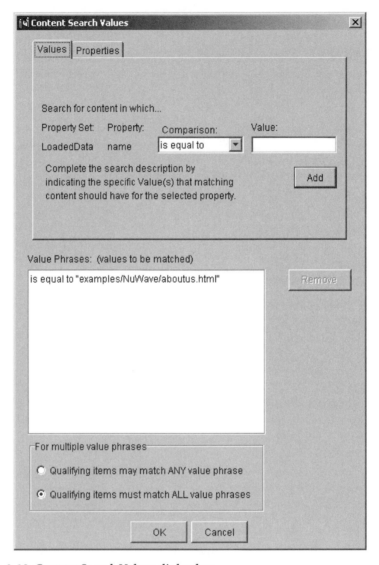

Figure 6-13. Content Search Values dialog box

Clicking the OK button in the Content Search Values dialog box brings you back to the Content Search dialog box again. Notice that the Preview button has been enabled. You can test the Content Selector you just created by clicking this button. Figure 6-14 shows the results of the Content Selector we created.

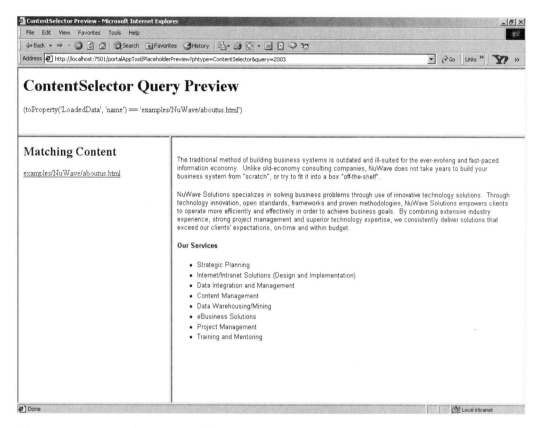

Figure 6-14. Testing the Content Selector

After testing the Content Selector, click the OK button in the Content Search dialog box. The Selection Rule screen appears. If you are finished defining rules for your Content Selector, you can click the OK button, and the Content Selector Editor is displayed. Figure 6-15 shows the Content Selector Editor with selection rules defined.

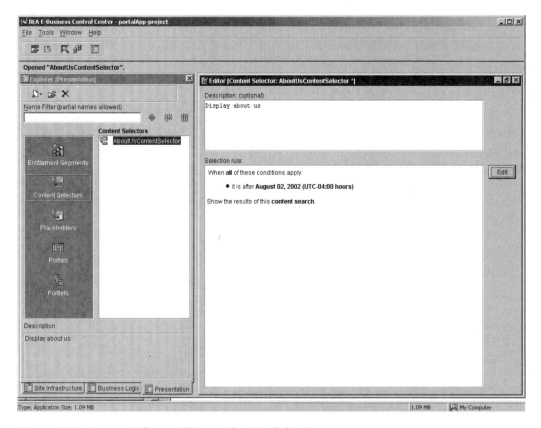

Figure 6-15. Content Selector Editor with rules defined

Now you can save the Content Selector. For this example, we save our Content Selector as AboutUsContentSelector. You will need the name of your Content Selector when you start using the Content Selector tags. Remember that you must synchronize all changes done in the EBCC.

Using Content Selector Tags in a Portlet

Now that a Content Selector has been created, you want to access it in code. The Content Selector definition that you create in the EBCC will determine the conditions that activate the Content Selector and the query that the active Content Selector runs.

To refer to this definition, use the following rule attribute:

```
<pz:contentSelector rule= { definition-name | scriptlet } >
```

To query the Content Selector, AboutUsContentSelector, created in the previous section, we would write the following code:

```
<pz:contentSelector rule="AboutUsContentSelector"
    contentHome="<%=ContentHelper.DEF_DOCUMENT_MANAGER_HOME %>"
    id="contentArray" />
```

Notice that the preceding code contains a reference to a variable, contentHome. The Content Selector tag must use the contentHome attribute to specify the JNDI home of the content management system. Because the code includes the ContentHelper class, you must first use the following tag to import the class into the JSP:

```
<%@ page import="com.bea.p13n.content.ContentHelper"%>
```

The tag <pz:contentSelector> will return an array. Use the <es:forEachInArray> tag to iterate over the array of content and display the results. The code that follows puts everything together:

```
<%-----------------------------------------------------------------
File: content_selector.jsp
Purpose: Use a content selector to retrieve content and display it.
---------------------------------------------------------------%>

<%@ page import="com.bea.p13n.content.ContentHelper" %>
<%@ page import="com.bea.p13n.content.Content" %>
<%@ page import="com.bea.p13n.content.document.Document" %>
<%@ page import="java.net.URLEncoder" %>

<%@ taglib uri="cm.tld" prefix="cm" %>
<%@ taglib uri="es.tld" prefix="es" %>
<%@ taglib uri="pz.tld" prefix="pz" %>
```

```
<%------------------------------------------------------------------
Retrieve the content using the content selector rule specified.
----------------------------------------------------------------%>
<pz:contentSelector rule="AboutUsContentSelector"
    contentHome="<%=ContentHelper.DEF_DOCUMENT_MANAGER_HOME %>"
    id="contentArray" />

<% if (contentArray.length <= 0) contentArray = null; %>

<table align="center" width="100%" border="0" cellspacing="2" cellpadding="2">
<tr>
    <td width="10%"> </td>
    <td width="40%"> </td>
    <td width="40%"> </td>
    <td width="10%"> </td>
</tr>

<%------------------------------------------------------------------
If the content selector does not return any values, display an
appropriate message.
----------------------------------------------------------------%>
<es:isNull item="<%=contentArray%>">
    <tr>
        <td> </td>
        <td colspan="2">
            <b>Sorry, The content selector did not find content based on
Selection
 Rules.<br><br>
            </b>
        </td>
        <td> </td>
    </tr>
</es:isNull>
<%------------------------------------------------------------------
If the content selector does return any values, display the Name of
the Document.
----------------------------------------------------------------%>
<es:notNull item="<%=contentArray%>">
```

```
<%------------------------------------------------------------------
Use the es:forEachInArray tag to iterate over the array of content.
----------------------------------------------------------------%>
<es:forEachInArray id="nextDoc"
array="<%=contentArray%>" type="Content">
    <cm:getProperty resultId="contentName" resultType="String"
    id="nextDoc" name="name" encode="html" />

    <%=contentName%>
    <es:notNull item="<%=contentName%>">
<table>
    <tr><td>
        <% // display the content %>
        <cm:printDoc id="nextDoc" blockSize="1000" >
    </td></tr></table>
        </es:notNull>
    </es:forEachInArray>
</es:notNull>
</table>
```

We place the preceding code in a portlet called contentselector and include this portlet on a page called contentselector. Figure 6-16 shows the content selector page. The system clock on the computer the portal is running on indicates the date is August 5, 2002. The Content Selector AboutUsContentSelector has a business rule defined that displays the content only if the date is after August 02, 2002. As you can see, the portlet displays the name of the content and then the actual content, aboutus.html.

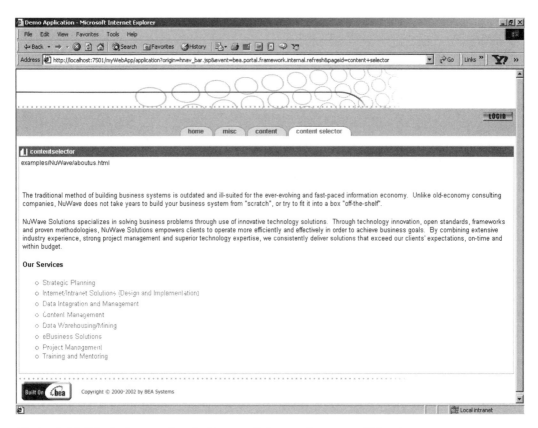

Figure 6-16. Displaying results of a Content Selector when a condition is met

Next, we change the system clock on the computer the portal is running on to August 1, 2002. Because the date is not after August 2, 2002, the rule defined in the Content Selector AboutUsContentSelector has not been met. As a result, the portlet indicates that it could not display the content based on selection rules (see Figure 6-17).

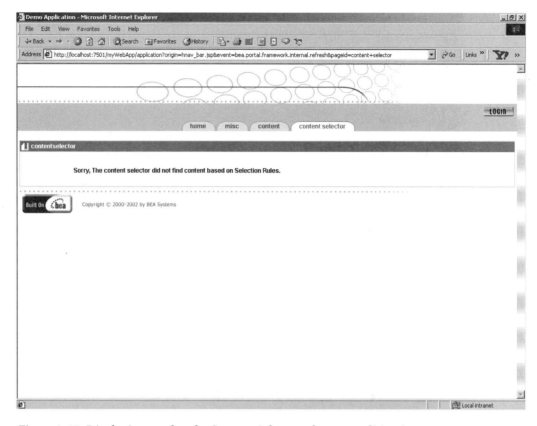

Figure 6-17. Displaying results of a Content Selector when a condition is not met

We have shown you the basics for implementing a Content Selector. As you can see, Content Selectors are very powerful, and they can be used to build very robust content delivery mechanisms.

Integrating Third-Party Content Management Systems

If you want features that the Content Manager does not provide, such as versioning, check-in/check-out, and an interface through which to enter content, then you might want to use one of the third-party content management systems, or CMSs. BEA partners with many third-party vendors to integrate their CMS with the BEA WebLogic Portal. Several companies such as Percussion Software, Interwoven, and Documentum provide excellent content management systems. The functionality, complexity of integration, and cost of these products vary. When deciding on which tool to integrate with, keep in mind the three strategies

BEA recommends for integrating a third-party CMS with the BEA WebLogic Portal. If the third-party tool you have selected does not use one of the three recommended strategies, you might want to look at alternatives. Following are the three recommended strategies for integrating a CMS with BEA.

Publishing to File System

The CMS can publish documents to a file system—specifically to the dmsBase directory, as we discussed earlier in the chapter. The BulkLoader can then load the content placed in the file system by the third-party CMS into the database.

Using a DocumentProvider Interface

The DocumentProvider interface that is provided by BEA includes methods that access an underlying content management system. Implementing a DocumentProvider interface involves writing implementations of the following Java interfaces contained in the com.beasys.p13n.content.document.spi package:

- DocumentProvider

- DocumentIterator

- DocumentMetadataDef

- DocumentDef

- DocumentSchemaDef

If you want more information on how to implement the DocumentProvider interface, refer to the javadoc provided by BEA.

Updating the Database and File System

This final strategy involves updating the DOCUMENT and DOCUMENT_METADATA tables, updating the dmsBase file directories with content, and updating the XML schema files. Many of the third-party CMSs have implemented this strategy—they have written java classes that integrate with the BEA WebLogic Portal and its content management solution.

Summary

Content is a very important aspect of any portal. This chapter gave you an overview of how content is incorporated within the BEA WebLogic Portal. We discussed how to publish content that can be used by the Content Manager. We then discussed the different Content Manager JSP tags and how you can use them in portlets to access the content you have published. We then showed you how to create and use Content Selectors. Finally, we touched on strategies for integrating a third-party CMS.

CHAPTER 7

Incorporating Webflow in Portlet Navigation

THE WORLD IS IN A STATE of constant change. There is a direct correlation between change and late nights at the office, and countless numbers of developers can attest to this, having been burdened with the weight of constant change.

Even simple changes, such as maintaining the flow of presentation within a Web application, come with a cost. Each link within a JSP has a hard-coded destination. If these links need to be changed, and according to Murphy's Law they will, this would result in many code changes. These modifications pale in comparison to those that would be needed for data validation changes or any other business logic changes. Efficiency and modularity would be greatly improved if these types of changes were centralized in one location. This is what Webflow provides.

This chapter takes you step by step through the various components of Webflow. We discuss each component in full and explore its role in the BEA Webflow Editor.

Introduction to Webflow

As previously discussed, it is important to maintain a clear, concise separation between the layers of a Web application. *Webflow* is a mechanism that is designed to help maintain the separation of the presentation layer from the business layer of a Web application. You can specify the flow of JSPs within the Web application through Webflow, greatly reducing the amount of development and testing time necessary for building and maintaining navigation subsystems. With Webflow, you can not only map out the entire flow of the Web application, but also use componentized modules for data validation and other business logic.

Every Web application has a flow that it follows. A user clicks links to navigate throughout the site. The process of navigating from an origin to a destination is the *flow*. This action is the result of an event, clicking a link. The user's state changes from one page to another and is hard-coded within the HTML or JSP in the form of the page source found within that link.

BEA Webflow maintains the user's state, without the need of hard-coding this information within the source code of the page. The origin and event are passed to Webflow via the request. Webflow processes this information and, based on the event and the origin of that event, calculates what the destination should be. It then forwards the request to the destination. This removes the state information from the presentation layer, making it easy to change later.

Webflow is said to enable the Model View Controller (MVC) design pattern. What exactly does it mean to enable a design pattern? Simply put, the components of Webflow, when pieced together, follow the specifications of the pattern. By implementing the use of Webflow for a Web application, you are almost guaranteed that Web application will follow the MVC pattern. Presentation nodes are decoupled from all business logic. These, of course, make up the View. Input processors and pipeline components represent the Model. The Controller is not in plain view. Within the implementation of Webflow, a Webflow servlet handles all requests from the presentation layer and delegates them to the appropriate Processor nodes.

Basic Components of Webflow

As complicated as Webflow may sound, only three basic types of components are used in creating Webflows. These are namespaces, nodes, and events. A Webflow transitions from node to node via an event. These nodes and events are defined within a namespace. Multiple namespaces are contained within the Webflow for the application.

Namespaces

In the BEA WebLogic Portal, a Web application can consist of only one Webflow. Knowing this, you can see how it would be difficult for a team of developers to work separately without some way to overcome this problem. Namespaces resolve this issue.

A Webflow can be separated into modules called *namespaces*. Namespaces can be considered a container of all the other components of Webflow. There is no limit to the number of namespaces that a Webflow may contain. The use of namespaces makes Webflow development a more maintainable chore and allows a team of developers to work simultaneously on application-specific tasks, since each namespace is a separate entity.

Nodes

Nodes are the origin and destination of Webflows. All nodes either present information to the user or process information sent from the user. Accordingly, nodes are categorized as either Presentation nodes or Processor nodes.

Presentation Nodes

Presentation nodes display information to the end user. The origin and destination of a Webflow is always a Presentation node. Presentation nodes can be in the form of JSPs, HTML, WML, or servlets.

Processor Nodes

Processor nodes are components that process information from the user's request. There are two types of Processor nodes: Input Processors and Pipelines. Although discussed briefly in this chapter, Processor nodes are examined fully in Chapter 8.

Input Processors

Input Processors acquire data from the request object and also validate this information. They are embedded in the JSP as custom tags from the Webflow tag library. An Input Processor helps to eliminate using complex code directly in a JSP. For example, an Input Processor can be used to ensure that a password has the appropriate number of characters during a registration process, or that a date is displayed in a proper format. Having this logic directly within the JSP creates illegible source code that is a chore to maintain.

Pipelines

After input is processed and validated, most Web applications need to then persist this information in Java objects or in a relational database. All *Pipelines* are made up of groupings of *Pipeline Components*, which are server-side objects that process information from the request and perform certain business logic on this data. A Pipeline can be used through the registration process to store user information, once registration is complete, within a database. Also, a Pipeline can retrieve order information based on a certain product identification number passed via the user's request in an accounts receivable Web application.

A Pipeline Component can either succeed or fail. Failure throws an exception that can either terminate the entire Pipeline or cause Webflow to proceed down a branch that handles the exception and continues on with normal processing. An entire Pipeline can be designated as transactional. In the case of failure in a transaction Pipeline, a terminating failure will roll back all prior changes.

Events

The transition from one node to another within Webflow is the result of an *event* occurring. Each type of node can only process certain types of events; therefore, events are divided into two groups: presentation events and processor events.

Presentation Events

From a Presentation node, *presentation events* can occur in two ways: by clicking a link or by clicking a button. Each of these events will result in Webflow responding to the event and transitioning to the next node. That node can be another Presentation node or a Processor node. In the case of a link, usually what occurs is traversal to another JSP. In the case of a button press, the action would more than likely be the submission of information to an Input Processor.

Processor Events

Processor events respond to different events. These are either exceptions or success objects. An exception event, of course, is the result of a failure within an Input Processor or a Pipeline Component. A success object is merely an object that signals that this certain step of processing, accomplished by a Pipeline Component, has succeeded and normal flow can continue.

Additional Webflow Components

Webflow also contains several additional components other than the basic components mentioned. These components are employed during Webflow development and aren't truly part of the basic structure of Webflow. These objects aid development so that the developer's task can be accomplished more effectively and above all more efficiently.

PipelineSession Object

The PipelineSession object enables Processor nodes to store information in Java objects while transitioning from one node to the other. Information normally needs to be retained while traversing a Pipeline. An Input Processor stores information in the PipelineSession object so that Pipeline Components may retrieve it for further processing. Java objects are stored within the Pipeline Session as key/value pairs. This information is also accessible from within a JSP via tags in the Webflow tag library. Attributes stored within this object can be included in rollbacks of data on failure.

Attributes within the Pipeline Session can be of session scope or request scope. Storing vast amounts of information within the session object can be dangerous—it can result in performance problems, as the amount of attributes within a user's session can accumulate greatly. It also causes persistence problems in a clustered environment; if rollback needs to occur, it must occur on each server within the cluster.

The Configuration Error Page

When you develop a Webflow, more than likely it will not be configured correctly the first time. Like any other type of development, Webflow will have to be debugged. The Configuration Error page is a special kind of Presentation node that can be used in case of a configuration error in Webflow. Configuration errors could occur for many reasons. For instance, it is possible for Webflow not to be able to find the destination node for a transition. In such a situation, the defined Configuration Error page would be displayed. This page is only used in development; configuration errors should obviously be corrected before you give the public access to your Web application.

Configuration Error pages are specified on a per-namespace basis. Each namespace can use its own error page. However, an error page is not a requirement, rather an option that the developer can choose to include in Webflow. If a configuration error were to occur within a namespace that has no Configuration Error page set up, Webflow would attempt to use the error page from the default namespace. We recommend that, at a minimum, the default namespace of a Web application define a Configuration Error page.

Wildcard Nodes

Many times, an common event can occur throughout a Web application. For instance, it is not unusual for the same link to be present on several pages throughout a portal. This link could take the user to a login page, a help page, or the home page. Also, considering that Processor nodes will potentially throw errors from time to time, it would be useful to have a single JSP display all errors thrown by processors no matter what their origin might be. It would be incredibly tedious to define these events over and over, and would result in a convoluted Webflow.

Wildcard nodes handle these situations. A Wildcard node can be in the form of either a Presentation node or a Processor node. These nodes can handle some behavior that may originate from numerous nodes with a Webflow. If a Webflow cannot find the required node to complete a transition, it will then search through Wildcard nodes. If a Wildcard node is found that matches the transition, the Webflow will use that node as the origin of the transition. This way, only one node need be defined to handle a transition that occurs throughout the Webflow.

Begin Node

The Begin node is the starting point of the namespace in which it is defined. This node can be either a Presentation node or a Processor node. Typically, a Presentation node in the form of a JSP is defined as the Begin node. If no event is specified within a URL, the Begin node of the current namespace becomes the Webflow's destination. It is possible for a URL not to specify an origin, namespace, or event. At this point, the Webflow must find a starting point on its own. If this were to occur, the Begin node of the default namespace would be used. This is why we recommend that at least the default namespace of the Web application have a Begin node defined.

Root Node

Much like the Begin node, the Root node is the initial state of a Pipeline. The only difference is that specifying a Root node for a Pipeline is required. Each Pipeline must define a Root node.

Predefined Events and lastContentUrl

The BEA WebLogic Portal has many predefined events that provide generic portal functionality and occur regularly throughout the portal. Events can be used in any Webflow by defining a Wildcard node. lastContentUrl is a node, rather than an event, defined within the portal namespace. This node is accessible from any namespace by using a Proxy node and is usually used in correlation with the predefined events. We explain the use of Wildcard nodes and Proxy nodes later in this chapter.

Predefined Events

Many events are predefined to handle generic portlet events. These events could be present in any portlet. When one of these events occurs, Webflow attempts to find an origin and event that match this event within the current namespace. For that reason, if a portlet will be using any of these events, it is necessary to include a Wildcard node for each event. The most frequently used events are as listed here:

- *Refresh event:* When the user refreshes the browser window, this event is called. Since it is impossible to stop users from clicking the refresh button in their browser, every Webflow should define this event.

  Webflow event name: bea.portal.framework.internal.refresh

- *Maximize event:* When the user maximizes a portlet by clicking the Maximize button, usually the same page is to be displayed.

  Webflow event name: bea.portal.framework.internal.portlet.maximize

- *Unmaximize event:* The Unmaximize button uses this event; like the Maximize event, the destination for this event is also usually the same page.

  Webflow event name: bea.portal.framework.internal.portlet.unmaximize

- *Minimize event:* When the user minimizes a portlet by clicking the Minimize button, this event is called.

  Webflow event name: bea.portal.framework.internal.portlet.minimize

- *Unminimize event:* Unminimizing with the Unminimize button will cause Webflow to look for this event.

  Webflow event name: bea.portal.framework.internal.portlet.unminimize

- *Edit event:* Clicking the Edit button on a portlet will cause Webflow to search for this event.

  Webflow event name: bea.portal.framework.internal.portlet.edit

- *Unedit event:* This event is fired off when a user clicks the Unedit button.

  Webflow event name: bea.portal.framework.internal.portlet.unedit

- *Float event:* Clicking the Float button on a portlet calls this event.

  Webflow event name: bea.portal.framework.internal.portlet.float

lastContentUrl

With most of the events mentioned in the previous section, the destination of the event transition would be the same location. For instance, when maximizing a portlet, the user would probably want to stay on the same page in order to view the information that needed maximizing in the first place. lastContentUrl is a node that can serve as the destination of this transition and all other transitions whose destination should be the current page.

The Webflow Editor

Webflows are created and modified in the Webflow Editor. This editor is part of the E-Business Control Center (EBCC). The Webflow Editor allows the developer or architect of the Web application to view Webflows and Pipelines in a hierarchical tree for each Web application within the BEA WebLogic Portal. This editor also allows for easy creation and modification of Webflows and Pipelines via a graphical user interface, which provides drag-and-drop functionality for adding and manipulating nodes and events within a Webflow.

Getting to the Webflow Editor

The first step in getting to the Webflow Editor is to start the EBCC. As you learned in earlier chapters, the EBCC is comprised of an Explorer window and a workspace. Three tabs exist within the Explorer window: Site Infrastructure, Business Logic, and Presentation. The Site Infrastructure tab is where the Webflow Editor can be found, and this is shown in Figure 7-1.

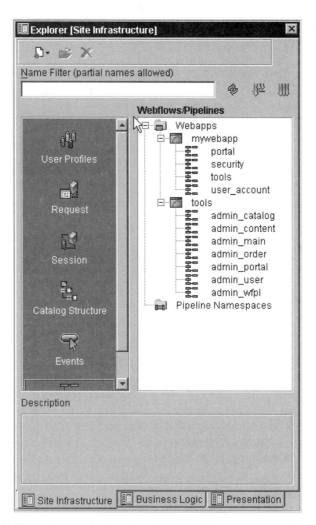

Figure 7-1. EBCC Explorer window showing Site Infrastructure tab

When you click the Webflows/Pipelines button, the Explorer window displays all Webflows within BEA WebLogic Portal, categorized by Web application. Also displayed are all Pipelines categorized by their namespaces. You can expand a particular Web application to display all Webflows associated with that Web application; likewise, Pipeline Namespaces can be expanded to show all Pipelines contained within the namespace. Figure 7-1 shows an expanded view of Webflows and Pipelines.

Table 7-1 contains a description of the icons on the Site Infrastructure tab. Web applications are displayed at the topmost level. Webflows can be found underneath the Web application node. Since the BEA WebLogic Portal is built using Webflow, a newly created Web application will already have several Webflows within it.

Beneath the Web applications, at the same level, are Pipeline Namespaces. Namespaces are not associated with a certain Web application. Each namespace can be accessed by any number of Web applications. Expanding the Pipeline Namespace component reveals the Pipelines contained within the namespace.

Table 7-1. Icons on the Site Infrastructure Tab

ICON	NAME
🖼	Web Applications
🗂	Webflows
🗃	Pipeline Namespaces
🎞	Pipelines

Exploring the Webflow Editor

You access the Webflow Editor by either double-clicking a currently created object, Webflow, or Pipeline, or creating a new object. The New Object button, located within the Explorer window, allows you to create a new object. Figure 7-2 demonstrates using the New Object button within the Explorer window to create a new Webflow or Pipeline. The File menu also provides a means of creating a new Webflow or Pipeline.

Figure 7-2. Creating a new Webflow or Pipeline via the New Object button

Once you select the menu option Webflow/Pipeline, a New Webflow/Pipeline dialog box appears, as shown in Figure 7-3. This dialog box allows you to choose to create either a Webflow or a Pipeline, and is where the initial setup of the node occurs. Choosing New Webflow brings up the Webflow Editor in the EBCC work-space. The New Pipeline option also opens an editor, much like the Webflow Editor; however, this editor is Pipeline specific and will be discussed in a later chapter. We also cover the New Webflow/Pipeline dialog box and the creation of Webflows later in this chapter. Before beginning to create a Webflow or Pipeline, we first want to give you an overview of the Webflow Editor so that you grasp the functionality of the tool.

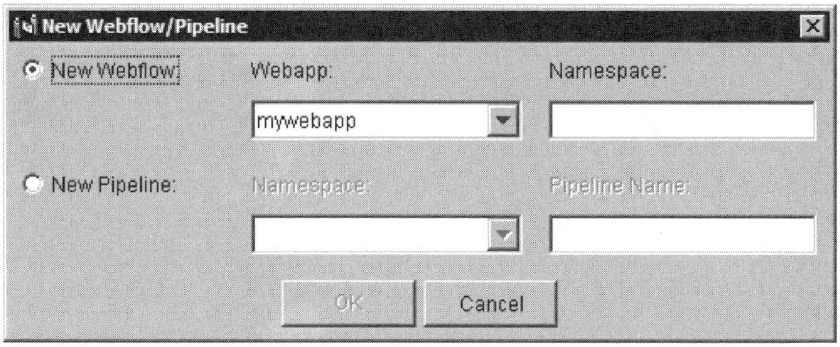

Figure 7-3. New Webflow/Pipeline dialog box

Once you enter the appropriate information in the New Webflow/Pipeline dialog box, you are presented with the Webflow Editor within the EBCC work-space (see Figure 7-4). We will explain the tools within the utility to give you a strong working knowledge of them.

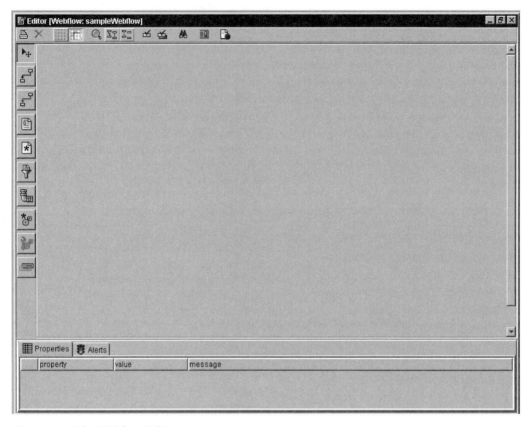

Figure 7-4. The Webflow Editor

There are two groups of tools within the Webflow Editor. Tools are located either within the toolbar, displayed horizontally across the top of the editor pane, or within the editor palette, vertically displayed at the left of the pane. The next two sections describe the functionality of every tool within the Webflow Editor.

Command Tools Within the Toolbar

The toolbar is located at the top of the editor window, and the tools that appear there affect the editor workspace and the Webflow as a whole. These tools, described in Table 7-2, are more administrative than developmental.

Table 7-2. Command Tools on the Toolbar

TOOL	DESCRIPTION
🖨	Prints the entire Webflow or Pipeline.
✕	Deletes the selected component. Once a component is selected, this button is enabled and can be used to remove the component from the Webflow.
⋮⋮	Shows or hides the gridline. Determines whether gridlines will be displayed within the editor workspace.
⊞	Enables or disables the Snap to Grid feature. Snap to Grid can be used to help align Webflow components in the editor workspace for visual appeal. Gridlines do not have to be displayed for Snap to Grid to function.
🔍	Displays the Zoomed Overview view. Since Webflows can become large, this button enables an entire Webflow to be reviewed at once.
⯑	Enables and disables link optimization. This is not as useful as it may sound. Link optimization, when enabled, merely ensures that, while moving a node within the editor workspace, an associated event moves with the node so that it may remain entirely visible.
⯑	Shows or hides exception events.
✓	Validates the selected node. Validation messages will appear on the Alert tab at the bottom of the editor workspace. This button is disabled when no component is selected.
✓	Validates all components within the entire namespace. Validation messages, again, are displayed within the Alert tab.
🔍	Finds a node based on many advanced search features.
🔲	Designates a node as the Begin node. This tool will assign an already existing node to be the Begin node of the namespace.
📄	Sets up the Configuration Error page. This page will display any error that may occur in case there is a configuration error within the Webflow.

Editor Tools Within the Editor Palette

The editor palette is located on the left side of the editor, vertically aligned. The tools in the editor palette are used to develop and design Webflows, as described in Table 7-3.

Table 7-3. Editor Tools on the Editor Palette

TOOL	DESCRIPTION
	The Selection tool allows you to select and manipulate components within the Webflow.
	The Event tool draws event transitions between two nodes.
	The Exception tool draws exception transitions between two nodes.
	The Presentation Node tool places a Presentation node within the workspace.
	The Wildcard Presentation Node tool handles generic events that occur on multiple Presentation nodes.
	The Input Processor Node tool places an Input Processor in the workspace.
	The Pipeline Node tool places a Pipeline node in the workspace.
	The Wildcard Processor Node tool handles generic events that occur within multiple Processor nodes.
	The Custom Processor Node tool places a custom processor in the workspace. This tool is only used if you are extending BEA's Webflow mechanism by creating your own custom Processor nodes.
	The Proxy Node tool adds a Proxy node to the editor workspace. These nodes make it possible to access nodes from separate namespaces.

The majority of these tools are used within the Webflow examples in this chapter. In the next chapter, we explain Pipeline-specific components.

Tab Palette

The last palette within the Webflow Editor is the tab palette, located at the bottom of the editor window. This palette contains two tabs, Properties and Alerts. Figure 7-5 shows the tab palette.

Figure 7-5. The tab palette

The Properties Tab

The Properties tab, as you might guess, displays the properties of the currently selected components within the Webflow. On this tab, you can enter or modify such properties. Figure 7-6 shows the properties of a Presentation node.

	property	value	message
	name*	Presentation	
	type*	jsp	
	page-relative-path		
	page-name*		*The required processorInfo tag [page-name] on Presentation is undefined*
	event*		*The event [ ] on [Presentation] is not connected*

Figure 7-6. The Properties tab

As you can see, the Properties tab is comprised of a four-column table, where each row contains property information.

The first column, which has no column heading, is the status column. Contained within this column is either a traffic light image or a connection image. The traffic light reflects the status of the property as follows:

A green light represents a good status.

A yellow light represents a warning or information status.

A red light represents an alert status.

The connection image has two states:

The closed connection represents a good event.

The open connection represents a disconnected event.

The second column displays the property name. A trailing asterisk (*) indicates that this property is required. Figure 7-6 shows the properties for a Presentation node. Each node that can be added to the canvas has certain properties associated with it. These properties are explained in a later section of this chapter, "Component Properties."

Property values are contained within the third column. Clicking the field either reveals a text box (see Figure 7-7) or a drop-down list (see Figure 7-8), depending on the property, allowing the property value to be set.

Figure 7-7. Property text box

Figure 7-8. Property drop-down list

When setting a text box value, you need to either press Enter or click elsewhere within the Properties tab to set the value. After setting a value, if the text box is still active and the focus is set on the canvas, the new value will not be stored.

A drop-down list that has no value set will display the string "No Data Available". Clicking the right-hand side of the property value column displays the drop-down list. If the drop-down list refuses to display, it helps to take the focus off of the Properties tab and then reselect the node to continue setting its properties.

The fourth and last column is a message column. In the case of an error or warning with a property, an alert will be displayed in this column specifying the details of the problem. In Figure 7-6, the page-name property has a trailing *, meaning that it is required. However, no value has been set. Therefore, the traffic light status displays a red light and the alert is listed in the last column.

The Alert Tab

Selecting each component contained in a Webflow to debug any possible alerts would quickly turn into a tedious process. To prevent this from happening, the tab palette provides the Alert tab. All alerts for the entire Webflow are displayed on this tab, so that you can easily view all errors in one central location. Double-clicking an event selects the offending node and displays its properties.

A Clear button located at the bottom of the tab pane will clear all alerts from the Alert tab. With the Alert tab cleared, you could then use the Validate tool to debug the component of your choice. Validation adds to the Alert tab the specific errors for the selected component. The Validate All tool refills the Alert tab with the errors for the entire Webflow. Figure 7-9 displays a sample Alert tab.

Figure 7-9. The Alert tab

Component Properties

Each component that can be added to the Webflow Editor canvas has properties associated with it that you can view and modify via the Properties tab. The following sections list these properties on a per-component basis.

Event Property

Table 7-4 shows the event property.

Table 7-4. Event Property

PROPERTY NAME	REQUIRED	EXPLANATION
name	Yes	Name of the event. This value will be used in links within the JSP.

Exception Property

Table 7-5 shows the exception property.

Table 7-5. Exception Property

PROPERTY NAME	REQUIRED	EXPLANATION
name	Yes	Name of the exception. This value will be used in links within the JSP.

Presentation Node Properties

Table 7-6 shows the presentation properties.

Table 7-6. Presentation Node Properties

PROPERTY NAME	REQUIRED	EXPLANATION
name	Yes	Name of the node. This field is filled with a default value when the node is added to the canvas. Once the page-name property is set, this value will automatically be filled.
type	Yes	Type of file this node represents. Valid values are presented in a drop-down list for selection. The default value is JSP.
page-relative-path	No	Path to file this node represents, relative to the Web application.
page-name	Yes	Name of the file this node represents, located in page-relative-path. This value minus the file extension will be used as the name property.

Wildcard Presentation Node Properties

Table 7-7 shows the Wildcard Presentation node properties.

Table 7-7. Wildcard Presentation Node Properties

PROPERTY NAME	REQUIRED	EXPLANATION
name	Yes	Name of the node. This field is filled with a default value when the node is added to the canvas. Once the event property is set, this value will automatically be filled.
type	Yes	Type of file this node represents. The default value is JSP.
event	Yes	Event associated with this node. The default value is the name.

Input Processor Node Properties

Table 7-8 shows the Input Processor node properties.

Table 7-8. Input Processor Node Properties

PROPERTY NAME	REQUIRED	EXPLANATION
name	Yes	Name of the Input Processor
class-name	Yes	Package and class name of the Input Processor

Pipeline Node Properties

Table 7-9 shows the Pipeline Node properties.

Table 7-9. Pipeline Node Properties

PROPERTY NAME	REQUIRED	EXPLANATION
name	Yes	Name of the Pipeline to be displayed on the canvas.
pipeline-name	Yes	Name of the Pipeline to be invoked.
pipeline-namespace	No	Namespace in which the Pipeline resides.
event	Yes	By default the success event is included without a transition. It is the developer's responsibility to assign the transition of the event.

Wildcard Processor Node Properties

Table 7-10 shows the Wildcard Processor node properties.

Table 7-10. Wildcard Processor Node Properties

PROPERTY NAME	REQUIRED	EXPLANATION
name	Yes	Name of the node. This field is filled with a default value when the node is added to the canvas. Once the exception property is set, this value will automatically be filled.
type	Yes	Type of Processor node that this node represents.
exception	Yes	Exception associated with this node. The default value is the name.

Custom Processor Node Properties

Table 7-11 shows the Custom Processor node properties.

Table 7-11. Custom Processor Node Properties

PROPERTY NAME	REQUIRED	EXPLANATION
name	Yes	Name of the node to be displayed on the canvas.
type	Yes	Type associated with the custom node.
...	Yes/No	Additional properties could be included. These properties are dynamically listed based on the definition of the custom node.

Proxy Node Properties

Table 7-12 shows the Proxy node properties.

Table 7-12. Proxy Node Properties

PROPERTY NAME	REQUIRED	EXPLANATION
referent-namespace	Yes	Namespace where the referenced node resides
entity-name	Yes	Name of the node to be referenced

Alerts and Visual Cues

BEA has gone to great lengths to build in many visual cues to let you know when there are problems within a Webflow. We already discussed the status column on the Properties tab that indicates status of a property using different traffic light images. This traffic light image is also included as the icon of the Alert tab. Even though the Properties tab is the default tab for the workspace, you can quickly see that there are errors within the Webflow with a glance at this icon.

There is one additional visual cue for alerts, represented by another image. This image is displayed in several locations as an added means of error notification:

As Table 7-1 also shows, the icon displayed for a Webflow in the Explorer pane is as follows:

However, in the case of a Webflow that contains a component with an error status, this icon is displayed:

Even without opening a Webflow in the Webflow Editor, you can see that there are errors that require your attention.

The error icon is also displayed on node representations within the workspace. For instance, when you are adding a Presentation node to the workspace, an icon much like the one in Figure 7-10 would be displayed. Notice that the error icon is embedded into the node icon. By viewing the properties of the node or the Alert tab icon, you can see that there is an alert associated with the node. The alert says, basically, that the page-name property is required and no value has been set. After setting a value for this property, the error icon is no longer displayed in the node icon (see Figure 7-11).

	Presentation

Figure 7-10. Presentation node with alert

	Presentation

Figure 7-11. Presentation node without alert

Using the Webflow Editor

As you've seen earlier in this chapter, many tools are included in the Webflow Editor. This section demonstrates the functionality of these tools by guiding the reader through the creation of an example Webflow.

Adding Nodes to the Canvas

Nodes are the building blocks of all Webflows, and there are several nodes available to a Webflow. Since the primary focus of this chapter is navigation using Webflow, only Presentation nodes are needed here. Processor nodes will be explored in the next chapter.

To add nodes to the Webflow Editor canvas, follow these steps:

1. Select one of the node tools on the editor palette.

2. Position the mouse pointer on the canvas. The cursor should be a crosshair icon.

3. Click the canvas to place the node icon. It is not necessary to click the exact location you want the node to be displayed. A node can be moved by simply dragging and dropping its icon.

4. Fill in the necessary properties for the node in the Properties tab.

Figure 7-12 shows two Presentation nodes added to the canvas. Notice that the gridlines help to align the nodes in a vertical line. Of course, prettiness is not necessary in developing a functional Webflow. It does add visual appeal that can be used in presentation or reports, however. Also, a well-aligned Webflow is easier to read and will aid in future modifications.

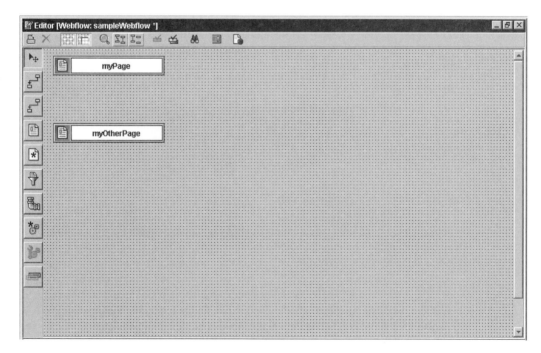

Figure 7-12. Adding nodes to the Webflow Editor canvas

Specifying the Begin Node

After all of the nodes have been added to the canvas, one node should be specified as the Begin node. As previously discussed, the Begin node is the default node for the namespace.

To specify the Begin node, click the Begin Node tool on the Toolbar. A dialog box will appear resembling the one in Figure 7-13.

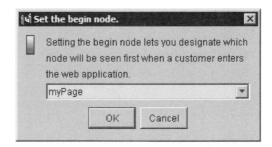

Figure 7-13. The Set the Begin node dialog box

The dialog box that appears features a drop-down containing all of the potential nodes available to be assigned as the Begin node. Select the appropriate node, as shown in Figure 7-14.

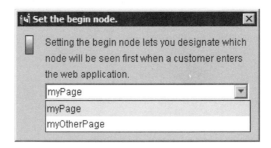

Figure 7-14. Selecting the Begin node

Click OK. After specifying a node to be the Begin node, the icon displayed on the canvas for that node will change slightly. Figure 7-15 shows the myPage node specified as the Begin node.

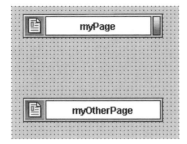

Figure 7-15. Specified Begin node

Adding Event Transitions

Once the nodes have been added to the canvas and the Begin node has been specified, it is time to create event transitions between the nodes.

To add an event, start by selecting the Event tool from the editor palette.

On the canvas, hover the mouse pointer along the edge of the node that is to be the origin of the event. The mouse pointer changes and an orange square appears along the edge of the node, as shown in Figure 7-16.

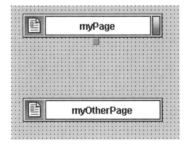

Figure 7-16. Selecting the Origin node

Hold the primary mouse button down and drag the mouse to the edge of the destination node. What is referred to as a connection port is displayed on the edge of the Origin node, and an orange square appears on the edge of the Destination node, as shown in Figure 7-17.

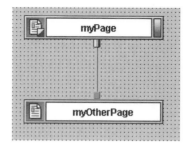

Figure 7-17. Selecting the Destination node

Release the mouse button. The orange square on the edge of the Destination node is now an arrowhead. Figure 7-18 shows a completed transition.

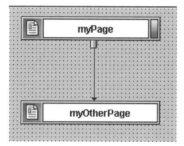

Figure 7-18. Completed event component

Specify the name of the event on the Properties tab.

If the selected Origin or Destination node for the event cannot support the event, a red square and X is displayed rather than the orange square, as shown in Figure 7-19. This occurs when attempting to add an event to a Pipeline node or an exception to a Presentation node. These types of transitions are not valid.

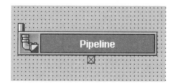

Figure 7-19. Attempting an invalid transition

Moving Components on the Canvas

Moving components is very straightforward. Any component can be selected and dragged to a new location on the canvas. Albeit easy, some functionality within the Webflow editor does come into play when moving components.

Moving Event Transitions

There will be many instances when you need to change a currently defined event's origin or destination. In these cases, it's not necessary to re-create the entire event. It can simply be moved to a new node.

To move an event transition, first select either the connection port or arrowhead of the appropriate transition by holding down the primary mouse button.

Drag the transition to the edge of the new node. The orange square appears, if the transition is valid. The original connection port or arrowhead remains fixed to the original node, highlighted in orange, until the moving of the transition is complete. Figure 7-20 shows a transition being moved to another destination.

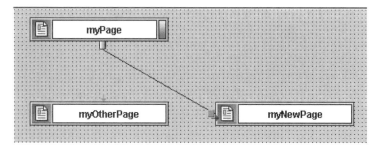

Figure 7-20. Moving an event transition

Release the mouse button when you have finished moving the transition to its new location.

Elbowing Event Transitions

Another way to keep Webflow legible is by elbowing, or bending, transitions. A transition can be bent at any number of points along its line. When developing Webflows with many nodes, elbowing is the only way to keep entire transitions visible. Figure 7-21 shows a situation where elbowing would be beneficial.

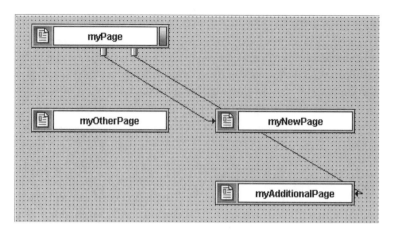

Figure 7-21. A partially hidden transition

To elbow a transition, select the point on the transition line from which to bend. When selected, the transition should turn orange.

Hold the primary mouse button down and drag the transition line to an appropriate position. A joint is displayed at the bending point. In Figure 7-22, the small orange square on the transition line represents an elbow.

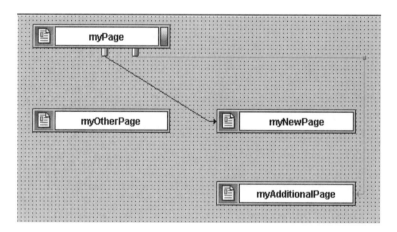

Figure 7-22. Elbowing a transition

Release the mouse button, and continue to elbow the transition until desirable.

Link Optimization

The Link Optimization tool helps to keep event transitions visually appealing by allowing the position of the connecting point of the event transition to rotate around the edge of the node as it is moved around the canvas. The event transition will be the shortest length between the two nodes. With link optimization disabled, when moving a node the connecting point will remain fixed to the edge of the node. This usually results in part of the event transition being hidden underneath a node icon. Using the Webflow shown earlier in Figure 7-18, moving the myOtherPage node to the right of the myPage node would result in the Webflow shown in Figure 7-23.

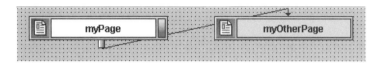

Figure 7-23. Moving components with link optimization disabled

With link optimization enabled, the probable expected result would be the Webflow in Figure 7-24. Unfortunately, it's not. The event is only optimized in respect to the selected node. To achieve the Webflow shown in Figure 7-24, the myPage node had to be nudged.

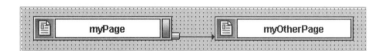

Figure 7-24. Expected result

Looking at the preceding example, link optimization may seem to be rather frivolous, but after all this example only shows two nodes. Imagine the time that could be spent on the layout of a Webflow if there were many more nodes to be moved.

Setting Up the Configuration Error Page Name

The Configuration Error page is a page that displays all configuration errors that may occur while debugging Webflow.

To set up the Configuration Error page, follow these steps:

1. Click the Set Up Configuration Error Page Name button located on the Webflow Editor Toolbar. The Configuration Error Page Dialog box appears, as shown in Figure 7-25.

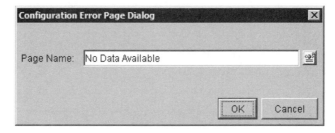

Figure 7-25. The Configuration Error Page Dialog box

2. Enter the path to the Configuration Error page, relative to the Web application, or browse to the location by clicking the Browse button:

3. Click OK.

Using Webflow Events Within a Portlet

Building a Webflow within the Webflow Editor is only half of the task, as it constitutes the foundation of the Web application flow. This flow must now be incorporated into the presentation layer of the portal. This is where the Webflow tag library comes into play. The Webflow tags are included in a portlet's source code to make use of the events specified within the Webflow.

Importing the Webflow Tag Library

Like any Java class, before a tag library can be used it must be imported. In the case of tag libraries, you do this through the taglib directive. The following line of code can be used in any JSP to import the Webflow tag library:

```
<%@ taglib uri="portlet.tld" prefix="pt" %>
```

The prefix specified is entirely left to your discretion. All that is necessary is that it be unique to the tag library. Of course, it never hurts to have a good naming convention that is standardized application wide. It is common practice to use a two-letter nomenclature as in the preceding example, or to use the entire name of the tag library as such:

```
<%@ taglib uri="portlet.tld" prefix="portlet" %>
```

Creating Webflow URLs

In order to access Webflow events, you need a properly constructed URL. This URL will pass to the Webflow servlet the origin and destination of the event. This URL can be assembled by hand:

```
<a href="./myPortal?origin=theOrigin&event=theEvent">theLink</a>
```

Although the preceding link would cause the Webflow event to be fired, resulting in the proper destination, it nullifies the usefulness of Webflow. This no longer represents a dynamic separation of the presentation layer from the underlying business infrastructure. The createWebflowURL tag, included in the Webflow tag library, accomplishes dynamic formation of links like these.

The simplest form of the createWebflowURL tag is this:

```
<portlet:createWebflowURL event="theEvent"/>
```

This tag would be placed directly in the href attribute of an anchor tag in a JSP.

```
<a href="<portlet:createWebflowURL event="theEvent"/>">theLink</a>
```

Many attributes can be associated with this tag, giving you the ability to pass values via the request, specify a separate origin or namespace, and even designate what protocol should be used. The following sections describe each of the attributes associated with the createWebflowURL tag.

domainName Attribute

The domainName attribute allows you to specify what domain name will be used within the URL. It may be hard to see why it might be necessary to use a separate domain name rather than the one specified for the Web application server. In cases when proxy servers or switches are placed in front of the Web application server, the domain name that you would need to use is that of the proxy or switch, rather than the Web application server.

If this attribute is not specified, then Webflow will use the optional context parameter, P13N_URL_DOMAIN. You can enter this value into the application descriptor via the BEA Console application. Application descriptors are covered in detail in Chapter 14.

If neither of the preceding is specified, Webflow defaults to the Web application server's domain name.

doRedirect Attribute

By default, Webflow forwards requests. You may choose to have it perform a redirect instead of a forward. If this is the case, then you want to set the value of the doRedirect attribute to true. The valid values for this attribute are either true or false. However, specifying false or not specifying the attribute at all produces the same results.

encode Attribute

Webflow encodes all URLs by default. An encoded URL is one that contains the user's session state information. Normally, this information is stored within a cookie on the user's browser. If the user's browser is configured not to accept cookies, then it is necessary to encode the session state within the URL. Valid values for this attribute are true and false.

event Attribute

The event attribute is the only required attribute of the createWebflowURL tag. This attribute value refers to an event that has been defined in a namespace. As you learned previously, an event is the action that causes a transition to occur between two nodes. Within the Webflow Editor, the Event tool creates these.

extraParams Attribute

A URL is used to navigate from one Web page to another by specifying the page as a parameter. Usually, a URL uses additional parameters to pass various information to the destination page. This can be accomplished within createWebflowURL by using the extraParams attribute. As you learned in Chapter 3, request parameters are separated by an ampersand (&) character on a URL. The format remains the same when using this attribute, only the leading & is left off, as such:

```
<portlet:createWebflowURL event="theEvent" extraParams="fname=David&lname=Hritz"/>
```

httpsInd Attribute

This attribute specifies the protocol that should be used. For instance, it may be necessary to force a URL in SSL if it specifies a login page or out of SSL when navigating to the public portion of the Web application. In these cases, the value of the attribute would be set to https or http, respectively.

The BEA WebLogic Portal allows for the dynamic calculation of protocol. Within the application descriptor, it is possible to specify URL patterns that are to use the HTTPS protocol. A URL pattern is a portion of the URL itself. For example, /login could be contained in a URL, and this is what would be specified within the application descriptor. If the pattern /login is matched anywhere on the URL, the HTTPS protocol is automatically used. When the value "calculate" is specified for the httpsInd attribute, Webflow will dynamically calculate the protocol based on the values present in the application descriptor.

namespace Attribute

With many developers working on different namespaces within Webflow, more than likely it will be necessary to transition to a node contained in a namespace different from the one that is currently being used. In these cases, use the namespace attribute to navigate to these nodes by setting the value to the namespace containing the Origin node and the event.

origin attribute

Any node can be specified as the origin of the event. By default, the name of the JSP is used as the origin. Depending on the purpose of the event, the origin could be set to another JSP or a servlet.

pathPrefix Attribute

When using a proxy server on the same machine as a Web application server, it may be necessary to prefix the paths with some pattern that the proxy server is listening on. The pathPrefix attribute allows you to prefix the path in this way.

If this attribute is not specified, then Webflow will use the optional context parameter, P13N_URL_PREFIX. This value can be entered in the application descriptor via the BEA Console application. We cover application descriptors in detail in Chapter 14.

pathSuffix Attribute

It also may be necessary to add to the end of the path of the Webflow URL. This could be helpful when using a servlet that accesses the file system. The getPathInfo() method of the request object returns this information.

Webflow Walkthrough Example

This section is a step-by-step walkthrough of the creation of a Webflow. The example that we show you how to create in this section is a help portlet. Many Web applications have to provide the user with help screens to various subsystems of the application. These help screens guide the user in performing various tasks. Creating the Webflow should be one of the first steps. This can be accomplished in the Portlet Wizard, or the Webflow can be created by hand. We will not show you how to use the Portlet Wizard method in this example. The wizard definitely saves time in developing Webflows; however, it is necessary that you fully understand the process of integrating Webflows into portlet navigation to ensure that no crucial steps are missed during the process. For this reason, we demonstrate all development by hand and cut no corners. After the process comes as second nature to you, you can use the wizard to save time.

Example Overview

As mentioned previously, this example creates a help system for a Web application. For simplicity, this system will contain only three help pages: Contents, Topic One, and Topic Two. These pages will be linked to provide optimal navigational options to the user.

The pages will be linked together in the following way:

- From the Contents page, the user should be able to navigate to either topic.

- From the Topic One page, the user should be able to navigate to Topic Two and back to the Contents page.

- From the Topic Two page, the user should be able to navigate to Topic One and back to the Contents page.

Creating the Help Webflow

The first step in the example is to create the Webflow for the help system. After reading the overview of the example, it's probably easy to envision how this Webflow will look.

Creating a New Webflow

The first step is to create the Webflow to be used with the Webflow Editor.

1. Click the New icon in the Explorer pane and choose Webflow/Pipeline. Figure 7-26 highlights the Webflow/Pipeline option.

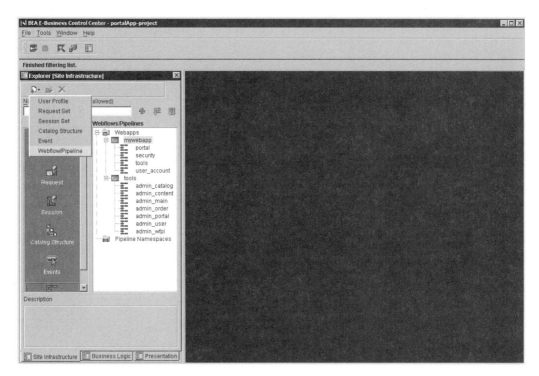

Figure 7-26. Creating a new Webflow

2. Select the appropriate Web application. For this example, use mywebapp.

3. Enter a namespace for the Webflow—"help" in this example, as shown in Figure 7-27.

4. Click OK.

Figure 7-27. Selecting the Web application and namespace

Adding the Presentation Nodes

Three Presentation nodes are needed to support this example.

1. Select the Presentation Node tool from the editor palette.

2. Add three nodes to the canvas as shown in Figure 7-28.

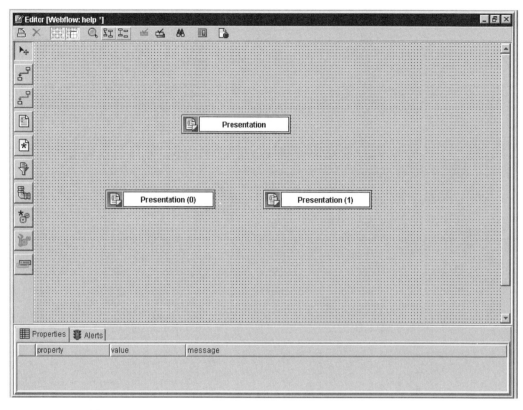

Figure 7-28. Adding the Presentation nodes

Setting the Node Properties

Each node needs to be associated with a presentation page. To do so, follow these steps:

1. Select the node named Presentation. This will be the Contents node.

2. Set the page-relative-page property to /portlets/help.

3. Set the page-name property to contents.jsp; the name property is automatically set.

4. Accept the default value for the type property, JSP.

5. The help Webflow should now resemble the Webflow in Figure 7-29.

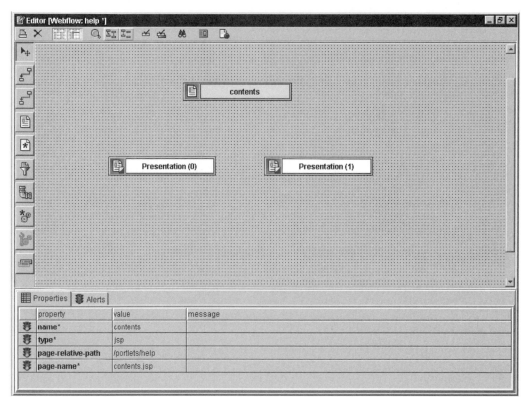

Figure 7-29. The Contents node

6. Select the node named Presentation (0). This will be the Topic One node.

7. Set the page-relative-page property to /portlets/help.

8. Set the page-name property to topicOne.jsp.

9. The help Webflow should now resemble the Webflow in Figure 7-30.

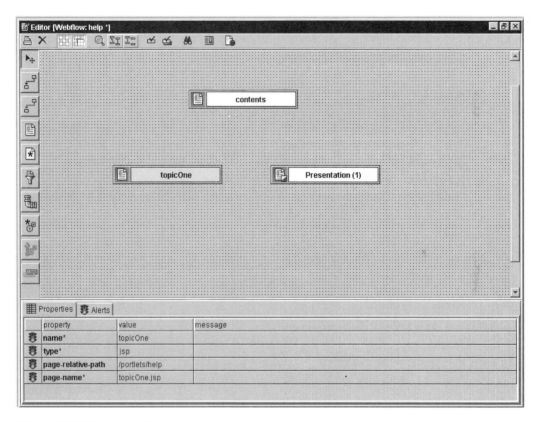

Figure 7-30. The Topic One node

10. Select the node named Presentation (1). This will be the Topic Two node.

11. Set the page-relative-page property to /portlets/help.

12. Set the page-name property to topicTwo.jsp.

13. The help Webflow should now resemble the Webflow in Figure 7-31.

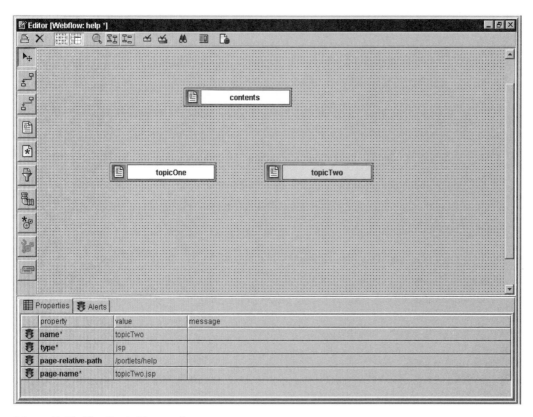

Figure 7-31. The Topic Two node

Adding a Wildcard Presentation Node

Since both the Topic One and Topic Two nodes will contain a link back to the Contents node, a Wildcard Presentation node can be used to handle this behavior. Follow these steps:

1. Select the Wildcard Presentation Node tool from the editor palette.

2. Add a node to the canvas, as shown in Figure 7-32.

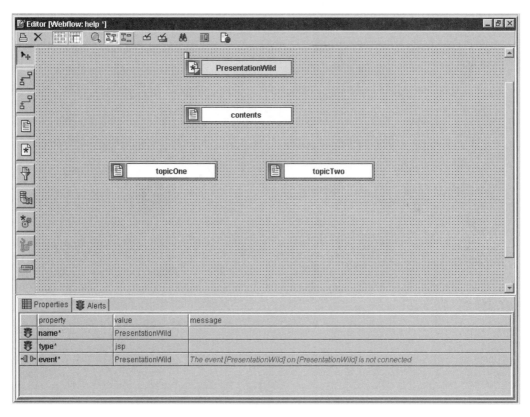

Figure 7-32. Adding a Wildcard Presentation node

Setting the Properties for the Wildcard Presentation Node

You must associate the Wildcard node with the common link to the Contents node, as described in the following steps:

1. Select the node named PresentationWild.

2. Set the event property to link.contents.

3. The help Webflow should now resemble the Webflow in Figure 7-33.

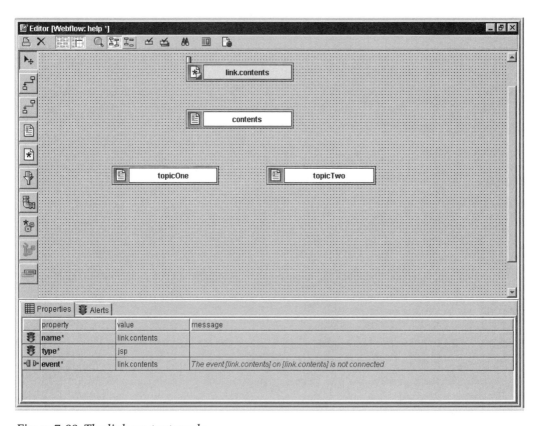

Figure 7-33. The link.contents node

Connecting the link.contents Transition

Now that the link.contents transition has been created, the next step is to connect the event:

1. Select the Event tool from the editor palette.

2. Select the connection port for the link.contents event.

3. Connect the transition to the contents node.

4. Nudge the link.contents node for link optimization to occur.

5. The help Webflow should now resemble the Webflow in Figure 7-34.

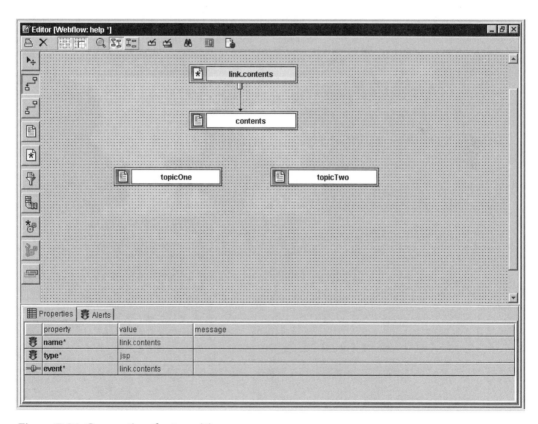

Figure 7-34. Connecting the transition

Creating the Event Transitions

The remaining nodes also have transitions as dictated in the overview of the example.

1. Select the Event tool from the editor palette.

2. Create a transition from the contents node to the topicOne node.

3. Set the name property to link.topicOne.

4. The help Webflow should now resemble the Webflow in Figure 7-35.

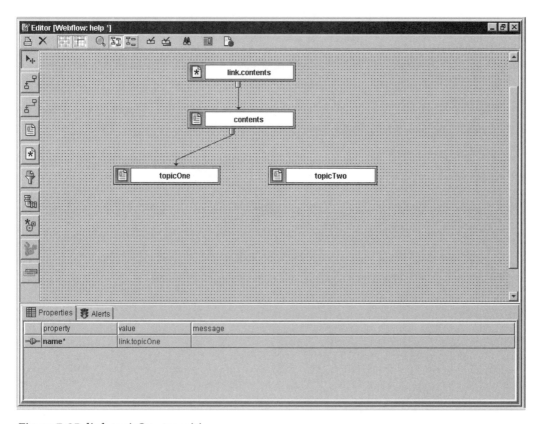

Figure 7-35. link.topicOne transition

5. Create a transition from the contents node to the topicTwo node.

6. Set the name property to link.topicTwo.

7. The help Webflow should now resemble the Webflow in Figure 7-36.

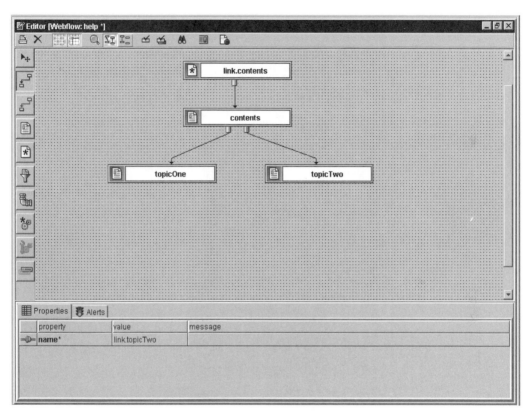

Figure 7-36. link.topicTwo transition

8. Create a transition from the topicOne node to the topicTwo node.

9. Set the name property to link.next.

10. The help Webflow should now resemble the Webflow in Figure 7-37.

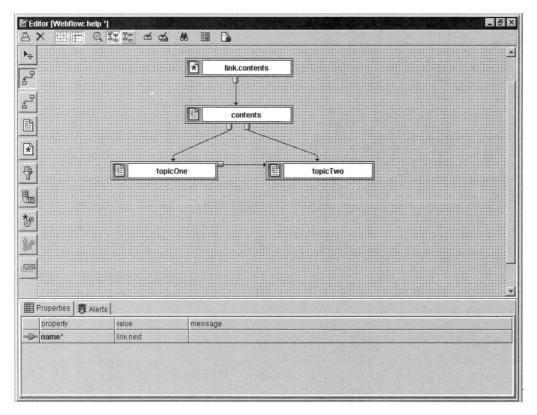

Figure 7-37. link.next transition

11. Create a transition from the topicTwo node to the topicOne node.

12. Set the name property to link.back.

13. The help Webflow should now resemble the Webflow in Figure 7-38.

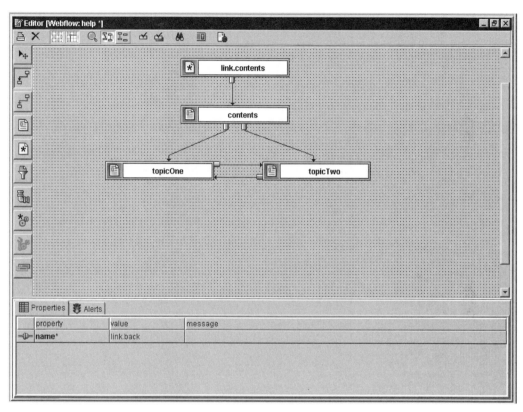

Figure 7-38. link.back transition

Adding the Refresh Portal Event

Other portal functionality, such as the Maximize or Minimize events, can be added at this point. For simplicity, this example will only concern itself with the Refresh event.

1. Add another Wildcard Presentation node to the canvas.

2. Select the Proxy Node tool.

3. Add a Proxy node to the canvas, as shown in Figure 7-39.

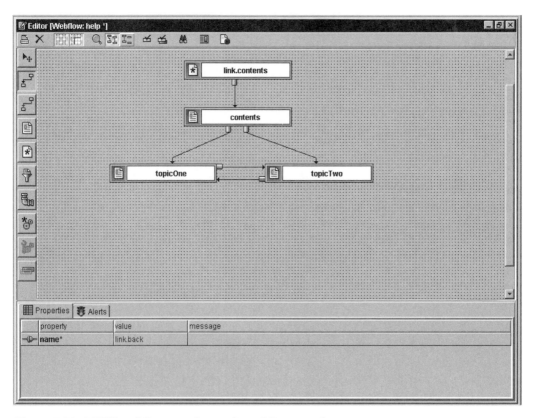

Figure 7-39. A Wildcard Presentation node and Proxy node

4. Select the Proxy node.

5. Set the referent-namespace property to portal.

6. Set the entity-name to lastContentUrl, as shown in Figure 7-40.

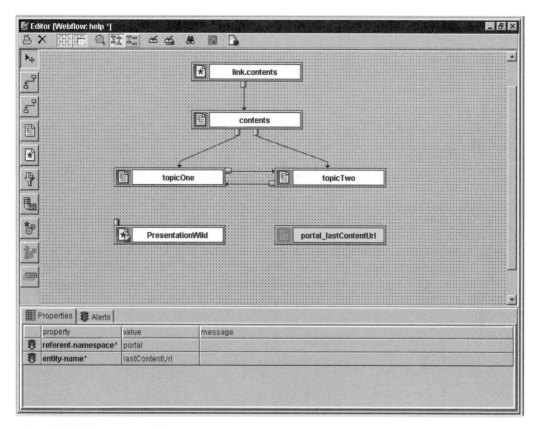

Figure 7-40. Proxy properties

7. Select the Wildcard Presentation node.

8. Set the event property to bea.portal.framework.internal.refresh.

9. Use the Event tool to connect the transition to the Proxy node.

10. The help Webflow should now resemble the Webflow in Figure 7-41.

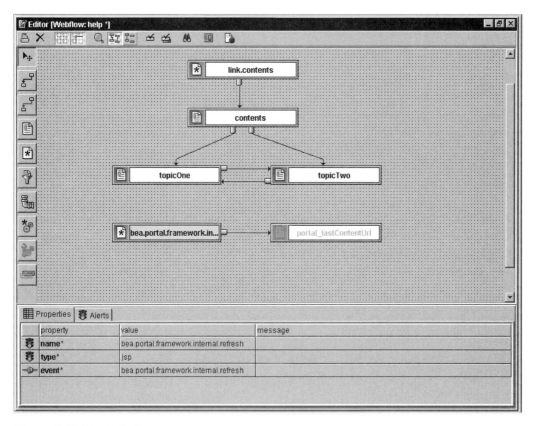

Figure 7-41. The Refresh event

Setting the Begin Node

In this example, the contents node will be the entry point into the Webflow, and thus set as the Begin node.

1.   Select the Begin Node tool from the toolbar.

2.   Select the contents node as the Begin node.

3.   Click OK.

4.   The help Webflow should now resemble the Webflow in Figure 7-42.

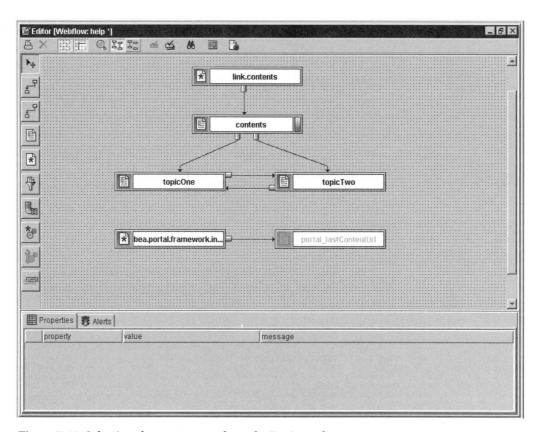

Figure 7-42. Selecting the contents node as the Begin node

Saving the Webflow

The Webflow is now complete and can be saved.

1. Select the File menu.

2. Choose Save.

Creating the Help JSPs

Now that you have created the Webflow, the next step is to incorporate this Webflow into the JSPs for the portlet using the Webflow tag library. According to the Webflow just created, the JSPs for the Presentation nodes were named content.jsp, topicOne.jsp, and topicTwo.jsp.

Creating a Help Portlet Directory

All portlets are stored in separate directories to keep portlet JSPs conveniently separated. Create the help portlet directory as follows:

1. Navigate to the sample portal's portlet directory.

2. Create a new directory named help.

Creating the contents.jsp

The main JSP for the help system is contents.jsp. Its node is designated as the Begin node for the Webflow. A JSP should be created using the following Webflow tags:

- <%@ taglib uri="portlet.tld" prefix="portlet"%>

- <portlet:createWebflowURL namespace='help' event='link.topicOne'/>

- <portlet:createWebflowURL namespace='help' event='link.topicTwo'/>

An example JSP is shown in Listing 7-1.

Listing 7-1. contents.jsp

```
<%@ taglib uri="portlet.tld" prefix="portlet"%>


<h3>Help Contents</h3>


<br>


<table>
  <tr>
    <td><a href="<portlet:createWebflowURL namespace="help"
        event='link.topicOne'/>">Topic One</a></td>
  </tr>
  <tr>
    <td><a href="<portlet:createWebflowURL namespace="help"
        event='link.topicTwo'/>">Topic Two</a></td>
  </tr>
</table>
```

Creating the topicOne.jsp

The first page in the help system is topicOne.jsp. A JSP should be created using the following Webflow tags:

- <%@ taglib uri="portlet.tld" prefix="portlet"%>

- <portlet:createWebflowURL namespace='help' event='link.next'/>

- <portlet:createWebflowURL namespace='help' event='link.contents'/>

An example JSP is shown in Listing 7-2.

Listing 7-2. topicOne.jsp

```
<%@ taglib uri="portlet.tld" prefix="portlet"%>


<h3>Topic One</h3>


<br>
This is Help Topic One.  Use the links below to navigate to the next topic,
or to return the Help Contents.
```

```
<table>
  <tr>
    <td><a href="<portlet:createWebflowURL namespace="help"
        event='link.next'/>">Next</a></td>
  </tr>
  <tr>
    <td><a href="<portlet:createWebflowURL namespace="help"
        event='link.contents'/>">Help Contents</a></td>
  </tr>
</table>
```

Creating the topicTwo.jsp

The last JSP for the help system is topicTwo.jsp. A JSP should be created using the following Webflow tags:

- <%@ taglib uri="portlet.tld" prefix="portlet"%>

- <portlet:createWebflowURL namespace='help' event='link.topicTwo'/>

- <portlet:createWebflowURL namespace='help' event='link.contents'/>

An example JSP is shown in Listing 7-3.

Listing 7-3. topicTwo.jsp

```
<%@ taglib uri="portlet.tld" prefix="portlet"%>

<h3>Topic Two</h3>

<br>
This is Help Topic Two.  Use the links below to navigate back to
the previous topic, or to return the Help Contents.

<table>
  <tr>
    <td><a href="<portlet:createWebflowURL namespace="help"
event='link.back'/>">Back</a></td>
  </tr>
  <tr>
    <td><a href="<portlet:createWebflowURL namespace="help"
event='link.contents'/>">Help Contents</a></td>
  </tr>
</table>
```

Creating the Help Portlet

The final step is to create the Help Portlet and add it to a page.

1. Create a new portlet.

2. Set the content URL to /portlets/help/contents.jsp.

3. Set the Webflow to help.

4. Compare with Figure 7-43.

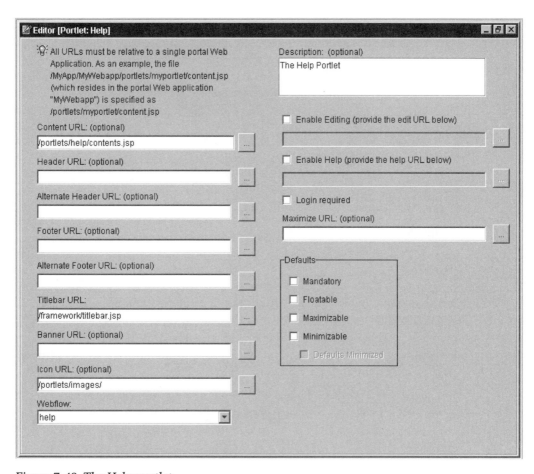

Figure 7-43. The Help portlet

5. Save the portlet as Help.portlet.

6. Add the portlet to a page.

7. Synchronize the Web application.

8. Specify portlet attributes using the portalAppTools utility.

Testing the Webflow Integration

The example is now complete. Access the portal through a Web browser. Navigate to the page that the portlet was placed on. In this example, the portlet was placed on the home page. The portlet should look similar to the one displayed in Figure 7-44. The links should successfully navigate through the help system.

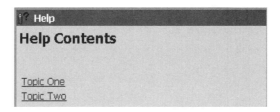

Figure 7-44. Help portlet

Summary

This chapter has only begun our discussion of Webflow. With the concepts covered in this chapter, you should be able to easily accomplish future navigation integrations. Although portlet navigation makes up a large portion of portal development, it is merely half of the functionality of Webflow. We further discuss Webflow in Chapter 8.

CHAPTER 8

Processing Input with Webflow

THE PREVIOUS CHAPTER COVERED much information concerning Webflow. That chapter discussed in brief the ability to process input with components such as Input Processors and Pipeline Components. This chapter explores these topics in full and provides a functional example to demonstrate their usefulness in Web application development.

As we discussed in the last chapter, Webflow can make developing navigation systems for Web applications easy. Also, Webflow can be used to obtain and validate data entered by a user, and then persist this information in a Java object or in a relational database. Webflow accomplishes this task by use of Input Processors, Pipeline Components, and some additional elements that tie the two nodes together.

Input Processors

An Input Processor is a processor node within a Webflow. Each Webflow can have any number of Input Processors or none at all. Usually, when developing a Web application, there are many times when you must acquire and validate user data. An Input Processor provides this functionality.

Another possible task of an Input Processor is branching to separate pieces of business logic. Many decisions will need to be made within a Web application. Input Processors can act as funnels by deciphering information and passing flow to the appropriate nodes.

An Input Processor is a class that you create by either implementing a special Input Processor interface or by extending an abstract Input Processor support class. The choice is solely up to you, depending on what is trying to be accomplished.

InputProcessor Interface

Implementing the com.bea.p13n.appflow.webflow.InputProcessor interface is one way of starting a new Input Processor. This interface has one public method that needs to be implemented, process(). The signature of this method is as follows:

```
public java.lang.Object process(javax.servlet.http.HttpServletRequest req,
    java.lang.Object requestContext) throws ProcessingException
```

InputProcessorSupport Class

Rather than implementing the InputProcessor interface directly, Input Processors may extend com.bea.p13n.appflow.webflow.InputProcessorSupport, an abstract class that implements the InputProcessor interface. The process() method needs to be implemented in this case as well. The advantage of creating an Input Processor by extending this class is the ability to use the static methods it provides. These methods are listed in Table 8-1.

Table 8-1. Methods of InputProcessorSupport

METHOD NAME	REFERENCE
getCurrentNamespace	Returns the current Namespace
getPipelineSession	Returns the PipelineSession object
getRequestAttribute	Obtains attributes of request scope
getSessionAttribute	Obtains attributes of session scope
setRequestAttribute	Sets an attribute of scope request in the PipelineSession object
setSessionAttribute	Sets an attribute of scope session in the PipelineSession object

Although these methods are convenient, it may not be possible for an Input Processor to extend the InputProcessorSupport class if it needs to extend another class. In this case, you could design a class hierarchy so that the base class extends InputProcessorSupport. Otherwise, you can implement these methods easily in a new base class.

Returning from the Process Method

As seen previously, the process() method of an Input Processor returns an object. This object can be any object that has a valid implementation of the toString() method. Inside the mechanism of Webflow, the toString() method is called on the returning object, and the resulting value is used to calculate the event transition. A single Input Processor may have several destination nodes. Based on this return object, branching can occur.

Naming an Input Processor

BEA has suggested a naming convention for Input Processors such that each class name be suffixed with "IP". By no means is this a requirement. It is, however, important to have a clear, concise naming convention for classes within a Web application. Through the development cycle of any enterprise application, multitudes of classes will be created. Having a naming convention for these classes will help to maintain structure in a large application. Appending "IP" to Input Processor class names is a straightforward standard to follow.

More on Business Logic

As discussed, the Model View Controller pattern dictates that presentation logic is separate from business logic. Input Processors aid in this separation in that they allow complex validation and branching code to be compiled in one reusable, central location, instead of being embedded in the application's JSPs. It is important that Input Processors not attempt to handle too much functionality. Although within an Input Processor it is possible to implement data persistence mechanisms, this methodology is frowned upon. Accessing databases or EJBs should be done primarily in Pipeline Components, which we discuss later in this chapter.

Validation Support

One of the most common uses of an Input Processor is to acquire information and then validate it. Validation can range from ensuring that a phone number is numeric to restricting the number of characters entered for a password or user name. The BEA WebLogic Portal supplies numerous interfaces for handling validation. These interfaces will be used from within an Input Processor as well as a JSP. We explain the most frequently used of these in the following sections.

ValidatedValues

The com.bea.p13n.appflow.webflow.forms.ValidatedValues interface provides functionality to validate HTML form fields. This interface maintains a separate status for each field. ValidatedValues can report if a field is valid or invalid and even unspecified. For each field processed, the ValidatedValues object will retain the field value, the status of the field. The ValidatedValues object may also include a validation message to display to the user upon error.

Within an Input Processor, a reference to a ValidatedValues object can be obtained by accessing the getValidatedValues() method of the com.bea.p13n.appflow.webflow.forms.ValidatedValuesFactory class. This method is static, so there is no need to instantiate a ValidatedValuesFactory class. The getValidatedValues() method has one argument, a reference to the HttpServletRequest. The following code sample demonstrates how to instantiate a ValidatedValues object:

```
ValidatedValues values = ValidatedValuesFactory.getValidatedValues(request);
```

You can use this object independently to perform the validation process within an Input Processor. However, the ValidatedForm interface is much easier to use. We demonstrate the ValidatedValues interface, along with the ValidatedForm interface, in the examples at the end of this chapter.

When using ValidatedValues with the ValidatedForm object, you work primarily with one method. The getInvalidFieldCount() method retrieves the number of validation failures for the given ValidatedValues object. This method is called after validation of all fields is complete. The method signature is as follows:

```
public int getInvalidFieldCount()
```

If this method returns a value that is greater than zero, an InvalidFormDataException should be thrown, at which point the origin JSP may be redisplayed to the user. The form fields are filled based on the data stored in the ValidatedValues object and appropriate validation messages may be displayed at the field level.

ValidatedForm

The com.bea.p13n.appflow.webflow.forms.ValidatedForm interface validates HTML form data. You use this interface within an Input Processor along with the <webflow:validatedForm> tag library. When used in conjunction, a functional validation mechanism is achieved, easing the development of validation code.

To obtain a reference to an instantiated ValidatedForm object within an Input Processor, use the com.bea.p13n.appflow.webflow.forms.ValidatedFormFactory class. This class has one static method, getValidatedForm(). Following is an example of this class:

```
ValidatedForm form = ValidatedFormFactory.getValidatedForm();
```

In correlation with the ValidatedValues object and a Validator object, ValidatedForm validates form fields on a per-field basis via the validate() method or the validateMultiple method. While the validate() method validates single values, the validateMultiple() method validates collections of values. Collection of values occurs from a select box field that allows multiple values to be selected. Both methods have been overloaded, allowing validation to occur in many different ways. A summary of the more commonly used method signatures rounds out this section.

The following method signature, using the specified Validator class, validates a request parameter:

```
public java.lang.String validate(ValidatedValues validatedValues,
                                 java.lang.String validatorClassName,
                                 java.lang.String requestParam,
                                 java.lang.Object expression)
                        throws MissingFormFieldException
```

The expression object is optional since not all Validators use expressions. In this case, a null value may be passed. Error messages are retrieved from the ValidationException.xml file. Results of validation are stored in the ValidatedValues object. This method throws a MissingFormFieldException if the specified parameter is not in the request object, and may also throw an InvalidValidatorException if the Validator is incorrect. This method returns the validated value.

This next version of the validate() method again uses a Validator class to validate a request parameter:

```
public java.lang.String validate(ValidatedValues validatedValues,
                                 java.lang.String validatorClassName,
                                 java.lang.String requestParam,
                                 java.lang.Object expression,
                                 java.lang.String message)
                        throws MissingFormFieldException
```

The expression object is optional, depending on the Validator used. A message is supplied as the last argument, which will be displayed instead of a message from the message catalog. This method throws a MissingFormFieldException if the specified parameter is not in the request object, and may also throw an InvalidValidatorException if the Validator is incorrect. This method returns the validated value.

As oddly as it sounds, this next validate() method does no validation whatsoever:

```
public java.lang.String validate(ValidatedValues validatedValues,
                                 java.lang.String RequestParam)
```

It is possible that a form field may not require validation. For instance, the check-box field usually does not need to be validated. However, it is important to retain the value of this field for display. In this case, the method supplies the desired functionality. It merely stores the value of the parameter within the ValidatedValues object. This method returns the validated value or null.

The following example retrieves the specified collection of values:

```
public java.util.Collection validateMultiple(ValidatedValues validatedValues,
                                 java.lang.String paramName,
                                 int minimum)
                             throws MissingFormFieldException
```

If the indicated number of values, specified by the minimum argument, are not retrieved, validation fails and the validation message will be obtained from the ValidationException.xml file. This method throws a MissingFormFieldException if the specified parameter is not in the request object. The return value is the collection of values.

The next example functions similarly to the previous method:

```
public java.util.Collection validateMultiple(ValidatedValues validatedValues,
                                 java.lang.String paramName,
                                 int minimum,
                                 java.lang.String message)
                             throws MissingFormFieldException
```

Here a collection of values is retrieved from the request. If the specified number of values is not obtained, validation will fail. This method, however, uses the message parameter rather than the message catalog. This method also throws MissingFormFieldException and returns the collection of values.

The following method does not perform any validation on the field. Instead it attempts to find the parameter on the request and store it for display purposes.

```
public java.util.Collection validateMultiple(ValidatedValues validatedValues,
                                   java.lang.String requestParam)
```

If the parameter is not found, an empty Collection object is returned.

Expressions

In some of the various implementations of the validate() method shown in the preceding section, an expression object is passed. An *expression* is an object, used by the Validator, that specifies additional information pertaining to the validation of a particular field. In some cases this object can be as simple as a String or a Boolean object. Some of the Validators implemented within the BEA WebLogic Portal can employ a MinMaxExpression object. This object allows you to specify that the length of a parameter value must fall between a certain minimum and maximum value, inclusively.

Validators

All Validators implement the com.bea.p13n.appflow.webflow.forms.Validator interface. Validator objects are passed into the ValidatedForm object to perform the actual validation. It is the duty of a Validator to update the ValidateValues status and message fields. The BEA WebLogic Portal has implemented many Validators to provide a moderate level of functionality. Each of these Validators can be used with the ValidatedForm object. Constants have been provided for these objects in the com.bea.p13n.appflow.webflow.forms.ValidatedFormConstants interface. We summarize these Validators next.

EmailValidator

This Validator validates e-mail addresses in that it ensures the "@" character is present within the parameter value. A Boolean object may be passed in as an expression specifying that the field is required.

- *Constant:* EMAIL_VALIDATOR

NumberValidator

To validate numerical data, try the NumberValidator. This Validator ensures that the parameter value is numeric and that the number of characters within the value is between 0 and 999999. The MinMaxExpression may be used with this Validator, in which case the Validator will ensure that the number of characters in the entered value falls between the specified minimum and maximum values, inclusively.

- *Constant:* NUMBER_VALIDATOR

PhoneValidator

A phone number may be validated with this Validator. After stripping off all parentheses, hyphens, periods, and whitespace characters, the parameter value is checked whether it has 7, 10, or 11 numerical characters. If the value is valid, the value is then formatted using the hyphen (-) character as a separator. This Validator has no expressions.

- *Constant:* PHONE_VALIDATOR

SpecialCharacterValidator

Some field data may have characters that are not permitted. For instance, an HTML form may not allow users to enter in the double quote (") character. In such a case, you may want to use this Validator. An expression of class String, containing all characters that are invalid for the particular field, is passed to this Validator. The Validator will check that each character does not exist within the parameter value.

- *Constant:* SPECIAL_CHARACTER_VALIDATOR

NOTE *This Validator will perform a String.trim() operation on the expression. This makes it difficult to check for whitespace in a parameter value. To accomplish this, wrap the whitespace in a special character as shown here:*

```
String invalidCharacters = '\uFFFF' + " " + '\uFFFF';
```

StringValidator

This Validator ensures that the number of characters within the parameter value is between 0 and 999999. The MinMaxExpression may be used with this Validator, in which case the Validator will ensure that the number of characters in the entered value falls between the specified minimum and maximum values, inclusively.

- *Constant:* STRING_VALIDATOR

Custom Validators

The packaged Validators may not meet all of your needs. In this situation, you can create custom Validators and plug them into the Web application. All custom Validators must adhere to the following specifications:

- The custom Validator must implement the Validator interface.

- The value, status, and message fields of the ValidatedValues object must be set by the custom Validator.

- The custom Validator must be stateless.

Pipeline Session

When navigating between presentation and processor nodes, it is usually necessary to retain information. This information may need to be persisted, or may just be used as a means of communication between Input Processors and Pipeline Components. The com.bea.p13n.appflow.common.PipelineSession object serves this function.

The PipelineSession object provides the ability to store data in one central location. Any type of object may be stored within the PipelineSession object. This information can then be used by any number of nodes anywhere within the Web application. Objects are stored within the PipelineSession object under one of two different degrees of scope: either the scope of the request or the scope of the session.

Obtaining the PipelineSession

The PipelineSession object is accessible from JSPs, Input Processors, and Pipeline Components. Like the HttpSession object, objects can be stored within the PipelineSession object in key/value pairs referred to as attributes. The PipelineSession object will be used extensively in Web application development.

From within a JSP, the PipelineSession object can be obtained by using custom Pipeline Session JSP tags contained within the Webflow tag library. These tags are explained fully in the next section of this chapter.

As mentioned previously, Input Processors that extend the InputProcessorSupport class have a method in the base class that provides access to the PipelineSession object. From within this type of Input Processor, the getPipelineSession() method can obtain a reference to the Pipeline Session. The signature for this method is as follows:

```
public static PipelineSession getPipelineSession
    (javax.servlet.http.HttpServletRequest request)
```

It may not always be possible to extend the InputProcessorSupport class. In cases like this, the PipelineSession object can be obtained by using the SessionManagerFactory class. The following code sample demonstrates the use of this factory in obtaining the PipelineSession object:

```
PipelineSession pipelineSession =
SessionManagerFactory.getSessionManager().getPipelineSession(request);
```

The PipelineSession object is passed to Pipeline Components. Pipeline Components heavily rely on the data within the Pipeline Session since they are usually the bulk of a Web application's business logic. We further explore Pipeline Components in the next section.

Using the PipelineSession Object

Attributes are stored in the PipelineSession object to be accessed by other nodes within the Webflow when necessary. There are two scopes in which an attribute may live: request and session. These scopes have been thoroughly discussed in Chapter 3, and we summarize them in the context of PipelineSession later.

If extended, the support classes for Input Processors and Pipeline Components provide functionality for getting and setting attributes in a specific scope. The PipelineSession object also may be used to set and get attributes. Since the support class methods for Input Processors and Pipeline Components is covered in their respective sections, this section concentrates on the

PipelineSession methods. Following is the method signature for each method along with a short summary of each.

The following method can be used to get an attribute, via its key, that has request scope:

```
public java.lang.Object getRequestScopedAttribute(java.lang.String key,
                                  java.lang.Object namespace,
                                  java.lang.Object requestContext)
                       throws InvalidArgumentException
```

This throws an InvalidArgumentException if any argument is invalid.

Next is the setter method for request-scoped attributes:

```
public void setRequestScopedAttribute(java.lang.String key,
                                  java.lang.Object attribute,
                                  java.lang.Object namespace,
                                  java.lang.Object requestContext)
                       throws InvalidArgumentException
```

This method throws an InvalidArgumentException if any argument is invalid. There can only be one object set for each key; therefore, if an object already exists within the request with the specified key, the object will be overwritten.

The next method is used to obtain an attribute with the specified key from the session:

```
public java.lang.Object getSessionScopedAttribute(java.lang.String key,
                                  java.lang.Object namespace)
                       throws InvalidArgumentException
```

This method throws an InvalidArgumentException if any argument is invalid.

The following method sets an attribute of session scope:

```
public void setSessionScopedAttribute(java.lang.String key,
                                  java.lang.Object attribute,
                                  java.lang.Object namespace)
                       throws InvalidArgumentException
```

Once again, if the key already exists within the session, the original object is overwritten. This method throws an InvalidArgumentException if any argument is invalid.

Request-Scoped Attributes

Request-scoped attributes are stored within the HttpRequest object. Therefore, these properties will live until the next JSP is displayed. Since the lifetime of these attributes is limited and they are automatically removed when the next request begins, request-scoped attributes are less expensive than session-scoped attributes. Request-scoped attributes should be used wherever possible to make for the most efficient Web application. Attributes should never be overscoped for convenience sake.

Session-Scoped Attributes

More than likely, each Web application will have a handful of attributes that should be persisted for the HTTP session. In these cases, attributes should be specified as session scoped. These attributes will live as long as a user remains within the context of the Web application.

Other PipelineSession Considerations

A final note on PipelineSession objects we would like to make is that each object stored on the Pipeline Session must implement the Serializable interface. The PipelineSession object itself is serialized by Webflow. If an object within the Pipeline Session fails to serialize, it will throw an exception and cause the Pipeline to fail.

Pipeline Components

As previously discussed, Webflows may also contain Pipelines. A Pipeline is a mechanism that provides complex business logic such as accessing EJBs or executing database transactions. Pipelines can be made up of any number of Pipeline Components, acting together to accomplish a certain piece of functionality. A Pipeline Component is an encapsulated piece of functionality. Usually, Pipeline Components access the Pipeline Session and acquire information. This information is then processed, and possibly persisted. The PipelineSession object may then be updated and returned.

Like Input Processors, Pipeline Components can also be created by implementing a special interface or by extending an abstract class. These two methodologies are described next, and again the choice of which to use is up to you depending on your application's needs.

PipelineComponent Interface

Implementing the com.bea.p13n.appflow.pipeline.PipelineComponent interface is one possible method to create a new Pipeline Component. In order to implement this interface, the process() method must be included within the class. The signature of this method is as follows:

```
public PipelineSession process(PipelineSession pipelineSession,
                               java.lang.Object requestContext)
               throws PipelineException,
                      java.rmi.RemoteException
```

Notice that the method receives a reference to the PipelineSession object and returns a PipelineSession object. This method may not return a null value. If a null value is returned from any Pipeline Component, the Pipeline to which the Pipeline Component belongs will terminate.

When creating an EJB Pipeline Component, the remote interface of the EJB will extend this interface as well as the EJBObject interface. For assistance in creating EJBs, consult Chapter 10.

PipelineComponentSupport Class

Alternatively, Pipeline Components may extend the com.bea.p13n.appflow.pipeline.PipelineComponentSupport class. This abstract class implements the PipelineComponent interface, so naturally the process() method needs to be implemented. This class provides additional functionality you may use to your advantage. These methods, shown in Table 8-2, match those of the InputProcessorSupport class.

Table 8-2. Methods of PipelineComponentSupport

METHOD NAME	REFERENCE
getCurrentNamespace	Returns the current Namespace
getPipelineSession	Returns the PipelineSession object
getRequestAttribute	Obtains attributes of request scope
getSessionAttribute	Obtains attributes of session scope
setRequestAttribute	Sets an attribute of scope request in the PipelineSession object
setSessionAttribute	Sets an attribute of scope session in the PipelineSession object

This class is also used when creating EJB Pipeline Components. As discussed in the next chapter, the main class of an EJB is known as an "impl" class, and it performs the bulk of the processing. To aid in Pipeline Component development, this impl class may extend the PipelineComponentSupport class.

Once again, you may need to extend a different base class, rather than the PipelineComponentSupport class. It these cases, these methods can easily be reimplemented in the base class of your choice.

Naming a Pipeline Component

BEA has dictated a naming convention for Pipeline Components similar to what is specified for Input Processors. In the case of Pipeline Components, BEA suggests that all class names be suffixed with "PC". Once again, this is not mandatory, merely a suggestion that may help bring order to a multitude of classes. You need not apply this specific naming convention , but you should follow some naming convention.

Transactional Pipelines

As mentioned earlier, Pipelines comprise any number of Pipeline Components. It is possible to dictate that a pipeline be transactional. This means that any failure that may occur during the execution of the pipeline would cause the transaction to be rolled back. Items included in the rollback are database operations as well as any modification made to the Pipeline Session. Of course, this can be crucial when performing any all-or-none type of process.

Exploring the Webflow Tag Library

The Webflow tag library is used within JSP development to build Webflows. This section covers all tags available to you, which encapsulate all of the functionality needed in Webflow development. By using these tags, you can eliminate the need for complex Java code within a JSP.

Importing the Tag Library

The process of importing a tag library into a JSP has been covered in a previous chapter. For reference the following line will import the Webflow tag library. At further locations within the JSP, the tag library will be referenced by the prefix.

```
<%@ taglib uri="webflow.tld" prefix="wf"%>
```

URL Creation Tags

The prior chapter introduced you to URL creation tags. These tags, which we take a closer look at in the following sections, create link transitions for Webflow, and they can also create resource URLs for elements such as images and static resources.

createResourceURL

The createResourceURL tag creates a URL to be used for static resources such as images, style sheets or files. Two attributes can be included within the tag: encode and resource.

Encode

By setting this parameter to true or false, you specify whether the URL for the resource should be encoded. By default, this attribute is set to true.

Resource

This attribute specifies the relative URL to the resource. This URL is relative to the Web application, unless the P13N_STATIC_ROOT context parameter has been specified in the application's web.xml file.

createWebflowURL

The createWebflowURL tag allows you to create dynamic URLs to be used in transitions between Webflow's presentation nodes. This tag has many attributes, as we specify next.

domainName

This attribute sets the domain name that will be used in generating the URL. This attribute overrides the domain name set in the P13N_URL_DOMAIN context parameter. When a proxy server or a content switch fronts a Web server, it is necessary to specify a different domain name.

doRedirect

By default, Webflow forwards the request to the destination node. In some circumstances, it may be necessary to perform a redirect instead. Valid values for this attribute are true and false.

encode

This attribute encodes the Webflow URL. Valid values for this attribute are true and false. The default is true, which results in URLs being encoded. URLs will be encoded when the client browser does not support or accept cookies. In this case, session information will be encoded within the URL.

event

Webflow uses the event attribute in correlation with the origin attribute to calculate the destination node for the transition. This attribute specifies the event to be used. (Events are discussed in Chapter 7.)

extraParams

It is usually necessary to pass additional information via the URL. The extraParams attribute allows the addition of parameters to the dynamically generated URL. Parameters are specified in key/value pairs and separated by the ampersand (&) character.

httpsInd

This attribute specifies the mode to be used in the generated URL. Valid values are HTTP, HTTPS, and CALCULATE. By setting this attribute to HTTP or HTTPS, as expected, the generated URL is forced into the specified mode. CALCULATE causes Webflow to calculate which mode needs to be used. Within the application's web.xml file, you can specify values in the HTTPS_URL_PATTERNS parameter. If any origin and event pair is matched within this list, HTTPS is used; otherwise, the mode generated is HTTP.

namespace

The namespace attribute specifies in which namespace the origin and event are defined. If not specified, the current namespace is used. The current namespace, as specified in the prior chapter, is the last namespace to be successfully used.

origin

By default, the name of the JSP is used as the origin in Webflow transitions. The origin attribute allows you to specify a different origin as necessary. The origin, along with the event attribute, is used by Webflow to calculate the destination of the transition.

pathPrefix

The value specified in this attribute is used to prefix the URL. Setting this attribute overrides the value set for the P13N_URL_PREFIX context parameter. A prefix may be necessary if a proxy server is being used, and the server resides on the same machine.

pathSuffix

Additional path information can be added to the URL by using this attribute. The value specified as the pathSuffix is appended to the end of the URL. This path information can then be accessed by the request.getPathInfo() method.

Examples of URL Creation Tags

Here are examples showing the many uses of the URL creation tags.

```
<a href="<wf:createResourceURL resource="/pdf/some.pdf" encode="false"/>">
    Some File</a>
<img src="<wf:createResourceURL resource="/images/btn_continue.gif"/>"
    border="0">
<a href="<wf:createWebflowURL event="link.load"  encode="false"
    pathSuffix="/loadfiles" pathPrefix="/proxyListens"/>">
    Path Suffix and Prefix (Encoded URL)</a>
<a href="<wf:createWebflowURL event="link.cancel" origin="home.jsp"
    namespace="homeNamespace"/>">Specifying Events, Origins and Namespaces</a>
<a href="<wf:createWebflowURL event="link.foward" httpsInd="HTTPS"
    doRedirect="true"/>">Secure Redirecting Link</a>
<a href="<wf:createWebflowURL event="link.goto"
    domainName="switch.domainName.com"
    extraParams="param1=value1&param2=value2"/>">Specifying a Domain Name</a>
```

The Form Tag

You can create basic Webflow forms through the form tag. These tags can handle the simplest to the most complicated forms. The form tag is used to create simple HTML forms.

form

This tag generates a simple HTML form action. This form does not include validation, as discussed earlier. We describe the many attributes that can be used with this tag in the following sections.

domainName

This attribute sets the domain name that will be used in generating the URL, overriding the domain name set in the P13N_URL_DOMAIN context parameter. A proxy server or a content switch may front a Web server, in which case it would be necessary to specify a different domain name.

doRedirect

By default, Webflow forwards the request to the destination node. In some circumstances, it may be necessary to perform a redirect instead. Valid values for this attribute are true and false.

encode

This attribute specifies whether to encode the Webflow URL. Valid values for this attribute are true and false. By default this is set to true, so URLs are encoded when the client browser does not support or accept cookies. In this case, session information is encoded within the URL.

event

Webflow uses the event attribute in correlation with the origin attribute to calculate the destination node for the transition. This attribute specifies the event to be used. (Events were discussed in Chapter 7.)

extraParams

It is usually necessary to pass additional information via the URL. The extraParams attribute allows the addition of parameters to the dynamically generated URL. Parameters are specified in key/value pairs and separated by the ampersand (&) character.

hide

By default, the namespace, origin, and event of the transition are displayed in hidden form fields within the HTML form. By setting this attribute to false, these values are displayed in the URL instead.

httpsInd

This attribute specifies the mode to be used in the generated URL. Valid values are HTTP, HTTPS, and CALCULATE. By specifying HTTP or HTTPS, as expected, the generated URL is forced into the indicated mode. CALCULATE causes Webflow to calculate which mode needs to be used. Within the application's web.xml file, values can be specified in the HTTPS_URL_PATTERNS parameter. If any origin and event pair is matched within this list, HTTPS is used; otherwise, the mode generated is HTTP.

method

By default, the method used to submit the form is post. Valid values for this attribute are get and post.

name

This attribute specifies the name of the form.

namespace

The namespace attribute specifies in which namespace the origin and event are defined. If not specified, the current namespace is used. The current namespace, as specified in the prior chapter, is the last namespace to be successfully used.

origin

By default, the name of the JSP is used as the origin in Webflow transitions. The origin attribute allows you to specify a different origin as necessary. The origin, along with the event attribute, is used by Webflow to calculate the destination of the transition.

317

pathPrefix

The value specified in this attribute serves as a prefix to the URL. Setting this attribute overrides the value set for the P13N_URL_PREFIX context parameter. A prefix may be necessary if a proxy server is being used, and the server resides on the same machine.

pathSuffix

Additional path information can be added to the URL through this attribute. The value specified as the pathSuffix is appended to the end of the URL. This path information can then be accessed via the request.getPathInfo() method.

Example of the Form Tag

Following is a very simple example of a functioning Webflow form:

```
<wf:form event="button.search">
        <input type="text" name="query">
</wf:form>
```

Validated Form Tags

The form tags described in this section create HTML forms with validation.

validatedForm

Use the validated form tag in combination with the other tags in this section to build an HTML form with validation. The following sections describe the attributes contained within the validatedForm tag.

applyStyle

This attribute refers to the style of validation messages to display. Valid values are message, field, and none. Setting the value of this attribute to message displays validation messages concisely in one central location. The field value displays the validation messages at the appropriate HTML field. Obviously, setting the style to none results in no validation messages being displayed.

domainName

This attribute sets the domain name that is used in generating the URL. This attribute overrides the domain name set in the P13N_URL_DOMAIN context parameter. This is useful in cases where a proxy server or a content switch fronts a Web server, as it would then be necessary to specify a different domain name.

doRedirect

By default, Webflow forwards the request to the destination node. In some circumstances, it may be necessary to perform a redirect instead. Valid values for this attribute are true and false.

encode

This attribute specifies whether to encode the Webflow URL. Valid values for this attribute are true and false. By default, this is set to true, so URLs are encoded when the client browser does not support or accept cookies. In this case, session information is encoded within the URL.

event

Webflow uses the event attribute in correlation with the origin attribute to calculate the destination node for the transition. This attribute specifies the event to be used. (Events were discussed in Chapter 7.)

extraParams

It is usually necessary to pass additional information via the URL. The extraParams attribute allows the addition of parameters to the dynamically generated URL. Parameters are specified in key/value pairs and separated by the ampersand (&) character.

hide

By default, the namespace, origin, and event of the transition are displayed in hidden form fields within the HTML form. By setting this attribute to false, these values are displayed in the URL instead.

httpsInd

This attribute specifies the mode to be used in the generated URL. Valid values are HTTP, HTTPS, and CALCULATE. By specifying HTTP or HTTPS, as expected, the generated URL is forced into the indicated mode. CALCULATE causes Webflow to calculate which mode needs to be used. Within the application's web.xml file, values can be specified in the HTTPS_URL_PATTERNS parameter. If any origin and event pair is matched within this list, HTTPS is used; otherwise, the mode generated is HTTP.

invalidStyle

This attribute specifies the style to be used when a form field has a validation error. This style formats either the form message or the form field message depending on the applyStyle attribute.

messageAlign

This message sets the alignment of validation messages. Validation messages can be displayed on the top of the field, to the right of the field, or on the bottom of the field. Valid values are top, right, and bottom.

method

By default, the method used to submit the form is post. Valid values for this attribute are get and post.

name

This attribute specifies the name of the form.

namespace

The namespace attribute specifies in which namespace the origin and event are defined. If not specified, the current namespace is used. The current namespace, as specified in the prior chapter, is the last namespace to be successfully used.

origin

By default, the name of the JSP serves as the origin in Webflow transitions. The origin attribute allows you to specify a different origin as necessary. The origin, along with the event attribute, is used by Webflow to calculate the destination of the transition.

pathPrefix

The value specified in this attribute serves as a prefix to the URL. Setting this attribute overrides the value set for the P13N_URL_PREFIX context parameter. A prefix may be necessary if a proxy server is being used, and the server resides on the same machine.

pathSuffix

Additional path information can be added to the URL through this attribute. The value specified as the pathSuffix is appended to the end of the URL. This path information can then be accessed by using the request.getPathInfo() method.

text

This tag attribute enables you to include an HTML text field, and attributes you can use with this tag are described next.

htmlAttributes

This attribute specifies additional parameters within the HTML text field tag.

maxlength

This sets the maximum length of the text field.

name

This required attribute is the name of the text field.

retainValue

Upon validation error, the form is redisplayed. This attribute specifies whether or not to redisplay the value entered into the text field.

size

This attribute sets the size of the text field.

style

This attribute specifies a style for the text field to use.

value

This attribute specifies an initial value for the text field.

Password

This tag allows you to include an HTML password field within a validated form. The attributes for this tag are discussed in the following sections.

htmlAttributes

This attribute specifies additional parameters within the HTML password field tag.

maxlength

This sets the maximum length of the password field.

name

This required attribute is the name of the password field.

retainValue

Upon validation error, the form is redisplayed. This attribute specifies whether or not to redisplay the value entered into the text field.

size

This attribute sets the size of the password field.

style

This attribute specifies a style for the password field to use.

value

This attribute specifies an initial value for the password field.

radio

This tag lets you add an HTML radio button to the validated form. Attributes of this tag are described in the following text.

checked

A radio button has two states, checked and unchecked. This attribute sets the initial state of the radio button. Valid values for this attribute are true and false.

htmlAttributes

This attribute specifies additional parameters within the HTML radio button tag.

name

This required attribute indicates the name of the radio button.

value

This required attribute specifies the value for the radio button.

checkbox

This tag includes a check box in a validated form. The attributes of this tag are the same as the radio tag, as described in the following text.

checked

A check box has two states, checked and unchecked. This attribute sets the initial state of the check box field. Valid values for this attribute are true and false.

htmlAttributes

This attribute specifies additional parameters within the HTML check box field tags.

name

This required attribute is the name of the check box field.

value

This required attribute specifies the value for the check box field.

textarea

This tag generates the HTML for a text area in a validate form. We describe this tag's attributes next.

cols

This attribute sets the number of columns to be used within the text area.

name

This required attribute indicates the name of the text area field.

retainValue

Upon validation error, the form is redisplayed. This attribute specifies whether or not to redisplay the value entered into the text area field.

rows

This attribute sets the number of rows to be used within the text area.

style

This attribute specifies a style for the text area field.

value

This attribute specifies the value for the text area field.

wrap

This attribute specifies whether or not to wrap the text. By default, the generated text area wraps the text that is entered into it. Valid values are true and false.

select

This tag, together with the attributes described in the following text, allows you to include an HTML select box in the validated form.

htmlAttributes

This attribute specifies additional parameters within the HTML select box field tag.

multiple

This attribute specifies that the select box can have multiple items selected. Valid values are true and false.

name

This required attribute is the name of the select box field.

size

This attribute sets the size of the select box.

style

This attribute specifies a style for the select box field to use.

option

Use this tag within the select tag to include items in a select box that is contained within a validate form. The attributes for this field are listed next.

selected

This attribute specifies the initially selected option. By default the value is false. Valid values are true and false.

style

This attribute specifies a style for the option field.

value

This required attribute specifies the value for the option field.

Example of Validated Form Tags

Following is an example form using the validated form tags previously discussed:

```
<wf:validatedForm event="form.submit">
<wf:text name="userName" size="25" maxlength="25"/>
<wf:password name="password" size="30"/>
<wf:radio name="status" value="1" checked="true"/>
<wf:checkbox name="email" checked="true" value="Y"/>
<wf:select name="pets" size="25" multiple="true">
    <wf:option value="dog">Dog</wf:option>
    <wf:option value="cat">Cat</wf:option>
    <wf:option value="platypus">Platypus</wf:option>
    <wf:option value="fish">Fish</wf:option>
    <wf:option value="hamster">Hamster</wf:option>
</wf:select>
<wf:textarea name="comments" cols="40" rows="20"/>
</wf:validatedForm>
```

Pipeline Session Tags

As described in the previous chapter, the PipelineSession object stores values to be retrieved by Webflow components. The tags we discuss here are used to get and set these values from within a JSP.

setProperty

This tag sets a property within the PipelineSession object. The attributes for this tag are as follows.

namespace

This specifies the namespace containing a certain origin and event; otherwise, the current namespace is used.

property

This required attribute is the name of the property to set.

scope

Properties can either be of session or of request scope. This attribute specifies the scope of the property being set. By default, properties have session scope. Valid values are session and request.

value

This required attribute sets the value of the property.

getProperty

This tag gets a property within the Pipeline Session object, and its attributes are described next.

namespace

Specifies the namespace containing a certain origin and event; otherwise, the current namespace is used.

id

This attribute specifies the name of a variable that stores the property. This variable is the instance that is used within the JSP. If an ID is not specified, the object is converted to a string, using the object's toString() method, and displayed as template text within in the JSP.

property

This required attribute is the name of the property to get.

scope

Properties can be either of session or of request scope. This attribute sets the scope of the property being retrieved. By default, properties have session scope. Valid values are session and request.

type

This attribute is the class name of the object being retrieved.

setValidatedValue

This tag sets the value and status of fields on an HTML form in which a validation error has occurred. This tag allows you to specify which fields on the HTML form a user must correct. Although this tag provides low-level functionality that may be very useful to you, the validatedForm tag is used more often in these circumstances. An Input Processor usually sets the validation values, but this tag allows for this to be accomplished within a JSP. The following sections describe the attributes of this tag.

fieldName

This attribute is the name of the HTML field element in question.

fieldStatus

This is the status of the HTML field. Valid values are unspecified, invalid, and valid. If a field is required by the system, but the user does not enter anything in this field, unspecified is used. Invalid signifies that the data entered by the user is incorrect. Valid, of course, is set if there are no errors with the field validation.

fieldValue

This is the new value of the field.

getValidatedValue

Much like setValidatedValue, use of this tag is usually replaced with the validatedForm tag. This tag retrieves the validation values of HTML fields. These values have either been set by an Input Processor or by use of the setValidatedValue tag. The attributes of this tag are described next.

fieldColor

This attribute changes the color of the field or message.

fieldDefaultValue

This attribute is the default value of the field. This value is used if the fieldValue attribute is not specified.

fieldMessage

This attribute sets a specific message for display in the HTML field.

fieldName

This required attribute is the name of the HTML field element in question.

fieldStatus

This is the status of the HTML field. Valid values are unspecified, invalid, and valid. If a field is required by the system, but the user does not enter anything in this field, unspecified is used. Invalid signifies that the data entered by the user is incorrect. Valid, of course, is set if there are no errors with the field validation. This field is required.

fieldValue

This required attribute indicates the value of the field.

invalidColor

By default, when a field status is invalid, its message is displayed in red. This attribute allows you to set the color of invalid messages.

unspecifiedColor

By default, when a field status is unspecified, its message is displayed in red. This attribute allows you to set the color of unspecified messages.

validColor

By default, when a field status is valid, its message is displayed in black. This attribute allows you to set the color of the valid messages.

getException

In Webflow, when an exception occurs within a processor, either an InvalidFormFieldException or a ProcessingException is thrown. This exception can be obtained within a JSP by using the getException tag. Its attributes are described in the following sections.

id

This required attribute specifies the name of a variable that stores the exception. This variable is the instance that will be used within the JSP.

type

This attribute refers to the type of exception. It casts the exception that is thrown by the processor.

Example of Pipeline Session Tags

The example that follows demonstrates setting and getting properties, as well as getting an exception from the PipelineSession object.

```
<% Date now = new java.util.Date(); %>
<wf:setProperty property="NOW" value="<%=now%>" scope="request"/>

<wf:getProperty property="NOW" id="theDate" type="java.util.Date" scope="request"/>
Today's Date: <%= theDate.toString() %>

Validation Exception: <span color="red"><wf:getException/></span>
```

Exploring the Portlet Tag Library

Previously in this chapter we described the tags in the Webflow tag library that you use to build Webflows. However, the portlet tag library contains some of the same tags and is also used to build Webflows. What is the difference between these tag libraries? The difference is in what is affected by the Webflow. The tags in the Webflow tag library build a Webflow that affects the portal as a whole. The portlet tags, on the other hand, only affect the portlet in which the Webflow is being executed. The examples in this chapter make use of both tag libraries.

Importing the Tag Library

The following line imports the Portlet Tag Library. At further locations within the JSP, the tag library is referenced by the prefix.

```
<%@ taglib uri="portlet.tld" prefix="pt"%>
```

Duplicated Tags

The following is a listing of the tags that are common to both the Webflow tag library and the portlet tag library. (Refer to earlier sections in this chapter for a description of each tag and its attributes.) Functionality remains the same in either version; only the scope of the Webflow is different. When developing Webflows that are used within portlets, you should use these tags rather than their Webflow tag library counterparts.

- createWebflowURL

- form

- validatedForm

- getException

The Pipeline Editor

Now that you are familiar with the many objects described previously in this chapter, it is time to delve into another editor. The Pipeline Editor, within the E-Business Control Center (EBCC), closely resembles the Webflow Editor and is, not surprisingly, used to create Pipelines. After you create all of the Pipeline Component classes necessary to perform some task, the components are assembled in this editor. Input Processors and Pipelines, as you learned in Chapter 7, are then added to a new or existing Webflow using the Webflow Editor.

Exploring the Pipeline Editor

The Pipeline Editor can be found within the EBCC on the Site Infrastructure tab of the Explorer window. You access the Pipeline Editor by either double-clicking a currently existing Pipeline or by creating a new object. Figure 8-1 shows the Site Infrastructure tab and highlights existing Pipelines.

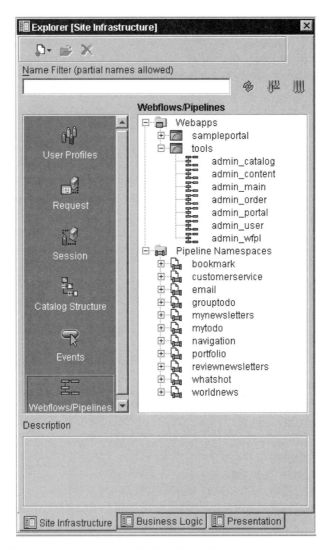

Figure 8-1. The Explorer window with Pipelines displayed

A new Pipeline may be created through either the File menu or the New Object button within the Explorer window (see Figure 8-2).

Figure 8-2. Using the New Object button

Upon your choosing to create a new Pipeline, by either methodology, the New Webflow/Pipeline dialog box is displayed (see Figure 8-3). You saw this dialog box in the context of creating Webflows in the previous chapter. To create a Pipeline, choose the second option, New Pipeline, and enter the appropriate namespace and Pipeline name. If the entered namespace does not exist, it will be created.

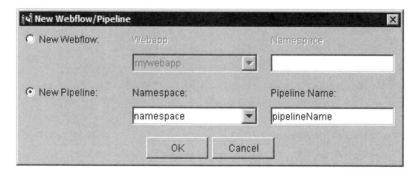

Figure 8-3. The New Webflow/Pipeline dialog box

Once you click the OK button, the Pipeline Editor appears, as shown in Figure 8-4. Many of the tools within this editor will be familiar. A lot of functionality was seen when exploring the Webflow Editor in the prior chapter. For that reason, this chapter will only explain the new tools.

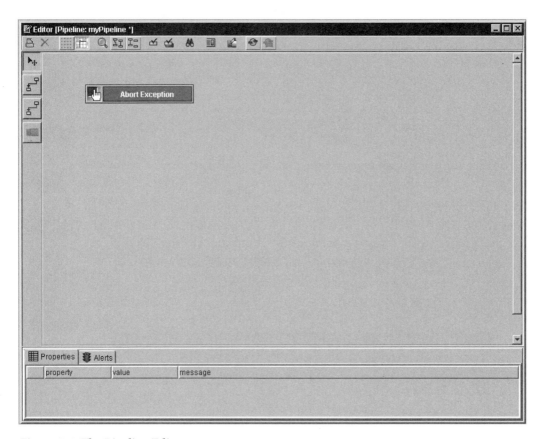

Figure 8-4. The Pipeline Editor

Like the Webflow Editor, the Pipeline Editor comprises two sets of tools. These tools are located either within the toolbar, displayed horizontally across the top of the editor pane, or within the editor palette, vertically displayed at the left of the pane. The next two sections describe the functionality of every tool within the Pipeline Editor.

Command Tools Within the Toolbar

The Toolbar is located at the top of the editor window, and the tools it contains affect the editor workspace and the Webflow as a whole. These tools, which are for the most part the same as those in the Webflow Editor Toolbar, are more administrative than developmental. There are three additional tools available on the Toolbar within the Pipeline Editor, and these are shown in Table 8-3.

Table 8-3. Additional Command Tools in the Pipeline Editor Toolbar

TOOL	DESCRIPTION
	Opens the Pipeline Component Editor, which is used to manage Pipeline Components
	Specifies that the Pipeline is transactional
	Specifies that the Pipeline Session should be included in the transaction

Editor Tools Within the Editor Palette

The editor palette is located on the left side of the editor, vertically aligned, and it features tools for developing and designing Pipelines. While the editor palette of the Pipeline Editor has much less functionality than that of the Webflow Editor, it does contain an additional tool, the Pipeline Component Node tool.

This tool allows you to place a Pipeline Component in the workspace.

Tabs Within the Tab Palette

The Pipeline Editor also contains a tab palette. This palette is exactly the same as the Webflow Editor's tab palette. Two tabs exist on this palette: Properties and Alerts (see Figure 8-5).

Figure 8-5. The tab palette in the Pipeline Editor

Using the Pipeline Editor

As you can see, there are only a few pieces of functionality to master in the Pipeline Editor. This section describes this functionality by demonstrating its use, and we show you an actual example at the end of this chapter. This section's purpose is to familiarize you with the tools and the processes behind Pipeline development.

Defining Pipeline Components

Once you start a new Pipeline, the Pipeline Components have to be defined using the Pipeline Component Editor before a node can be added. The Pipeline Component Node tool will be disabled if no Pipeline Components have been defined within the current namespace.

To define a Pipeline Component, follow these steps:

1. Click the Pipeline Component Editor tool on the Toolbar. The Pipeline Component Editor window pops up (see Figure 8-6).

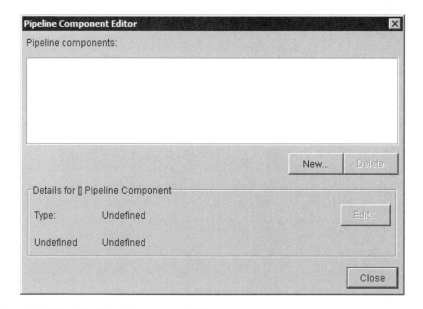

Figure 8-6. The Pipeline Component Editor

2. Click the New button. The Pipeline Component Creator dialog box appears, as shown in Figure 8-7.

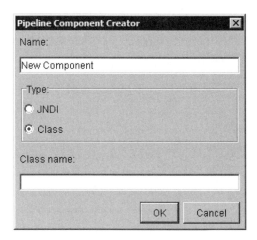

Figure 8-7. The Pipeline Component Creator dialog box

3. Enter the name of the Pipeline Component.

4. Choose the type of Pipeline Component that you want created. Choose JNDI if this Pipeline Component is an EJB. Choose Class if this Pipeline Component is a Java class.

5. Enter the absolute JNDI name or Class Name depending on the chosen type.

6. Click OK.

7. The Pipeline Component Editor now lists the details of the newly created Pipeline Component (see Figure 8-8). The editor provides functionality to edit and delete Pipeline Components as well.

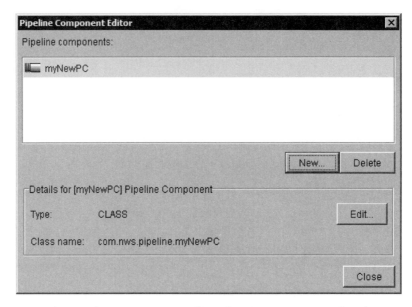

Figure 8-8. The Pipeline Component Editor showing component details

8. Click Close. The Pipeline Component is now ready to be added to the canvas.

Adding Pipeline Component Nodes to the Canvas

Pipeline Components, once defined, can be added to the canvas in the same way any other node is added to the canvas.

To add a node to the canvas, follow these steps:

1. Select the Pipeline Component Node tool from the editor palette.

2. Position the mouse pointer on the canvas. The mouse cursor should turn into a crosshair icon.

3. Click the canvas to place the node icon. It is not necessary to click in the exact location you want the node to be displayed. Nodes can be moved by simply dragging and dropping the icon.

4. Select the Properties tab on the tab palette. The component property must be set.

5. Click the component property field to display a drop-down list containing all of the Pipeline Components defined for the namespace (see Figure 8-9).

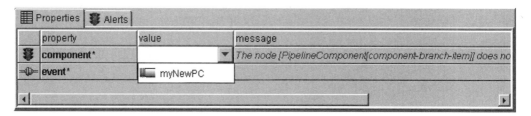

Figure 8-9. Pipeline Component properties

6. Choose the appropriate Pipeline Component name.

Selecting the Begin Node

It is not necessary to define a Begin node for a Webflow; however, you do need to do so for Pipelines. You accomplish this process in the same way as you do for Webflows.

To select the Begin node, do the following:

1. Click the Begin Node tool on the Toolbar. The Begin Node dialog box appears.

2. The Set the begin node dialog box, depicted in Figure 8-10, holds a list of Pipeline Components being used in the Pipeline. These are nodes that have been added to the canvas, not the list of components defined in the Pipeline Component Editor.

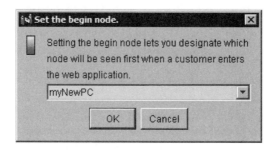

Figure 8-10. The Set the begin node dialog box

3. Choose the appropriate node at which to begin the Pipeline.

4. Click OK.

Adding Event and Exception Transitions

You can draw transitions in the Pipeline Component Editor as you did in the Webflow Editor.

To add a transition, follow these steps:

1. Select either the Event tool or the Exception tool from the editor palette.

2. Hover the mouse cursor around the edge of the node that you want to be the origin.

3. Drag the mouse to the destination node.

Revisiting the Webflow Editor

After a Pipeline has been created with the Pipeline Editor, it is time to include it in a Webflow. You will more than likely also want to add Input Processors to the Webflow Editor canvas, thereby forming a complete flow from the presentation tier to the business tier.

Adding Input Processors to the Canvas

Input Processors can be added to the canvas as easily as any other node. Once you have created the Java class for the Input Processor, you can place a node on the canvas representing that class.

To add an Input Processor to the canvas, do the following:

1. Select the Input Processor Node tool from the editor palette.

2. Position the mouse pointer on the canvas. The cursor should turn into a crosshair icon.

3. Click the canvas to place the node icon. It is not necessary to click in the exact location you want the node to be displayed. Nodes can be moved by simply dragging and dropping the icon. Figure 8-11 shows the image representation of an Input Processor on the canvas.

Figure 8-11. Input Processor node

4. Select the Properties tab on the tab palette.

5. Set the class-name property to the absolute class name for the Input Processor class. The name property will be filled automatically based on the class name. Figure 8-12 shows the properties for an Input Processor.

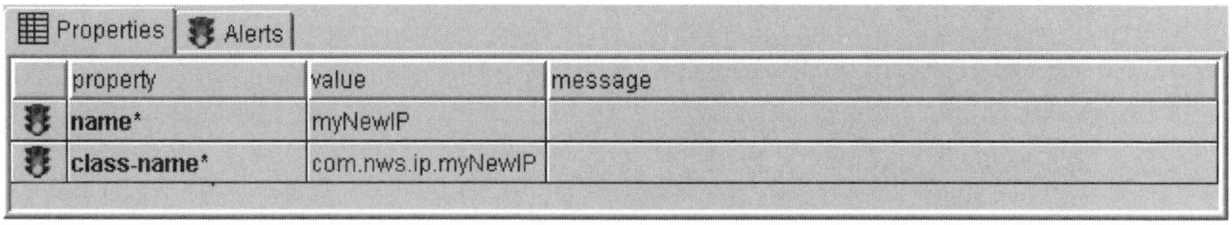

property	value	message
name*	myNewIP	
class-name*	com.nws.ip.myNewIP	

Figure 8-12. The Properties of the Input Processor node

Adding Pipeline Components to the Canvas

If you want to add a Pipeline Component to the canvas, you must have created it via the Pipeline Editor. After creation of the Pipeline Component, you can add a node representing this class to the canvas.

To add a Pipeline Component to the canvas, follow these steps:

1. Create the Pipeline Component with the Pipeline Editor.

2. While editing a Webflow, click the Pipeline Component Node tool on the editor palette.

3. Click the canvas to place the node icon. It is not necessary to click in the exact location you want the node to be displayed. Nodes can be moved by simply dragging and dropping the icon. Figure 8-13 shows the image representation of a Pipeline Component on the canvas.

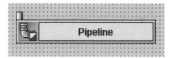

Figure 8-13. Pipeline Component node

4. Select the Properties tab on the tab palette.

5. Set the pipeline-namespace property, if necessary.

6. The pipeline-name property now displays a drop-down list of all available pipelines contained within the selected namespace (see Figure 8-14).

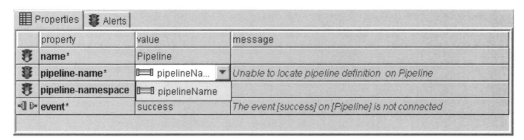

Figure 8-14. Available Pipelines

7. Complete the event transition.

8. Complete the exception transition.

Input Processing Walkthrough Examples

In this chapter, we have covered a lot of information pertaining to Webflow, Pipelines, and Input Processing in general. For this reason, to encapsulate all of the knowledge presented in this chapter, more than one example is necessary.

The first example is a simple HTML form. This form uses an Input Processor, but it is not validated. It demonstrates the nonvalidated Webflow form tag as well as process branching.

The second example is much more in depth. This example also uses an HTML form, but this time the Input Processor validates the data prior to passing it through a Pipeline for further processing.

Basic Form Example

This example combines the <portlet:form> JSP tag with an Input Processor. We show you how to create a JSP that contains a form with a single select box. A user will be able to select an option from this select box to navigate to different JSPs within the portlet.

Example Overview

This example comprises four JSPs and an Input Processor. The main JSP, jumpto.jsp, contains the select box that enables users to navigate to the other three JSPs, info1.jsp, info2.jsp, and info3.jsp. The form, contained on the main JSP, will submit information to the Input Processor. The Input Processor will read the value off of the request and then branch the flow to the appropriate JSP based on the user's selection.

The JSPs

The JSPs in this example are very basic. It is not the objective of this example to demonstrate advanced form processing. You may presume that this will be covered in the advanced form example later in this chapter. This example is merely an attempt to refamiliarize you with Webflow and to add to this knowledge with some of the topics you learned in this chapter.

This example will use the following JSPs:

- jumpto.jsp

- info1.jsp

- info2.jsp

- info3.jsp

The jumpto.jsp File

The jumpto.jsp file, which will contain the form, is the main file for the Webflow and therefore serves as the Begin node. The source code for this JSP appears in Listing 8-1.

Listing 8-1. jumpto.jsp

```
<%@ taglib uri="portlet.tld" prefix="pt"%>

<pt:form event="submit.jumpto">
  <select name="NEXTPAGE">
    <option value="info1">info 1</option>
    <option value="info2">info 2</option>
    <option value="info3">info 3</option>
  </select>
  <input type="submit" value="Go!"/>
</pt:form>
```

The Info JSP Files

The three info JSPs, info1.jsp, info2.jsp, and info3.jsp, are all primarily the same. They include the jumpto.jsp so that further navigation can occur from these pages. Listing 8-2 shows the code for info.jsp. This file differs from the others only in message text.

Listing 8-2. info.jsp

```
<jsp:include page="jumpto.jsp"/>
<br>
This is the Info 1 page.
```

The Input Processor

As shown in Listing 8-1, jumpto.jsp submits a form with the event submit.jumpto. A Wildcard node is used within a Webflow to direct this event to an Input Processor. The Input Processor then parses the request and navigates to a different JSP based on the user's selection. If nothing was selected, the Input Processor returns main, which in turn navigates to the main JSP, jumpto.jsp. Listing 8-3 is the source code for the Input Processor used for this example.

Listing 8-3. BasicIP.java

```
package com.nws.examples;

import com.bea.p13n.appflow.webflow.InputProcessorSupport;
import com.bea.p13n.appflow.exception.ProcessingException;
import javax.servlet.http.HttpServletRequest;

public class BasicIP extends InputProcessorSupport {

  private static final String PARAM_NEXTPAGE = "NEXTPAGE";
  public BasicIP() {
  }

  public Object process(HttpServletRequest request, Object requestContext)
      throws ProcessingException {

    String jumpToPage = request.getParameter(PARAM_NEXTPAGE);
    if (jumpToPage == null) jumpToPage = "main";

    return jumpToPage;
  }
}
```

Assembling the Webflow

A Webflow must be created to combine the JSPs and Input Processor. The layout of this Webflow is rather simple and can probably be guessed after looking at the preceding source code. You can follow these steps to build the necessary Webflow:

1. Create a new Webflow, and specify the Web application and namespace.

2. Add a Wildcard Presentation node to the canvas.

3. Set the event property to submit.jumpto.

4. Add an Input Processor node to the canvas.

5. Set the class-name property to com.nws.examples.BasicIP.

6. Connect the submit.jumpto event to BasicIP.

7. Add a Presentation node to the canvas.

8. Set the page-relative-path property to the proper path, i.e., /portlets/jumpto.

9. Set the page-name property to info1.jsp.

10. Create an event from BasicIP to info1.

11. Set the name property of this event to info1.

12. Add a Presentation node to the canvas.

13. Set the page-relative-path property to the proper path, i.e., /portlets/jumpto.

14. Set the page-name property to info2.jsp.

15. Create an event from BasicIP to info2.

16. Set the name property of this event to info2.

17. Add a Presentation node to the canvas.

18. Set the page-relative-path property to the proper path, i.e., /portlets/jumpto.

19. Set the page-name property to info3.jsp.

20. Create an event from BasicIP to info3.

21. Set the name property of this event to info3.

22. Add a Presentation node to the canvas.

23. Set the page-relative-path property to the proper path, i.e., /portlets/jumpto.

24. Set the page-name property to jumpto.jsp.

25. Create an event from BasicIP to jumpto.

26. Set the name property of this event to main.

27. Set jumpto as the Begin node for this JSP.

28. Compare your Webflow to Figure 8-15.

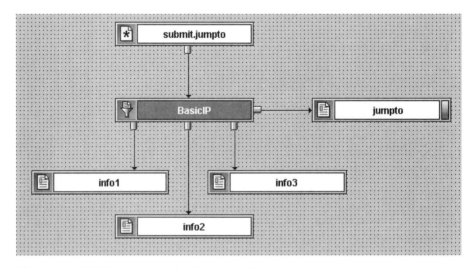

Figure 8-15. Webflow created for the example

The submit.jumpto event occurs on all of the JSPs contained within this portlet. For that reason it needs to be a Wildcard Presentation node. This way, it matters not which JSP originated the event—the destination is always BasicIP.

The Input Processor, BasicIP, represents the class com.nws.examples.BasicIP, as shown previously. This node has four events associated with it. By looking at the source code, you can see that these are the possible return values from the Input Processor: "info1", "info2", or "info3", the page names from the drop-down list, or "main", in the case that no value was selected from the select box.

 NOTE   *The Webflow used for this example also handles the BEA intrinsic refresh event, not shown in Figure 8-15. See Chapter 7 for details.*

Putting It All Together

At this point, there are some final steps that need be taken prior to viewing the results of this effort. However, we will not go into detail here since these steps have already been explored thoroughly in prior chapters. The following is a list of the final steps that need to be done:

- The com.nws.examples.BasicIP class must be visible to the Web application. This class should either be in the exploded classes directory or packaged within the lib directory.

- A portlet needs to be created using the jumpto.jsp file as its source. The portlet should also use the jumpTo Webflow shown earlier.

- The jumpto portlet also needs to be placed on a page and be made visible.

Please refer back to the preceding chapters to review this information if necessary.

The Result

Now that all of the files have been assembled, the results can be seen within the BEA WebLogic Portal. Figure 8-16 shows the jumpto portlet within the portal, and Figure 8-17 shows the result after selection of a page.

Figure 8-16. Initial view of the jumpto portlet

Figure 8-17. Result after selection

To the end user, this example does not look like much. However, you know that the selection made is passed through Webflow to the Input Processor. Based on the parameter selected, the Input Processor branches navigation and the resulting JSP is used within the portlet. This basic functionality can be expanded to facilitate some of the many needs of the Web application developer.

Advanced Form Example

Now that you have seen an example of a basic form, it is time to delve more deeply into Webflow and create an advanced form. In this example, we show you how to use the <portlet:validatedForm> tags to create a user information form. This information will be validated and processed and then presented to the user.

Example Overview

This example demonstrates the use of <portlet:validatedForm> tags to create a user information form. This form will be submitted once again to an Input Processor, only this time the Input Processor will validate the values. If validation fails, error messages will be displayed to the user. If validation succeeds, the information will be passed through a Pipeline for persistence in a database. If persistence succeeds, a second Pipeline Component will be executed in order to create a password string that is suitable for display, i.e., all asterisks (*). Finally, the information will be redisplayed to the user.

The JSPs

This example includes three JSPs. One JSP will be the form the user fills out. Validation errors will be displayed here. Another JSP will be needed to redisplay the information that was entered. Finally, an error page will capture all other errors that may occur outside of validation errors.

This example will use the following JSPs:

- userform.jsp

- userinfo.jsp

- usererror.jsp

userform.jsp

This is the beginning JSP for the portlet, and naturally the Begin node for the Webflow. This JSP contains a validated form. Note in Listing 8-4, which shows the source code for userform.jsp, the use of <portlet:validatedForm> rather than <webflow:validatedForm>.

Listing 8-4. userform.jsp

```
<%@ taglib uri="portlet.tld" prefix="pt"%>
<%@ taglib uri="webflow.tld" prefix="wf"%>

<% String textStyle="color: #000000; font-size: 12px;
    font-family: Arial, Geneva, sans-serif; text-decoration: none;"; %>

<pt:getException/>
<br>
<pt:validatedForm event="userform.submit" namespace="userinfo" applyStyle="field"
  messageAlign="right">
  <table>
    <tr>
      <td width="35%">Username:</td>
      <td><wf:text name="username" size="25" maxlength="25"
        style="<%=textStyle%>"/></td>
    </tr>
    <tr>
      <td>Password:</td>
      <td><wf:password name="password" size="25" maxlength="25"
```

```
            style="<%=textStyle%>"/></td>
      </tr>
      <tr>
        <td>Marital Status:</td>
        <td><wf:radio name="maritalStatus" value="S" checked="true"/> Single</td>
      </tr>
      <tr>
        <td> </td>
        <td><wf:radio name="maritalStatus" value="M"/> Married</td>
      </tr>
      <tr>
        <td> </td>
        <td><wf:radio name="maritalStatus" value="D"/> Divorced</td>
      </tr>
      <tr>
        <td> </td>
        <td><wf:radio name="maritalStatus" value="W"/> Widowed</td>
      </tr>
      <tr>
        <td>Language Expertise:</td>
        <td><wf:select name="expertise" size="3" multiple="true">
            <wf:option value="Java">Java</wf:option>
            <wf:option value="C">C</wf:option>
            <wf:option value="C++">C++</wf:option>
            <wf:option value="Ada">Ada</wf:option>
            <wf:option value="Fortran">Fortran</wf:option>
            <wf:option value="Cobol">Cobol</wf:option>
            </wf:select>
        </td>
      </tr>
      <tr>
        <td>Comments:</td>
        <td><wf:textarea name="comments" cols="30" rows="5"
          style="<%=textStyle%>"/></td>
      </tr>
      <tr>
        <td>Check to receive Email:</td>
        <td><wf:checkbox name="email" checked="true" value="Y"/></td>
      </tr>
      <tr>
        <td colspan="2" align="right"><input type="submit" value="Save"></td>
      </tr>
    </table>
</pt:validatedForm>
```

userinfo.jsp

If all processing succeeds, this page is used to redisplay the information to the user. This page uses a series of <webflow:getProperty> tags to retrieve the information from the Pipeline Session. Listing 8-5 shows the source code for userinfo.jsp.

Listing 8-5. userinfo.jsp

```
<%@ page import="java.util.*" %>

<%@ taglib uri="webflow.tld" prefix="wf"%>

<wf:getProperty property="expertise" id="expertise" type="java.util.Collection"
  scope="request" namespace="userinfo"/>

<% Iterator i = expertise.iterator(); %>

<table>
  <tr>
    <td width="25%">Username:</td>
    <td><wf:getProperty property="username" scope="request"
      namespace="userinfo"/></td>
  </tr>
  <tr>
    <td>Password:</td>
    <td><wf:getProperty property="displayPassword" scope="request"
    namespace="userinfo"/></td>
  </tr>
  <tr>
    <td>Marital Status:</td>
    <td><wf:getProperty property="maritalStatus" scope="request"
    namespace="userinfo"/></td>
  </tr>
  <tr>
    <td>Language Expertise:</td>
    <td><%=i.next()%></td>
  </tr>
<% while (i.hasNext()) { %>
  <tr>
    <td> </td>
    <td><%=i.next()%></td>
  </tr>
```

```
<% } %>
  <tr>
    <td>Comments:</td>
    <td><wf:getProperty property="comments" scope="request"
      namespace="userinfo"/></td>
  </tr>
  <tr>
    <td>Email:</td>
    <td><wf:getProperty property="email" scope="request"
      namespace="userinfo"/></td>
  </tr>
</table>
```

usererror.jsp

This JSP is very simple. It merely displays an exception, using the
<portlet:getException> tag, as you can see in Listing 8-6.

Listing 8-6. usererror.jsp

```
<%@ taglib uri="portlet.tld" prefix="pt"%>

<table>
  <tr>
    <td><pt:getException/></td>
  </tr>
</table>
```

The Input Processor

In this example, the Input Processor, AdvancedIP, validates all of the fields from
the HTML form. As shown in Listing 8-7, if validation succeeds, it places these
values in the Pipeline Session so that the information can be retrieved later during further processing.

Listing 8-7. AdvancedIP

```
package com.nws.examples;

import javax.servlet.http.HttpServletRequest;
import com.bea.p13n.appflow.common.PipelineSession;
import com.bea.p13n.appflow.exception.ProcessingException;
import com.bea.p13n.appflow.webflow.InputProcessorSupport;
```

```
import com.bea.p13n.appflow.webflow.forms.ValidatedValues;
import com.bea.p13n.appflow.webflow.forms.ValidatedValuesFactory;
import com.bea.p13n.appflow.webflow.forms.ValidatedForm;
import com.bea.p13n.appflow.webflow.forms.ValidatedFormFactory;
import com.bea.p13n.appflow.webflow.forms.MinMaxExpression;
import com.bea.p13n.appflow.webflow.forms.InvalidFormDataException;
import java.util.Collection;

public class AdvancedIP extends InputProcessorSupport {

  private static final String SUCCESS = "success";

  public AdvancedIP() {
  }
  public Object process(HttpServletRequest request, Object requestContext)
    throws com.bea.p13n.appflow.exception.ProcessingException {

    PipelineSession pipelineSession = getPipelineSession(request);
    String namespace = getCurrentNamespace(pipelineSession);

    ValidatedValues values = ValidatedValuesFactory.getValidatedValues(request);
    ValidatedForm form = ValidatedFormFactory.getValidatedForm();
    MinMaxExpression minMax = new MinMaxExpression();

    String username = form.validate(values, STRING_VALIDATOR, "username",
      minMax.set(1, 25), "Username is required");

    String password = form.validate(values, STRING_VALIDATOR, "password",
      minMax.set(1, 25), "Password is required");

    String maritalStatus = form.validate(values, "maritalStatus");

    Collection expertise = form.validateMultiple(values, "expertise", 2,
      "Please select at least two areas of expertise");

    String comments = form.validate(values, STRING_VALIDATOR, "comments",
      minMax.set(0,500), "Please limit your comment to 500 characters");

    String email = form.validate(values, "email");

    if (values.getInvalidFieldCount() > 0) {
      throw new InvalidFormDataException("Form data is invalid!");
    }
```

```
        setRequestAttribute("username", username, namespace, requestContext,
          pipelineSession);

        setRequestAttribute("password", password, namespace, requestContext,
          pipelineSession);

        setRequestAttribute("maritalStatus", maritalStatus, namespace,
          requestContext, pipelineSession);

        setRequestAttribute("expertise", expertise, namespace, requestContext,
          pipelineSession);

        setRequestAttribute("comments", comments, namespace, requestContext,
          pipelineSession);

        setRequestAttribute("email", email, namespace, requestContext,
          pipelineSession);

        return SUCCESS;
    }
}
```

The Pipeline

The Pipeline in this example is made up of two Pipeline Component objects, persistToDBPC and setDisplayPasswordPC, as discussed next.

persistToDBPC

The persistToDBPC object is specified as the Begin node for the Pipeline. Upon execution, the user's information is acquired from the Pipeline Session. This information is passed to the persist function, which in turn could execute the proper SQL to insert this record into a database. Listing 8-8 shows the persistToDBPC source code.

Listing 8-8. persistToDBPC

```
package com.nws.examples;

import com.bea.p13n.appflow.common.PipelineSession;
import com.bea.p13n.appflow.pipeline.*;
import java.util.Collection;
import java.util.Iterator;
```

```java
public class persistToDBPC extends PipelineComponentSupport {

  public persistToDBPC() {
  }

  public PipelineSession process(PipelineSession pipelineSession,
    Object requestContext) throws
    com.bea.p13n.appflow.exception.PipelineException, java.rmi.RemoteException {

    String namespace = getCurrentNamespace(pipelineSession);

    String username = (String)getRequestAttribute("username", namespace,
      requestContext, pipelineSession);

    String password = (String)getRequestAttribute("password", namespace,
      requestContext, pipelineSession);

    String maritalStatus = (String)getRequestAttribute("maritalStatus",
      namespace, requestContext, pipelineSession);

    Collection expertise = (Collection)getRequestAttribute("expertise",
      namespace, requestContext, pipelineSession);

    String comments = (String)getRequestAttribute("comments", namespace,
      requestContext, pipelineSession);

    String email = (String)getRequestAttribute("email", namespace,
      requestContext, pipelineSession);

    persist(username, password, maritalStatus, expertise, comments, email);

    return pipelineSession;
  }

  private void persist(String username, String password, String maritalStatus,
    Collection expertise, String comments, String email) {

    // A Database connection would be made here to store all of the values
    // contained within the Pipeline Session
  }
}
```

setDisplayPasswordPC

After successful execution of persistToDBPC, processing continues with the setDisplayPasswordPC. This Pipeline Component creates a display string consisting of a asterisk (*)for each character in the entered password. This is merely for redisplay to the user. The source code for setDisplayPasswordPC appears in Listing 8-9.

Listing 8-9. setDisplayPasswordPC

```
package com.nws.examples;

import com.bea.p13n.appflow.common.PipelineSession;
import com.bea.p13n.appflow.pipeline.PipelineComponentSupport;

public class setDisplayPasswordPC extends PipelineComponentSupport {

  public setDisplayPasswordPC() {
  }

  public PipelineSession process(PipelineSession pipelineSession,
    Object requestContext) throws
    com.bea.p13n.appflow.exception.PipelineException, java.rmi.RemoteException {

    StringBuffer sb = new StringBuffer();
    String namespace = getCurrentNamespace(pipelineSession);

    String pwd = (String)getRequestAttribute("password", namespace,
      requestContext, pipelineSession);

    for(int i = 0; i < pwd.length(); i++) {
      sb.append("*");
    }

    setRequestAttribute("displayPassword", sb.toString(), namespace,
      requestContext, pipelineSession);

    return pipelineSession;
  }
}
```

Assembling the Pipeline

The two classes described previously will be used to create a Pipeline. Follow these steps to construct this Pipeline:

1. Create a new Pipeline, and specify the namespace and Pipeline name.

2. Launch the Pipeline Component Editor.

3. Click New.

4. Name the Pipeline Component persistToDBPC.

5. Set the Class Name to com.nws.examples.persistToDBPC.

6. Click OK.

7. Click New.

8. Name the Pipeline Component setDisplayPasswordPC.

9. Set the Class Name to com.nws.examples.setDisplayPasswordPC.

10. Click OK.

11. Click Close.

12. Add a Pipeline Component node to the canvas.

13. Set the component property to persistToDBPC.

14. Add another Pipeline Component node to the canvas.

15. Set the component property to setDisplayPasswordPC.

16. Connect the persistToDBPC nodes success event to setDisplayPasswordPC.

17. Connect persistToDB.exception to the Abort Exception node.

18. Connect setDisplayPassword.exception to the Abort Exception node.

19. Specify the persistToDBPC node as the Begin node for this Pipeline.

20. Compare your Pipeline to the one in Figure 8-18.

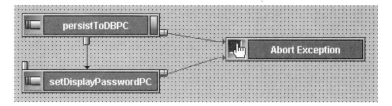

Figure 8-18. The completed Pipeline

The Pipeline almost speaks for itself. Each component throws an exception on failure. These exceptions have been transitioned to the Abort Exception node, which will cause any failure, in either component, to abort processing.

Assembling the Webflow

Now that the Pipeline has been created, it is time to create the Webflow for this application. The following steps can be used as a guide in creating the Webflow:

1. Create a new Webflow, and specify the Web application and namespace.

2. Add a Presentation node to the canvas.

3. Set the page-relative-path property to the proper path, i.e., /portlets/userinfo.

4. Set the page-name property to userform.jsp.

5. Specify this node as the Begin node.

6. Add an Input Processor node to the canvas.

7. Set the class-name property to com.nws.examples.AdvancedIP.

8. Add an event to the userform node with a destination of AdvancedIP.

9. Set this event's name property to userform.submit.

10. Add an exception event to the AdvancedIP node with a destination of userform.

11. Set this event's name property to com.bea.p13n.appflow.exception.ProcessingException.

12. Add a Pipeline node to the canvas.

13. Set the name property to userinfo.

14. Add an event to the AdvancedIP node with a destination of the userinfo Pipeline node.

15. Set this event's name property to success.

16. Add another Presentation node to the canvas.

17. Set the page-relative-path property to the proper path, i.e., /portlets/userinfo.

18. Set the page-name property to userinfo.jsp.

19. Select the event on the userinfo Pipeline node and complete the transition with a destination of the userinfo Presentation node.

20. Set this event's name property to success.

21. Add another Presentation node to the canvas.

22. Set the page-relative-path property to the proper path, i.e., /portlets/userinfo.

23. Set the page-name property to usererror.jsp.

24. Connect setDisplayPassword.exception to the usererror node.

25. Connect persistToDB.exception to the usererror node.

26. Add a Wildcard Processor node to the canvas.

27. Set the type property to pipeline.

28. Set the exception property to com.bea.p13n.appflow.exception.PipelineException.

29. Connection the exception to the usererror node.

30. Add another Wildcard Processor node to the canvas.

31. Set the type property to pipeline.

32. Set the exception property to java.rmi.RemoteException.

33. Connection the exception to the usererror node.

34. Compare your Webflow to the one in Figure 8-19.

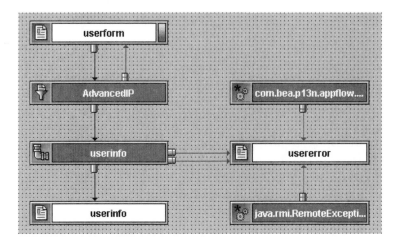

Figure 8-19. The completed Webflow

In this completed Webflow, the AdvancedIP Input Processor will throw a ProcessingException if validation were to fail. For this reason, the exception is directed back to the userform page. Pipelines can throw an RMIException or a PipelineException; these exceptions could have just as easily transitioned from the userinfo Pipeline node. This example demonstrated catching these exceptions using Wildcard Processor nodes.

NOTE *The Webflow used for this example also handles the BEA intrinsic refresh event, not shown in Figure 8-19. See Chapter 7 for details.*

Putting It All Together

Pipeline Components must be made visible at the enterprise application level. For this reason, these classes cannot simply be placed in the exploded class directory or in the lib directory of the Web application. Several methods can be used to accomplish this depending on whether the Pipeline Components are EJBs or simple Java classes.

Deploying Pipeline Components as EJBs

If at least one of the Pipeline Components you want to deploy is an EJB, deployment is a breeze. EJB development is covered in depth in Chapter 10 of this book. Follow the steps in creating an EJB module and deploy. The Pipeline Components will automatically be picked up and the Webflow will work.

Deploying Pipeline Components as Java Classes

If the Pipeline Components you want to deploy are not EJBs, deployment is trickier. But by no means is it necessary to have the components be EJBs. There are two methods for deploying these types of components. Either deploy a dummy EJB or piggyback on an already existing EJB.

If none of the components are EJBs, you can create a dummy class in order to achieve an EJB deployment. This EJB would never be used as an actual EJB. It would be deployed only so that the Pipeline Components could be added to the deployment and picked up by the class loader. This does result in functional Pipeline Components; however, this creates an EJB that would just be floating out in the Web application with the sole purpose of holding the component classes.

Piggybacking on an existing EJB still may not seem like the proper way of doing things. But it does accomplish the same goal without creating an EJB that is not used. The Pipeline Components in this example were deployed using this method.

To piggyback an existing EJB, follow these steps:

1. Create a jar file containing the Pipeline Components.

2. Place this jar file in the application directory, i.e., <BEA_HOME>/user_projects/mydomain/beaApps/portalApp.

3. Open the EJB jar file that will be used to deploy the components.

4. Extract the manifest.mf file to a root directory, e.g., C:\.

5. Edit the manifest.mf file.

6. Add the jar file created in step 1 to the class path. In the manifest.mf file shown in Listing 8-10, my.jar was added.

7. Save the manifest.mf file.

8. Add the manifest.mf file back to the EJB jar.

9. Ensure that the file has been added back with the path meta-inf\.

 NOTE *If no existing EJB deployment is available, use the pipeline.jar file located in the previously mentioned directory.*

Listing 8-10. Modified manifest.mf File

```
Manifest-Version: 1.0
Implementation-Version: 7.0.0.0
Specification-Title: BEA WebLogic Portal 7.0 Mon Jun 24 15:26:20 MDT 2
 002 61568
Specification-Version: 7.0.0.0
Implementation-URL: http://www.bea.com/
Implementation-Title: BEA WebLogic Portal 7.0 Mon Jun 24 15:26:20 MDT
 2002 61568
Class-Path: existing.jar my.jar
Implementation-Vendor: BEA Systems, Inc.
Specification-Vendor: BEA Systems, Inc.
```

Final Steps

At this point there are some final steps that need be taken prior to viewing the results of this effort. However, we will not go into detail in this chapter, since these steps have already been explored thoroughly in prior chapters. The following is a list of the final steps for finishing the advanced form example:

- The com.nws.examples.AdvancedIP class must be visible to the Web application. This class should either be in the exploded classes directory or packaged within the lib directory.

- The Pipeline Components must be deployed using one of the previously mentioned techniques.

- A portlet needs to be created using the userform.jsp file as its source. The portlet should also use the userinfo Webflow shown previously.

- The userform portlet also needs to be placed on a page and made visible.

Please refer back to the prior chapters to review this information if necessary.

The Result

At this point the portlet is ready to execute. Figure 8-20 shows the initial userinfo portlet.

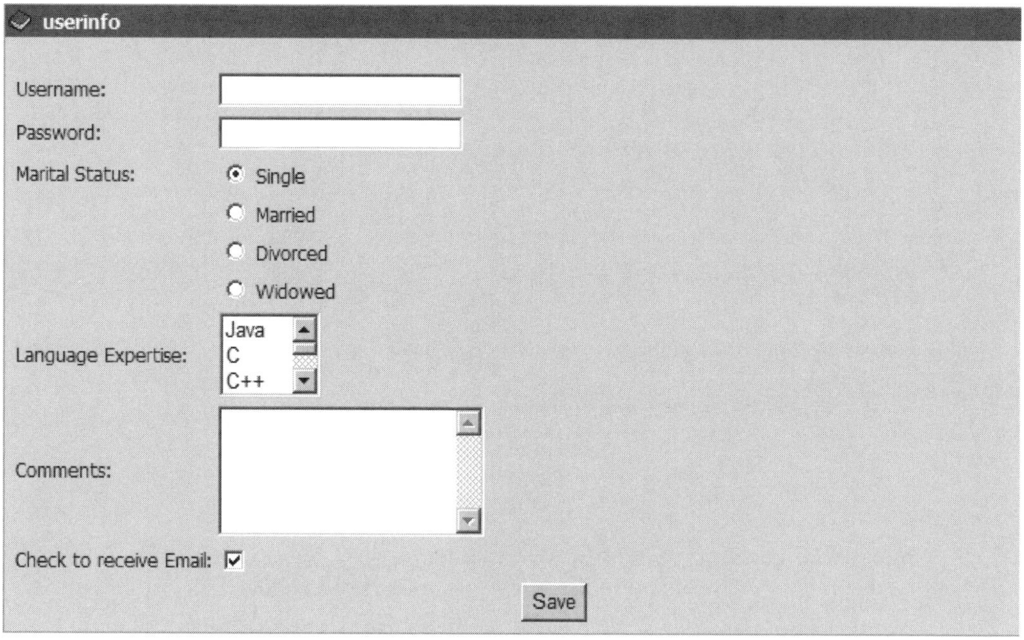

Figure 8-20. userinfo portlet

Validation will fail if the Username or Password field is left blank. Not making at least two selections for Language Expertise will also cause a validation error. If the Comments field contains more than 500 characters, another failure will occur. Figure 8-21 shows the validation messages for all of these fields, and also the warning message at the top of the form.

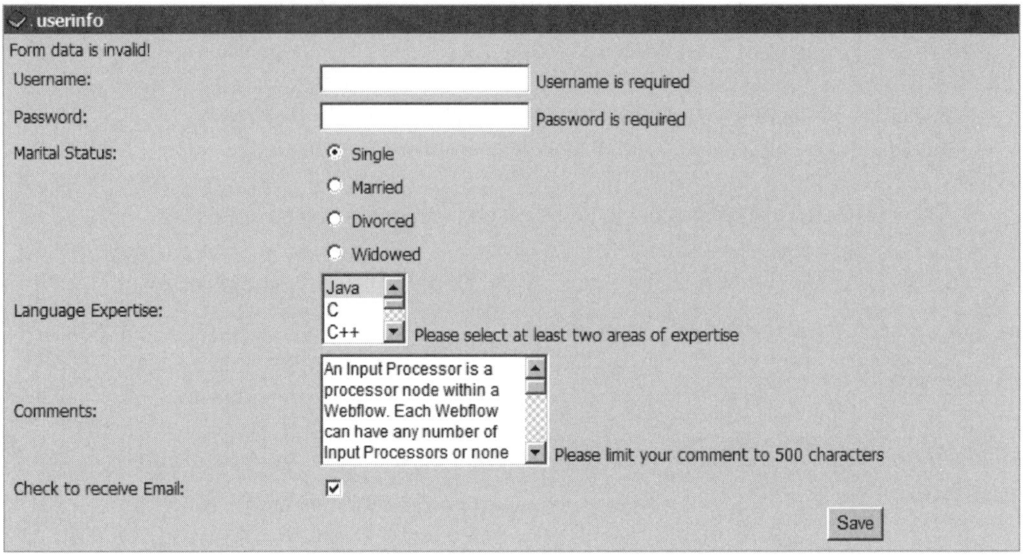

Figure 8-21. Validation failure

After correcting the mistakes on the form, processing will be successful and the Portlet will then display the information that the user has entered. Results similar to Figure 8-22 should appear.

Figure 8-22. Results of successful form processing

Summary

This chapter has finished our discussion of Webflow. The BEA WebLogic Portal provides much functionality. You may not feel comfortable using Webflow as it has been discussed in this chapter, since it adds several layers of abstraction that you may not be used to. The next chapter will discuss an alternative to using Webflow to process user input, one that you may be more accustomed to.

CHAPTER 9

Implementing a Front Controller

THE PREVIOUS TWO CHAPTERS covered Webflow. However, you may choose not to use Webflow in your application modules, in which case you should follow a standardized methodology. One of these methodologies involves using a Front Controller. In this chapter, we discuss Front Controllers and their advantages, and we include an example Front Controller at the end of this chapter.

What Is a Front Controller?

A *Front Controller* can be thought of as a doorway. The presentation tier uses this doorway in order to mingle within the world of the business tier. A Front Controller is a centralized entry point for the presentation tier requests. As you learned in Chapter 3, a servlet can handle many types of requests. When processing user input, a Front Controller mainly concerns itself with the doGet() and doPost() methods. All requests pass through the Front Controller and are then interpreted and pushed off to the proper handler routine. This handler routine could simply be a specialized method of the servlet. In larger enterprise applications, this handler would be a class that the Front Controller uses to handle the specific action or request. There is no limit to the number of Front Controllers that can exist within a Web application. Numerous controllers could be included, each handling a subset of functionality within the system.

Figure 9-1 shows how a Front Controller acts as a mediator for requests from any number of pages.

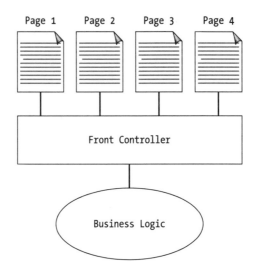

Figure 9-1. How a Front Controller works

Advantages of Using Front Controllers

Since the controller code is centralized, obviously one of the main advantages of using a Front Controller is reduced duplication of code. If it were up to the presentation tier to directly handle business logic, such as database connections, each JSP would need to have this code included within its source. This creates a maintenance nightmare. Any change to the business logic would more than likely cause a change in the bulk of the application's JSPs. If any change is missed, system stability would be threatened.

Another advantage is reduced complexity at the presentation tier. Complex code is removed from within the JSP and placed in controller objects. This aids development and maintenance of the JSP. When a JSP is cluttered with scriplets, readability is greatly hindered. A good rule of thumb is to keep JSP code down to template text and tag libraries. This methodology creates a clean presentation tier.

You should always strive for reuse in enterprise application development. With business logic centralized in one object, reuse is greatly improved. Many views may have similar processes that could all be handled by the same controller, rather than each view containing the same logic.

Types of Front Controllers

Basically, there are two types of Front Controllers: Servlet Front Controllers and JSP Front Controllers. The difference between the two is where the controller code is implemented.

Servlet Front Controller

The controller code can be implemented within a servlet, rather than within a JSP. This business logic is related to processing information and controlling the flow of the Web application. For this reason, using a servlet over a JSP to implement the controller code is the preferred methodology.

Depending on the type of request, the information is processed once within either the doPost() or doGet() method. Usually a special parameter signifies the action that has taken place. In Listing 9-1, the OPERATION parameter is used to inform the Front Controller of the action that has taken place.

Listing 9-1. Example Servlet Front Controller

```
package com.nws.examples;

import javax.servlet.ServletException;
import javax.servlet.ServletConfig;
import javax.servlet.http.HttpServlet;
import javax.servlet.http.HttpServletRequest;
import javax.servlet.http.HttpServletResponse;
import java.io.IOException;

public class sampleController extends HttpServlet {

  public void init(ServletConfig config) throws ServletException {
    super.init(config);
  }

  public void doGet(HttpServletRequest request, HttpServletResponse response)
    throws ServletException, IOException {
    doPost(request, response);
  }
```

```java
public void doPost(HttpServletRequest request, HttpServletResponse response)
  throws ServletException, IOException {

  String op = request.getParameter("OPERATION");

  if ((op != null) && (op.equalsIgnoreCase("SOMETHING"))) {
    doSomething(request);
  }

  getServletConfig().getServletContext().
    getRequestDispatcher("/application?pageid=somepage").
      forward(request, response);

}

private void doSomething(HttpServletRequest request) {
  //This method would process the request.
}

public void destroy() {
}

}
```

JSP Front Controller

When using a JSP Front Controller, the controller code is implemented within a JSP. We do not cover this approach in detail since we do not recommend that it be used. If you place controller code (i.e., business logic) within a JSP, everything that you have gained with the Model View Controller pattern will be lost. If code does not help with the display, it does not belong in a JSP. Also, JSPs would be more complex and convoluted since page markup would be intermingled with processing coded.

Within the BEA WebLogic Portal, using a JSP Front Controller can cause additional problems. Many times in a Web application, after processing user information, flow should be transferred to another page. Unfortunately, it is not possible to redirect the response object from the middle of a JSP. Since the results of several framework JSPs have already been written out, the response object has been committed and cannot be changed. This only adds to the reasons for not to using a JSP Front Controller.

Although this approach has a few warning signs, with proper implementation this methodology can work for enterprise applications. It is up to the architect to create his or her design. The example shown in Listing 9-2 demonstrates the JSP Front Controller methodology.

Listing 9-2. Example JSP Front Controller

```
<%
  String firstname = "";
  String lastname = "";
  StringBuffer sb = new StringBuffer();

  if (request.getParameter("SUBMIT") != null) {
    boolean isValid = true;

    firstname = request.getParameter("FIRSTNAME");
    lastname = request.getParameter("LASTNAME");

    if ((firstname == null) || (firstname.equals(""))) {
      sb.append("First Name is required<BR>");
      isValid = false;
    }

    if ((lastname == null) || (lastname.equals(""))) {
      sb.append("Last Name is required<BR>");
      isValid = false;
    }
```

```
      if (isValid) {
        //Perform what ever processing is neccessary
        firstname = "";
        lastname = "";
      }


    }

  %>


  <form name="PersonForm" method="post" action="/mywebapp/application?pageid=misc">
  <table>
    <tr>
      <td colspan="2"><span style="color:red"><%=sb%></span></td>
    </tr>
    <tr>
      <td>First Name:</td>
      <td><input type="text" value="<%=firstname%>" name="FIRSTNAME"></td>
    </tr>
    <tr>
      <td>Last Name:</td>
      <td><input type="text" value="<%=lastname%>" name="LASTNAME"></td>
    </tr>
    <tr>
      <td colspan="2"><input type="submit" value="Submit" name="SUBMIT"></td>
    </tr>
  </table>
  </form>
```

How Webflow Fits In

Within the BEA WebLogic Portal exists a servlet that is mapped to the URL /application. All requests within the portal should traverse through this servlet, which is a Front Controller. When using the Webflow URL creation process, the Webflow URLs that are dynamically created all contain the node /application. Once a request is passed to the servlet, whether that request is by a get or post method, the servlet dispatches the request to the appropriate handler.

Front Controller Example

The example presented in this section expands on what you have just learned about Servlet Front Controllers. The purpose of the controller is to validate user information and then persist this information in a JavaBean.

This example demonstrates validating information from within a servlet and forwarding control based on the result of validation.

If validation fails, the user should be presented once more with the form. The form should include all data previously entered as well as validation messages dictating which fields need corrections. These validation messages can be presented either in one block at the top of the form, or each message can be presented at its corresponding field.

If validation succeeds, information is persisted in a JavaBean that is accessible from the session. Also, after persistence, the flow of the Web application is forwarded to a different page, where the data is then displayed.

Only a few components need to be assembled for this example. The following is a list of components that we show you how to create:

- ControllerForm.jsp

- ControllerDisplay.jsp

- UserController

- UserBean

ControllerForm.jsp

The ControllerForm.jsp contains an HTML form. Once the user completes the form and clicks the Submit button, the request is processed by a servlet. If validation fails, the servlet forwards the request to the current page so the user may correct his or her mistakes. Upon successful validation, the servlet forwards the request to a new page. Listing 9-3 shows the ControllerForm.jsp component.

Listing 9-3. ControllerForm.jsp

```jsp
<jsp:useBean id="userBean" class="com.nws.examples.UserBean" scope="request"/>

<form name="userForm" method="post" action="./user">
<table>
  <tr>
    <td colspan="2"><span style="color:red"><%--userBean.getErrorMessage()--%>
      </span></td>
  </tr>
  <tr>
    <td width="25%">First Name:</td>
    <td width="75%"><input type="text" value="<jsp:getProperty name="userBean"
      property="firstname"/>" name="FIRSTNAME"> <span style="color:red">
      <%=userBean.getFieldError("FIRSTNAME")%></span></td>
  </tr>
  <tr>
    <td>Last Name:</td>
    <td><input type="text" value="<jsp:getProperty name="userBean"
      property="lastname"/>" name="LASTNAME"> <span style="color:red">
      <%=userBean.getFieldError("LASTNAME")%></span></td>
  </tr>
  <tr>
    <td>Email:</td>
    <td><input type="text" value="<jsp:getProperty name="userBean"
      property="email"/>" name="EMAIL"> <span style="color:red">
      <%=userBean.getFieldError("EMAIL")%></span></td>
  </tr>
  <tr>
    <td colspan="2"><input type="submit" value="Submit" name="SUBMIT"></td>
  </tr>
</table>
</form>
```

Notice that both the getErrorMessage() method and the getFieldError() method are used in this JSP. Yet the getErrorMessage() method has been commented out. As mentioned previously, one of the specifications for this example is to demonstrate displaying validation messages as a block of text as well as a single line associated with a particular field. To include both of these messages at once would produce unsatisfactory results, as each validation message would appear twice. As we show later, we use these method calls separately in this example. The results of validation will be illustrated using each method. We cover the logic behind these methods in the section "UserBean JavaBean," and you can see this logic later in Listing 9-6.

ControllerDisplay.jsp

Once validation succeeds for the HTML form, the servlet forwards the request to a page containing ControllerDisplay.jsp. This JSP obtains the JavaBean from the request object and displays the validated fields. Listing 9-4 shows the ControllerDisplay.jsp component.

Listing 9-4. ControllerDisplay.jsp

```
<jsp:useBean id="userBean" class="com.nws.examples.UserBean" scope="request"/>

<table>
  <tr>
    <td>First Name:</td>
    <td><jsp:getProperty name="userBean" property="firstname"/></td>
  </tr>
  <tr>
    <td>Last Name:</td>
    <td><jsp:getProperty name="userBean" property="lastname"/></td>
  </tr>
  <tr>
    <td>Email:</td>
    <td><jsp:getProperty name="userBean" property="email"/></td>
  </tr>
</table>
```

UserController Servlet

The HTML form posts its data to this servlet. The servlet retrieves the information entered by the user and then populates a JavaBean, which is passed to a validation method to ensure that the data entered is valid. This bean is stored within the request object, and it displays validation error messages back to the user upon validation failure. If validation succeeds, this bean obtains the data for display. Depending on the status of the validation, the servlet is in charge of forwarding the request to the proper page. Listing 9-5 displays the source code for the UserController servlet.

Listing 9-5. UserController Servlet

```
package com.nws.examples;

import javax.servlet.ServletException;
import javax.servlet.ServletConfig;
```

```java
import javax.servlet.http.HttpServlet;
import javax.servlet.http.HttpServletRequest;
import javax.servlet.http.HttpServletResponse;
import java.io.IOException;

public class UserController extends HttpServlet {

  private static final String PARAM_FIRSTNAME = "FIRSTNAME";
  private static final String PARAM_LASTNAME = "LASTNAME";
  private static final String PARAM_EMAIL = "EMAIL";

  public void init(ServletConfig config) throws ServletException {
    super.init(config);
  }

  public void doGet(HttpServletRequest request, HttpServletResponse response)
      throws ServletException, IOException {
    doPost(request, response);
  }

  public void doPost(HttpServletRequest request, HttpServletResponse response)
      throws ServletException, IOException {
    String url = "";
    UserBean userBean = getBean(request);

    if (isValid(userBean)) {
      url = "/application/?pageid=home";
    }
    else {
      url = "/application/?pageid=misc";
    }

    request.setAttribute("userBean", userBean);

    getServletConfig().getServletContext().getRequestDispatcher(url).
forward(request, response);

  }

  public void destroy() {
  }
```

```java
    private UserBean getBean(HttpServletRequest request) {

        UserBean bean = new UserBean();
        bean.setFirstname(request.getParameter(PARAM_FIRSTNAME));
        bean.setLastname(request.getParameter(PARAM_LASTNAME));
        bean.setEmail(request.getParameter(PARAM_EMAIL));
        return bean;
    }

    private boolean isValid(UserBean userBean) {
        boolean isValid = true;

        if ((userBean.getFirstname() == null) ||
(userBean.getFirstname().equals(""))) {
            userBean.setFieldError(PARAM_FIRSTNAME, "First Name is required.");
            isValid = false;
        }

        if ((userBean.getLastname() == null) ||
(userBean.getLastname().equals(""))) {
            userBean.setFieldError(PARAM_LASTNAME, "Last Name is required.");
            isValid = false;
        }

        if ((userBean.getEmail() == null) || (userBean.getEmail().equals(""))) {
            userBean.setFieldError(PARAM_EMAIL, "Email is required.");
            isValid = false;
        }
        else if (!validEmail(userBean.getEmail())) {
            userBean.setFieldError(PARAM_EMAIL, "Email is not valid.");
            isValid = false;
        }

        return isValid;
    }

    private boolean validEmail(String email) {
        int position = email.indexOf("@");

        if (position == -1) {
            return false;
        }
```

```
        else if (email.substring(position).indexOf(".") == -1) {
          return false;
        }

      return true;
    }
}
```

UserBean JavaBean

The final object we need in this example is a JavaBean. UserBean follows the same guidelines that we explained in Chapter 3. It is serializable, it contains a constructor with no arguments, and it includes a get and set method for each of its properties. In addition to these items, it also contains a HashMap that stores validation messages on a per-field basis or as one entire block. The source code for UserBean appears in Listing 9-6.

Listing 9-6. UserBean JavaBean

```
package com.nws.examples;

import java.io.Serializable;
import java.util.HashMap;
import java.util.Set;
import java.util.Iterator;

public class UserBean implements Serializable{

  private HashMap errors = new HashMap();

  private String firstname;
  private String lastname;
  private String email;

  public UserBean() {
  }

  public String getFirstname() {
    return firstname;
  }
```

```java
  public void setFirstname(String firstname) {
    this.firstname = firstname;
  }

  public String getLastname() {
    return lastname;
  }

  public void setLastname(String lastname) {
    this.lastname = lastname;
  }

  public String getEmail() {
    return email;
  }

  public void setEmail(String email) {
    this.email = email;
  }

  public void setFieldError(String field, String error) {
    errors.put(field, error);
  }

  public String getFieldError(String field) {
    return (String)errors.get(field);
  }

  public String getErrorMessage() {
    StringBuffer error = new StringBuffer();
    Set keys = errors.keySet();

    if (keys.size() > 0) {
      error.append("Errors have occured<br>");
    }

    for (Iterator i = keys.iterator(); i.hasNext();) {
      error.append(getFieldError((String)i.next()));
      error.append("<br>");
    }

    return error.toString();
  }
}
```

Putting It All Together

After creating these classes and JSPs, you need to assemble them within the Web application. Use the JSPs to create two separate portlets. In this example, the ControllerForm portlet is placed on a page entitled misc. The ControllerDisplay portlet is placed on the home page to demonstrate how the request can be forwarded between pages.

You can include the two classes, UserController and UserBean, within the exploded class directory, or assemble these classes in a JAR file and deploy them in the lib directory.

The UserController class is a servlet. For this reason, you need to map it to a URL. Within the WEB-INF directory of the Web application, the web.xml file contains all mappings for servlets. The following sections should be included in the web.xml file:

```
<servlet>
    <servlet-name>userController</servlet-name>
    <servlet-class>com.nws.examples.UserController</servlet-class>
</servlet>

<servlet-mapping>
    <servlet-name>userController</servlet-name>
    <url-pattern>/user/*</url-pattern>
</servlet-mapping>
```

The Results

Upon accessing the misc page of the portal, depending on the configuration of the page, you should see a portal that resembles the one shown in Figure 9-2. The ControllerForm portlet should display a simple, empty HTML form.

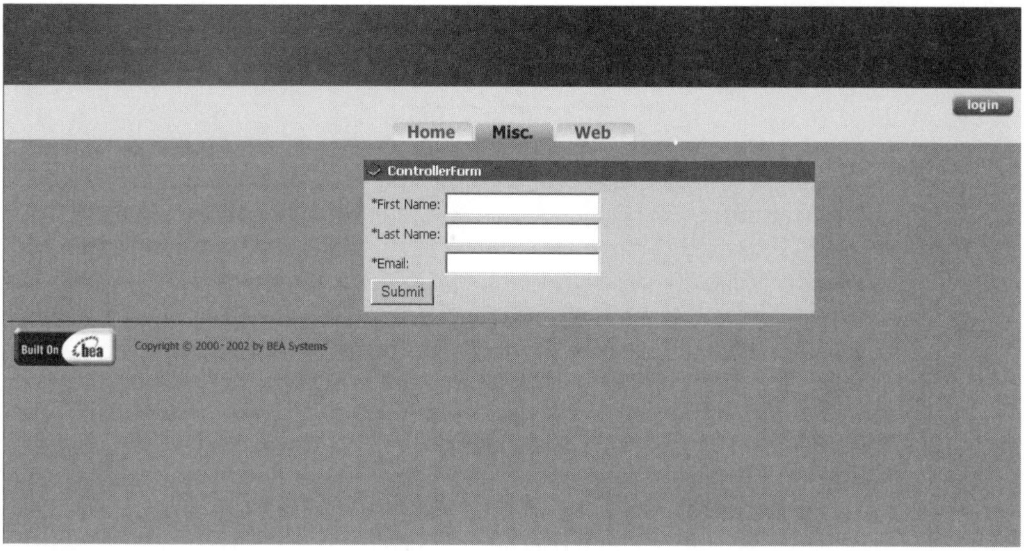

Figure 9-2. The ControllerForm portlet

If you were to click the Submit button at this point, validation would certainly not succeed. This action would result in the error messages being displayed in one of the two manners mentioned previously. Figures 9-3 and 9-4 display error messages using the getErrorMessage() method and the getFieldError() method, respectively.

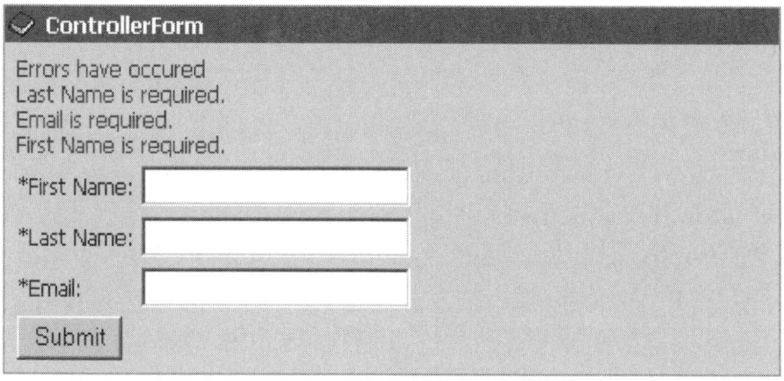

Figure 9-3. Block of error messages

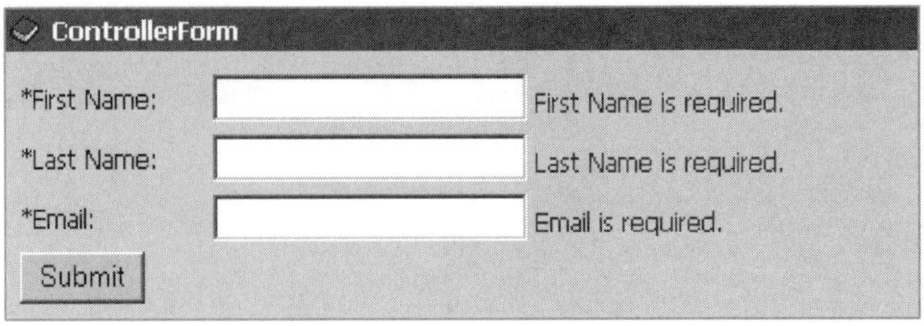

Figure 9-4. Field error messages

In this example, you can see by examining the isValid() method of UserController that not only are all of the fields required, but the email address field also must be entered in a proper format. When validation fails and the user is returned to the misc page to correct errors, it is common practice to repopulate the fields so that the user need not reenter all of the data again, valid or not. The information is gathered from UserBean, which has been placed within the request object via introspection. Figure 9-5 displays a repopulated form with an e-mail validation error.

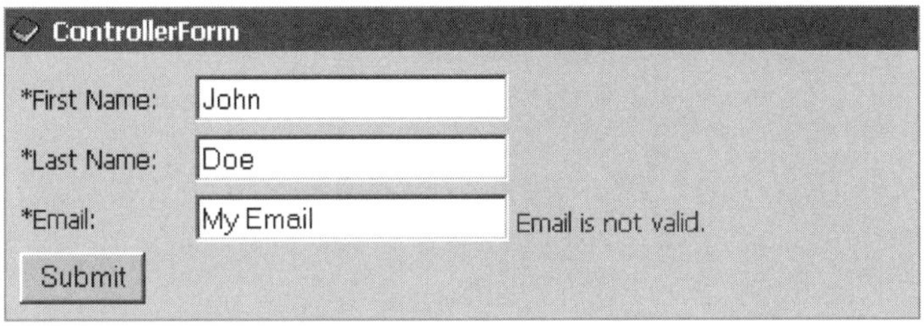

Figure 9-5. Repopulated form

Finally, after the user enters all field data correctly, the UserController servlet forwards the user to the home page. Again, depending on the configuration of the page, the home page should somewhat resemble the one in Figure 9-6. The ControllerDisplay portlet, like the ControllerForm portlet, gathers the user information via UserBean within the request.

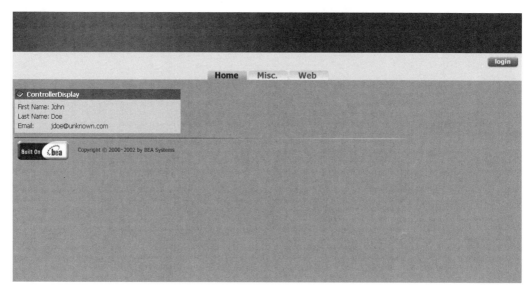

Figure 9-6. The ControllerDisplay portlet

Summary

Although the Webflow mechanism implemented in the BEA WebLogic Portal is useful, you are not required to use it. You may not be comfortable with the level of abstraction created by Webflow, or you may not be fond of using a visual editor to piece together the flow of business logic. In these cases, a Front Controller strategy can take the place of all that is accomplished by Webflow.

CHAPTER 10

EJBs Within the Portal

THE TOPIC OF THIS CHAPTER, Enterprise JavaBeans (EJBs), is a broad one. In fact, many books have been written on EJBs. The purpose of this chapter is to give simple instructions on creating, deploying, and using EJBs within the WebLogic Portal Server. It is not our intention to give comprehensive coverage of EJBs. This chapter will give you a basic understanding of EJBs and how they can be used in the WebLogic Portal Server to provide distributed functionality. Though we touch on all the types of EJBs in this chapter, our examples and discussions mainly focus on stateless session beans. After reading this chapter, you will be able to create distributed EJB functionality in your application by following the examples provided here.

EJB Overview

EJBs are Java objects that can be executed remotely to perform functionality for your application. Enterprise JavaBeans, a Java standard, were developed to provide interoperability among disparate environments. Because EJBs are based on a standard followed by all vendors who support EJBs, these objects can be reused across vendor platforms without changing your code.

One of the concepts integral to EJBs is the *container*. An EJB is executed within an EJB container. The container takes care of things like security, persistence, concurrency, and transaction management. This allows the developer to focus on functionality and defer to the container to handle those items. Each vendor may have a slightly different approach to implementing the container functionality. However, because vendors as well as EJB developers follow the EJB standard, interoperability is maintained regardless of the container implementation.

EJBs deployed to a WebLogic server have the benefit of access to WebLogic system services. Since the container for a WebLogic EJB is the WebLogic Server, services such as security, database connection management, Java messaging, and others are easily accessible to the EJB.

EJB Types

The WebLogic Portal Server supports the following types of EJBs specified in the J2EE specification:

- *Stateless session:* These objects provide distributed functionality to a client without saving any data or state information from call to call. These EJBs are not tied to a client or a session. Any client can use any instance of these EJBs.

- *Stateful session:* These objects store state information from call to call. Each client that calls this type of EJB is associated with a specific instance of the EJB.

- *Entity:* This type of EJB stores and retrieves persistent data from the data store using a primary key as a unique identifier. The data store can be a SQL database or file system or any other type of storage system.

- *Message-driven:* This type of EJB acts as a message consumer within the Java Message Service (JMS) to perform distributed functionality. The WebLogic Server container directly interacts with a message-driven bean by creating bean instances and passing JMS messages to those instances as necessary.

- *EJB classes:* An EJB consists of three class files that are used by the container to instantiate the remote object and execute it.

- *Home interface:* This object type is used to find the EJB within the network and retrieve a reference to it. Once the home object is found either in the JNDI directory or within the context of the local server, a reference to the remote interface can be created to call the business methods of the EJB.

- *Remote interface:* This object type is used by the client to reference the remote object and execute its functionality.

- *Bean class:* This class implements the functionality of the EJB object on the remote server.

EJB Descriptor Files

EJB descriptor files basically tell the container about the EJB objects contained within an EJB jar file. There are standard descriptor files and container-specific descriptor files. Because the container implementation may differ among vendors, vendor-specific EJB descriptor files may differ among vendors as well. However, the EJB code should be standard across vendors.

Stateless Session Bean Example

In the following example, we demonstrate how to create, deploy, and execute a stateless session bean. For our example, we use the same functionality that you saw in Chapter 4, where we created a portlet, named firstPortlet, to retrieve presidents' names from a file and display those names as links. In the EJB example that follows, we show you how to take the code from that portlet and move it to an EJB.

Creating the EJB Classes

Figure 10-1 shows the project directory for the example EJB as well as the three Java source files.

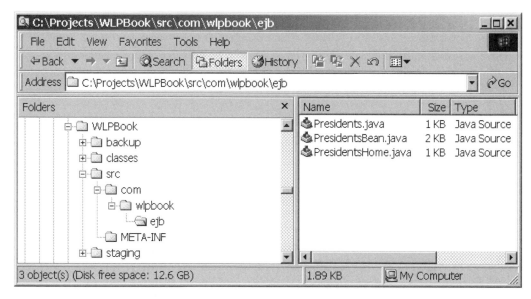

Figure 10-1. Project source directory

Notice that we named the Java files according to their position within the EJB standard. PresidentsHome.java contains the home interface, Presidents.java contains the remote interface, and PresidentsBean.java contains the bean class source code.

Creating the EJB Home Interface

Following is the code for the home interface. Notice that it only contains one method declaration, for the create method. The create method creates an instance of the remote object. Notice that it returns an instance of an object defined by our remote interface. You will see how this is used when we execute the EJB from our portlet.

```
package com.wlpbook.ejb;

public interface PresidentsHome extends javax.ejb.EJBHome
{
    Presidents create() throws
        java.rmi.RemoteException, javax.ejb.CreateException;
}
```

Creating the EJB Remote Interface

The remote interface, shown in the code that follows, defines all the methods and attributes contained in the EJB bean class. The client uses the remote interface to execute the code within the remote object. The remote interface tells the client everything it needs to know about the remote object to execute it and retrieve results from it.

```
package com.wlpbook.ejb;

import java.util.*;

public interface Presidents extends javax.ejb.EJBObject {

  public ArrayList getData()
        throws java.rmi.RemoteException;
}
```

Creating the EJB Bean Class

The EJB bean class is the implementation of the EJB functionality. Listing 10-1 shows the Java code for the PresidentsBean class.

Listing 10-1. PresidentsBean Class

```
package com.wlpbook.ejb;

import java.rmi.*;
import java.util.*;
import java.io.*;

public class PresidentsBean implements javax.ejb.SessionBean
{

    private javax.ejb.SessionContext m_context;

    public PresidentsBean()
    {
    }

    public ArrayList getData()
                throws java.rmi.RemoteException{



      BufferedReader br = null;
      ArrayList names = new ArrayList();

      String record = null;
      int recCount = 0;

      try{

                InputStreamReader isr = new InputStreamReader(
                    getClass().getResourceAsStream("presidents.txt"), "ASCII");
                br = new BufferedReader(isr);

            while ((record = br.readLine()) != null) {
                names.add(record);
      }
        } catch (IOException e) {
          // catch possible io errors from readLine()
```

```
                System.out.println("IOException error!");
                e.printStackTrace();
        }
        finally
        {
            try {
                    if (br != null) br.close();
            }
            catch (IOException ignore) {}
        }
        return names;
    }
/** required methods
These methods are used by the container during the life cycle of the EJB
For this example there is no need for code in these methods
**/

    public void setSessionContext( javax.ejb.SessionContext context ) throws
        java.rmi.RemoteException
    {
        m_context = context;
    }

    public void ejbCreate() throws
        java.rmi.RemoteException, javax.ejb.CreateException
    {
    }

    public void ejbRemove() throws
        java.rmi.RemoteException
    {
    }

    public void ejbPassivate() throws
        java.rmi.RemoteException
    {
    }

    public void ejbActivate()throws
        java.rmi.RemoteException
    {
    }
}
```

Notice that our example has one method, getData(). Notice also that this method corresponds to the declaration of the method in the remote interface. This is the same code that we used in the portlet JSP in Chapter 4, and it retrieves the presidents' names from the file and returns them in an ArrayList for use by the portlet.

Notice that this EJB implements the SessionBean interface. This class contains the functionality for the getData() method, but it also contains several methods that are used by the container to manage our session bean.

Compiling the EJB Classes

Although it is our preference to use a more robust tool for developing, compiling, and archiving Java classes, we use the command line tools provided by the JDK for this example to allow you to see the whole process required to build and deploy an EJB.

We use the following javac command to compile Java code into class files:

```
javac -classpath C:\bea\weblogic700\server\lib\weblogic.jar;classes -sourcepath
src -d classes
src\com\wlpbook\ejb\*.java
```

Some things you should note about this command:

- We include the -classpath option to point the compiler to the weblogic.jar, since we are using the WebLogic environment to run our code, and to point the compiler to our classes directory so that all three classes can see each other at compile time.

- The -sourcepath option tells the compiler to look in the src directory for our source code.

- The -d option tells the compiler to output the compiled classes to the classes directory.

- The last argument indicates the files we want to compile.

Figure 10-2 shows the class files that were created by this compile command.

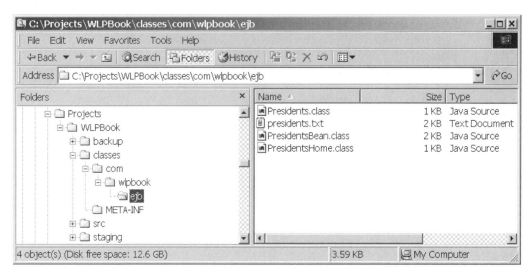

Figure 10-2. Project class files

Creating EJB Deployment Descriptors

The next step is to create the EJB deployment descriptors. In our case, we create two deployment descriptors ejb-jar.xml and weblogic-ejb-jar.xml. Figure 10-3 shows the XML descriptors, in the META-INF directory, which is at the root of the classes directory. We place this directory and the deployment descriptors here so that they can be archived into the jar file in this same structure relative to the classes that we created previously.

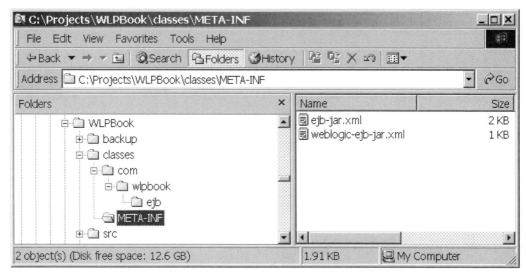

Figure 10-3. META-INF project directory

ejb-jar.xml

The ejb-jar.xml file describes the EJB to the container. We've only included the options that are required to deploy our example EJB in Listing 10-2.

Listing 10-2. ejb-jar.xml for Presidents EJB

```xml
<?xml version="1.0"?>

<!DOCTYPE ejb-jar PUBLIC
'-//Sun Microsystems, Inc.//DTD Enterprise JavaBeans 2.0//EN'
'http://java.sun.com/dtd/ejb-jar_2_0.dtd'>

<ejb-jar>
  <enterprise-beans>
    <session>
      <ejb-name>Presidents</ejb-name>
      <home>com.wlpbook.ejb.PresidentsHome</home>
      <remote>com.wlpbook.ejb.Presidents</remote>
      <ejb-class>com.wlpbook.ejb.PresidentsBean</ejb-class>
      <session-type>Stateless</session-type>
      <transaction-type>Container</transaction-type>
    </session>
  </enterprise-beans>
  <assembly-descriptor>
```

```
    <container-transaction>
      <method>
        <ejb-name>Presidents</ejb-name>
            <method-name>*</method-name>
      </method>
      <trans-attribute>Required</trans-attribute>
    </container-transaction>
  </assembly-descriptor>
  <ejb-client-jar>WLPEjb_client.jar</ejb-client-jar>
</ejb-jar>
```

The <enterprise-beans> node describes all the Enterprise Java Beans in the jar file. Our session bean is described by the <session> tag.

The <ejb-name> tag can be any name; however, you should be consistent with this name throughout your own deployment descriptors.

The <home>, <remote>, and <ejb-class> nodes specify the home interface, remote interface, and bean class names that we created earlier. The container uses these class names to instantiate and reference the EJB in the deployed environment.

The <session-type> tag specifies that we are deploying a stateless session EJB. If we were deploying a stateful session bean, we would specify that by using the value Stateful in this tag.

The <transaction-type> tag specifies that this is a container-managed EJB.

The <method> tag describes the methods that the container should expose to the outside world. In this example, we only have one method. Note that we use * to indicate that we want all methods in this EJB to be exposed. If you want a limited number of methods exposed from your EJB, specify the methods that you want to make available in the <method-name> tag for each EJB that you are deploying.

Note also that we specify with the <ejb-client-jar> tag that we want to generate a client. This causes the EJBC application to generate a client jar file. If you will be referencing your EJB from a Java client application or some other application outside of this virtual machine, you may want to generate a client jar. This jar will contain all the files necessary for a client application to reference this EJB. Since our example is a portlet running in the same virtual machine, this option is not required.

weblogic-ejb-jar.xml

The weblogic-ejb-jar.xml file shown in this section is a WebLogic-specific descriptor that describes the EJBs contained in a jar. Notice that the <ejb-name> tag contains the same value that we used to name the EJB in ejb-jar.xml. Place an entry inside the <weblogic-enterprise-bean> node for each EJB that you are deploying.

Notice that for our EJB we specify a value in the <jndi-name> node. This is the value that the server will use to find the EJB in the directory when it is referenced, and it can be any value in your environment. For our example, we use the fully qualified class name with dot notation.

```
<?xml version="1.0"?>

<!DOCTYPE weblogic-ejb-jar PUBLIC
'-//BEA Systems, Inc.//DTD WebLogic 7.0.0 EJB//EN'
'http://www.bea.com/servers/wls700/dtd/weblogic-ejb-jar.dtd'>

<weblogic-ejb-jar>

  <weblogic-enterprise-bean>

    <ejb-name>Presidents</ejb-name>
    <jndi-name>com.wlpbook.ejb.Presidents</jndi-name>

  </weblogic-enterprise-bean>

</weblogic-ejb-jar>
```

Archiving the EJB Classes

Like other applications and components within the WebLogic environment, you can deploy an EJB in exploded or archived format. For this example, we want to deploy our EJB in archived format. Following is the command to archive our EJB classes. Notice we use the jar utility from the Java JDK. Also, when the command is finished, it is returned to the prompt without any output because there were no errors.

```
c:\bea\jdk131\bin\jar -cf WLPEjb.jar -C classes
```

The -c option tells the jar utility to create a new archive file, and the -f option specifies the filename to create. The -C option (note the capital C) tells the utility to change to the directory specified as the first item after this option and to archive the file(s) specified as the second item after this option. We want the package structure in our archive to start at the root of our archive. Since we are running this command from our project directory, we need to archive to compensate for this. With this option, we also specify that we want the utility to archive all the files and subdirectories of the classes directory by using the dot (.).

Generating Container Classes

We've now shown you how to create a standard EJB and archive it. This is basically the process you would follow to create an EJB on any application server. To deploy an EJB to the WebLogic Portal Server, you must generate some WebLogic-specific files that the portal server will use to reference and execute the functionality within the EJB.

To do this in our example, we use the EJBC utility, which is provided with the WebLogic Portal Server. This utility is a Java program, so we use java.exe to execute it. Following is the command syntax that generates the required files within our archive:

```
C:\bea\jdk131\bin\java -cp C:\bea\weblogic700\server\lib\weblogic.jar;
weblogic.ejbc WLPEjb.jar WLPEjb_wl.jar
```

The -cp option places the weblogic.jar into the class path. The second parameter is the class that we are executing (weblogic.ejbc). The third and fourth parameters are the parameters for the ejbc class. The first is the input archive file and the second is the output archive file. Notice that we are using different output filenames for our example. This is not required, but it is good practice, as it allows you to reuse the jar file without the ejbc-generated items if necessary.

NOTE   *The ejbc utility displays a message indicating the results when it is completed.*

If you open the archive, you can see the files that the ejbc utility has generated. Figure 10-4 shows a WinZip window displaying ejbc-generated files. Notice that this file contains the class files and deployment descriptors that we previously created and archived as well as some ejbc-generated files.

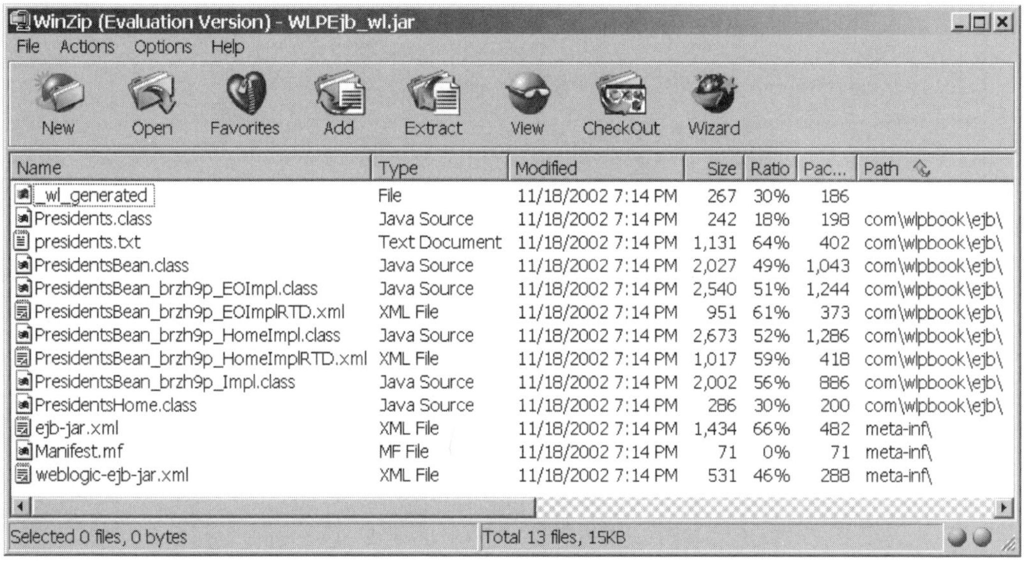

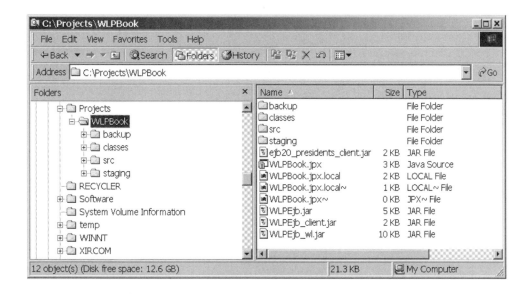

Figure 10-4. ejbc files

The Explorer window in Figure 10-5 shows the results of the process that we've followed so far. Notice the source directory that we started with and the classes directory that was created when we compiled the code. The WLBEjb.jar file is the jar file created by the archive process. Finally, notice the WLBEjb_wl.jar file. This is the file that we will be deploying to the WebLogic Portal Server.

Figure 10-5. Project results

Deploying EJB Jar File

Now that we've created an EJB and made it ready to deploy, we can deploy it to the portal server. The following steps walk you through this process:

1. As shown in Figure 10-6, copy the WLBEjb_wl.jar to the portalApp directory.

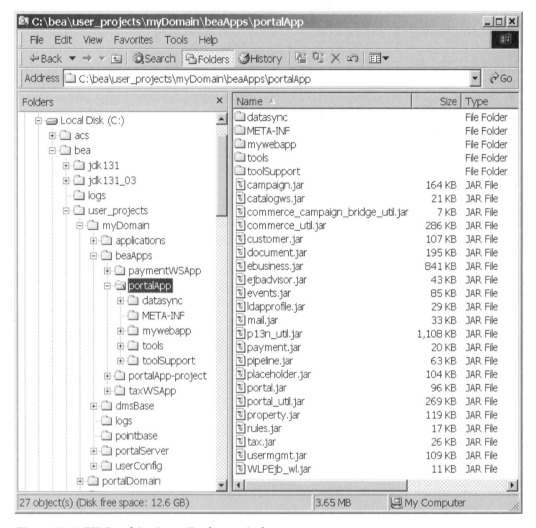

Figure 10-6. EJBC archive in an Explorer window

2. Log in to the WebLogic Server Console. Browse to
   http://*server:port*/console and enter the user ID and password that
   you created using the Domain Configuration Wizard in Chapter 4. In our
   case, we use weblogic for the user ID and weblogic for the password.

3. Navigate to the myDomain/Deployments/Applications/portalApp node
   of the navigation tree as shown in Figure 10-7. Click the Edit Application
   Descriptor link. This opens the Application Descriptor editor window in
   a new browser.

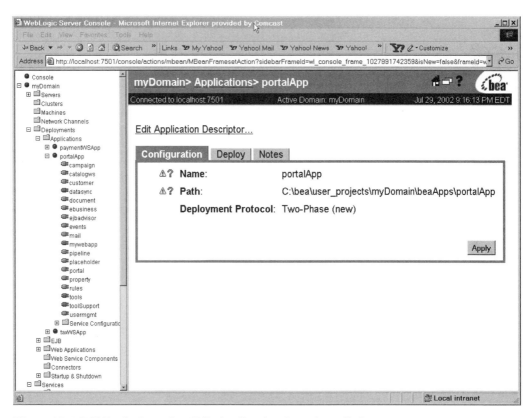

Figure 10-7. WebLogic Console—Edit Application Descriptor link

4. Select the BEA Portal Application ➤ EJB Modules node from the navigation tree in the Application Descriptor editor window. Click the Configure a new EJBModule link as shown in Figure 10-8.

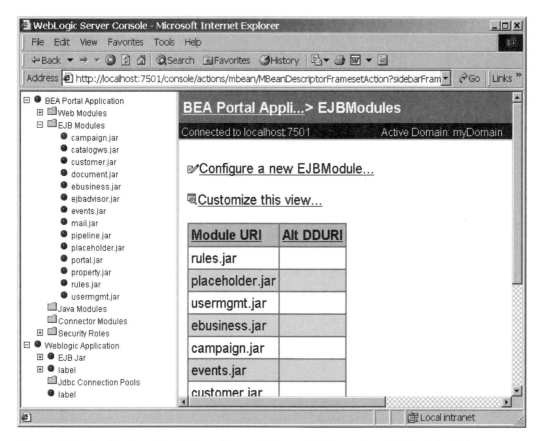

Figure 10-8. Application Descriptor editor window—Configure New EJBModule link

5. Enter the jar name, WLPEjb_wl.jar, in the Module URI field and leave the Alt DDURI field blank as shown in Figure 10-9. Click the Create button.

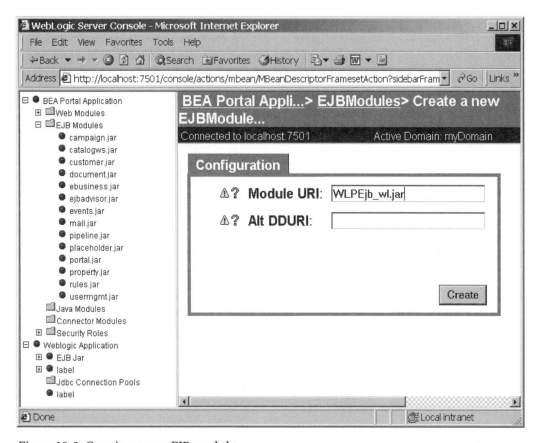

Figure 10-9. Creating a new EJB module

6. Now navigate to the top node of the navigation tree in the Application Descriptor editor window and click the Persist button in the right pane as shown in Figure 10-10.

NOTE   *This will cause the WebLogic Server to save the information you just entered into the portalApp/META-INF/application.xml file.*

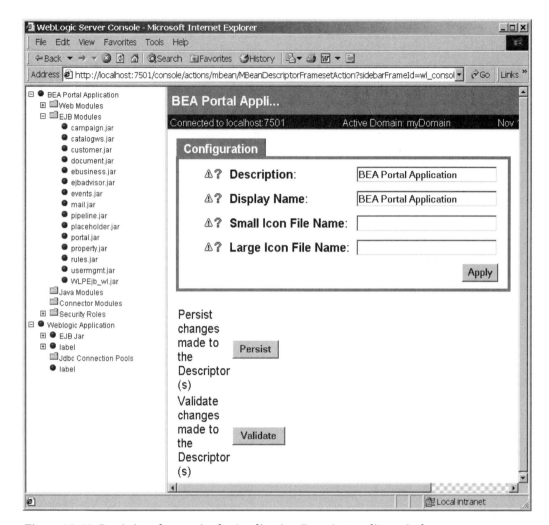

Figure 10-10. Persisting changes in the Application Descriptor editor window

7. Close the Application Descriptor editor window.

8. Figure 10-11 shows the main WebLogic Server Console window. Clicking the Undeploy Application button undeploys the portalApp enterprise application. You need to scroll all the way down in the right-hand pane to see this button. You then click the Deploy Application button to redeploy the portalApp enterprise application.

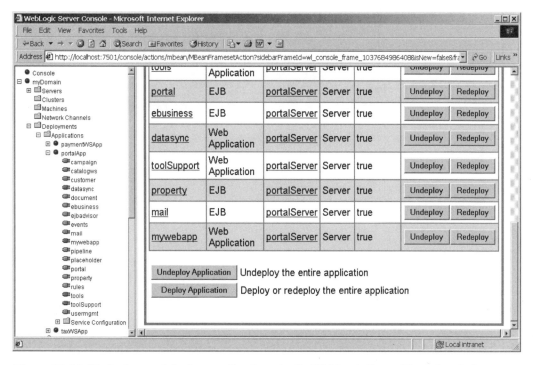

Figure 10-11. Undeploy and deploy applications in the WebLogic Server Console window.

9. Refresh the browser window. This allows the browser to display the EJB that you just entered into the application descriptor.

10. Navigate to the myDomain ➤ Deployments ➤ Applications ➤ portal App ➤ WLPEjb_wl.jar node in the navigation tree of the console window. Select the Targets tab, move portalServer from the Available list to the Chosen list, and click the Apply button (see Figure 10-12). This makes the new EJB available to be deployed on the portalServer.

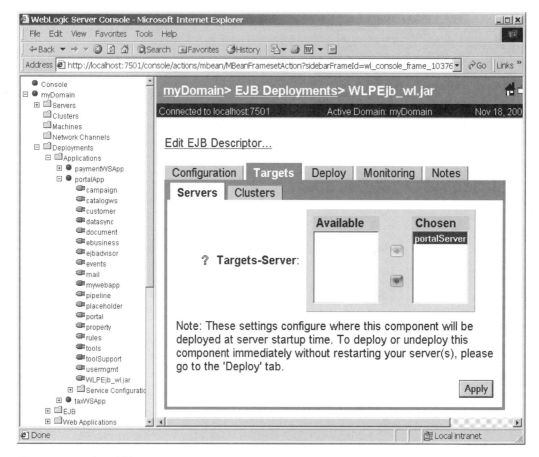

Figure 10-12. Specifying target servers

11. Finally, go to the Deploy tab shown in Figure 10-12 and deploy the EJB by clicking the Deploy button.

Building the EJB Client Code

Once you have built your EJB and deployed it, you need to build the client code to access its functionality. The client for your EJB could be anything. For example, it could be a Java application running on a user's desktop or a servlet. For this example, we modify the presidents portlet we created in Chapter 4 to call the EJB for the data instead of reading it within the portlet, as shown in Listing 10-3. If you are following along with our example, use this code to replace the code in the content.jsp file in the firstPortlet directory.

Listing 10-3. Modified Presidents Portlet JSP Code

```
<%@ page import="java.util.*"%>
<%@ page import="java.io.*"%>
<%@ page import="javax.naming.*"%>
<%@ page import="com.wlpbook.ejb.*"%>

<%

    // Declare the names ArrayList
    ArrayList names = null;

    // Get the initial context
    Context initialContext = new InitialContext();

    // Get the presidents home object from the initial context
    PresidentsHome presidentsHome =
        (PresidentsHome) initialContext.lookup("com.wlpbook.ejb.Presidents");

    // Get the presidents remote object
    Presidents presidents = presidentsHome.create();

    // Use the remote object to call the ejb method
    names = presidents.getData();

%>

<table width=100%>
<%

String rowclass = "row1";
String item = null;

Iterator i = names.iterator();
while (i.hasNext()) {
        item = (String)i.next();

%>
<tr class='<%=rowclass%>'><td><%= item %></td></tr>

<%

        // Alternate row class
        if(rowclass.equals("row1")){
                        rowclass = "row2";
        }
```

```
        else{
                    rowclass = "row1";
        }
}
%>
</table>
```

We first get a reference to InitialContext. With this reference, we get a reference to the home object (PresidentsHome) in the EJB. Notice that the string used in the lookup method is the value that we included in the jndi-name element of the weblogic-ejb-jar.xml file. For this value, we use the class name of the remote interface. You could specify any value here as long as you are consistent in the descriptor and the call.

With the home object, we use the create method to create an object of type Presidents. This is the remote interface that we create in our EJB. Using this reference, we can call any of the methods in the EJB that we made available in the remote interface class.

For our example, we call the getData() method to get the ArrayList of formatted president names. From this point on, our example is the same as the portlet we created previously.

Summary

In this chapter, we discussed the basics of EJBs, and we created a simple stateless session EJB. This showed how you can take portal functionality and move it to an EJB to provide distributed functionality. In our example, the EJB was deployed within the same server as the portal itself; however, in a production environment you could use this technology to balance the processing among the resources that are available.

CHAPTER 11

Portal Security

DEPENDING ON THE NATURE of the portal that you are building, you may need to add
security to it. You can use portal security to allow users to access the entire portal
or selected portions of the portal. You can also use security to allow different levels of access to the user group that a user belongs to.

In this chapter, we discuss how to manage portal users and groups and how
to manage portal access. In previous chapters, we talked about creating portals,
pages, and portlets. For our discussion here, we have set up our example portal
with three pages, each page having one portlet on it. Figure 11-1 shows our portal
with tabs for each page therein.

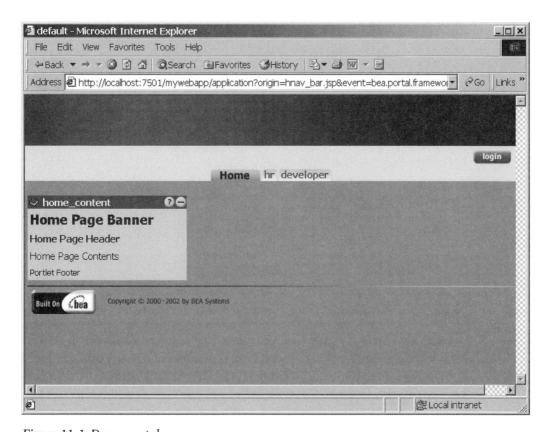

Figure 11-1. Demo portal

User Management

If your portal is a public portal with no access control, then you don't necessarily need to create any users for your portal. However, if your portal requires access control for the whole portal or portions of the portal, you need to create users.

The following steps show how to create users within the WebLogic Portal:

1. In your browser go to the following url:
    http://*server*:*port*/portalAppTools.

2. Log in using administrator/password as the user ID and password, respectively.

3. From the Administration Tools main window, click the User Management link as shown in Figure 11-2.

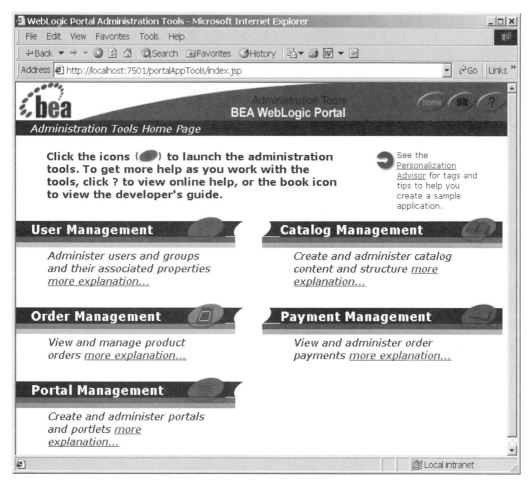

Figure 11-2. Administration Tools main window

4. From the User Management main window, choose the create users link on the user management bar as shown in Figure 11-3.

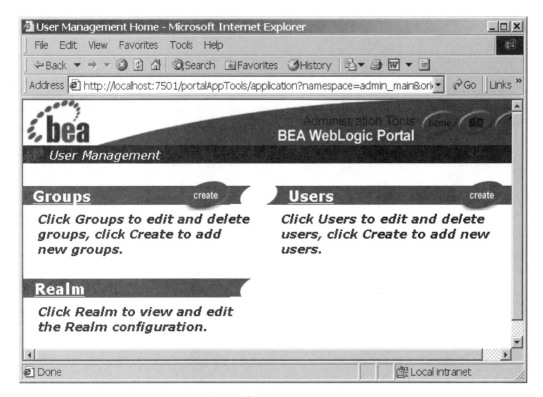

Figure 11-3. User Management main window

5. From the Create New Users window, shown in Figure 11-4, enter the information for the new user and click the create link.

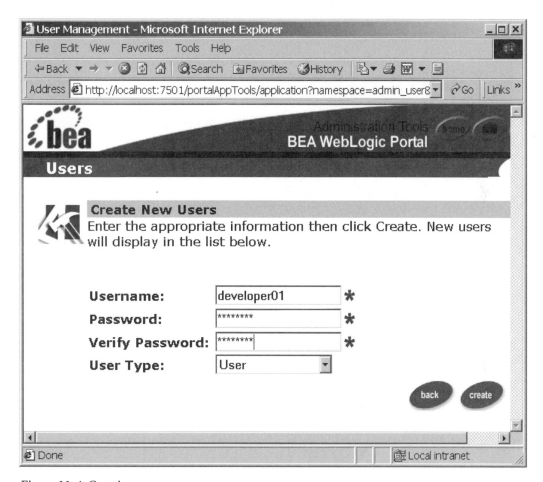

Figure 11-4. Creating a new user

For our access control example, we add three developer users (developer01, developer02, developer03) and three hr users (hr01, hr02, hr03). If you are following along, repeat the steps in this section for each user.

Group Management

Instead of specifying access control for each user in the portal, we specify access levels for groups of users. This will allow us to more easily manage user access within the portal.

Creating Groups

The following steps show how to create new groups of users within the WebLogic Portal:

1. From the User Management main window, click the create group link on the Group Management bar.

2. Choose to add a new group to the top level as shown in Figure 11-5 or click one of the groups to drill down and add the new group as a sub-group.

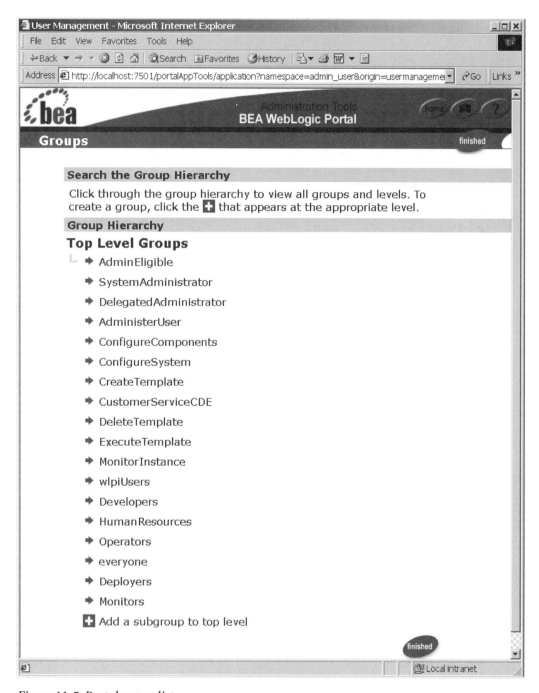

Figure 11-5. Portal group list

3. Enter the new group name in the Group Name text box as shown in Figure 11-6 and click the create link.

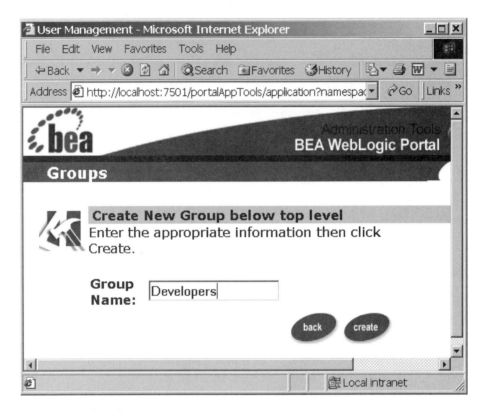

Figure 11-6. Creating a new group

To add other groups to the WebLogic Portal, repeat the preceding steps. For our access control example, we add two groups, Developers and HumanResources. If you are following along, go ahead and create these groups before moving on to the next section.

Adding Users to Groups

The next step is to associate the users that we created earlier with these new groups. The steps that follow show how to add a user to an existing group:

1. From the User Management main window, click the Groups link.

2. From the Group Hierarchy window, shown in Figure 11-7, click the group that you want to manage.

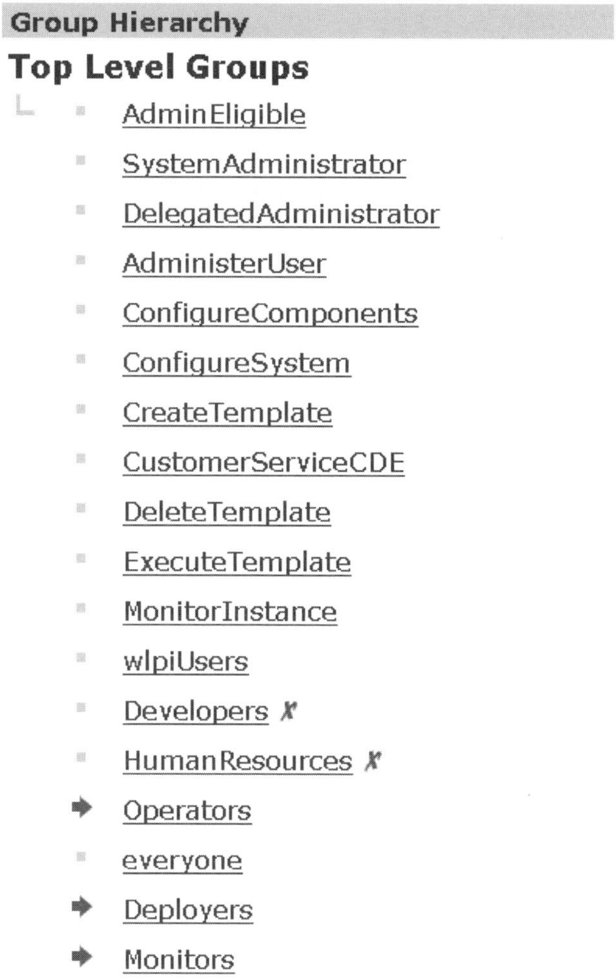

Group Hierarchy

Top Level Groups

- AdminEligible
- SystemAdministrator
- DelegatedAdministrator
- AdministerUser
- ConfigureComponents
- ConfigureSystem
- CreateTemplate
- CustomerServiceCDE
- DeleteTemplate
- ExecuteTemplate
- MonitorInstance
- wlpiUsers
- Developers 𝑋
- HumanResources 𝑋
- Operators
- everyone
- Deployers
- Monitors

Figure 11-7. Group list

3. Click the +/- image next to the Add/Remove Users From Group.

4. From the Group Management window, shown in Figure 11-8, use the search box or the letter search to find the users you want to add to the group.

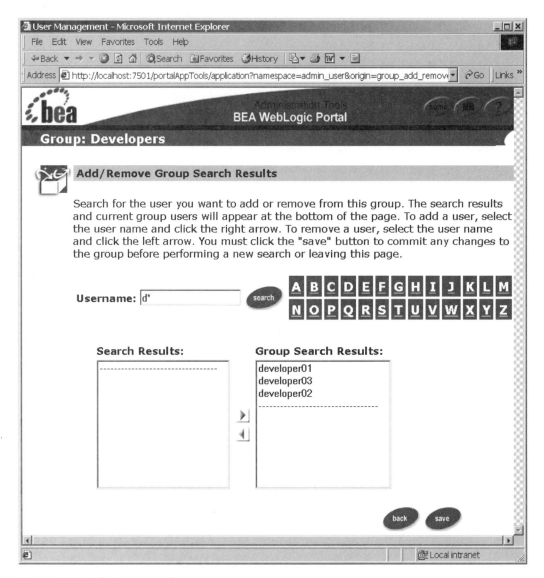

Figure 11-8. Selecting users for a group

5. Move the users you want to add to the group to the Group Search Results list and click the save link.

Access Control with Group Portals

A *group portal* is a set of pages and portlets and other portal resources that is associated with a portal user group. This association of portal resources with a user group defines the portal access for the user group.

When you create a portal, a default group portal is generated automatically. The default group portal is associated with the everyone group. In previous chapters we used this default group portal to define the pages and portlets that were available in the portal. Since the default group portal is associated with the everyone group, the portals that we created previously were public access portals.

Now that we have created users and groups for our portal, we can set up access control for the portal using group portals in the same way that we associated portal resources with the default group portal.

The following steps show how to create a new group portal:

1. From the Administration Tools main window, click the Portal Management link.

2. Click the Create group portal link on the Portal Management Home page, shown in Figure 11-9.

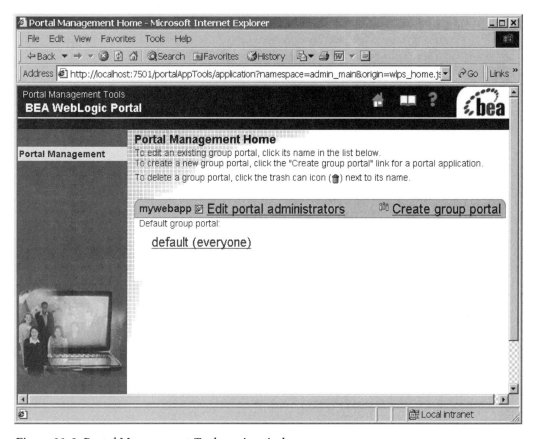

Figure 11-9. Portal Management Tools main window

3. From the Create Group Portal window, enter the group portal display name as shown in Figure 11-10.

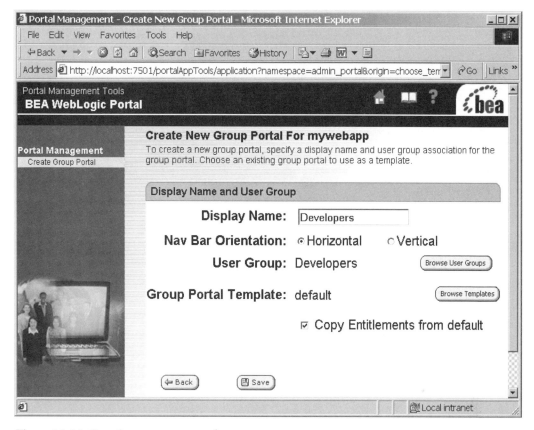

Figure 11-10. Creating a group portal

4. Specify the nav bar orientation—in this example, we select the Horizontal option.

5. Using the Browse User Groups button, select the user group that will be associated with the group portal.

6. Select a template to associate with this group portal.

7. Click the Save button to save the new group portal.

In the preceding example, we created a group portal associated with the Developers group. To create other group portals, repeat the previous steps. For our access control demo, we also create a group portal associated with the HumanResources group.

Now that we've created our group portals, we can set up the access controls for them. In Figure 11-11, you can see the group portals that we have created.

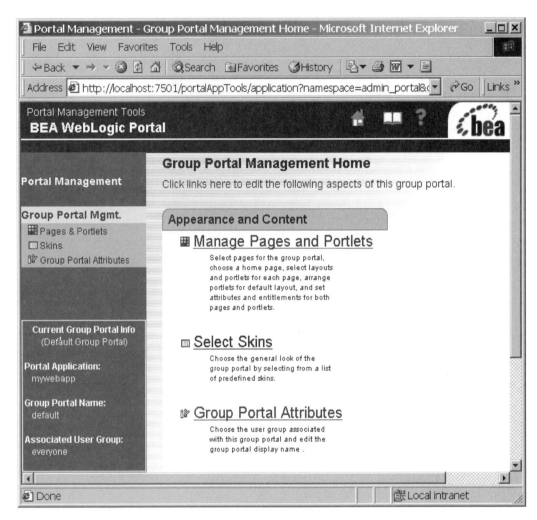

Figure 11-11. Group portal list

The following steps show how to set up the access control for a group portal.

1.   Select the group portal that you want to manage as shown in
     Figure 11-11. We will first assign resources to the default group portal.

2.   Select the Manage Pages and Portlets link as shown in Figure 11-12.

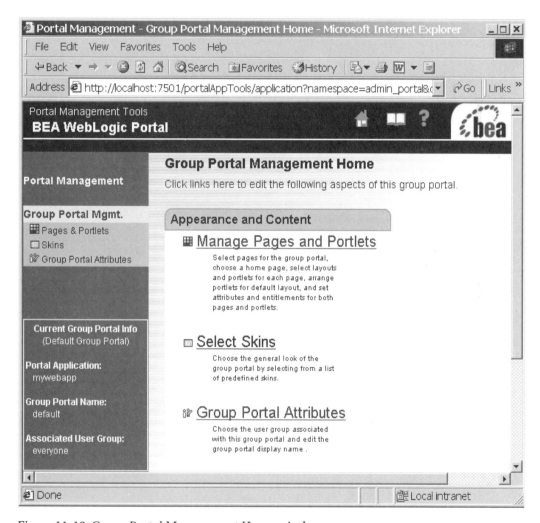

Figure 11-12. Group Portal Management Home window

3. Click the Select and Order Pages link as shown in Figure 11-13.

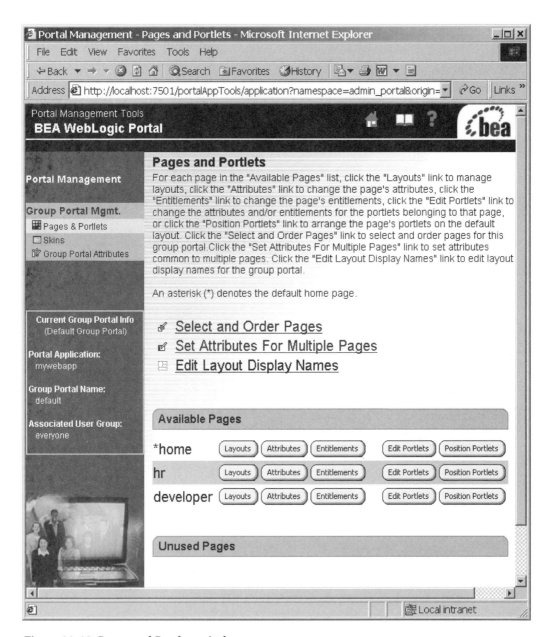

Figure 11-13. Pages and Portlets window

4. Select the pages that you want to be associated with the everyone group and click the Save button as shown in Figure 11-14. For our example, we want the everyone group to only have access to the home page.

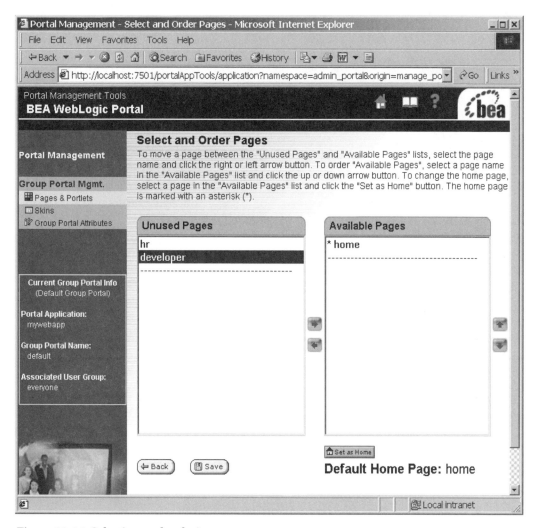

Figure 11-14. Selecting and ordering pages

In the same way that we assigned pages to the default (everyone) group portal, we could also assign portlets, skins, and other resources to the newly created group portal by clicking the appropriate links from the Group Portal Management window.

To assign resources to other group portals, repeat these steps. For our example, we also assign pages to the other two group portals as shown in Table 11-1.

Table 11-1. Group Portal Page Assignments

GROUP PORTAL	PAGES
Developers	home, developer
HumanResources	home, hr

NOTE *Make sure that the visible attribute is set for each of the pages here.*

Figure 11-15 shows our portal home page. Notice that the hr and developer tabs are not visible because we have not logged in as a user yet.

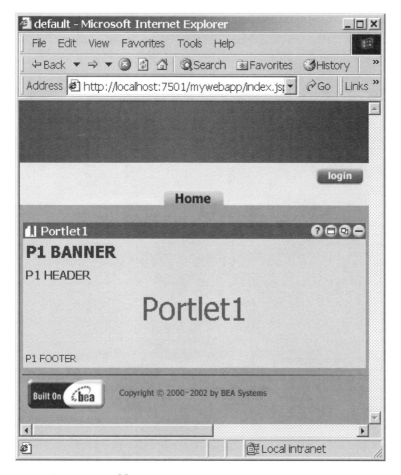

Figure 11-15. Demo portal home page

Now click the login button and log in through the Portal Login window as shown in Figure 11-16.

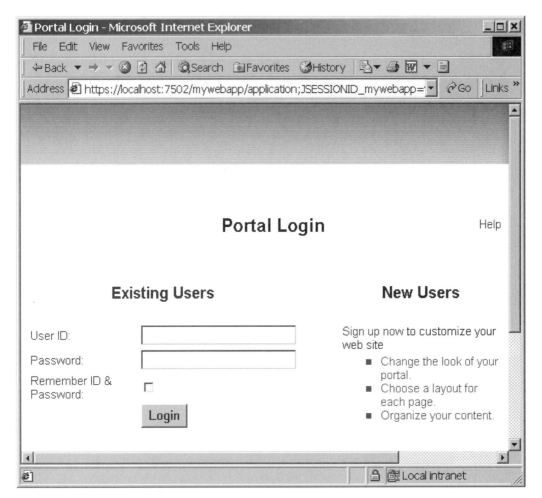

Figure 11-16. Portal Login Window for our demo portal

Let's say we log in as an hr user. Notice in Figure 11-17 that we now have access to the hr tab and can navigate to the hr page.

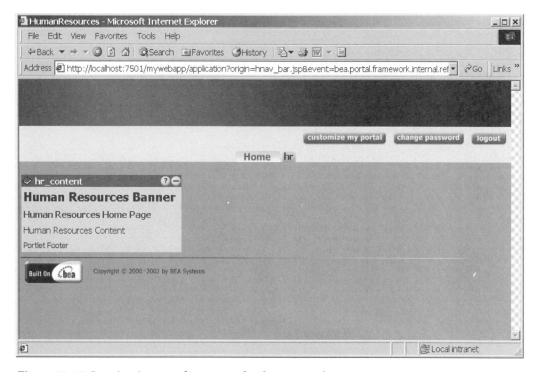

Figure 11-17. Logging in as an hr user to the demo portal

Access Control Using Entitlements

Entitlements are rules that can be set up in the EBCC. The WebLogic Portal can use these rules to determine whether or not and in which circumstances to display a portal page. You can use these rules to control access to pages within the portal.

For our example, we discuss how to create an entitlement that will determine whether a user has a specific value for a user profile attribute. User profile properties are discussed in Chapter 13. This discussion will assume that a user profile attribute named hrtest exists.

Creating an Entitlement

To create and manage entitlements, you must use the EBCC. The following steps show how to create a new entitlement within the EBCC:

1. From the File menu, select New ➤ Presentation ➤ Entitlement Segment. The Entitlement Editor window will display in the right-hand pane of the EBCC.

2. Click the Edit button in the Entitlement Editor.

3. In the Conditions pane of the pop-up window that appears, select the condition "The visitor has specific characteristics".

4. In the Actions pane of the pop-up window, select the characteristics link. This brings up the actions pop-up window.

5. Select the visitor property set that the hrtest visitor property was created in.

6. Select the hrtest visitor property.

7. Click the Add button, which will bring up another window.

8. From the pop-up window that appears, specify that "hrtest is equal to true".

9. Click the Add button.

10. Click the OK button to close the window and return the condition to the previous window.

11. Click the OK button to close the next window.

12. Click the OK button to close the next window and return the new rule to the entitlement.

13. Select Save from the File menu and save the entitlement as HREntitlement.

14. Use the synchronize functionality within the EBCC to synchronize the new entitlement with the WebLogic Portal Server.

Implementing the Entitlement

Once you create an entitlement within the portal, you must use the portalAppTools application to implement access control using the entitlement. In this section, we discuss how to associate a new entitlement to a page to control access to the page.

The following steps show how to set up access control in portalAppTools using the entitlement discussed in the previous section.

NOTE *If you followed the example for controlling access using group portals, you will need to remove the Developers and HumanResources group portals and add the hr page to the default portal before continuing on with this example.*

---

1. From the main window in portalAppTools, click the Portal Management link.

2. Click the default portal link

3. Click the Manage Portlets and Pages link.

4. Click the Entitlements button next to the hr page.

5. From the Set Page Entitlements page, click the Add or Remove Entitlement Segments link.

6. Move HREntitlementSegment to the Selected Entitlement Segments pane by using the right arrow button.

7. Select the Save button to save your selection.

8. For the EVERONE entitlement segment, select the Deny privilege for Can See and Can Remove.

9. Verify that for the HREntitlementSegment the Grant privilege is selected for Can See and Can Remove.

10. Click the Save button.

NOTE *This example assumes that the hrtest user profile property has been set to true for users who can see the hr page. For information on managing User Profile Properties, see Chapter 13.*

Now that we've created an entitlement using the EBCC and we've associated that entitlement with a page, access to that page will be controlled by the rules defined in the entitlement. In the case of our example, you will see that when you browse to the portal without logging in, the tab for the hr page does not appear. If you log in as a user with the hrtest property set to true, you will see the tab for the hr page and can navigate to it.

Controlling Access to Portlets

Another way to control access to the portal is by requiring a user to be authenticated before a portlet can be displayed. This is accomplished by enabling the Login required check box on the Portlet Editor within the EBCC. If this check box is checked for a portlet, the portlet will not be displayed to the user unless the user has authenticated to the portal.

Summary

In this chapter, we showed you how to manage users and groups. We also showed you how to create group portals and manage access control using group portals. You can use the same tools and processes to manage users and groups and restrict access to portal resources within your portal.

CHAPTER 12

Portal Deployment

IN SEVERAL PREVIOUS CHAPTERS, we have discussed how to create portal domains, enterprise applications, Web applications, and portals. We've also discussed the directory structure and components of an enterprise application. In this chapter, we talk about how to take a portal application that has been created in the development environment and move it to a staging or production environment. Most of this discussion focuses on the technical information required to move all the components of your portal from one environment to another. However, we first look at the process that must be in place to facilitate the portal deployment.

Deployment Process

The success of your production system from release to release will depend heavily on a well-defined deployment process and strict adherence to it. The portal deployment process may vary from project to project and from organization to organization. For instance, some organizations may have four release environments within their deployment process (i.e., development, testing, staging, and production). Other organizations, because of financial or other resource limitations, may only have two or three release environments within their process. Regardless of the organizational or project differences, successful portal deployments must begin with a deployment process.

Though the deployment process may vary from project to project or organization to organization, it should contain several key components. Following is a discussion of some of the key components of a successful deployment plan.

Source Control

Source control is an important part of the whole system development process. It should be used as part of the deployment process in the following ways:

- A source control system should be used to control the integrity of the source code and other resources during the development process.

- Each developer should have a sandbox environment. This is an environment that the developer uses to develop and perform unit testing of code changes that have been assigned to him or her.

- Developers should check out to their own sandbox the specific Java files, JSP files, and other resources required to work on each new feature or system defect that they have been assigned.

- As shown in Figure 12-1, developers should check in to the source control system the specific Java files, JSP files, and other resources modified or added to address each new feature or system defect that they were assigned.

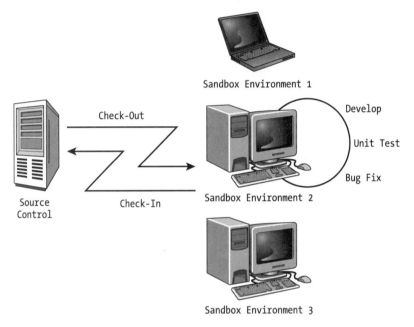

Figure 12-1. Source control

Deployment Request

Deployment requests are important in ensuring the integrity of the code within the deployment process. They should be used in the following ways:

- Each developer should submit a deployment request specifying the resources changed or added for each new feature or system defect addressed in the deployment request.

- Each developer should also specify any metadata changes that must be made using the EBCC.

- The deployment request should contain a list of new features that have been added or system defects that have been corrected.

- The deployment request should also contain instructions for testing the new features or system defects that have been corrected.

Deployment-Staging Environment

The deployment-staging environment is a computer and directory structure that is used to stage the files and resources from the deployment requests prior to deploying them to the release process.

- The directory structure within the deployment-staging environment should mirror the directory structure of the portal environment within the release environments. We discuss the specific required directories and resources for the portal deployment later in this chapter.

- The deployment manager should check out the files and resources for each deployment request that will compose a release from the source control system. Each file or resource that is checked out for the release should be placed in its proper location within the deployment-staging environment.

- Each release may contain multiple deployment requests. However, the number of deployment requests should be limited to make it easier to find the source of problems during regression testing.

- Deployments into any of the release environments should only be performed from the deployment-staging environment. Deployments into the release environments from other environments could introduce extraneous files and unintended consequences.

- Once a release has been compiled within the deployment-staging environment, it should be deployed to the first stage of the release environment for unit testing and regression testing.

Establishing Deployment Environments

The deployment process mentions several environments: the developer's sandbox, the deployment-staging environment, and the release environments. Each of these environments should be initially established using the tools and steps discussed in the previous chapters. Following is an overview of the steps required to create each of these environments for use within the deployment process:

- Install the WebLogic Portal Server on the target server.

- Use the Domain Configuration Wizard to create a new portal domain and enterprise application on the target server.

- Create the metadata database for the specific environment using the installation instructions on the WebLogic Web site. The instructions for creating the metadata database schema will vary depending on the database server being used to store the metadata.

Manual Release Deployment

Once the release environments have been established, new releases can be deployed as follows.

Deploy the Web Application Source Code

As shown in Figure 12-2, copy the Web application directory from the source control system into the enterprise application directory on the target server.

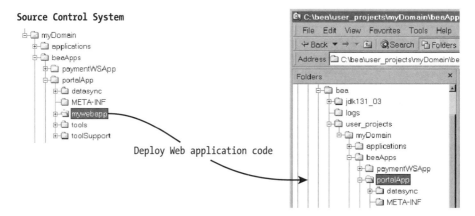

Figure 12-2. Deploying Web application code

Deploy the EBCC Project Directory

If the target environment is a developer's sandbox or the deployment-staging environment, the portal project directory may also be copied to the target server so that the developer can make EBCC changes to his or her environment and the deployment manager can make EBCC changes for new releases (see Figure 12-3).

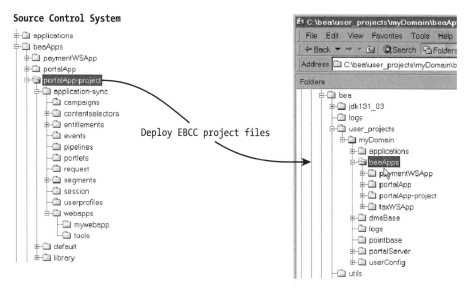

Figure 12-3. Deploy EBCC project files

Deploy the Web Application

Deploy the Web application and portal using the server console on the target
server:

1. Browse to the following URL in your browser:
   `http://server:port/console`.

2. Navigate to the *domain* ➤ Deployments ➤ Applications *enterprise app*
   node in the WebLogic Server Console as shown in Figure 12-4.

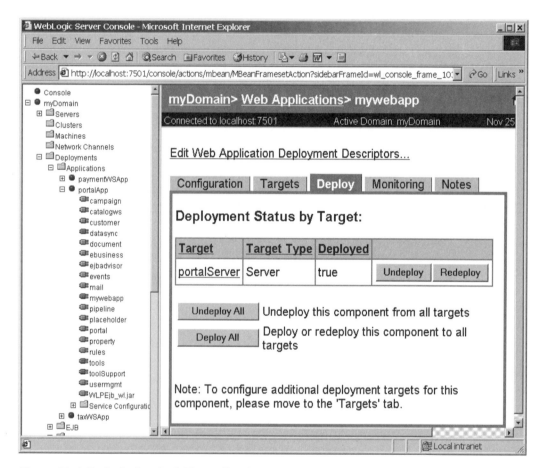

Figure 12-4. Redeploying the Web application

3. Undeploy the portal application using the Undeploy button.

4. Redeploy the portal application using the Redeploy button.

5. Open the portal project within the EBCC.

6. As shown in Figure 12-5, choose the Synchronize menu item on the Tools menu to begin the synchronization process.

Figure 12-5. Synchronizing portal metadata

7. You may have to enter a user name and password to continue the synchronization process. As shown in Figure 12-6, enter the user name/password combination you specified when you created the domain.

Figure 12-6. Synchronize portal metadata

8. The synchronization process is completed when the progress meter displays "Synchronization Finished" as shown in Figure 12-7.

9. Close the synchronization progress meter as well as the Reset Campaigns dialog box that displays.

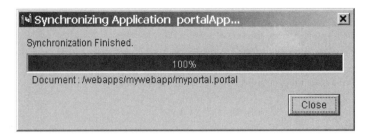

Figure 12-7. Synchronizing portal metadata

Deploy Other Web Application Resources

Your specific portal application may have other files and resources associated with it. For example, your application may have content stored in the WebLogic Portal content management system. In order to complete the deployment process, you need to copy or otherwise deploy any other resources from your deployment-staging environment to the target release environment.

> **NOTE**   *In order to maintain the integrity of the code, metadata, and other resources, code deployment and synchronization into the release environment should be done from a central location. In our process, this central location is the deployment-staging environment.*

Deployment Files

The WebLogic Portal installation provides many library files to support your portal application. You will need to include the appropriate libraries in your deployed portal application depending on the portal services that are used in your portal application. In this section, we present several lists of these files.

Following are the taglib jars that are required to support base portal instance. These files are included in your portal application when you choose the base portal template from the Web application wizard in the EBCC.

These files can also be found in the following directory within the WebLogic Portal installation: weblogic700\common\templates\webapps\portal\ baseportal\j2ee\WEB-INF\lib.

ent_taglib.jar	ren_taglib.jar
es_taglib.jar	res_taglib.jar
i18n_taglib.jar	um_taglib.jar
lic_taglib.jar	util_taglib.jar
portal_servlet.jar	visitor_taglib.jar
portal_taglib.jar	webflow_servlet.jar
portlet_taglib.jar	webflow_taglib.jar
p13n_servlet.jar	weblogic-tags.jar

The following taglib jars are required to support all portal services:

/weblogic700/portal/lib/commerce/web/cat_taglib.jar

/weblogic700/portal/lib/commerce/web/eb_taglib.jar

/weblogic700/portal/lib/commerce/web/productTracking_taglib.jar

/weblogic700/portal/lib/p13n/web/ad_taglib.jar

/weblogic700/portal/lib/p13n/web/cm_taglib.jar

/weblogic700/portal/lib/p13n/web/ph_taglib.jar

/weblogic700/portal/lib/p13n/web/ps_taglib.jar

/weblogic700/portal/lib/p13n/web/pz_taglib.jar

/weblogic700/portal/lib/p13n/web/tracking_taglib.jar

Following are the enterprise application jar files that are required by the portal:

campaign.jar	mail.jar
catalogws.jar	p13n_util.jar
commerce_campaign_bridge_util.jar	payment.jar
	pipeline.jar
commerce_util.jar	placeholder.jar
customer.jar	portal.jar
document.jar	portal_util.jar
ebusiness.jar	property.jar
ejbadvisor.jar	rules.jar
events.jar	tax.jar
ldapprofile.jar	usermgmt.jar

Automated Deployment

A Web application can also be deployed automatically using the ant utility that is installed with WebLogic. In this section, we discuss the process of automatically deploying the mywebapp Web application containing our portal. Our example will deploy our Web application in archived form.

Before we discuss the automated deployment, we must first set up our project directory. Notice in Figure 12-8, shown later, that in our project directory we have an src directory, a portlets directory, and a staging directory. These directories contain the source files that will be used by the automated deployment utility. Following are the steps required to create these source directories:

1. Check out the Java source files from the source control system and place them in the src directory, organizing them in a directory structure corresponding to their location within the project package structure.

2. Check out the portlet jsp files and other portlet resources from the source control system and place them in the portlets directory. The directory structure within the portlets directory should mimic that in the portlets directory within our Web application.

3. Check out the latest version of the Web application from the source control system and place it in the staging directory. This version of the Web application will be used as a base to retrieve those files from the Web application that will not need to be updated from version to version.

4. Run the set-environment.bat utility from the DOS environment in which you will run the deployment utility.

Figure 12-8 shows a build and a classes directory. These directories are created by the build utility during the build process.

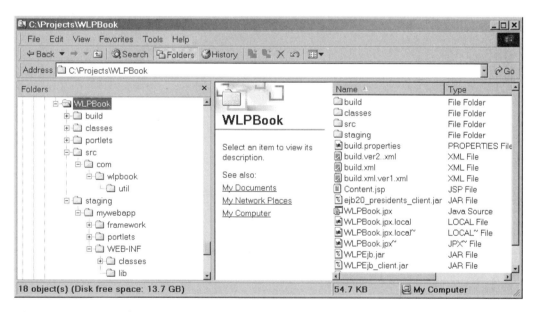

Figure 12-8. Project directory structure

Deployment Utility

Ant is a batch command utility from the Apache group that has become a standard for creating deployment utilities. For more information on the ant utility, go to http://jakarta.apache.org/ant.

The ant utility uses an XML file to define the actions that it will execute. This XML file can have any name; however, the default name for this XML file is build.xml. In this section we explain the build.xml file used in our example and the steps required to run the deployment utility.

Following are the deployment steps that the automated utility accomplishes:

- Compile the Java source files into class files in the classes directory.

- Copy the base portal files from the staging directory into the build directory.

- Copy the Java class files into the build directory.

- Copy the portlet files, directories, and resources into the build directory.

- Archive the files in the build directory into a war file.

The code that follows shows the build.xml file that the ant utility uses to deploy our example Web application:

```
<?xml version="1.0"?>
<project name="project" default="core" basedir=".">
```

This next section describes the files and directories that will be used by the deployment utility:

```
<target name="init">
      <!-- include top-level common properties -->
      <property file="./build.properties"/>
      <!-- The root directory of the workspace -->
      <property name="project.home" value="."/>
      <!-- The destination directory for the builds -->
      <property name="project.build" value="${project.home}/build"/>
      <property name="project.buildjardir" value="${project.home}/build/ejbjar"/>
      <property name="project.build.war" value="${project.home}/build/war"/>
      <property name="project.src" value="${project.home}/src"/>
      <property name="project.lib" value="${project.home}/src/lib"/>
      <property name="project.portlets" value="${project.home}/portlets"/>
      <!-- The destination directory for all the compiled classes. -->
      <property name="project.classbindir" value="${project.build}/classes"/>
      <!-- The staging directory of all the components -->
      <property name="project.staging" value="${project.home}/staging/mywebapp"/>
      <property name="project.staging.framework"
```

```
value="${project.staging}/framework"/>
      <property name="project.staging.portlets" value="${project.staging}/portlets"/>
      <property name="project.staging.webinf" value="${project.staging}/WEB-INF"/>
      <!-- The root directory of all the components. -->
      <property name="project.war.framework"
value="${project.build.war}/framework"/>
      <property name="project.war.portlets" value="${project.build.war}/portlets"/>
      <property name="project.war.webinf" value="${project.build.war}/WEB-INF"/>
      <property name="project.war.lib" value="${project.build.war}/WEB-INF/lib"/>
      <property name="project.war.classes"
value="${project.build.war}/WEB-INF/classes"/>
      <!-- Deployment directories -->
      <property name="bea.home" value="/bea"/>
      <property name="weblogic.home" value="${bea.home}/weblogic700"/>
      <property name="weblogic.lib" value="${weblogic.home}/server/lib"/>
      <property name="deploy.dir"
value="${bea.home}/user_projects/myDomain/beaApps/portalApp"/>
      <!-- project Components -->
      <property name="project.war" value="mywebapp.war"/>
      <property name="project.ear" value="portalApp.ear"/>
      <property name="project.ejbjar" value="projectEjb.jar"/>
      <!-- Classpaths -->
      <property name="portal.dir" value="${weblogic.home}/portal"/>
      <!-- Setup the system classpath -->
      <path id="system.classpath">
          <!-- WLS stuff -->
          <pathelement path="${bea.home}"/>
          <pathelement path="${weblogic.lib}/weblogic.jar"/>
          <pathelement path="${weblogic.lib}/weblogic_sp.jar"/>
          <pathelement path="${weblogic.lib}/webservices.jar"/>
          <pathelement path="${weblogic.lib}/xmlx.jar"/>
          <!-- WLP stuff -->
          <fileset dir="${portal.dir}/lib">
              <include name="*_system.jar"/>
              <include name="ext/*.jar"/>
          </fileset>
      </path>

      <property name="project.classpath"
value="${project.classbindir}"/>
</target>
```

The section that follows tells the ant utility to compile the files in the source directory into class files. The first two elements of this section tell the ant utility to display the class path to the console. The next element makes the output classes directory if it doesn't exist. The last element of this section tells the ant utility to run the javac command to do the compile operation and tell it the options and arguments to use.

```
<target name="compile" depends="init">
    <echo message="project.classpath = "/>
    <echo message="${project.classpath}"/>
    <mkdir dir="${project.classbindir}"/>
    <!-- Compile classes -->

    <javac debug="${javac.debug.option}" srcdir="${project.src}"
      destdir="${project.classbindir}" includes="com/**">
        <classpath>
            <path refid="system.classpath"/>
        </classpath>
    </javac></target>
```

The following section tells the ant utility to move all the required files for the Web application into the build directory and then archive them in a war file:

```
<target name="war" depends="init">
    <!-- Make the war directory -->
```

The following elements tell the ant utility to make directories required to build the war file:

```
<mkdir dir="${project.build.war}"/>
<mkdir dir="${project.war.lib}"/>
<mkdir dir="${project.war.webinf}"/>
<mkdir dir="${project.war.classes}"/>
<mkdir dir="${project.war.framework}"/>
<mkdir dir="${project.war.portlets}"/>
```

The next code snippet tells the ant utility to copy the portal framework directory from the staging directory to the build directory:

```
<copy todir="${project.war.framework}">
<fileset dir="${project.staging.framework}"/>
</copy>
```

The following element tells the ant utility to copy the portal portlets directory from the project portlets directory to the build directory:

```
<copy todir="${project.war.portlets}">
<fileset dir="${project.portlets}"/>
</copy>
```

The next code lines tell the ant utility to copy the WEB-INF directory from the project staging directory to the build directory:

```
<copy todir="${project.war.webinf}">
<fileset dir="${project.staging.webinf}"/>
</copy>
```

The following element tells the ant utility to delete the WEB-INF/classes directory from the build directory:

```
<delete dir="${project.war.classes}"/>
```

Now replace the WEB-INF/classes directory with the classes that were compiled previously:

```
<copy todir="${project.war.classes}">
<fileset dir="${project.classbindir}"/>
</copy>
```

This final element tells the ant utility to archive the Web application files in a war file:

```
<jar jarfile="${project.build}/${project.war}"
basedir="${project.build.war}" excludes="cvs"/>
</target>
```

The next section copies the war file from the build directory to the enterprise application directory on the WebLogic Portal server:

```
<target name="deploywar" depends="init">
    <copy todir="${deploy.dir}">
        <fileset dir="${project.build}/${project.war}"/>
    </copy>
</target>
<target name="clean" depends="init">
    <delete dir="${project.build}"/>
```

```
</target>
<target name="banner">
      <echo>+---------------------------------------+</echo>
      <echo>+    Building project Application       +</echo>
      <echo>+---------------------------------------+</echo>
</target>
<target name="core"
depends="banner, clean, compile, war, deploywar"/>
</project>
```

Summary

The specifics of deploying a portal application in a particular environment will vary depending on the architecture of the application functionality and the portal services used. Every organization has its own processes and standards. And every application has its own individual architecture to support its specific requirements. However, you can use the instructions and example provided in this chapter as a guide to building a deployment strategy for your specific application.

CHAPTER 13

Personalization Services

Personalization services help you deliver dynamic and personalized content. This includes content management and user/group management. In this chapter, we discuss the following areas of personalization:

- *User profiles:* How to set and retrieve values

- *Personalization of content:* Segments, Content Selectors, and placeholders

User Profiles

User profiles allow you to store information about each customer. If you want to personalize anything in the portal you are creating, you need to store information about each user. In the BEA WebLogic Portal, you implement user profiles with property sets. *Property sets* are the schemas for personalization attributes, and they provide a convenient way to give a name to a group of properties for a specific purpose. Suppose you want to capture work information for each user. You could set up a property set that captures the work name and the work type for each user of the portal. You can use the EBCC to create property sets and define the properties therein. Once you set up a property set, you can then enter values for the different properties in a user profile by using the Administration Tool or when creating a portlet.

Setting Up User Profiles

In the EBCC, you must go to the Site Infrastructure tab and click User Profiles to see any user profiles created. To create a new user profile, you click the New button in the EBCC and select User Profile. The User Profile Editor appears in the right pane as shown in Figure 13-1.

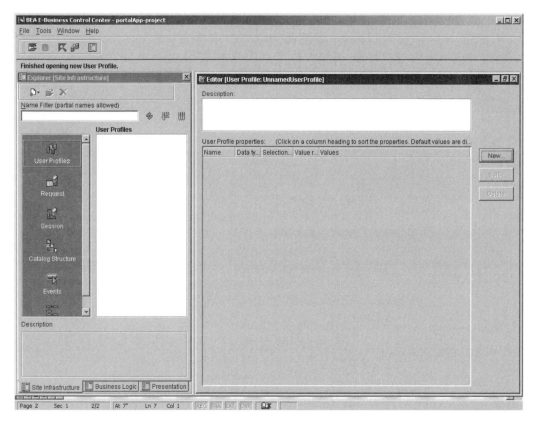

Figure 13-1. User Profile Editor in the EBCC

You can now add user properties by clicking the New button in the editor. This brings up the Edit Property dialog box, shown in Figure 13-2, in which you can define the different properties you want to capture for this property set.

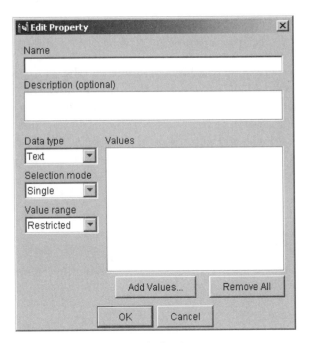

Figure 13-2. User Profile Edit Property dialog box

In the this dialog box, enter the following information:

- In the Name field, enter a unique name for the property that is no longer than 100 characters (required). Do not enter LDAP in the Name field.

- In the Description field, which is optional, you may enter a description of the property that is no longer than 254 characters.

- In the Data type drop-down list, select the data type. The data type selection can influence the Selection mode and Value range drop-downs. If you select Boolean as the data type, for example, the Selection mode and Value range drop-down lists are no longer available, as the default values for Boolean are Single and Restricted, respectively.

- In the Selection mode drop-down list, select either Single or Multiple. The value you select here determines the number of property values you can set: one (Single) or multiple (Multiple).

- In the Value range drop-down list, specify whether the value is restricted or unrestricted.

After you have entered the property information, click the Add Values button. One of two types of Enter Property Value dialog boxes appears, depending on the values selected. To show you how to specify the different types of property values, let's take a look at setting up two different properties. The first, called the WorkName property, will be used to track the name of the company the user works for. The second, called the WorkType property, will be used to track one of three work types for that user. The WorkName property has a data type of text, selection mode of single, and value range of unrestricted. Figure 13-3 shows how you would enter this type of property. To enter a default value press the AddValues button and enter the default property. You would press the OK button to save this.

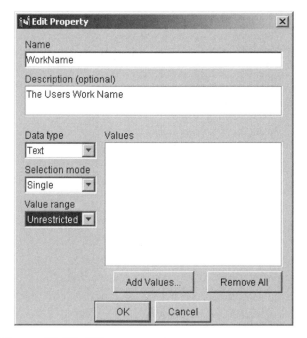

Figure 13-3. User profile WorkName property

Give the WorkType property a data type of text, selection mode of single, and value range of restricted. Figure 13-4 shows how you would enter this type of property.

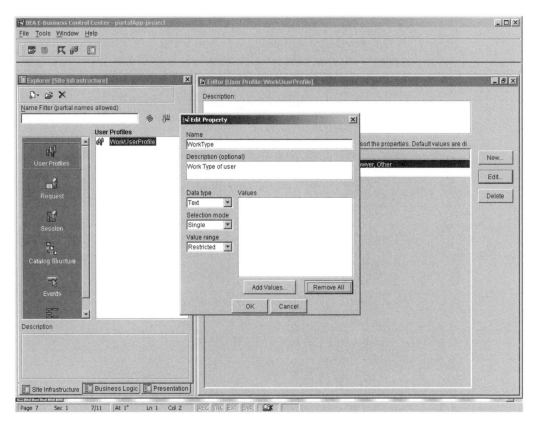

Figure 13-4. User profile WorkType property

Because you elected to make the value range restricted, you need to enter the values for this range. To enter the restricted values for this property, click the Add Values button on the Edit Property dialog box. The Enter Property Value dialog box opens as shown in Figure 13-5. The default value is checked.

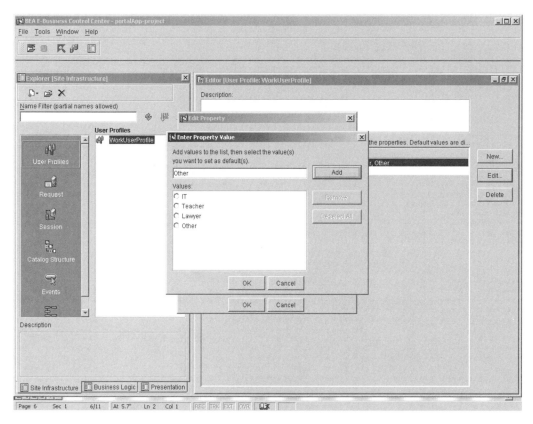

Figure 13-5. User profile Enter Property Value dialog box

As you can see in Figure 13-5, you can enter the different values for this property. If you have selected a selection mode of single, the values appear as radio button options since only one choice will be allowed. If you specified a selection mode of multiple, then check box options will be displayed.

You have created two properties, WorkName and WorkType, for the user profile. You must now click the Save button at the top of the EBCC to name and save this user profile. Figure 13-6 shows the EBCC after this example user profile is saved with the name WorkUserProfile.

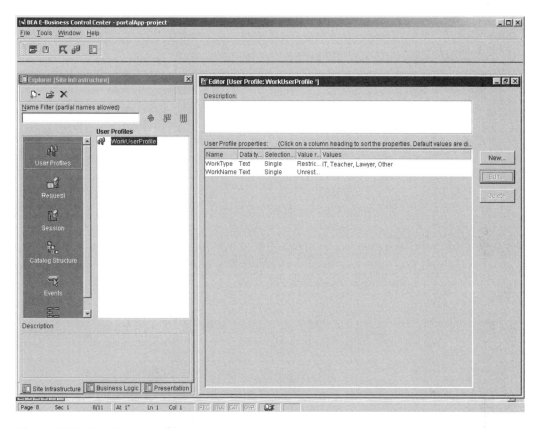

Figure 13-6. Saved user profile

Save the changes and synchronize the EBCC to have the newly created property sets available for the portal.

Tracking User Profile Information

Now that you have created a user profile, you want to track this information for each user. There are two ways that you can enter the user profile information for each user: by using the Administration Tools or by creating a portlet that captures the information.

If you choose to use the Administration Tools method, each user who is added to the portal will need this information entered. This strategy could work in a controlled user environment in which an administrator enters users. Any time a new user is added to the portal, the administrator would enter the user profile information after entering the general user information. If you are creating a portal in which new users can sign themselves up, you need to create a portlet that will capture the user profile information.

In the following sections, we first show you how to use the Administration Tools to enter user profile information. We then show you how to write a portlet to capture user profile information.

Using the Administration Tools to Enter User Profile Information

In the Administration Tools, select User Management and then Users to begin entering user profile information. We enter user profile information for an existing user that we created, testuser. If you are following along, create this user through the Administration Tools. Figure 13-7 shows the Users page from the Administration Tools for testuser.

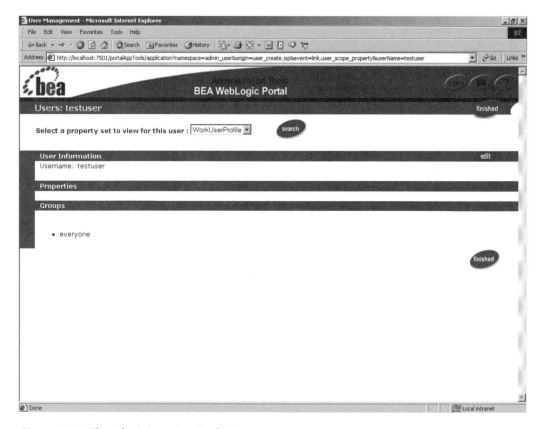

Figure 13-7. The Administration Tools Users page

If you select the property set WorkUserProfile from the drop-down list and click Search, you will be able to enter the user profile information for this user. Figure 13-8 shows the property set information.

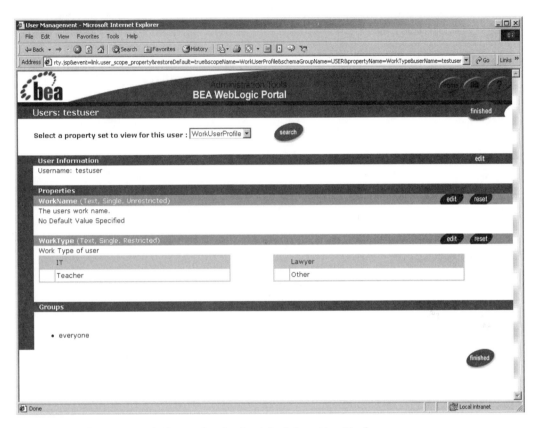

Figure 13-8. Property set information in the Administration Tools

To enter information for a particular property, click Edit to the right of that property. First enter information for the WorkName property as shown in Figure 13-9. As you can see, since you defined this property as having a data type of text, selection mode of single, and value range of unrestricted, you are presented with an entry field in which to enter the work name for this user.

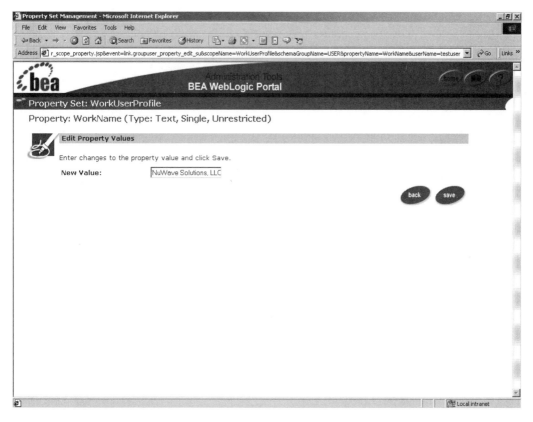

Figure 13-9. Entering WorkName property information in the Administration Tools

Next, enter information for the property WorkType as shown in Figure 13-10. Because you defined this property as having a data type of text, selection mode of single, and value range of restricted, you are presented with radio button options and restricted values that you can select for the property WorkType.

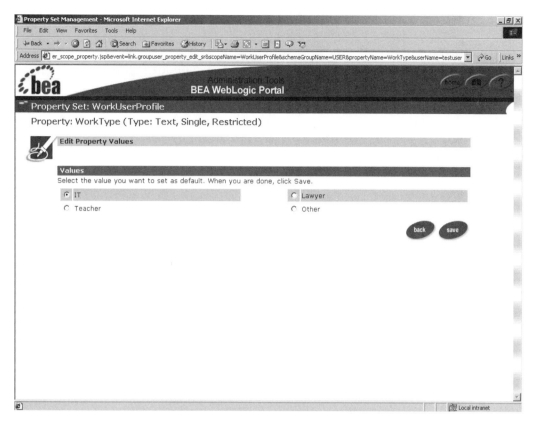

Figure 13-10. Entering WorkType property information in the Administration Tools

You have now entered all the information for the user profile that you created earlier for testuser.

Using a Portlet to Enter User Profile Information

Before you can use the JSP tags, you must verify that the property set taglib is configured. You need to copy the *PORTAL_HOME*/lib/p13n/web/ps_taglib.jar into WEB-INF/lib.

You must map the ps.tld tag library to /WEB-INF/lib/ps_taglib.jar in a <taglib> entry in your Web application's WEB-INF/web.xml file. You then verify that the following XML is located in the web.xml file within the <web-app></web-app> tokens:

```
<taglib>
    <taglib-uri> ps.tld </taglib-uri>
    <taglib-location> WEB-INF/lib/ps_taglib.jar </taglib-location>
</taglib>
```

There are several JSP tags that you can use to retrieve and update user profile property sets: <um:getProfile>, <um:getProperty>, <um:setProperty>, and <ps:getRestrictedPropertyValues>. We discuss these tags in the following sections.

<um:getProfile>

The <um:getProfile> tag retrieves the profile corresponding to the provided profile key and profile type. Here is an example of how this tag is used:

```
<um:getProfile scope="session" profileKey="<%= userName %>"/>
```

Table 13-1, from the WebLogic Portal 7.0 documentation, lists all attributes for this tag. WebLogic Portal 7.0 documentation reprinted with permission from BEA Systems, Inc. Copyright© 2002 BEA Systems, Inc. All rights reserved.

Table 13-1. <um:getProfile> Tag Attributes

TAG ATTRIBUTE	REQUIRED*	TYPE	DESCRIPTION	R/C**
profileKey	Yes	String	A unique identifier that can be used to retrieve the profile which is sought. Example: "<%=username%>"	R
successorKey	No	String	A unique identifier that can be used to retrieve the profile successor. Example: "<%=defaultGroup%>"	R
scope	No	String	The HTTP scope of the retrieved profile. Pass "request" or "session" as the values. Defaults to session.	C
groupOnly	No	String	Specifies to retrieve a group profile named by the profileKey, rather than a user profile. No successor will be retrieved when this value is true. Defaults to false.	C
profileId	No	String	A variable name from which the retrieved profile is available for the duration of the JSP's page scope.	C
successorId	No	String	A variable name from which the retrieved successor is available for the duration of the JSP's page scope.	C
result	No	String	A variable name from which the result of the operation is available. Possible values: *Success:* UserManagementTagConstants.GET_PROFILE_OK *Errorencountered:* UserManagementTagConstants.GET_PROFILE_FAILED UserManagementTagConstants.NO_SUCH_PROFILE UserManagementTagConstants.NO_SUCH_SUCCESSOR	C

* The Required column specifies if the attribute is required (yes) or optional (no).

**In the R/C column, C means that the attribute is a compile-time expression, and R means that the attribute can be either a request-time expression or a compile-time expression.

<um:getProperty>

The <um:getProperty> tag retrieves the property value for a specified property set–property name pair. The tag is usually used after the <um:getProfile> tag is invoked to retrieve a profile for session use. The property to be retrieved is taken from the session profile. Here is an example of how this tag is used:

```
<um:getProperty propertyName="WorkName" propertySet="WorkUserProfile"
id="work_name"/>
```

Table 13-2, from the WebLogic Portal 7.0 documentation, lists all attributes for this tag. WebLogic Portal 7.0 documentation reprinted with permission from BEA Systems, Inc. Copyright© 2002 BEA Systems, Inc. All rights reserved.

Table 13-2. <um:getProperty> Tag Attributes

TAG ATTRIBUTE	REQUIRED*	TYPE	DESCRIPTION	R/C**
propertySet	No	String	The property set from which the property's value is to be retrieved. Example: "Demographics" **Note:** If no property set is provided, the property is retrieved from the profile's default (unscoped) properties.	R
propertyName	Yes	String	The name of the property to be retrieved. Example: "Date_of_Birth"	R
id	No	String	If the id attribute is supplied, the value of the retrieved property will be available in the variable name to which id is assigned. Otherwise, the value of the property is inlined.	C

* The Required column specifies if the attribute is required (yes) or optional (no).

** In the R/C column, C means that the attribute is a compile-time expression, and R means that the attribute can be either a request-time expression or a compile-time expression.

<um:setProperty>

The <um:setProperty> tag updates a property value for the session's current profile. Here is an example of how this tag is used:

```
<um:setProperty propertyName="WorkName" propertySet="WorkUserProfile"
value="<%= worknameenter %>"/>
```

Table 13-3, from the WebLogic Portal 7.0 documentation, lists all attributes for this tag. WebLogic Portal 7.0 documentation reprinted with permission from BEA Systems, Inc. Copyright© 2002 BEA Systems, Inc. All rights reserved.

Table 13-3. <um:setProperty> Tag Attributes

TAG ATTRIBUTE	REQUIRED*	TYPE	DESCRIPTION	R/C**
propertySet	No	String	The property set in which the property's value is to be set. Example: "Demographics" **Note:** The property is set for the profile's default (unscoped) properties if no property set is provided.	R
propertyName	Yes	String	The name of the property to be set. Example: "Gender"	R
value	Yes	Object	The new property value.	R
result	No	String	The name of an Integer object to which the result of the set property operation is assigned. *Success:* UserManagementTagConstants.SET_PROPERTY_OK *Error encountered:* UserManagementTagConstants.SET_PROPERTY_FAILED	C

* The Required column specifies if the attribute is required (yes) or optional (no).

** In the R/C column, C means that the attribute is a compile-time expression, and R means that the attribute can be either a request-time expression or a compile-time expression.

<ps:getRestrictedPropertyValues>

The <ps:getRestrictedPropertyValues> tag returns a list of restricted values for a specific property definition, converted into strings. You use this to get a list of all the restricted values a user could select for a property. These values will be returned as an array of strings. In this example, this tag is used to get a list of all the work types so that a drop-down list can be created for the user to select from. To create the drop-down list, you would need to loop through the array. Here is an example of how this tag is used:

```
<ps:getRestrictedPropertyValues
        propertyName="WorkType"
        propertySetName="WorkUserProfile"
        propertySetType="USER"
        id="worktypeRestrictedValues"
        result="worktypeRestrictedValuesRet"/>
```

Table 13-4, from the WebLogic Portal 7.0 documentation, lists all attributes for this tag. WebLogic Portal 7.0 documentation reprinted with permission from BEA Systems, Inc. Copyright© 2002 BEA Systems, Inc. All rights reserved.

Table 13-4. <ps:getRestrictedPropertyValues> Tag Attributes

TAG ATTRIBUTE	REQUIRED*	TYPE	DESCRIPTION	R/C**
propertySetName	Yes	String	The name of the property set containing the property.	R
propertySetType	Yes	String	Type of property set containing the property.	R
propertyName	Yes	String	The name of the property to inspect.	R
id	Yes	String	The identifier of the variable to hold the list of property names, as a String array.	C
result	No	String	The identifier of an Integer variable that will be created and initialized with the result of the operation. Possible values: Query is successful: PropertySetTagConstants. PROPERTY_SEARCH_OK Problem accessing the property: PropertySetTagConstants. PROPERTY_SEARCH_FAILED Property set named by propertySetName and propertySetType could not be found: PropertySetTagConstants. INVALID_PROPERTY_SET The requested property is not restricted: PropertySetTagConstants. PROPERTY_NOT_RESTRICTED	C

* The Required column specifies if the attribute is required (yes) or optional (no).

** In the R/C column, C means that the attribute is a compile-time expression, and R means that the attribute can be either a request-time expression or a compile-time expression.

The portlet code in Listing 13-1 can be used to retrieve and update the user profile property set WorkUserProfile. It does these things:

- Checks to see if the user is logged in. If the user is not logged in, then an error message will be displayed.

- Retrieves the current user profile using the <um:getProfile> tag. The profile is received with a session scope, so that the next time this tag is invoked, the profile will be available.

- Gets the values of the text fields in the form. If the WorkName or WorkType fields have been filled, then update the property using the <um:setProperty> tag.

- Retrieves the restricted property values for WorkType using the <ps:getRestrictedPropertyValues> tag. This is done so that a drop-down list can be created that displays all the different work types that the user can select from.

- Retrieves all of user's property values using the <um:getProperty> tag so they can be displayed.

Listing 13-1. Retrieve and Update User Profile Code

```
<%@ taglib uri="um.tld" prefix="um" %>
<%@ taglib uri="weblogic.tld" prefix="wl" %>
<%@ taglib uri="ps.tld" prefix="ps" %>
<%@ taglib uri="es.tld" prefix="es" %>
<%@ taglib uri="webflow.tld" prefix="webflow" %>
<%@ page import=
"com.bea.p13n.usermgmt.servlets.jsp.taglib.UserManagementTagConstants" %>
<%@ page import=
"com.bea.p13n.property.servlets.jsp.taglib.PropertySetTagConstants" %>
<%@ page import="java.security.Principal" %>

<%
  // check to see if the user is logged in.
  java.security.Principal pr = request.getUserPrincipal();

  if ( pr == null )
  {
%>
    <b>Sorry, but you must log in for this example to work.</b>
<%
    return;
  }
%>
<%
  // get the user name
  String userName = pr != null ? pr.getName() : null;
%>
<%-------------------------------------------------------------------
```

Retrieve the current user profile using the <um:getProfile> tag.
The profile is received with a session scope, so that the next time
this tag is invoked, the profile will be available.
--%>

```
<um:getProfile scope="session" profileKey="<%= userName %>"/>

<form method="post" action="application?pageid=misc">
<table border="0" cellspacing="0" cellpadding="0" width="100%" class="accent">
  User '<%= userName %>'    <BR><BR>


<%----------------------------------------------------------------
Determine whether properties are to be updated.
------------------------------------------------------------------%>
<%
// get the values entered
String worktypeenter = request.getParameter("worktype");
String worknameenter = request.getParameter("workname");

// don't update workname property if nothing has been entered
if ((worknameenter != null)) {
%>
<um:setProperty propertyName="WorkType" propertySet="WorkUserProfile"
    value="<%= worktypeenter %>"/>
<%
}
// don't update worktype property if nothing has been entered
if ((worktypeenter != null)) {
%>
<um:setProperty propertyName="WorkName" propertySet="WorkUserProfile"
    value="<%= worknameenter %>"/>
<%
}
%>


<%----------------------------------------------------------------
Retrieve restricted property values for WorkType
------------------------------------------------------------------%>
    <ps:getRestrictedPropertyValues
        propertyName="WorkType"
        propertySetName="WorkUserProfile"
        propertySetType="USER"
        id="worktypeRestrictedValues"
        result="worktypeRestrictedValuesRet"/>
```

```
<%------------------------------------------------------------------
Retrieve all of user's property values.
-------------------------------------------------------------%>
<um:getProperty propertyName="WorkType"
propertySet="WorkUserProfile" id="work_type"/>
<um:getProperty propertyName="WorkName"
propertySet="WorkUserProfile" id="work_name"/>
        <tr>
            <td>Work Name:</td>
            <td><input type="text" name="workname" value="<%=work_name%>"></td>
        </tr>

            <tr>
            <td>Work Type: </td>
            <td><select size="1" name="worktype">
<%
// make sure that work_type is not null

if (work_type == null)
    work_type = "";
    // loop and get all restricted values to populate a drop down
    for (int i = 0; i < worktypeRestrictedValues.length; i++) {
{
            String worktypevalue = worktypeRestrictedValues[i];

            // if the retreived value is equal to the restricted value then
            // that value will be selected
            if (work_type.equals(worktypevalue))

%>
<option selected value="<%= worktypevalue %>"><%= worktypevalue %></option>
<%
    }
    else {
%>
<option value="<%= worktypevalue %>"><%= worktypevalue %></option>
<%
    }
}
%>
            </td>
        </tr>
</table>
<input type="submit" name="sbutton" value="Update">
</form>
```

Figure 13-11 shows the portlet when it is run within the portal and the user is logged in as testuser.

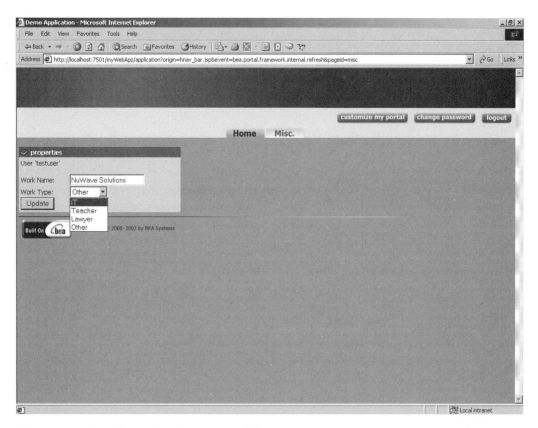

Figure 13-11. Display and update user profile property set portlet

Personalizing Content

Delivering content that is based on user characteristics is very important. This capability allows each user to have a unique experience using the portal. In Chapter 6 you learned how to use the content management capabilities of the BEA WebLogic Portal. We now show you how to personalize content.

Using Content Selectors

As you may recall from our discussion in Chapter 6, a Content Selector is one of several mechanisms that WebLogic Portal provides for retrieving documents from a content management system. In this chapter, we discuss how you can use a Content Selector to personalize the content you display in a portal by specifying conditions under which content is retrieved. We discuss two ways that you can personalize content through Content Selectors: using segments and user-specific characteristics. In order to use a segment with a Content Selector, you must first create the segment.

Creating a Segment

You can target users with Web content and campaigns by defining and using groups called *segments*. Segments are groupings of characteristics, such as users' work types. If a user matches the characteristics defined, he or she is automatically and dynamically a member of that segment and is shown specific Web content that you determine. To create a new segment, in the EBCC, you must first go to the Business Logic tab. Click the New button in the EBCC and select Segment. The Segment Editor appears. If you click the Edit button, the Characteristics dialog box is displayed as shown in Figure 13-12.

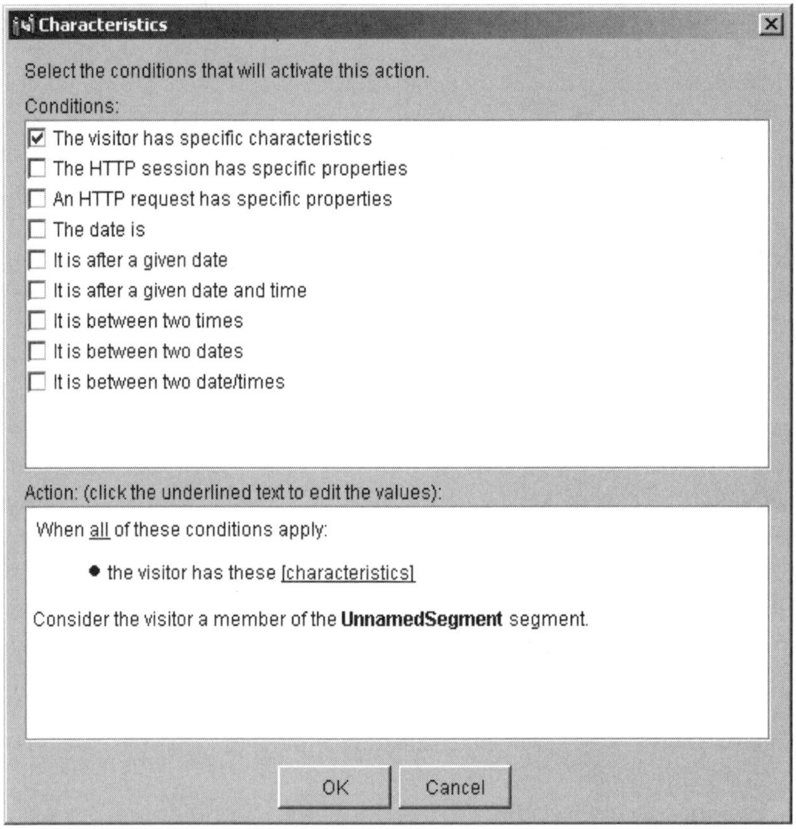

Figure 13-12. Segment Characteristics dialog box

Select the check box next to the option "The visitor has specific characteristics". Notice that when you click the check box, the Action portion of the dialog box changes. Click the [characteristics] link in the Action portion of the dialog box. The Visitor Characteristics dialog box is now displayed, as shown in Figure 13-13. This is where you define the type of properties you want this segment to be assigned to.

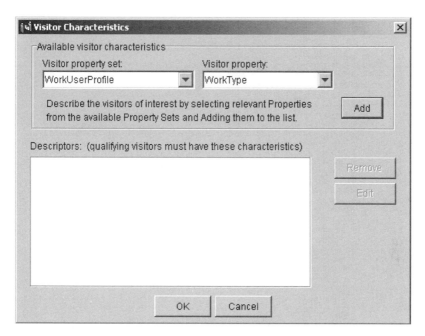

Figure 13-13. Segment Visitor Characteristics dialog box

A visitor property set and visitor property must be selected. Previously in this chapter you created a user profile property set called WorkUserProfile. Select WorkUserProfile for the visitor property set and WorkType for the visitor property. When you click the Add button, the Visitor Characteristic Values dialog box appears, as shown in Figure 13-14. This is where you define the value for the selected property. Since you selected WorkType as the property, you are given a list of choices to select for the value. Recall that when you created the WorkType property, you defined it to have a restricted list of values, which are displayed in the Value drop-down list.

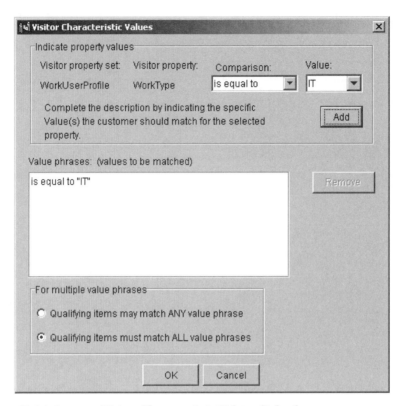

Figure 13-14. Segment Visitor Characteristic Values dialog box

Select the value IT and click the Add button. The value is then displayed in the Value phrases portion of the dialog box. All users who have a work type of IT will be part of this segment. You now need to save the changes and synchronize the EBCC to have the newly created segment available for the portal.

Creating the Content Selector

At this point, you are ready to start creating Content Selectors based on personalization. In the EBCC, you must go to the Presentation tab. In Chapter 6, we created a sample Content Selector called AboutUsContent. This displayed content based on a date. Here we show you how to modify this Content Selector so that it uses personalization. If you followed along with the example in that chapter and created your own AboutUsContent Content Selector, double-click this Content Selector to bring up the Content Selector Editor. If you click the Edit button, the Selection Rule dialog box is displayed. Deselect the check box next to the option "It is between two times" and select the check box beside "The visitor is a member of a predefined customer segment" as shown in Figure 13-15.

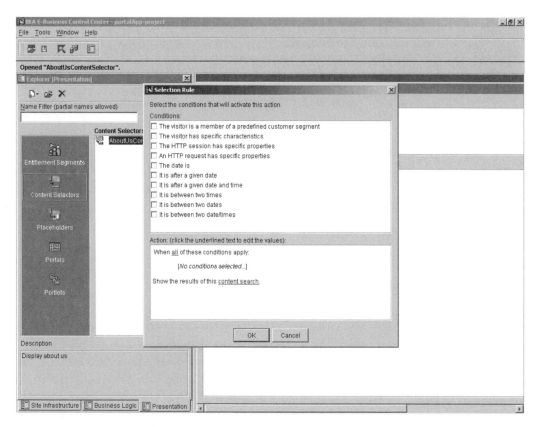

Figure 13-15. Content Selector Selection Rule dialog box

You can now select the condition for the display of the content. If you select the first check box option, "The visitor is a member of a predefined customer segment", you will see that the Action portion of the dialog box changes. If you click the customer segment link under Action, the Select Customer Segments dialog box is displayed as shown in Figure 13-16.

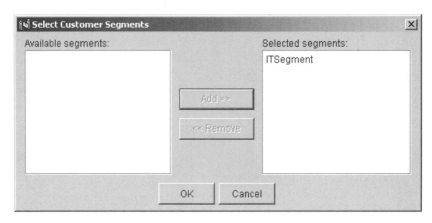

Figure 13-16. Content Selector Select Customer Segments dialog box

This dialog box displays the available segments that you can select. In our case, we created a segment called ITSegment so it is displayed under the Available segments. Select the segment you previously created and click the OK button. You have now created a Content Selector that will display the AboutUsContent only if the user who is logged in to the portal is part of the segment you created. You can use the search query that has already been defined for the Content Selector. Save the changes and synchronize the EBCC to have the modified Content Selector available for the portal.

To see how this works, you can use the content_selector.jsp portlet created in Chapter 6 to display the Content Selector. When you look at that this portlet, notice the use of the <pz:div> tag. To query the Content Selector AboutUsContentSelector, which you defined to use a segment, you would write the following code:

```
<pz:contentSelector rule="AboutUsContentSelector"
  contentHome="<%=ContentHelper.DEF_DOCUMENT_MANAGER_HOME %>"
  id="contentArray" />
```

If you displayed a page that contains the portlet without logging in to the portal, you would see that no content is displayed. If you logged in to the portal as a user with a work type of IT and then went to the page that contained the portlet, you would see the content displayed.

If you don't want to create a segment, you can still personalize the content you want displayed by selecting the check box option "The visitor has specific characteristics" in the Selection Rule dialog box. This allows you to select visitor characteristics just as you did when you created your segment. You can then select a visitor property set of WorkUserProfile and a visitor property of WorkType. This causes the content to be displayed only for users who have a work type of IT.

Using the <pz:div> Tag to Personalize a JSP

The <pz:div> tag is an additional way that you can personalize your JSP. You can use this tag in your JSP to specify that when a specific condition is met, your JSP will execute some code. An example of this would be to check if a user was a part of the customer segment ITSegment and display a welcome message that is different from that for other users of the portal. Table 13-5, from the WebLogic Portal 7.0 documentation, lists all attributes for this tag. WebLogic Portal 7.0 documentation reprinted with permission from BEA Systems, Inc. Copyright© 2002 BEA Systems, Inc. All rights reserved.

Table 13-5. <um:setProperty> Tag Attributes

TAG ATTRIBUTE	REQUIRED*	TYPE	DESCRIPTION	R/C**
Rule	Yes	String	The name of the rule such as the customer segment, ITSegment that was defined previously.	R
Id	No	String	A collection that contains the Classification objects that apply to the user for the given classifier rule.	C

*The Required column specifies if the attribute is required (yes) or optional (no).

**In the R/C column, C means that the attribute is a compile-time expression, and R means that the attribute can be either a request-time expression or a compile-time expression.

The following portlet can be used to display a welcome message to the customer segment ITSegment:

```
<pz:div rule="ITSegment">
Welcome, IT Employee!
</pz:div>
```

Using Placeholders

Placeholders represent an area in a portal page where predefined content is provided when certain criteria are met. When a visitor requests a JSP that contains a placeholder tag, the placeholder selects a single query to run and generates the HTML to display the results of the query. In this chapter, we explain how to create and use a placeholder. In the next chapter, we explain how you can personalize the placeholder when you set up a campaign.

In order to use placeholders, you must do the following:

- Verify placeholder configuration

- Create content to be displayed

- Create a placeholder

- Create a portlet to display the placeholder

Verifying Placeholder Configuration

In order to use placeholders, you must make sure that placeholders have been configured.

Checking the Taglib Configuration

You must first make sure the ph_taglib.jar file is in the Web application's WEB-INF/lib directory. It can be copied from the BEA_HOME/weblogic700/portal/lib/p13n/web directory. Check the mapping of the taglib by looking at your Web application's WEB-INF/web.xml file. It must contain the following within the <web-app></web-app> tokens:

```
<taglib>
            <taglib-uri> ph.tld </taglib-uri>
            <taglib-location>/WEB-INF/lib/ph_taglib.jar </taglib-location>
</taglib>
```

Checking the PlaceHolderService Session EJB Configuration

Check your Web Application's WEB-INF/web.xml file. It must contain the following within the <web-app></web-app> tokens:

```
<ejb-ref>
    <description>The PlaceholderService Session EJB for the placeholder
tag.</description>
    <ejb-ref-name>ejb/PlaceholderService</ejb-ref-name>
    <ejb-ref-type>Session</ejb-ref-type>
    <home>com.bea.p13n.placeholder.PlaceholderServiceHome</home>
    <remote>com.bea.p13n.placeholder.PlaceholderService</remote>
</ejb-ref>
```

Check your Web Application's WEB-INF/weblogic.xml file. It must contain the following within the <reference-descriptor> </reference-descriptor> tokens:

```
<ejb-reference-description>
    <ejb-ref-name>ejb/PlaceholderService</ejb-ref-name>
    <jndi-name>${APPNAME}.BEA_personalization.PlaceholderService</jndi-name>
</ejb-reference-description>
```

Creating Content

You must now create content that you want to be displayed through your placeholder. Once your content has been created, you load it into the portal. Figure 13-17 shows a file directory where we included four ads. We placed these ads in a directory called user_projects*domain*\dmsBase\examples\banners. These ads were saved from banner images that were displayed on a Web site under the names ad1.gif, ad2.gif, ad3.gif, and ad4.gif. If you want to follow this example, it is recommended that you find some GIF files and save them in the same directory as shown previously. Once the content has been moved to the proper file directory, run the BulkLoader (see Chapter 6 for more details). The BulkLoader loads the content into the portal.

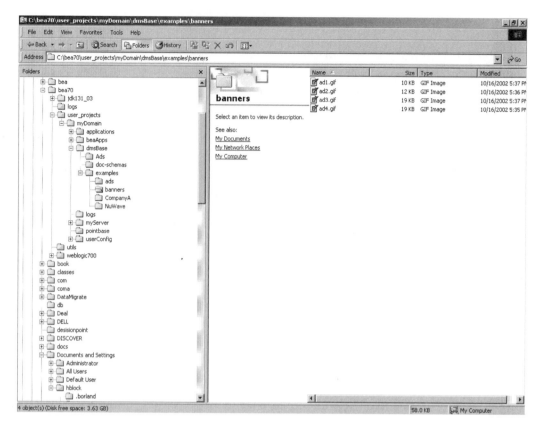

Figure 13-17. File directory for placeholder content

Creating a Placeholder

Next you create a placeholder to display the ad content you created. In the EBCC, go to the Presentation tab. To create a new placeholder, click the New button in the EBCC and select Placeholder. The Placeholder Editor is displayed. If you click the New button, the Ad Search dialog box appears as shown in Figure 13-18. Note that you might be prompted to connect to the portal.

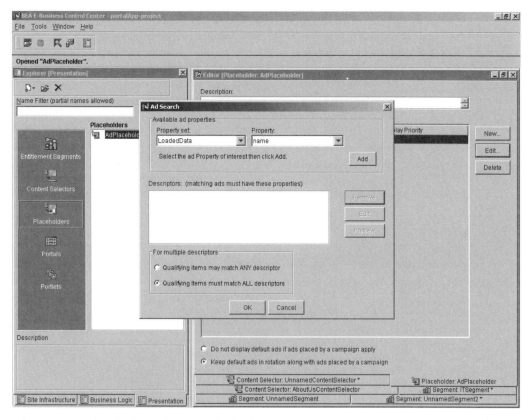

Figure 13-18. Placeholder Ad Search dialog box

In the Ad Search dialog box, select LoadedData for the property set and name for the property. This builds a query using the name of the content as the query. You can select other ways to query the content, including the modified date, width, comments, and author. Once you have entered values for the property set and property, click the Add button and the Ad Search Values dialog box is displayed. Figure 13-19 shows this dialog box.

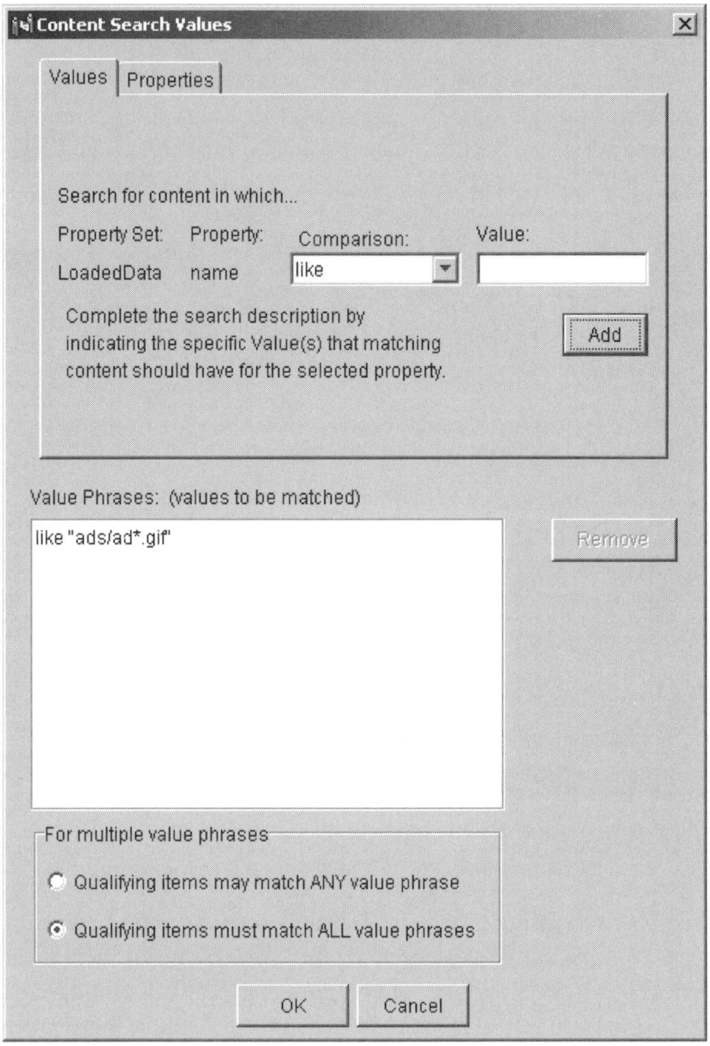

Figure 13-19. Placeholder Ad Search dialog box

This is where you enter the specific values for the content query. Previously, you chose name as the property, so you now have to enter a comparison and value. There are several choices you can enter for the comparison: is equal to, is not equal to, contains, and like. We showed you that we added four ads as the content to be displayed in the placeholder. The query that we want will use the comparison "like" to search for any file that matches ad*.gif. The query results will be the four ads. For the value, enter the filename that you want to search for. To display all the ads added to the portal, you would enter examples/banners//ad*.gif for the value. The wild card *, when used in conjunction with the like comparison, gives a result of the four ads that were loaded into the portal. You now need to save the changes and synchronize the EBCC to have the newly created placeholder available for the portal.

You can now preview the content that will be selected based on the ad query you just created. Figure 13-20 shows a browser with the results of the ad query. You can click any of the four Matching Content links to display the content.

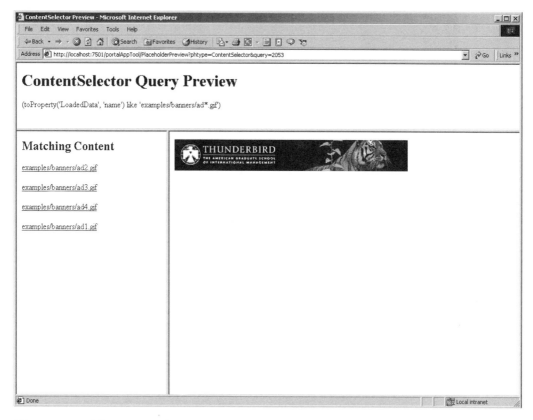

Figure 13-20. Ad query preview

Creating a Portlet

The <ph:placeholder> tag implements a placeholder that describes the behavior for a location on a JSP page. When a portal receives a request for a JSP that contains a placeholder, the <ph:placeholder> tag contacts the Ad Service, a session EJB that invokes business logic to determine which content to display. Here is an example of how this tag is used:

```
<ph:placeholder name="/placeholders/AdPlaceholder.pla"/>
```

Table 13-6, from the WebLogic Portal 7.0 documentation, lists all attributes for this tag. WebLogic Portal 7.0 documentation reprinted with permission from BEA Systems, Inc. Copyright© 2002 BEA Systems, Inc. All rights reserved.

Table 13-6. <ph:placeholder> Tag Attributes

TAG ATTRIBUTE	REQUIRED*	TYPE	DESCRIPTION	R/C**
name	Yes	String	A string that refers to a placeholder definition.	R
height	No	int	Specifies the height (in pixels) that the placeholder uses when generating the HTML that the browser requires to display a document. The placeholder uses this value only for content types to which display dimensions apply and only if other attributes have not already defined dimensions for a given document. If you do not specify this value and other attributes have not already been defined, the browser behavior determines the height of the document.	R
Width	No	int	Specifies the width (in pixels) that the placeholder uses when generating the HTML that the browser requires to display a document. The placeholder uses this value only for content types to which display dimensions apply and only if other attributes have not already defined dimensions for a given document. If you do not specify this value and other attributes have not already been defined, the browser behavior determines the height of the document.	R

* The Required column specifies if the attribute is required (yes) or optional (no).

** In the R/C column, C means that the attribute is a compile-time expression, and R means that the attribute can be either a request-time expression or a compile-time expression.

Take a look at the following code contained in a portlet called placeholder:

```
<%@ taglib uri="ph.tld" prefix="ph" %>

<table width="100%" height="100%" border="0" cellspacing="0" cellpadding="0">
<tr>
<td align="center">
<ph:placeholder name="/placeholders/AdPlaceholder.pla"/>
</td>
</tr>
</table>
```

Figure 13-21 shows how this portlet looks when it is placed on the home page. Every time the Refresh button is clicked, a new ad will be displayed.

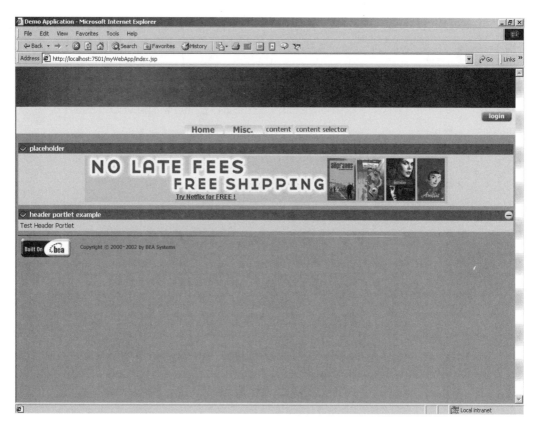

Figure 13-21. Placeholder portlet displayed in a portal

Summary

Personalization is very important in any portal you create. You want your users to have a unique experience based on their user profiles. This chapter gave an overview on how to start personalizing the portal you are creating. The next chapter will expand on personalization using campaigns.

CHAPTER 14

Campaign Services

THE LAST CHAPTER COVERED some of the different personalization aspects of the BEA WebLogic Portal. An additional way you can add personalization to your portal is through the use of a campaign. A *campaign* is a way to organize the different things you want to do to personalize the portal. A campaign allows you to target visitors with personalized actions. For example, users can register for access to your portal. Once they have registered, you can send them a customized e-mail message welcoming them to the portal. You can also target ads displayed to them on the portal based on the registration information. All of the business rules for these actions can be placed in a campaign. This chapter talks about the following:

- *Campaign prerequisites:* Things that must be done before a campaign can be set up

- *Setting up campaigns:* How you set up a campaign in the EBCC

- *Deactivating and reactivating campaigns:* How to start and stop a campaign that has been created

- *Running campaigns:* How to run the campaign you have created

Campaign Prerequisites

Before you can set up a campaign, you must create the pieces that cause campaign actions to occur, such as a user property or an event. These are called *triggers.* You must also create the content, discounts, or e-mail messages that visitors see or receive when an action is triggered. These are called content. Once you have created the triggers and content, you then set up your campaign using the EBCC. Finally, you must write code in your portlets to support the triggers and content you have set up.

Creating Triggers

When someone uses your site, a campaign action can be triggered by a number of factors that you define. In many cases, setting up triggers is a development task that involves coding and JSP work. Table 14-1 shows some of the different triggers you can define.

Table 14-1. Campaign Triggers

TRIGGER	DESCRIPTION
Create users and user profile properties	This triggers campaign actions based on specific information that is stored for a user in a user profile. An example that appears later in this chapter is a trigger based on a user having a WorkType property of IT as described in Chapter 13. In Chapter 13, we created a user profile called WorkUserProfile, which is used in an example later in this chapter.
Create segments	This triggers campaign actions based on users who belong to a specific segment. In Chapter 13 we created a segment called ITSegment, which is used in an example later in this chapter.
Create custom events	This triggers campaign actions based on events that occur, such as a user registering as a new user in the portal. The WebLogic Portal comes with a set of predefined events you can use. We use a predefined event, UserRegistrationEvent, in an example later in this chapter.
Create HTTP session and request properties	This triggers campaign actions based on HTTP session or request properties, such as character encoding or the type of browser being used. When creating a campaign action, this task maps to the HTTP session and request options.
Create a catalog and set up a shopping cart	This triggers campaign actions based on shopping cart contents or values. When creating a campaign action, this task maps to the shopping cart options.

Creating Content

Once you have created the different triggers you want for your campaign, you must create the Web content and placeholders, discounts, and e-mail messages you want to use in the campaigns. Table 14-2 shows the different content you can create.

Table 14-2. Campaign Content

TRIGGER	DESCRIPTION
Set content metadata, load content, and create placeholders	If you want to show a user personalized Web content as part of a campaign, that Web content must be created and stored in a database or content management system. The graphics properties must be made available in the EBCC for defining queries that retrieve the graphics. Placeholders must be defined in portlets and in the EBCC. In Chapter 13, we created a placeholder called AdPlaceholder, which we use in an example later in the chapter.
Create discounts	If you want to use discounts in campaigns, the discounts must already be defined in the EBCC and designated as campaign discounts. We will not talk about discounts beyond this point.
Create e-mail messages	If you want to send e-mail as part of a campaign, you must create and store the e-mail messages that are used in the campaigns.

Setting Up E-Mail Messages

In order to use e-mails in a campaign, there are several things you must do:

- Define e-mail properties

- Configure Campaign service settings

- Create e-mail messages you want to use

Define E-Mail Properties

Before a campaign can send e-mail, you must configure properties that the Campaign service will use to send and receive mail. To configure mail-related properties, you must define two properties in a user profile property set. Recall from Chapter 13 that we showed you how to define user profile property sets in the EBCC. In that chapter, we defined an example property set called WorkUserProfile. If you followed our example, you could now add the two necessary e-mail properties to that user profile:

- *Email:* The name of the property set and the property that defines customer e-mail addresses. This needs to be defined as a single-value, unrestricted text property.

- *Email_opt_in:* The name of the property set and the property that records a customer's preference for receiving campaign-related e-mail. This needs to be defined as a single-value, unrestricted Boolean property.

You can then modify the property JSP created in Chapter 13 to allow users to enter their e-mail address. The property that you would need to add to WorkUserProfile is Email.

Configuring Campaign Service Settings

You need to configure Campaign service settings in the BEA WebLogic Console. Select Deployments ➢ Applications ➢ portalApp ➢ Service Configuration ➢ Campaign Service. On the Campaign Service page, click the Configuration tab. You need to define the Base directory for e-mail browsing. This is the directory in which you place the e-mail JSPs that you want sent. The default is campaigns/emails. That translates to the file directory *domain*\beaApps\portalApp\myWebApp\campaigns\emails.

On the Campaign Service page shown in Figure 14-1, click the Mail Action tab. On this tab enter the following:

- In the Default From Email Address field, enter the default address that receives any replies from e-mail that the campaign sends. In a standard mail header, this is the From address. Each campaign scenario can specify its own From address that overrides this default property.

- In the Email Address Property Name field, indicate the name of the property that contains customer e-mail addresses.

- In the Property Set Name Containing Email Address Property field, enter the name of the property set that contains customer e-mail properties. For our example, this is specified as the WorkUserProfile property set we modified to contain the E-mail and E-mail_Opt_In properties.

- In the Email Opt In Property Name field, set the name of the property that specifies whether customers want to receive campaign-related e-mail. The reference applications store this preference in the Demographics property set in the E-mail_Opt_In property.

- In the Property Set Name Containing Opt In Property field, enter the name of the property set that contains the customer's opt-in property.

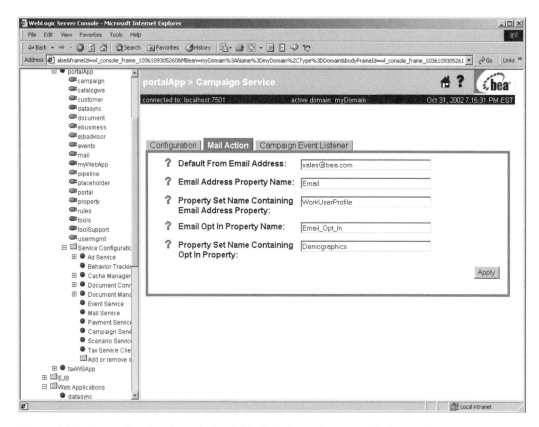

Figure 14-1. Campaign Service window's Mail Action tab, general information

Creating E-Mail Messages

You must create the different e-mail messages you want to be sent. Earlier you defined the Base directory for e-mail browsing as campaigns/emails. In the File directory *domain*\beaApps\portalApp\myWebApp\campaigns\emails you can start writing the different e-mail JSPs. When a scenario action requests an e-mail JSP, it passes a userID parameter, which specifies the login name of the customer who triggered the scenario action. By using the request.getParameter() method, you can retrieve the user ID and pass it to JSP tags in the e-mail JSP.

In addition, the scenario passes the following parameters:

- *scenarioId:* Specifies the ID of the scenario that triggered the e-mail

- *scenarioName:* Specifies the name of the scenario that triggered the e-mail

- *containerId:* Specifies the ID of the campaign to which the scenario belongs

- *containerName:* Specifies the name of the campaign to which the scenario belongs

Listing 14-1 shows a sample e-mail JSP, email.jsp, that we use later in the chapter. If you want to follow along with our example, be sure to place the following code in the directory specified previously.

Listing 14-1. Example E-Mail JSP

```
<%@ page session="false" %>
<%@ page contentType="text/plain" %>

Hello <%= request.getParameter("userId") %>,

Thank you for taking the time to become a registered member of the
NuWave Solutions website.
We hope you enjoy the website throughout the year.

In addition, your registration entitles you to premium services including:
    **Special "Members Only" discounts
    **Advance notice of new product releases
    **A personalized customer experience customized to your specific interests

Thanks again for becoming a registered member.

Best Regards
```

The Java class that the Campaign service uses to generate e-mail from a JSP, InternalRequestDispatcher, also generates an HTTPSession object. The HTTPSession object is usually already created when a user accesses your site. To disable the generation of an extraneous HTTPSession, add the following directive to the beginning of the JSPs that you use to generate e-mail for campaigns:

```
<%@ page session="false" %>
```

Adding this directive is necessary only if your application generates HTTPSession objects when customers access your site (or log in) and only for e-mail that is generated via the InternalRequestDispatcher.

Setting Up Campaigns

To create a new campaign, go to the Business Logic tab in the EBCC, click the New button in the EBCC and select Campaign. The Campaign Editor is now displayed. You should see three bars: General, Scenarios, and Start/Stop. You can click any of these three bars to enter information.

Entering General Information

If you click the General bar, it will expand, allowing you to enter general information (as shown in Figure 14-2). Campaign Sponsor and Description are required fields. Once you have finished entering general information, you can click the General bar to close it.

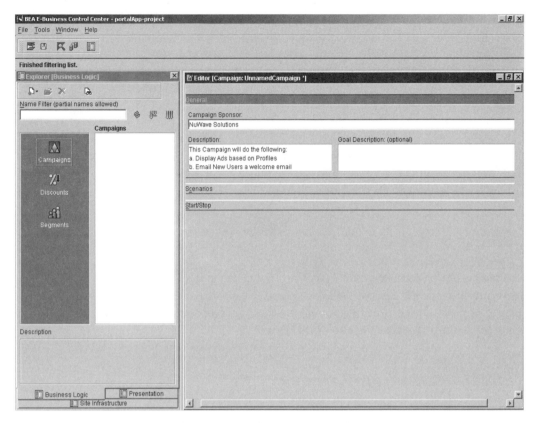

Figure 14-2. Adding general information in the Campaign Editor

Entering Scenarios

Now that you have entered general information for your campaign, you can click the Scenario bar and begin entering your different scenarios. When you click the New Scenario button, the New Scenario dialog box appears, displaying a list of scenario templates, as shown in Figure 14-3. The following list describes each scenario:

- *Default:* This is a blank template that allows you to manually build the scenario.

- *RegistrationConfirmationEmail:* This shows you how a registration confirmation e-mail can be sent to users who register.

- *DiscountAndAdActions:* This displays a discount ad in conjunction with an associated discount action.

- *OnlineContentTest:* This tests content effectiveness using probability-based branching.

- *EmailPilotTest:* This tests three different e-mail messages.

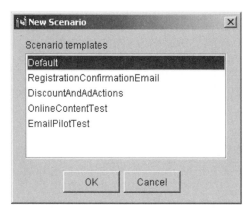

Figure 14-3. New Scenario dialog box in the Campaign Editor

Select Default and click OK. The Scenario Properties dialog box is now displayed as shown in Figure 14-4. Enter a scenario name and description. You can also select specific customer segments that you created to apply your scenario only to those segments.

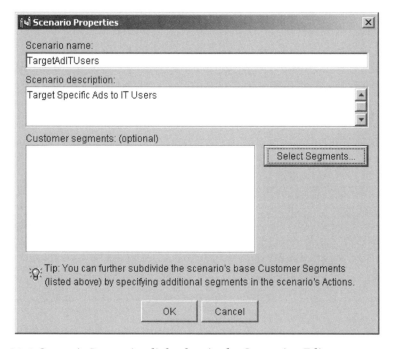

Figure 14-4. Scenario Properties dialog box in the Campaign Editor

Once you have entered all information in the Scenario Properties dialog box, click the OK button. You are returned to the Scenario Editor and ready to start defining actions. The three types of actions that you can set up within a scenario are ad, e-mail, and discount. Next we talk about setting up ad and e-mail actions.

NOTE *You must be connected to your server when you are setting up actions that rely on any content.*

Setting Up Ad Actions

Use this type of action to define the criteria for selecting content from your content management system to be displayed on a page or in a portlet. Because you are defining the query, the query can return more than one set of content. Make sure to define the query very narrowly if you want to return one specific piece of content. To show you how this is done, we build an ad action that selects a piece of content called it.gif. This is a banner ad that displays computer-related information. We want this ad to display for any user who logs in to our portal and has a work type of IT. In Chapter 13, we created a customer segment called ITSegment. That segment was defined for anyone who had a work type of IT in the WorkUserProfile property set.

For this example, click the New Action button and then select Ad. The New Ad Action dialog box now appears. In this dialog box you can define the condition(s) under which the content will be displayed. There are two ad actions we could use to select the content we want for our example:

- *The visitor is a member of a predefined customer segment:* Here we would just select ITSegment.

- *The visitor has specific characteristics:* Here we would have to define characteristics such as the Visitor property set and property to use.

To see how this works, select the first option, "The visitor is a member of a predefined customer segment." Once a check box has been selected, you must specify values for any bracketed hyperlinked text that appears in the Action portion of the window. Click the hyperlinked text and set the appropriate values. Figure 14-5 shows the different hyperlinked text that appears when the first check box option is selected. You can select the check box at the bottom if you only want this action to be performed once for each person who visits your portal.

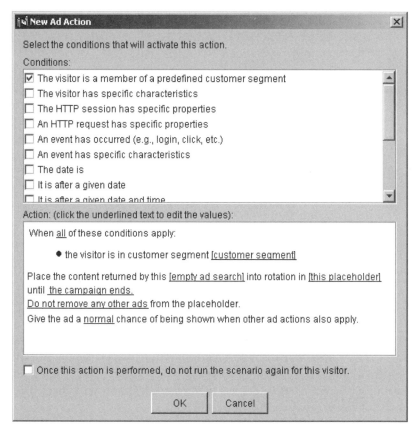

Figure 14-5. New Ad Action dialog box

 NOTE   *It is considered a best practice to always define scenario actions to include the "An event has occurred" condition as well as any others. In general, SessionLoginEvent can be used. Scenario actions without event checks can be a performance issue, since the campaign engine will have to check the action conditions upon every event received. If at least an event is specified, the campaign engine can filter based upon that first to avoid the overhead of invoking the rule engine.*

To continue with our example, click the link [customer segment]. The Select Customer Segments dialog box is displayed as shown in Figure 14-6. Select ITSegment and click OK.

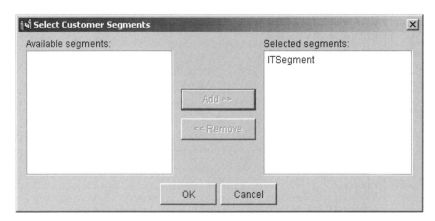

Figure 14-6. Select Customer Segments dialog box

You have selected an action that will be performed only when the user meets the conditions of the segment ITSegment defined in Chapter 13. If you selected more than one condition, enable the "When all of these conditions apply" option. When you click the word "all", it changes to "any". When you use the any option, only one of the conditions must be met to trigger the action. Next, you define the query that will determine which content to display. Before you can do this, however, make sure you have defined the content and placeholder prerequisite tasks described in Table 14-2. Click the hyperlink [empty ad search]. The Ad Search dialog box is displayed as shown in Figure 14-7.

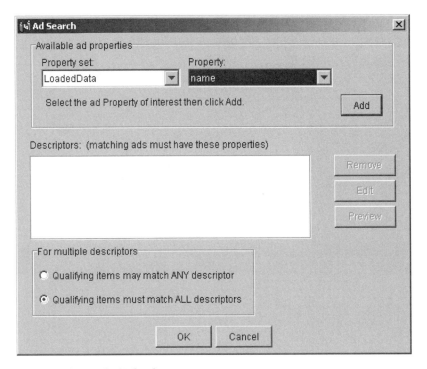

Figure 14-7. Ad Search dialog box

In the Ad Search dialog box, select a property set and property. Selecting
LoadedData for the property set results in searching all content that has been
loaded into the content management system. Selecting name for the property
results in a search based on the content's filename. Click the Add button to define
the query in the Ad Search Values dialog box. In the Ad Search Values dialog box
that appears, you set the comparison and value for your query. Figure 14-8
shows the Ad Search Values dialog box with the comparison of "is equal to"
and a value of examples/banners/it.gif. This will query for any content in the
examples/banners directory with a filename of it.gif.

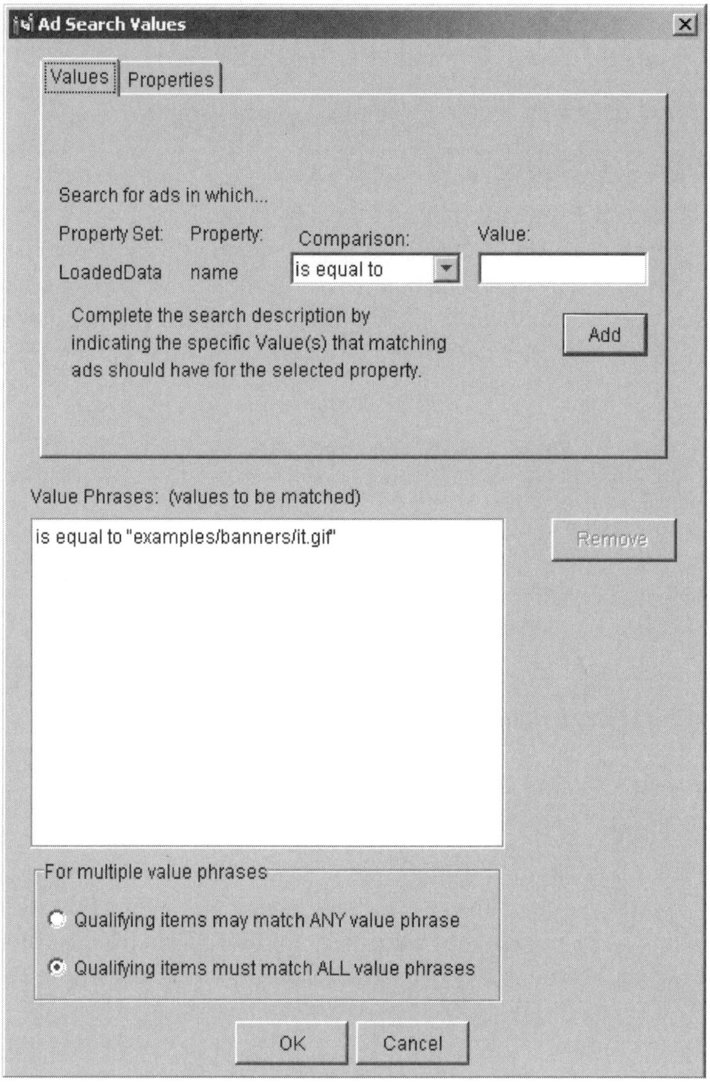

Figure 14-8. Ad Search Values dialog box

When you are finished adding values, set the appropriate For multiple value phrases option and click OK. The values appear in the Descriptors list in the Ad Search dialog box.

You can now select the appropriate For multiple descriptors option. If you select the "Qualifying items may match ANY descriptor" option, the query will return content matching any of the values you set. Selecting the "Qualifying items must match ALL descriptors" option narrows what the query will return, because any content to be displayed must match all of the criteria. Click the OK button on the Ad Search dialog box, and your query is defined.

You next have to define the placeholders for the query. Click [this placeholder] in the bottom portion of the Ad Action dialog box. The Select Placeholders dialog box is displayed. Select AdPlaceholder, the placeholder that you previously defined in Chapter 13.

There are several other links that you can define on the Ad Action dialog box. You can now set the priority for your content to be displayed by setting the "Give the ad a normal chance of being shown" option. Click the normal link to change priority. You can also improve the chances that your content is shown in a place-holder by automatically removing queries put in the placeholder by other scenarios or campaigns. To do this, click "Do not remove any other ads" and set the appropriate query-clearing option. If you want the Web content to stop being displayed in the placeholder before the campaign ends, click [the campaign ends] and set the end time. If you want the scenario to run only once per visitor, for example, to be displayed only when a user registers, select the "Once this action is performed, do not run the scenario again for this visitor" option.

After you have defined all links that you want, click the OK button and the Ad Action dialog box closes. The Campaign Editor now displays the ad scenario you just completed as shown in Figure 14-9.

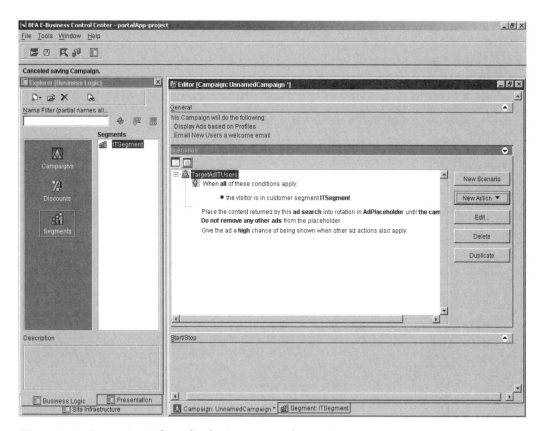

Figure 14-9. Campaign Editor displaying a new ad scenario

Setting Up E-Mail Actions

This type of action defines the criteria that you want to use to send a targeted e-mail message to a user. To show you how this is done, we demonstrate how to build an e-mail action that sends an e-mail to users once they have registered on the site. We use a predefined event to do this.

For this example, click the New Action button and then select E-mail. The New E-mail Action dialog box appears. In this dialog box, click the "An event has occurred (e.g., login, click, etc.)" check box option. Once the check box has been selected, you must specify values for any bracketed hyperlinked text that now appears in the Action portion of the dialog box. Click the hyperlinked text and set the appropriate values. Figure 14-10 shows the hyperlinked text that appears when the "An event has occurred (e.g., login, click, etc.)" option is selected. You can select the check box at the bottom if you want this action to be performed only once for each person who visits your portal.

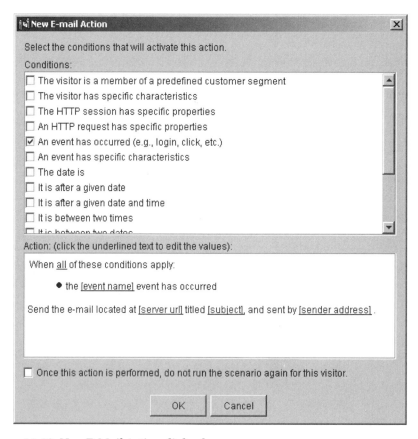

Figure 14-10. New E-Mail Action dialog box

To continue with this example, click the link [event name]. The Select Event dialog box is displayed as shown in Figure 14-11. Select UserRegistrationEvent and click the Add button to define that an e-mail will be sent every time the UserRegistrationEvent is triggered. Click the OK button to close the Select Event dialog box.

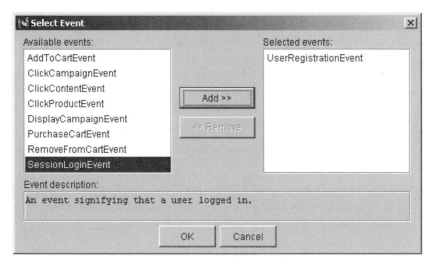

Figure 14-11. Select Event dialog box

Now click any of the hyperlinks—[server url], [subject], or [server address]—on the New Mail Action dialog box. The Enter E-Mail Information dialog box is now displayed as shown in Figure 14-12. In this window you define the URL where the campaign will find the e-mail message that you want to be sent. Recall that earlier we built a JSP called email.jsp (refer back to Listing 14-1) and placed it in the directory *domain*\beaApps\portalApp\myWebApp\campaigns\emails. We use this JSP as the e-mail that will be sent when the user registers on the portal. If you click the Browse button, you can select the email.jsp that was defined. You must also define the subject for the e-mail and optionally the sender's e-mail address.

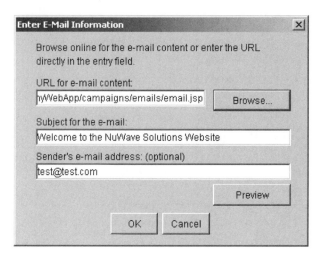

Figure 14-12. Enter E-Mail Information dialog box

Once this has been done, you can test how the e-mail looks by clicking the Preview button. You will be prompted for a user ID. Once the user ID has been entered, the e-mail is displayed as it would look when it is sent. Figure 14-13 shows how the e-mail preview looks.

Figure 14-13. Test e-mail in preview mode

After you have defined all links that you want, click the OK button to close the Mail Action dialog box. The Campaign Editor now shows the e-mail scenario under the ad scenario that was already defined.

Entering Stop/Start Criteria

Now that you have entered general information and defined an ad and e-mail scenario, you must enter the stop/start criteria. You can set a start date for a campaign, and you can end the campaign on a date and time or when certain campaign goals are met. Campaign goals are determined by the number of times content is viewed or clicked. To enter stop/start criteria, click the Stop/Start bar in the Campaign Editor window as shown in Figure 14-14.

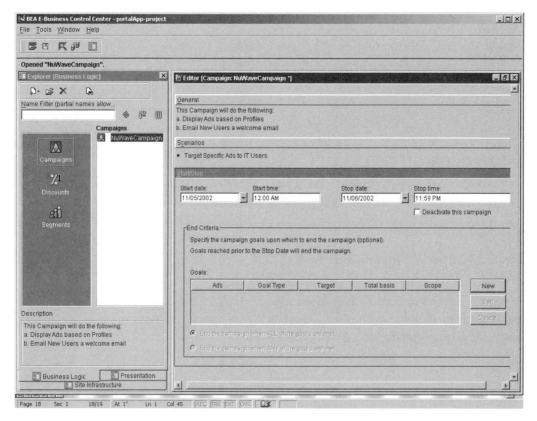

Figure 14-14. Start/Stop criteria in the Campaign Editor

You can enter the start date and start time that you want for the campaign as well as the stop date and stop time. If you plan on using ad actions in your scenarios and want to end your campaign when certain content-related goals are reached, you can end campaigns before the stop date when your goals are met. This is done by specifying the campaign end criteria based on the number of impressions (views) associated with the content, the number of content click-throughs, or a combination of both. To do so, click the New button to display the Goal Detail window. In this window you can end campaigns when a certain number of impressions or click-throughs occur.

Once you have defined the start/stop criteria, you must save the campaign and then synchronize all changes done in the EBCC.

You can test the campaigns you have created before you use them. This allows you to reset a campaign so it will work as if it was just deployed. To implement debugging, click Tools ➤ Reset Campaigns. The Reset Campaign States dialog box is displayed as shown is Figure 14-15.

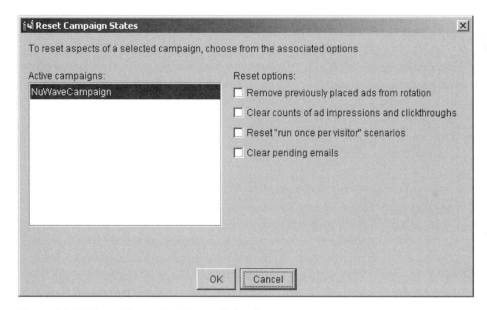

Figure 14-15. Reset Campaign States dialog box

NOTE *You can also set the E-Business Control Center to automatically display the Reset Campaign States dialog box after you synchronize. To do this, choose Tools ➤ Project Settings. On the Synchronization tab, select the "show reset options for active campaigns" option and click OK.*

Deactivating and Reactivating Campaigns

Once campaigns are saved, they are considered active. If you want to end an active campaign or stop a running campaign prior to the specified stop date, open the campaign and select the Deactivate this campaign option in the Start/Stop pane. After this has been done, save the campaign and synchronize the EBCC.

If at any time you want to reactivate a campaign, deselect the Deactivate this campaign option and click OK at the prompt. After this has been done, save the campaign and synchronize the EBCC.

Running the Campaign Created

Now that we have walked you through creating a campaign that has a scenario with ad and e-mail actions, in this section we tie everything together and show you how the scenario created is triggered.

Triggering the Ad

Recall that we demonstrated how to set up an ad action that was triggered by a user being part of the segment ITSegment. Anytime a user logs in to the portal and has a work type of IT, this action is triggered. When the ad action is triggered, it places the banner it.gif in the placeholder AdPlaceholder (created in Chapter 13) rotation. When the portlet called placeholder, also created in Chapter 13, is placed on a page, it displays the banners that are part of its query. Once the user logs in to the portal, the it.gif banner is added to the images that are displayed as part of the placeholder AdPlaceholder. The code for the portlet placeholder is listed here:

```
<%@ taglib uri="ph.tld" prefix="ph" %>

<table width="100%" height="100%" border="0" cellspacing="0" cellpadding="0">
<tr>
<td align="center">
<ph:placeholder name="/placeholders/AdPlaceholder.pla"/>
</td>
</tr>
</table>
```

Triggering E-Mail

If you have been following along up to this point, you have set up an e-mail
action to be triggered from a predefined event, UserRegistrationEvent. In order
for this event to be triggered, you have to place code in a portlet that will trigger
this event. When the event is triggered, the e-mail action occurs. You must periodically use a command to send the batched e-mail that is stored in the BEA
WebLogic Portal data repository. You can also use cron or any other scheduler
that your operating system supports to issue the command to send e-mail.

What follows is the code that needs to be added to the portlet that was
built in Chapter 13 for retrieving and updating the user profile property set—
WorkUserProfile. The code is only dispatched from this page if users actually
changed one of their properties.

```
<%@ page import="com.bea.p13n.tracking.TrackingEventHelper"%>
<%
    // check to see if the user changed a property
    if  (worknameenter != null || worktypeenter != null || emailenter != null)
        TrackingEventHelper.dispatchUserRegistrationEvent(request);
%>
```

Placing this code in this portlet triggers the event UserRegistrationEvent every
time a user uses this portlet to register his or her profile information. This in turn
triggers the e-mail action that will send an e-mail to the user who has registered.
This is just an example, and this event is triggered in this portlet to simplify
things.

NOTE *The UserRegistrationEvent is fired automatically from the
portal framework Webflow during the user registration process,
assuming the user registration process is configured via user_secu-
rity.wf.*

Now that e-mails have been placed in the BEA WebLogic Portal data repository, you need to learn how to send them.

TIP *You must set up the Mail service within Service
Configuration for your Web application in the BEA WebLogic
Console. The setting should be the SMTP host name that you want
to use to send mail.*

To send mail, you first open one of the following files in a text editor, depending on your operating system:

- *BEA_HOME*\weblogic700\portal\bin\win32\mailmanager.bat (Windows)

- *BEA_HOME*\weblogic700\portal\bin\win32\mailmanager.sh (Unix)

Please note that you might need to modify some of the settings in the file you open. Once you have configured the mailmanager script, you can run it from a shell. Note that the WebLogic Portal must be running for this script to execute correctly. The first thing that you need to do is run the mailmanager script to determine the names and contents of the e-mail batches in the data repository. If you are using Windows, enter the following command:

```
mailmanager.bat appName list
```

Or, if you are in Unix, enter this command:

```
mailmanager.sh appName list
```

In both cases, appName is the name of the enterprise application that generated the e-mail batch. The command prints to standard out. You can use shell commands to direct the output to files.

The following is the output after running mailmanager:

```
mailmanager portalApp list
Currently defined batches:
        Batch "/campaigns/NuWaveCampaign.cam" has 1 messages
```

Once you have the batch name, you can run mailmanager using send-delete. This sends all e-mails that have been stored and then deletes them from the BEA WebLogic Portal data repository. To send a batch and remove it from the data repository on a Windows system, enter the following command:

```
mailmanager.bat appName send-delete batch-name
```

In Unix, enter this command:

```
mailmanager.sh appName send-delete batch-name
```

Following is an example of this command using the batch name shown previously:

```
mailmanager portalApp send-delete /campaigns/NuWaveCampaign.cam
```

You will want to run the batch file mailmanager periodically or have a scheduler program run it to send all batched e-mails.

Summary

A campaign can be a very powerful mechanism for allowing personalization in the portal you have created. This chapter has covered some of the basic concepts for building a campaign. Once you have read this chapter, you should be able to create your own campaign that is based on the personalization requirements you have for your portal.

CHAPTER 15

Miscellaneous Topics

A FEW TOPICS DON'T WARRANT an entire chapter of their own but are important nonetheless in putting together a solid corporate portal. This chapter covers some of those topics.

Content Management Configuration

A typical portal configuration within a corporate environment has one or more portal servers serving its clients. Each of the portal servers usually accesses a single data repository for enterprise data. Although the default portal configuration for content system data has a data source for each server within the portal environment, it is sometimes desirable to use a single source for content system data.

Figure 15-1 shows this typical architecture. Notice that the data for the content management system consists of two parts. The content system files represent the directory structure that contains the actual data files (HTML, Word documents, etc.) stored in the content management system. The content system database contains the metadata for the content within the content management system.

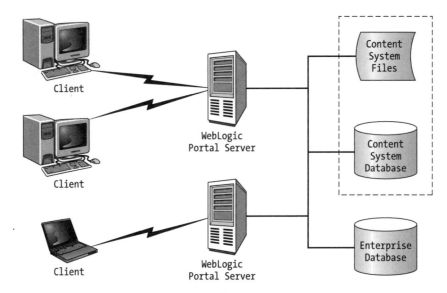

Figure 15-1. Content management overview

In this section, we discuss configuring content management systems within portal servers to point to a single data source for content system data. There are three main steps to configuring the content management systems in this way: You must configure the content management pool, the content management data source, and the content management service.

 NOTE *The example in this section uses Oracle for the metadata data source. This as well as the other configuration parameters may need to be adjusted for the specific portal environment being configured.*

Configuring the Content Connection Pool

The following steps show how to configure the content connection pool on each portal server:

1. In the console, navigate to myDomain ➤ Services ➤ JDBC ➤ ConnectionPools.

2. Click Configure a new JDBC Connection Pool.

3. Set Name to contentPool.

4. Modify the information for the pool as follows:

   URL: jdbc:oracle:thin:@*host*:*port*:*service name*

   Driver classname: oracle.jdbc.driver.OracleDriver

   Properties:

   user=<database user>

   weblogic.jts.waitSecondsForConnectionSecs=999999999999

   verbose=false

   server=<database server>

5. Set the password for the database user.

6. Click Create.

7. Under the Configuration tab, select the Connections subtab.

8. Set Maximum Capacity to 20.

9. Select Supports Local Transaction.

10. Click Apply.

11. Under the Configuration tab, select the Testing subtab.

12. Set Test Table Name to DUAL.

13. Select Test Reserved Connections.

14. Click Apply.

15. Select the Targets tab.

16. Move portalServer from Available to Chosen.

17. Click Apply.

Configuring the Content Data Source

The content data source specifies the data source for the content pool. To configure the content data source, do the following:

1. In the console, navigate to myDomain ➤ Services ➤ JDBC ➤ Data Sources.

2. Click Configure a new JDBC Data Source.

3. Set Name to contentPool.

4. Set JNDI Name to weblogic.jdbc.pool.contentPool.

5. Set Pool Name to contentPool.

6. Click Create.

7. Select the Targets tab.

8. Move portalServer from Available to Chosen.

9. Click Apply.

Configuring the Document Connection Pool Service

The document connection pool service tells the WebLogic Server where to look for the content data and the metadata.

1. In the console, navigate to portalDomain ➤ Deployments ➤ Applications ➤ portal ➤ Service Configuration.

2. Select the default Document Connection Pool service shown in Figure 15-2.

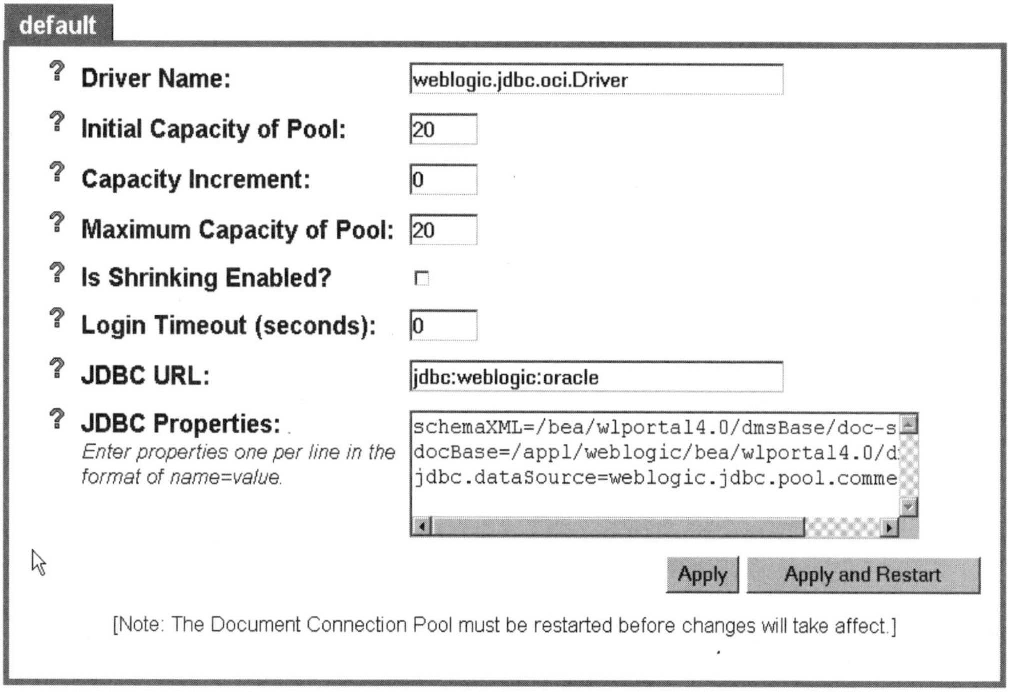

default

?	**Driver Name:**	weblogic.jdbc.oci.Driver
?	**Initial Capacity of Pool:**	20
?	**Capacity Increment:**	0
?	**Maximum Capacity of Pool:**	20
?	**Is Shrinking Enabled?**	☐
?	**Login Timeout (seconds):**	0
?	**JDBC URL:**	jdbc:weblogic:oracle

? **JDBC Properties:**
Enter properties one per line in the format of name=value.

```
schemaXML=/bea/wlportal4.0/dmsBase/doc-s
docBase=/appl/weblogic/bea/wlportal4.0/d
jdbc.dataSource=weblogic.jdbc.pool.comme
```

Apply   Apply and Restart

[Note: The Document Connection Pool must be restarted before changes will take affect.]

Figure 15-2. Document Connection Pool service

3. Set the JDBC properties as follows:

schemaXML=/bea/user_projects/mydomain/dmsBase/doc-schemas

docBase=/appl/weblogic/bea/user_projects/myDomain/dmsBase
jdbc.dataSource=weblogic.jdbc.pool.contentPool

NOTE   *The schemaXML, dmsBase, and docBase directories are mounted directories in Unix or mapped drives in Windows that all of the portal servers have access to.*

4.   Click Apply.

NOTE   *If the portal server that is being configured is running on Unix, you need to navigate to the /bea/wlportal4.0/applications/portal/META-INF directory and edit application-config.xml to remove ^M characters.*

5.   Restart the portal.

JSP Configuration

You may have noticed that you have to stop and restart the portal server for your JSP changes to take effect. This is because of the default configuration of the JSP descriptor for the Web application.

To get to the JSP descriptor, navigate to *Domain* ➤ Deployments ➤ *Enterprise Application* ➤ *Web Application* within the Server Console. Click the Edit Web Application Deployment Descriptors link. When the Web Application Deployment Descriptors window opens, click the *portal name* ➤ WebApp Ext ➤ JSP Descriptor node within the tree.

Page Check Seconds

By default, the Page Check Seconds setting is set to 300. The Page Check Seconds setting tells the server how often to check for new versions of JSPs. So by default the server will only check for new versions of JSPs every 5 minutes. To get the server to check for JSP changes immediately, change this setting to 1.

Precompile

The Precompile option tells the server to precompile JSPs when the server starts. This option enhances server performance since the server does not have to compile JSPs when they are accessed.

In a production environment where code isn't changing on a regular basis, you should enable the precompile option. You should also set the Page Check Seconds option to a wide interval or to 0, which tells the server not to check for changes in JSPs. If you have the Page Check Seconds setting set to 1 or a low number, performance of the server is degraded because the server has to check for new versions and possibly compile them every second.

Compiling JSPs

If you don't want the server startup to take so long or your users to have to wait for pages to compile the first time the JSPs are accessed, you might want to consider using the WebLogic JSP compiler. You can use the JSP compiler to compile your portal JSPs at deployment time to prevent automatic compiling at runtime. The WebLogic JSP compiler parses a JSP file into a Java source file and then compiles the source file into a Java class file.

Following is the syntax for running compiler:

```
$ java weblogic.jspc options filename
```

NOTE *The weblogic.jspc can be found in the weblogic.jar file in the \bea\weblogic700\server\lib package.*

The two most common compiler options that you may want to use are the -classpath and the -d options.

- The -classpath option allows you to specify a colon-separated list in Unix or a semicolon-separated list in Windows of directories that are required to compile the JSP.

- The -d option allows you to specify the output directly for the compiled class.

You can find more information on the WebLogic JSP compiler in the WebLogic documentation at http://e-docs.bea.com/wls/docs70/jsp/reference.html#57794.

Using Connection Pools

JDBC connection pools are a reusable set of connections to a database. A portal application can use these connection pools as needed without incurring the overhead of opening and closing these connections each time the application needs to access the database.

In this section, we discuss how to use connection pools within a portal application. We show you how to set up a connection pool in the WebLogic Portal Server and how to use the connection pool within a portal application.

To configure the connection pool for database access, you must create a JDBC pool and a JDBC data source and configure the ACL for the connection pool in the WebLogic Portal Server Console.

JDBC Pool Configuration

Following are the steps required to configure the JDBC pool in the WebLogic Portal Server.

NOTE *The settings in this example are for Oracle. If you are using another database, you need to modify these settings accordingly. For our example, we are using the SCOTT schema in the default Oracle database.*

1. Log in to the portal server console.

2. In the console go to *domain* ➤ Services ➤ JDBC ➤ ConnectionPools.

3. Select Configure a new JDBC Connection Pool.

4. Enter the name for the pool. For our example, we enter OrclPool as the name of the pool. Then enter the rest of the information for the pool using the information that follows as an example:

   URL: jdbc:oracle:thin:@<DBSERVER:1521:<SID>

   Driver classname: oracle.jdbc.driver.OracleDriver

   Properties: user=scott

5. Set the password to the current password for the paragon database.

6. Click Create.

7. Navigate to the Connection tab.

8. Set the information on the Connection tab as follows:

   • Set the Maximum Capacity to the maximum connections you want to allow. For development this can be set to 20.

   • Check the Supports Local Transaction check box.

9. Click Apply

10. Under the Configuration tab, select the Testing subtab.

11. Set Test Table Name to DUAL.

12. Select Test Reserved Connections.

13. Click Apply.

14. Select the Targets tab.

15. Move the server(s) that you are configuring from Available to Chosen.

16. Click Apply.

JDBC DataSource Configuration

The following shows how to set up the JDBC DataSource:

1. In the server console under *domain*/Services/JDBC/DataSources, create a data source by clicking the Configure a new JDBC Data Sources link.

2. Set the JNDI name to OrclDataSource.

3. Set the Pool name to the OrclPool that you created previously.

4. Click Create.

5. Click Apply.

Configure Connection Pool ACL

The following steps show how to configure an ACL to allow access to the content connection pool:

1. From the WebLogic Server Console, click the myDomain ➤ Compatibility Security ➤ ACLs node.

2. From the right pane click Create new ACL.

3. Click the Create button to create a new ACL called weblogic.jdbc.connectionPool.contentPool.

4. Click the Add a new Permission link.

5. As shown in Figure 15-3, create the new permission by entering "reserve" for the permission name and "everyone" in the Grant to Groups field and clicking the Apply button.

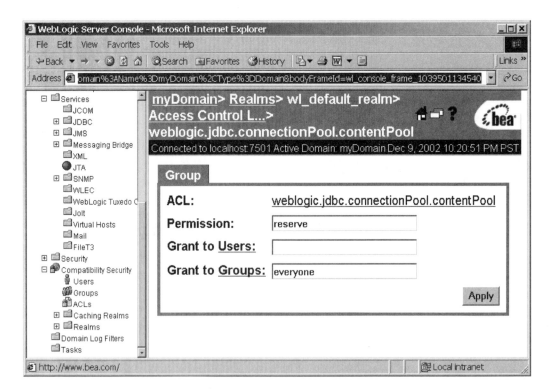

Figure 15-3. Creating a new ACL permission

Using the Connection Pool in Code

In Chapter 11, we set up a human resources page and portlet and a human resources group portal. Here we use the human resources portlet that we set up in that chapter to display employees names, job descriptions, and salaries.

Following is the code for the human resources portlet. As you can see, we are getting the connection from the pool that we just set up. Once we get the connection, we use it as we would a regular JDBC connection.

```
<!-- put the contents of your portlet here -->
<%@ page import="java.sql.*" %>
<%@ page import="javax.sql.DataSource"%>
<%@ page import="com.bea.p13n.util.jdbc.JdbcHelper"%>
<%@ page import="com.bea.p13n.util.JndiHelper"%>
<%
    String name = null;
    String job = null;
    Object sal = null;
    String html = null;
  Connection conn = null;
  Statement stmt = null;
  ResultSet rs = null;
try{
    DataSource dataSource = (DataSource)JndiHelper.lookupNarrow(
        "OrclDataSource", DataSource.class);
    conn = dataSource.getConnection();
    stmt = conn.createStatement();
    stmt.execute("select ename, job, sal from scott.emp");
  %>

<table>
<tr>
<td>Name</td>
<td>Job</td>
<td>Salary</td>
</tr>

<%
  rs = stmt.getResultSet();
  while (rs.next()){
```

```
        name = rs.getString("ENAME");
        job = rs.getString("JOB");
        sal = rs.getObject("SAL");

        html = "<tr><td>" + name + "</td><td>" + job +
                "</td><td>" + sal.toString() + "</td></tr>";

%>

<%=html %>

<%
    }
}
catch (SQLException ex)
{
    out.println("<pre><code>");
    StringWriter str = new StringWriter();
    PrintWriter pw = new PrintWriter(str);
    ex.printStackTrace(pw);
    pw.flush();
    out.println(str.toString());
    out.println("</code></pre>");
}
finally
{
    JdbcHelper.close(rs, stmt, conn);
}
%>

</table>
```

NOTE *By default the compatibility security for the WebLogic Portal is set up with several ACLs. If you are using a portal with this default configuration, this example may not work—you may get an Access Denied error.*

Some of these ACLs control access to JDBC resources. Since our HumanResources group isn't assigned to these ACLs, we will get an Access Denied error when we try to use the pool. You can work around this by assigning the HumanResources group to these ACLs or by deleting these ACLs.

If you followed our example, you can see the results by logging in to the portal as a human resources user and navigating to the hr page. Figure 15-4 shows the hr page from our example.

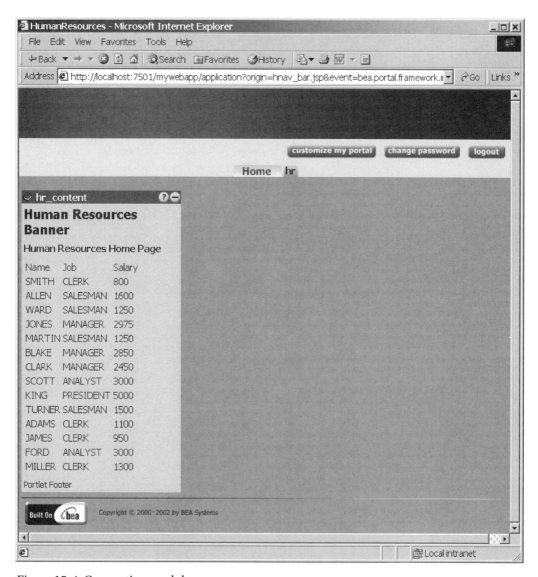

Figure 15-4. Connection pool demo

Configuring E-Mail

Being able to send and receive e-mail messages is a necessity in many portals. In order to send and receive e-mails, you must configure a mail session and then write code. This is the generic WebLogic Server/Java Mail way to send e-mail.

As discussed in Chapter 14, the WebLogic Portal provides another mechanism to send e-mail via the MailManager EJB (which can be accessed directly, not just through campaigns). The MailManager internally uses Java Mail to send e-mail by default. It has its own configuration in the console under Deployments ➤ Applications ➤ *app* ➤ Service Configuration ➤ MailService. The MailManager provides two features that Java Mail doesn't:

- Batching outbound e-mail messages that can be sent out in bulk. This allows the output e-mail to be sent offline from the user's request and gives an administrator control over how and when e-mail will be sent.

- Generating e-mail body text from a Web app resource, including JSPs and servlets. In this fashion, you can write a JSP that will generate the body of the e-mail.

Please see Chapter 14 if you want details on using e-mail this way. We discuss using the generic WebLogic Server/Java Mail way to send e-mail here.

Configuring a New Mail Session

To configure a new mail session, you must go into the WebLogic Server Administration Console. In the left pane of the Console, select Services ➤ Mail. In the right pane of the console, click the Configure a New Mail Session option. A window displays in the right pane showing the tabs associated with configuring a new mail session. In the Configuration tab shown in Figure 15-5, fill in the Name, JNDIName, and Properties (key=value) attribute fields.

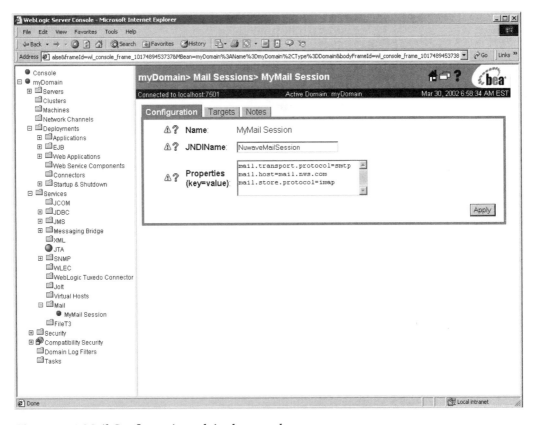

Figure 15-5. Mail Configuration tab in the console

The JNDI name is used to access the mail session. In the Properties field, you can define all the mail properties you want as defaults. You can change any of these properties in code.

In the Targets tab, indicate the server(s) for this configured mail session by moving the server from the Available list to the Chosen list. When you are done, click Apply to create a mail session instance with the name you specified in the Name field. The new instance is added under the Mail node in the left pane. Now you are ready to write code that accesses the mail session you just created.

Sending E-Mail

To send an e-mail, you must do the following:

1. Get the mail session created. The mail session created in the preceding section is named NuwaveMailSession.

2. Prepare the e-mail message.

3. Send the message.

The following JSP code could be placed in a portlet to send an e-mail:

```
<%@ page import="java.util.*" %>
<%@ page import="javax.activation.*" %>
<%@ page import="javax.mail.*" %>
<%@ page import="javax.mail.internet.*" %>
<%@ page import="javax.naming.*" %>
<%
// get the mailsession you created
InitialContext ic = new InitialContext();
Session mailsession = (Session) ic.lookup("NuwaveMailSession");

Message msg = new MimeMessage(mailsession);
msg.setFrom();
msg.setRecipients(Message.RecipientType.TO,
InternetAddress.parse("hblock@nuwavesolutions.com", false));
msg.setSubject("Test Email");

// Content is stored in a MIME multi-part message
// with one body part
MimeBodyPart mbp = new MimeBodyPart();
mbp.setText("this is a test message that is being sent.");
Multipart mp = new MimeMultipart();
mp.addBodyPart(mbp);
msg.setContent(mp);

//Send the message.
Transport.send(msg);
%>
```

Summary

In this chapter, we described a few items that will help you build a robust, industrial-strength portal within the WebLogic Portal Server. To find other advanced topics, refer to the WebLogic online documentation at `http://e-docs.bea.com`. You can also find other useful information on the support Web site at `http://support.bea.com`.

CHAPTER 16

Debugging

WHEN WALKING THROUGH ALL of the examples included in this book, you more than likely encountered errors as you went along. It is important to log these messages so that you may view the status of running modules and errors that might be occurring within them. During the debugging process, information messages are normally used to display the values of variables and to help track the flow of processing. In this chapter, we look at the logging mechanism of the BEA WebLogic Portal and also discuss some basic debugging techniques.

Instrumenting Java Code

Unfortunately, this chapter cannot magically turn a beginning Java developer into an expert. What it can do is serve as a foundation on which you can build. This section provides a basic discussion of instrumenting code for debugging to alleviate errors. You may choose to log application information when errors occur or to view the state of variables within a running class. The most basic methodology is simply logging this information to the standard output stream, using the System.out.println() method. This method writes any string message onto the output stream. When errors occur, just knowing what the error was may not be enough. In this case, you can use a stack trace, which traces the flow of the module to the point of exception.

System.out.println()

More than likely you are fully aware of the System.out.println() method. For reiteration's sake, this method writes information to the standard output stream. Although it may sound very useful and harmless, it is far from that. Littering source code with this method is not the preferred methodology and could even cause more work for you in the long run.

You can use System.out.println() to display a slew of messages. However, these messages are permanent, meaning they will be displayed and continue to be displayed until the containing class is modified and recompiled. At first, this doesn't sound all that bad. After debugging a piece of offending code, these messages may no longer be needed and could be removed from the source code. However, if at a later point they were needed, they would have to be replaced and the code recompiled. This could turn into a vicious cycle. BEA WebLogic Server has a built-in logging mechanism that you should use instead. This mechanism is covered within the bulk of this chapter.

Using Stack Traces

Writing the generic description of an exception to the standard output stream will give you a good idea of what has occurred. However, you will likely have to spend time determining the location and cause of the error. To pinpoint the offending line of code, a stack trace can be used. A stack trace generates more information than a simple message. This message gives a complete listing of each and every class invocation and method call that has occurred to reach the point of error. Also, the line number of the offending line of code is usually clearly noted. Figure 16-1 shows a sample stack trace.

```
java.lang.NullPointerException
        at com.nws.examples.MyClass.getValue(MyClass.java:10)
        at jsp_servlet._portlets._portlet1.__portlet.__jspService(__portlet.java:95)
        at weblogic.servlet.jsp.JspBase.service(JspBase.java:27)
        at weblogic.servlet.internal.ServletStubImpl$ServletInvocationAction.run(ServletStubImpl.java:1058)
        at weblogic.servlet.internal.ServletStubImpl.invokeServlet(ServletStubImpl.java:401)
        at weblogic.servlet.internal.ServletStubImpl.invokeServlet(ServletStubImpl.java:306)
        at weblogic.servlet.internal.RequestDispatcherImpl.include(RequestDispatcherImpl.java:542)
        at weblogic.servlet.internal.RequestDispatcherImpl.include(RequestDispatcherImpl.java:368)
        at weblogic.servlet.jsp.PageContextImpl.include(PageContextImpl.java:120)
        at jsp_servlet._framework.__portlet.__jspService(__portlet.java:266)
        at weblogic.servlet.jsp.JspBase.service(JspBase.java:27)
        at weblogic.servlet.internal.ServletStubImpl$ServletInvocationAction.run(ServletStubImpl.java:1058)
        at weblogic.servlet.internal.ServletStubImpl.invokeServlet(ServletStubImpl.java:401)
        at weblogic.servlet.internal.ServletStubImpl.invokeServlet(ServletStubImpl.java:306)
        at weblogic.servlet.internal.RequestDispatcherImpl.include(RequestDispatcherImpl.java:542)
        at weblogic.servlet.internal.RequestDispatcherImpl.include(RequestDispatcherImpl.java:368)
        at weblogic.servlet.jsp.PageContextImpl.include(PageContextImpl.java:120)
        at com.bea.portal.render.servlets.jsp.taglib.RenderTag.renderPortlets(RenderTag.java:172)
        at com.bea.portal.render.servlets.jsp.taglib.RenderTag.doStartTag(RenderTag.java:60)
        at jsp_servlet._framework._layouts._threecolumn.__template.__jspService(__template.java:124)
        at weblogic.servlet.jsp.JspBase.service(JspBase.java:27)
        at weblogic.servlet.internal.ServletStubImpl$ServletInvocationAction.run(ServletStubImpl.java:1058)
        at weblogic.servlet.internal.ServletStubImpl.invokeServlet(ServletStubImpl.java:401)
        at weblogic.servlet.internal.ServletStubImpl.invokeServlet(ServletStubImpl.java:306)
        at weblogic.servlet.internal.RequestDispatcherImpl.include(RequestDispatcherImpl.java:542)
        at weblogic.servlet.internal.RequestDispatcherImpl.include(RequestDispatcherImpl.java:368)
        at weblogic.servlet.jsp.PageContextImpl.include(PageContextImpl.java:120)
        at jsp_servlet._framework.__page.__jspService(__page.java:201)
        at weblogic.servlet.jsp.JspBase.service(JspBase.java:27)
        at weblogic.servlet.internal.ServletStubImpl$ServletInvocationAction.run(ServletStubImpl.java:1058)
        at weblogic.servlet.internal.ServletStubImpl.invokeServlet(ServletStubImpl.java:401)
        at weblogic.servlet.internal.ServletStubImpl.invokeServlet(ServletStubImpl.java:306)
        at weblogic.servlet.internal.RequestDispatcherImpl.include(RequestDispatcherImpl.java:542)
        at weblogic.servlet.internal.RequestDispatcherImpl.include(RequestDispatcherImpl.java:368)
        at weblogic.servlet.jsp.PageContextImpl.include(PageContextImpl.java:120)
        at jsp_servlet._framework.__portal.__jspService(__portal.java:734)
        at weblogic.servlet.jsp.JspBase.service(JspBase.java:27)
        at weblogic.servlet.internal.ServletStubImpl$ServletInvocationAction.run(ServletStubImpl.java:1058)
        at weblogic.servlet.internal.ServletStubImpl.invokeServlet(ServletStubImpl.java:401)
        at weblogic.servlet.internal.ServletStubImpl.invokeServlet(ServletStubImpl.java:306)
        at weblogic.servlet.internal.RequestDispatcherImpl$ForwardAction.run(RequestDispatcherImpl.java:341)
        at weblogic.security.service.SecurityServiceManager.runAs(SecurityServiceManager.java:744)
        at weblogic.servlet.internal.RequestDispatcherImpl.forward(RequestDispatcherImpl.java:251)
        at com.bea.portal.appflow.servlets.internal.PortalWebflowServlet.doGet(PortalWebflowServlet.java:176)
        at javax.servlet.http.HttpServlet.service(HttpServlet.java:740)
        at javax.servlet.http.HttpServlet.service(HttpServlet.java:853)
        at weblogic.servlet.internal.ServletStubImpl$ServletInvocationAction.run(ServletStubImpl.java:1058)
        at weblogic.servlet.internal.ServletStubImpl.invokeServlet(ServletStubImpl.java:401)
        at weblogic.servlet.internal.ServletStubImpl.invokeServlet(ServletStubImpl.java:306)
        at weblogic.servlet.internal.RequestDispatcherImpl$ForwardAction.run(RequestDispatcherImpl.java:341)
        at weblogic.security.service.SecurityServiceManager.runAs(SecurityServiceManager.java:744)
        at weblogic.servlet.internal.RequestDispatcherImpl.forward(RequestDispatcherImpl.java:251)
        at weblogic.servlet.jsp.PageContextImpl.forward(PageContextImpl.java:116)
        at jsp_servlet.__index.__jspService(__index.java:92)
        at weblogic.servlet.jsp.JspBase.service(JspBase.java:27)
        at weblogic.servlet.internal.ServletStubImpl$ServletInvocationAction.run(ServletStubImpl.java:1058)
        at weblogic.servlet.internal.ServletStubImpl.invokeServlet(ServletStubImpl.java:401)
        at weblogic.servlet.internal.ServletStubImpl.invokeServlet(ServletStubImpl.java:306)
        at weblogic.servlet.internal.WebAppServletContext$ServletInvocationAction.run(WebAppServletContext.java:5412)
        at weblogic.security.service.SecurityServiceManager.runAs(SecurityServiceManager.java:744)
        at weblogic.servlet.internal.WebAppServletContext.invokeServlet(WebAppServletContext.java:3086)
        at weblogic.servlet.internal.ServletRequestImpl.execute(ServletRequestImpl.java:2544)
        at weblogic.kernel.ExecuteThread.execute(ExecuteThread.java:153)
        at weblogic.kernel.ExecuteThread.run(ExecuteThread.java:134)
```

Figure 16-1. Sample stack trace

Although this may be confusing, the stack trace in Figure 16-1 gives a detailed roadmap to the error at hand. When debugging, first notice the error description on the topmost line. This gives an idea of what to look for in the code. The message in the sample stack trace, java.lang.NullPointerException, lets you know that some null object was referenced in the code. From the second line on in succession is the description of each method, in each class, that was called up to the point where the error occurred. Start with the first of these lines. The example shows

```
java.lang.NullPointerException
        at com.nws.examples.MyClass.getValue(MyClass.java:10)
```

The last section of this line, (MyClass.java:10), is most intriguing. This tells you that the exception occurred within MyClass.java on line 10. Now you can jump line by line, tracing the steps of the application to find why this object on line 10 is null.

Stack Traces Within Portlet JSPs

JSPs can be debugged in the same manner as discussed previously. However, keeping in mind that JSPs are converted to Java files in order to be compiled, the line numbers shown in a stack trace are not going to coincide with lines in the JSP. Instead, the stack trace displays line numbers of the Java file. This makes debugging a little more difficult.

Luckily, BEA has provided a mechanism to alleviate this issue. You can set a JSP parameter in the application descriptor for the Web application to enable JSP debugging. With JSP debugging enabled, the stack trace shows actual JSP line numbers, rather than those of the file's Java equivalent. To enable JSP debugging, follow these steps:

1. Log in to the BEA WebLogic Console.

2. Navigate to the Web application you want to use.

3. Select Edit Web Application Deployment Descriptors.

4. Navigate to myportal ➢ WebApp Ext ➢ JSP Descriptor.

5. Select Debug Enabled, as shown in Figure 16-2.

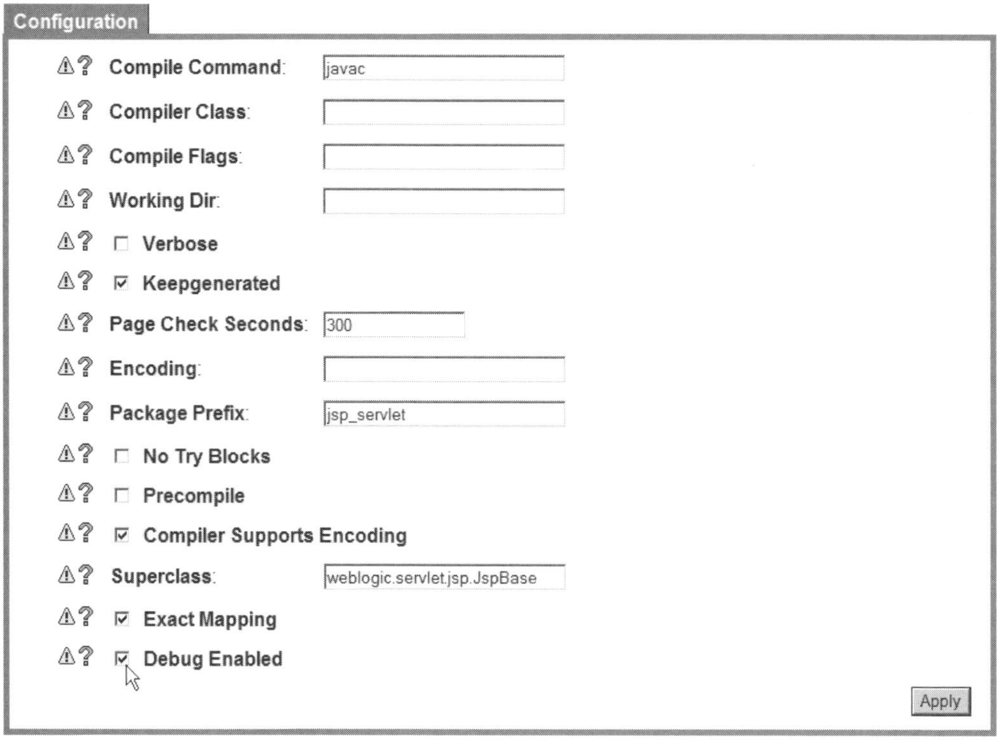

Figure 16-2. Enabling JSP debugging

Debugging Java Code

Instrumenting code is a very simple form of debugging; however, it is also time consuming. Naturally, you always want to log error and exception information. Otherwise, when would you know if a problem is occurring? State information, on the other hand, is not as necessary within logs as you may think. Certainly, logging this type of information gets the job done, but usually only after numerous compiles and deployments. For serious debugging of source code, it makes more sense to set break points within the code and step through the source line by line, to help track down the offending code.

In the BEA WebLogic Portal, it is possible to debug your source code via traditional debuggers while running it within the portal. This feature is a tremendous break when debugging enterprise applications. Any type of Java class can have break points set within and debugged using your favorite debugger. The following sections describe the steps necessary to debug code using the debugger within Borland JBuilder.

Creating a Runtime Configuration

Within the debugger you are using, it is necessary to attach to the Web server's debug port. Within JBuilder, this is accomplished by creating a runtime configuration. The following steps show this process. These steps can be applied to the debugger of your choice.

1. Choose Run ➤ Configurations.

2. Edit a current configuration or create a new one.

3. Select the Debug tab, shown in Figure 16-3.

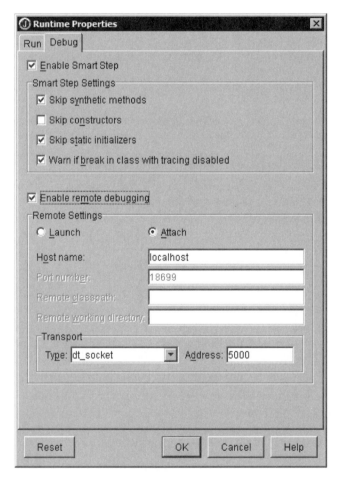

Figure 16-3. JBuilder runtime configuration

4. Select Enable remote debugging.

5. Select Attach.

6. Select a transport type.

7. Enter a transport address.

8. Save the configuration.

Starting the BEA WebLogic Portal in Debug Mode

After deploying the source code to the appropriate location within your Web application, it is necessary to start the portal in debug mode. This is a simple task: All that you need to do is place a few extra parameters within startPortal.bat. The following steps guide you through this process:

1. Navigate to and edit the startPortal.bat file in your domain directory.

2. Locate the line setting the JAVA_OPTIONS variable:

```
set JAVA_OPTIONS=
-Dcommerce.properties="%WLP_HOME%\weblogiccommerce.properties"
```

3. Add the following options:

```
-Xdebug
-Xnoagent
-Djava.compiler=NONE
-Xrunjdwp:transport=transport,server=y,address=address,suspend=n
```

 NOTE *The items* transport *and* address *must match the respective settings within the JBuilder Runtime Configuration previously created.*

4. Save the startPortal.bat file.

5. Start the BEA WebLogic Portal.

Stepping Through the Code

After finishing the previous steps, the code is now ready to be debugged. All that is left to do is to start the debugger using the previously created configuration and navigate through the Web application. While navigating through the portal, execution will break at any point set within the source code. You may now step through the code in the debugger while running within the BEA WebLogic Portal.

The Logging Mechanism

Using println() statements throughout your code does accomplish log messages, but at what cost? It is very possible to acquire enough statements to make the log illegible and unusable. On top of that, there is no good way to turn these statements on and off to debug a certain module of your Web application. Removing these statements means recompiling code, and remove them you must, since no client is going to want these statements in a production environment.

WebLogic has provided a means of writing messages to the WebLogic log based on levels. A switch exists in the server console allowing the developer to log messages at a certain level and even to turn off debugging completely. These console settings will be explored later. First, you should learn to use the logging mechanism in your code. System.out.println() messages should be avoided. It is only a fraction more difficult to use the logging mechanism instead. If you get into the habit of using the log rather than writing directly to the server console, precious time will be saved prior to production, when all println() statements will need to be replaced.

Message Levels

The WebLogic logging mechanism allows you to log messages at several different levels. The level of message that is actually printed out is controlled from within the console. BEA WebLogic provides four levels at which messages can be specified:

- Debug

- Info

- Warning

- Error

By specifying log message levels for an application, message levels can be turned down or up depending on what you want accomplished. For instance, say you have a bug in your application. This bug makes it necessary to display certain messages at different intervals in your code. You could easily access the BEA WebLogic Console to specify the log message level of Debug. This would in turn display all messages that are set at Debug or above. Once debugging is complete, you could set the log level higher, for example, to Warning. This would hide many of the messages from the log.

Using the NonCatalogLogger API

Logging a message in BEA WebLogic is almost as easy as using a println() statement. A message can be written to the log in three easy steps:

1. Import the weblogic.logging.NonCatalogLogger interface, as shown in the following code line. This interface can be found in the weblogic.jar.

   ```
   Import weblogic.logging.NonCatalogLogger;
   ```

2. Instantiate a NonCatalogLogger object:

   ```
   NonCatalogLogger log = new NonCatalogLogger("someApp");
   ```

   The constructor of the NonCatalogLogger interface takes a single String argument. This argument would be either an application name or a module name. In general, the argument is used within the log message to help discern where the message originated.

3. Use any of the available methods provided to write a message to the log. Table 16-1 describes the methods available, listed in ascending message level order.

Table 16-1. Methods of NonCatalogLogger

METHOD	DESCRIPTION
Debug(String message)	Logs a message at the Debug level
Debug(String message, Throwable t)	Logs a message at the Debug level and also logs a stack trace generated from the Throwable object
info(String message)	Logs a message at the Info level
info(String message, Throwable t)	Logs a message at the Info level and also logs a stack trace generated from the Throwable object
warning(String message)	Logs a message at the Warning level
warning(String message, Throwable t)	Logs a message at the Warning level and also logs a stack trace generated from the Throwable object
error(String message)	Logs a message at the Error level
error(String message, Throwable t)	Logs a message at the Error level and also logs a stack trace generated from the Throwable object

Figure 16-4 is an example of how a log message looks within the BEA WebLogic log. This message was generated by calling the warning(String msg, Throwable t) method.

```
<Nov 5, 2002 7:44:13 PM EST> <Info> <HTTP> <101047> <[ServletContext(id=6385630,name=mywebapp,context-path=/mywebapp)]
user_projects\portalDomain\portalServer\.wlnotdelete\portalApp_mywebapp_6385630\jsp_servlet\_portlets\_portlet1\__port
java.lang.NullPointerException
        at com.nws.examples.MyClass.getValue(MyClass.java:10)
        at jsp_servlet._portlets._portlet1.__portlet._jspService(__portlet.java:95)
        at weblogic.servlet.jsp.JspBase.service(JspBase.java:27)
        at weblogic.servlet.internal.ServletStubImpl$ServletInvocationAction.run(ServletStubImpl.java:1058)
        at weblogic.servlet.internal.ServletStubImpl.invokeServlet(ServletStubImpl.java:401)
        at weblogic.servlet.internal.ServletStubImpl.invokeServlet(ServletStubImpl.java:306)
        at weblogic.servlet.internal.RequestDispatcherImpl.include(RequestDispatcherImpl.java:542)
        at weblogic.servlet.internal.RequestDispatcherImpl.include(RequestDispatcherImpl.java:368)
        at weblogic.servlet.jsp.PageContextImpl.include(PageContextImpl.java:120)
        at jsp_servlet._framework.__portlet._jspService(__portlet.java:266)
        at weblogic.servlet.jsp.JspBase.service(JspBase.java:27)
        at weblogic.servlet.internal.ServletStubImpl$ServletInvocationAction.run(ServletStubImpl.java:1058)
        at weblogic.servlet.internal.ServletStubImpl.invokeServlet(ServletStubImpl.java:401)
        at weblogic.servlet.internal.ServletStubImpl.invokeServlet(ServletStubImpl.java:306)
        at weblogic.servlet.internal.RequestDispatcherImpl.include(RequestDispatcherImpl.java:542)
        at weblogic.servlet.internal.RequestDispatcherImpl.include(RequestDispatcherImpl.java:368)
        at weblogic.servlet.jsp.PageContextImpl.include(PageContextImpl.java:120)
        at com.bea.portal.render.servlets.jsp.taglib.RenderTag.renderPortlets(RenderTag.java:172)
        at com.bea.portal.render.servlets.jsp.taglib.RenderTag.doStartTag(RenderTag.java:60)
        at jsp_servlet._framework._layouts._threecolumn.__template._jspService(__template.java:124)
        at weblogic.servlet.jsp.JspBase.service(JspBase.java:27)
        at weblogic.servlet.internal.ServletStubImpl$ServletInvocationAction.run(ServletStubImpl.java:1058)
        at weblogic.servlet.internal.ServletStubImpl.invokeServlet(ServletStubImpl.java:401)
        at weblogic.servlet.internal.ServletStubImpl.invokeServlet(ServletStubImpl.java:306)
        at weblogic.servlet.internal.RequestDispatcherImpl.include(RequestDispatcherImpl.java:542)
        at weblogic.servlet.internal.RequestDispatcherImpl.include(RequestDispatcherImpl.java:368)
        at weblogic.servlet.jsp.PageContextImpl.include(PageContextImpl.java:120)
        at jsp_servlet._framework.__page._jspService(__page.java:201)
        at weblogic.servlet.jsp.JspBase.service(JspBase.java:27)
        at weblogic.servlet.internal.ServletStubImpl$ServletInvocationAction.run(ServletStubImpl.java:1058)
        at weblogic.servlet.internal.ServletStubImpl.invokeServlet(ServletStubImpl.java:401)
        at weblogic.servlet.internal.ServletStubImpl.invokeServlet(ServletStubImpl.java:306)
        at weblogic.servlet.internal.RequestDispatcherImpl.include(RequestDispatcherImpl.java:542)
        at weblogic.servlet.internal.RequestDispatcherImpl.include(RequestDispatcherImpl.java:368)
        at weblogic.servlet.jsp.PageContextImpl.include(PageContextImpl.java:120)
        at jsp_servlet._framework.__portal._jspService(__portal.java:734)
        at weblogic.servlet.jsp.JspBase.service(JspBase.java:27)
        at weblogic.servlet.internal.ServletStubImpl$ServletInvocationAction.run(ServletStubImpl.java:1058)
        at weblogic.servlet.internal.ServletStubImpl.invokeServlet(ServletStubImpl.java:401)
        at weblogic.servlet.internal.ServletStubImpl.invokeServlet(ServletStubImpl.java:306)
        at weblogic.servlet.internal.RequestDispatcherImpl$ForwardAction.run(RequestDispatcherImpl.java:341)
        at weblogic.security.service.SecurityServiceManager.runAs(SecurityServiceManager.java:744)
        at weblogic.servlet.internal.RequestDispatcherImpl.forward(RequestDispatcherImpl.java:251)
        at com.bea.portal.appflow.servlets.internal.PortalWebflowServlet.doGet(PortalWebflowServlet.java:176)
        at javax.servlet.http.HttpServlet.service(HttpServlet.java:740)
        at javax.servlet.http.HttpServlet.service(HttpServlet.java:853)
        at weblogic.servlet.internal.ServletStubImpl$ServletInvocationAction.run(ServletStubImpl.java:1058)
        at weblogic.servlet.internal.ServletStubImpl.invokeServlet(ServletStubImpl.java:401)
        at weblogic.servlet.internal.ServletStubImpl.invokeServlet(ServletStubImpl.java:306)
        at weblogic.servlet.internal.RequestDispatcherImpl$ForwardAction.run(RequestDispatcherImpl.java:341)
        at weblogic.security.service.SecurityServiceManager.runAs(SecurityServiceManager.java:744)
        at weblogic.servlet.internal.RequestDispatcherImpl.forward(RequestDispatcherImpl.java:251)
        at weblogic.servlet.jsp.PageContextImpl.forward(PageContextImpl.java:116)
        at jsp_servlet.__index._jspService(__index.java:92)
        at weblogic.servlet.jsp.JspBase.service(JspBase.java:27)
        at weblogic.servlet.internal.ServletStubImpl$ServletInvocationAction.run(ServletStubImpl.java:1058)
        at weblogic.servlet.internal.ServletStubImpl.invokeServlet(ServletStubImpl.java:401)
        at weblogic.servlet.internal.ServletStubImpl.invokeServlet(ServletStubImpl.java:306)
        at weblogic.servlet.internal.WebAppServletContext$ServletInvocationAction.run(WebAppServletContext.java:5412)
        at weblogic.security.service.SecurityServiceManager.runAs(SecurityServiceManager.java:744)
        at weblogic.servlet.internal.WebAppServletContext.invokeServlet(WebAppServletContext.java:3086)
        at weblogic.servlet.internal.ServletRequestImpl.execute(ServletRequestImpl.java:2544)
        at weblogic.kernel.ExecuteThread.execute(ExecuteThread.java:153)
        at weblogic.kernel.ExecuteThread.run(ExecuteThread.java:134)
```

Figure 16-4. Log message

As you can see from Figure 16-4, the debug message appears to be the same as the stack trace printed in Figure 16-1, but with two main differences. The debug message prints more verbose information, including a timestamp as well as the subsystem generating the error. The other main difference is that this message can easily be turned off by a simple console setting. In the prior example, in order to stop the printout of the message, code has to be recompiled.

Console Logging Settings

Now that the logging mechanism has been integrated into your code, it is necessary to administer these messages so that you can take full advantage of the functionality provide by BEA.

Control of the logging mechanism is present within the BEA WebLogic Console. This application has been discussed in previous chapters. To explore the functionality of the logging mechanism, follow these steps:

1. Log in to the BEA WebLogic Console.

2. Navigate to portalDomain ➤ Servers ➤ portalServer.

3. Choose the tab titled Logging.

The General Tab

The steps in the previous section will lead you to a screen similar to Figure 16-5.

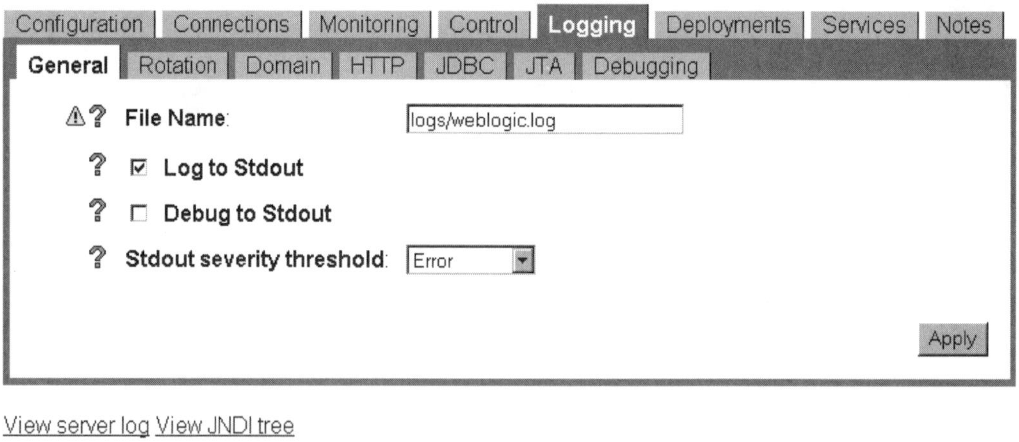

Figure 16-5. The General tab

As you can see in Figure 16-5, the General tab is the first tab shown when Logging is chosen in the BEA WebLogic Console. This tab contains the most generic features of the BEA logging mechanism, which are described in Table 16-2.

Table 16-2. Features of the General Tab

FEATURE	EXPLANATION
File Name	This input box contains the location of the BEA WebLogic log relative to the portal domain directory. Changing this property dictates restarting the BEA WebLogic Portal.
Log to Stdout	By selecting this check box, the WebLogic log will not only be written to the file you specify in the File Name text box, but it will also be displayed in the console window.
Debug to Stdout	This check box will enable debug messages to be written to the console window. This feature makes it very easy to disable all debug messages systemwide with no need to recompile or even restart the server. This is very handy in a production environment.
Stdout severity threshold	This drop-down list contains all the severity levels to which you have access. This feature is used to increase or decrease the message logging level as necessary. Figure 16-6 shows the available severities.

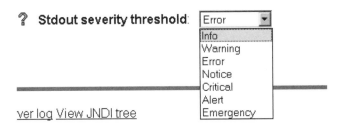

Figure 16-6. Logging severities

Notice that there are more severities within the drop-down list in Figure 16-6 than can be selected using the NonCatalogLogger API. The BEA WebLogic Portal retains the use of the last four severity levels for internal application purposes.

The Rotation Tab

The next tab in succession is the Rotation tab. Use this tab for specifying when the log file should be rotated and by what means. Figure 16-7 shows this tab.

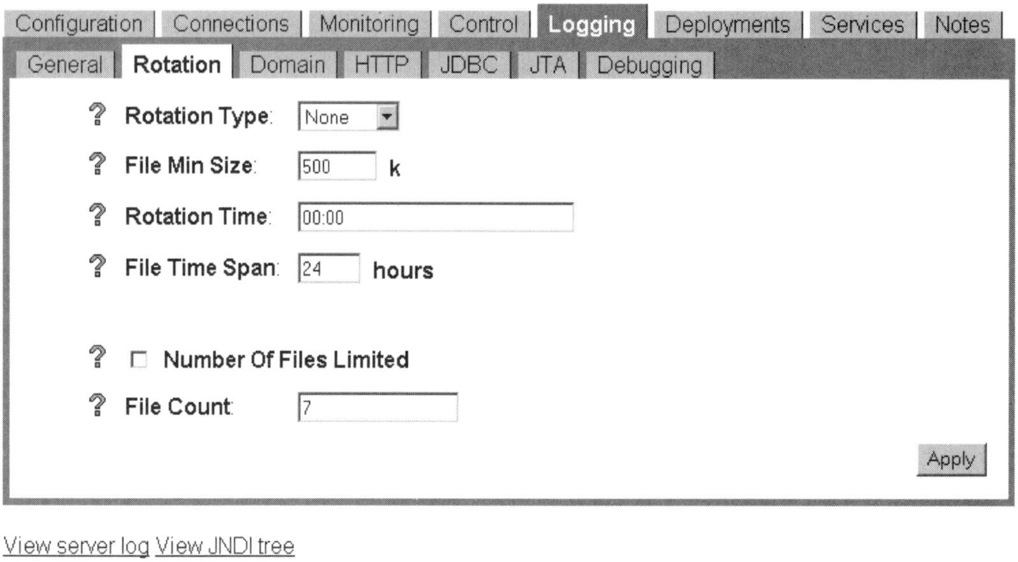

View server log View JNDI tree

Figure 16-7. The Rotation tab

The functionality available on this tab is described in Table 16-3.

Table 16-3. Features of the Rotation Tab

FEATURE	EXPLANATION
Rotation Type	Specifies by which means the log will be rotated. Valid values are None, By Size, and By Time. If None is selected, the log will never be rotated. If either By Size or By Time is selected, the log will be rotated according to the selection.
File Min Size	Specifies the size, in kilobytes, at which the log file will be rotated. This is only valid when the rotation type is By Size. Valid values are any integer between 1 and 65535.
Rotation Time	Specifies the time at which the log file will be rotated. This function is only used when the specified rotation type is By Time. Times need to be specified in MM-dd-yyyy-h:mm:ss format.
File Time Span	Specifies a time span in hours that the server will continue to write old messages to another file.
Number Of Files Limited	Specifies that the server will limit the number of files it creates. If this feature is not used, the server will create an indefinite number of log files and it will be the duty of the administrator to clean the log directory as necessary.
File Count	Specifies the number of files that the server will create. This feature is only used if Number Of Files Limited is selected. After this limit is reached, the oldest existing log file will be reused.

The Domain Tab

The Domain tab allows you to modify domain logging preferences. Figure 16-8 displays this tab.

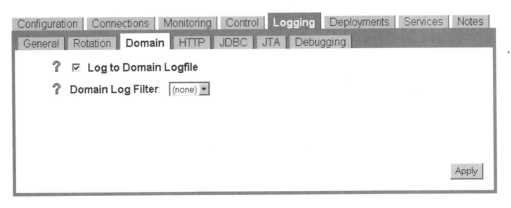

Figure 16-8. The Domain tab

This tab only has two features, and these are described in Table 16-4.

Table 16-4. Features of the Domain Tab

FEATURE	EXPLANATION
Log to Domain Logfile	Specifies that log messages should be written to the domain log as well.
Domain Log Filter	Filters the messages that will be sent to the domain log. This feature is only available when Log to Domain Logfile is selected.

The HTTP Tab

This tab, shown in Figure 16-9, contains the features available for the logging of HTTP requests.

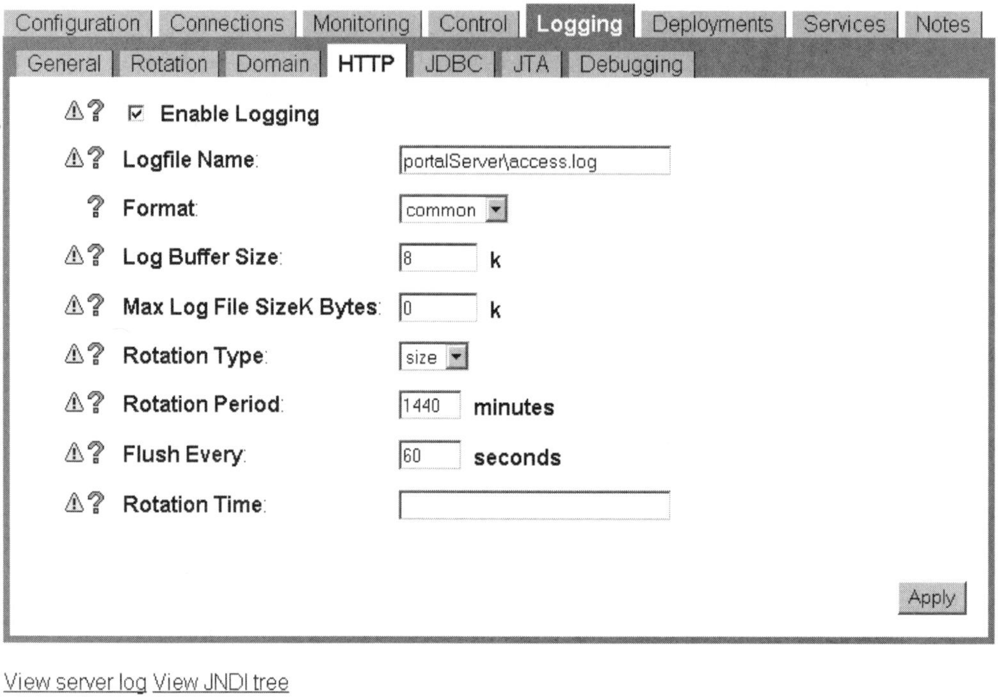

Figure 16-9. The HTTP tab

As shown in Figure 16-9, this tab encompasses the functionality of the first two tabs, but is directed toward the logging of HTTP requests. An overview of this tab is given in Table 16-5.

Table 16-5. Features of the HTTP Tab

FEATURE	EXPLANATION
Enable Logging	Specifies whether to log HTTP requests. Changing this feature requires that the portal be restarted.
Logfile Name	Specifies the name of the HTTP request log file. Changing this feature also requires restarting the portal. A relative path will be assumed to be relative to the root directory of the server.
Format	The W3C format of HTTP request that will be recorded in the log. Values are common or extended.
Log Buffer Size	The HTTP requests are stored in a buffer prior to being written to the log. Once this buffer is full, it will then be written to the log. This feature specifies the size in kilobytes of this buffer. Valid values are integers between 0 and 1024. Changing this feature requires that the portal be restarted.
Max Log File SizeK Bytes	Specifies the maximum size of the HTTP log file in kilobytes. Used only when Rotation Type is set to size. Changing this features requires that the portal be restarted.
Rotation Type	Specifies by what means the HTTP log file will be rotated. Valid values are size or date. Changing this feature requires that the portal be restarted.
Rotation Period	The time period, in minutes, that the server will write old log messages to another log file. Changing this feature requires that the portal be restarted.
Flush Every	Time, in seconds, that the server will check the size of the buffer in which the HTTP request information is stored. Once Log Buffer Size is reached, the information will be written to the log. Changing this feature requires that the portal be restarted.
Rotation Time	Specifies the time at which the log file will be rotated. This function is only used when the specified Rotation Type is By date. Times shall be specified in MM-dd-yyyy-h:mm:ss format. Changing this feature requires that the portal be restarted.

The JDBC Tab

JDBC information can also be logged into its own specific log file. This is configurable on the JDBC tab, which is displayed in Figure 16-10.

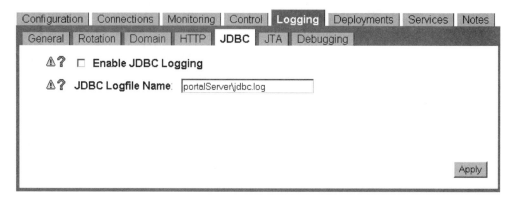

View server log View JNDI tree

Figure 16-10. The JDBC tab

Configuring JDBC logging is as simple as configuring domain logging. The
two functions on this tab are described in Table 16-6.

Table 16-6. Features of the JDBC Tab

FEATURE	EXPLANATION
Enable JDBC Logging	Specifies whether to write JDBC information to the log. Modifying this feature requires restarting the portal.
JDBC Logfile Name	Specifies the name of the JDBC log file. Changing this feature also requires restarting the portal. A relative path will be assumed to be relative to the root directory of the server.

The JTA Tab

The JTA tab is responsible for transaction log requirements. This tab, shown in
Figure 16-11, allows you to configure the transaction logs.

| Configuration | Connections | Monitoring | Control | **Logging** | Deployments | Services | Notes |

| General | Rotation | Domain | HTTP | JDBC | **JTA** | Debugging |

⚠? **Transaction Log File Prefix**: `logs/`

⚠? **Transaction Log File Write Policy**: `Cache-Flush ▾`

`Apply`

View server log View JNDI tree

Figure 16-11. The JTA tab

Transaction logs are written automatically. This cannot be disabled. However, there is a small amount of configuration that can be accomplished, as reviewed in Table 16-7.

Table 16-7. Features of the JTA Tab

FEATURE	EXPLANATION
Transaction Log File Prefix	This is the prefix path of the transaction log destination. If this path is not absolute, the server assumes that the path is relative to the root directory of the server.
Transaction Log File Write Policy	Specifies the policy to use when writing transaction logs to disk. By default, the policy used is Cache-Flush. When using this policy, the server will flush the on-disk and system caches after each write. The Direct-Write policy performs better than the two policies. When using this policy, the operating system writes directly to the disk, by passing any caching.

NOTE   *The Direct-Write policy in the Windows environment may not write transitional log messages immediately to the disk. This is dangerous in the case of a power failure. Transaction messages may be lost. To overcome this problem, disable write caching for the server's disks.*

The Debugging Tab

The last tab in logging configuration is the Debugging tab. This tab has two features that add useful functionality to the server's debug logs. See Figure 16-12 for a view of the Debugging tab.

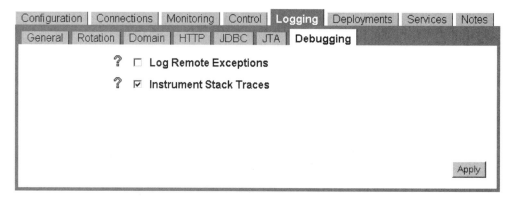

View server log View JNDI tree

Figure 16-12. The Debugging tab

The two features of this tab are described in Table 16-8.

Table 16-8. Features of the Debugging Tab

FEATURE	EXPLANATION
Log Remote Exceptions	Specifies whether to write log messages for exceptions that are thrown from remote servers.
Instrument Stack Traces	Specifies whether to include stack traces when logging exceptions.

Summary

Debugging code is one of the most tedious operations. However, it is eased with the ability to debug the code while it is running in the portal. In the past, after a developer had finished debugging a certain module, he or she would then have to edit the code once more to remove debug messages. This final edit of the code could in turn create other bugs within the application and increase the developer's workload. Using BEA WebLogic, it is no longer necessary to take that last step of removing debug lines from the application source code. The logging mechanism provided allows for easy configuration of logs. This saves you time and your client money.

CHAPTER 17

Best Practices

Now that you are at the point of beginning development on a portal project, it is important for you to know some best practices of the development process. The knowledge gained in this book is enough to build the simplest to the most advanced portals. However, there are rules and guides that will aid you in this process. None of the topics we discuss in this chapter are necessary. However, it is globally suggested that these best practices be given consideration.

Design Best Practices

The design process of any application is the most crucial. The design of an application can dictate its success or failure. If you have worked on projects with only a few developers, you may not realize how important this step is. Some shortcuts may have been taken and their implications not realized. However, after you've worked on projects with 40+ developers and a dozen managers, you will find the need for a proper design process becomes vividly apparent. The design process can weed out a lot of mistakes prior to writing one line of code. On large projects, that one mistake could affect each developer and waste plenty of man-hours and the client's money. The following best practices should be considered prior to starting any project.

Design Patterns

Design patterns have been discussed in part throughout this book. The use of design patterns will help develop an application that has a greater chance of success. Design patterns are reusable, well-proven solutions for object-oriented application design. Every developer has more than likely used a design pattern or two without even knowing it. Design patterns are a simple concept—they merely catalog common interactions and procedures that developers have frequently found useful. Turning away from design patterns means turning away from the insight of experienced developers.

UML Design

Unified Modeling Language (UML), a graphical language for visualizing software components, has become a standard for building object-oriented software. Classes, components, workflow, and use cases are just some of the elements that can be defined by UML as well as the relationship of these elements to each other. UML is a great organizational tool that can be used by software engineers to build maintainable models that cover the full software development life cycle.

Portlet Best Practices

There are a few considerations involving portlet development. The ones we cover in this section pertain directly to the BEA WebLogic Portal. The rules presented later in the section "JSP Best Practices" also apply to portlets.

HTML Tag Usage

Usually when creating an HTML page or JSP, the first tag would be the <HTML> tag, and then the <HEAD> and </HEAD> tags followed by the <BODY> tag. These basic beginning tags and their associated ending tags are not used within a portlet JSP. It is important to remember that all of the JSPs within the BEA WebLogic Portal are included in other JSPs. With this in mind, you can see that the HTML header and footer tags exist within the base JSP, portal.jsp. For that reason, these tags are not included in portlets. Inclusion would result in the HTML that is returned to the browser containing multiple heading and footing tags, and the browser would potentially have problems displaying the page.

Use the Skins

Another best practice in portlet development is to never include fonts, colors, or any other style element hard-coded in the portlet. Style elements should be inherited from the selected portal skin. Otherwise, the usefulness of the portal skins is diminished. All styles are defined in a skin since it consolidates style information in one place. This way, one style change can affect the entire portal, rather than your having to modify each JSP.

Use the Tags

You should familiarize yourself with the available tag libraries contained within the BEA WebLogic Portal. The portal product ships with tag libraries such as User Management, Content Management, Personalization, Webflow/Pipeline as well as Portal and Portlet utility tags. These tags will greatly enhance the portal and aid in the development process.

JSP Best Practices

This section describes the coding methodologies to be followed in JSP development. The flexibility of embedding Java in HTML pages is helpful for creating Web applications quickly. However, this flexibility can be abused, resulting in complex applications that are extremely difficult to maintain.

Watch the Java

It is necessary to be wary of the number of Java scriptlets within any given JSP. The more Java that is embedded into the HTML, the more complex it becomes. Readability is severely lessened with this approach. Also, reusability is completely halted.

Instead of embedding in the JSP every line of logic necessary for performing the task at hand, separate the logic into custom tag libraries and/or JavaBeans. These concepts are handled in the next two sections.

Use Custom Tags

Presentation logic can be separated from the JSP and placed into custom tag libraries. This increases modularity through separation of HTML and Java. Also, this greatly enhances reusability. The same presentation logic can either be placed as a scriptlet in each and every JSP, or a Java developer can create a custom tag for this functionality and lighten the load of the JSP developer.

Use JavaBeans

JavaBeans can be used to separate clumsy business logic from the JSP. The concept behind this closely matches the reasoning behind using custom tags—modularity and reuse. Also, keeping the MVC approach in mind, the presentation layer is no place for business logic in the first place. As JavaBeans, the business logic can easily be reused across multiple JSPs, functionality that will likely be needed, and also by other portions of the application.

Including the Proper Include

As covered in Chapter 3 of this book, there are two methodologies for including content within a page:

- *Include directive:* `<%@ include file="some.jsp"%>`

- *Include action:* `<jsp: include page="some.jsp"/>`

There is a big difference in these two approaches. When using the directive, the file is included during the translation phase, whereas when using the action the file is included during the request phase. Since the directive includes the page at translation time, there is no impact on the performance of the JSP. Unfortunately, using the directive does have its downside. As the inclusion is evaluated at compile time, the file parameter of the tag may not be an expression.

Always Use the Proper Scope

Many times developers use session scope because it is easier or they are just plain lazy, rather than actually deciding on and using a scope that is accurate for the data at hand. When using the useBean tag, a bean can be specified as being anywhere between page and application scope. When data is only necessary for the current request, and you specify that the bean has session scope, this object resides in memory unnecessarily past its required scope. This imposes overhead on memory as well as garbage collection. Always use the exact scope necessary for the object to ensure performance is at its peak.

Disable JSP Reloading

In the BEA WebLogic Portal, as well as in many other application servers, it is possible to allow JSPs to automatically be reloaded. This is a great feature during development, since it means you don't need to restart the server after modifying a JSP. However, in a production system, when there are infrequent changes, this functionality is unnecessary and costly to performance.

In the BEA WebLogic Portal, this feature can be accessed via the server console application by a property within the JSP descriptor. To access this value, follow these steps:

1. Open the BEA WebLogic Console.

2. Navigate to the Web application in question.

3. Edit the application deployment descriptor.

4. Choose JSP Descriptor.

5. Modify the Page Check Seconds property, as shown in Figure 17-1.

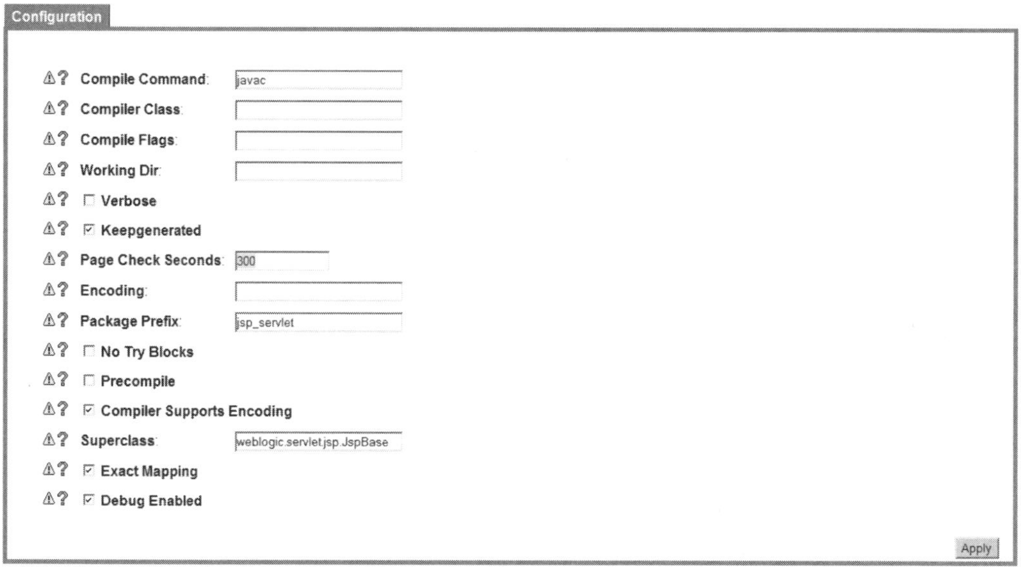

Figure 17-1. The JSP descriptor

Servlet Best Practices

When it comes to developing servlets, there are several items that can greatly increase their performance. Consider some of the following best practices when developing servlets.

Use init() for Initialization

Often, for some reason developers neglect to use the init() method of servlets. As discussed earlier in this book, the servlet's init() method is called once for the lifetime of the application. This makes the init() method a great place to cache values. This technique is displayed in the following code example:

```java
private static String header;
private static String footer;

public void init(ServletConfig config) throws ServletException {
    String email = config.getInitParameter("EMAIL");
    StringBuffer sbHeader = new StringBuffer(100);
    sbHeader.append("Welcome to this site!");
    sbHeader.append("<br>");
    sbHeader.append("Email us at: <a href=\"mailto:");
    sbHeader.append(email);
    sbHeader.append("\">");
    sbHeader.append(email);
    sbHeader.append("</a>");
    sbHeader.append("<br>");

    StringBuffer sbFooter = new StringBuffer(32);
    sbFooter.append("<br>");
    sbFooter.append("Copyright 2003");

    header = sbHeader.toString();
    footer = sbFooter.toString();
}

public void service(HttpServletRequest request, HttpServletResponse response)
                            throws ServletException, IOException {
    response.setContentType("text/html");
    ServletOutputStream out = response.getOutputStream();
    out.println(header);
    out.println("Some Dynamic Content");
    out.println(footer);
}
```

NOTE *Instead of building the content for each request in the service method, it has been built ahead of time in the init() method and cached for the lifetime of the application. The service method need only write out the cached values and add any dynamic content necessary.*

Writing It Out Right

You can use either the PrintWriter object or the ServletOutputStream object to send content to the client. However, some consideration should be taken when choosing which will be used. The PrintWriter object is meant to be used with character data and internally encodes the characters to bytes. When writing binary data to the client, you should use ServletOutputStream directly. This saves the extra conversion step and increases performance.

Don't Forget to Flush

When writing huge amounts of data involving content as well as images, the user has to wait until the ServletOutputStream or PrintWriter flushes the data. Depending on the amount of data and the processing time spent on assembling the content, the user may have to wait for a seemingly excruciating amount of time. To avoid users viewing the big white screen and considering leaving the site, it may be a good idea to flush periodically while writing the content. Using the example from the prior section (although it wouldn't be necessary for such a small amount of content), we demonstrate partial flushing in the following code:

```
public void service(HttpServletRequest request, HttpServletResponse response)
                    throws ServletException, IOException {
    response.setContentType("text/html");
    ServletOutputStream out = response.getOutputStream();
    out.println(header);
    out.flush();
    out.println("Some Dynamic Content");
    out.flush();
    out.println(footer);
    out.flush();
}
```

Be Thread-Safe

By design servlets are thread-safe. However, developers can change this feature of servlets by improper use of class variables. To have a servlet retain its thread-safety, you should declare all member variables as static. If it is not possible to have no nonstatic class variables, then the servlet must implement the SingleThreadModel interface. This interface guarantees thread-safety since the servlet is no longer multithreaded.

EJB Best Practices

EJBs were covered in detail in Chapter 10. This section discusses some methods for improving performance as well as general programming methodologies concerning EJBs.

Reduce Method Calls

Calling methods on remote objects is a time-consuming process. Often developers like to program methods in such a way that fine-grained data is retrieved and set. The following code example demonstrates setting fine-grained data on a remote object:

```
remote.setFirstName("David");
remote.setLastName("Hritz");
remote.setEmail("dhritz@mail.com");
```

In this example, three separate network calls are made to the remote object. When using a coarse-grained approach, the network calls are lessened, thus improving performance. The following example demonstrates the coarse-grained approach:

```
PersonBean bean = new PersonBean();
bean.setFirstName("David");
bean.setLastName("Hritz");
bean.setEmail("dhritz@mail.com");
remote.setPerson(bean);
```

Set Transaction Age

Some EJBs may declare transactional elements. It is possible that some of these transactions are very large and expensive. You may want to specify a transaction time-out in cases like this to ensure that a transaction only occupies a set time limit. This setting can be added to BEA WebLogic's weblogic-ejb-jar.xml file. The following sample XML shows the nodes used in setting this limit:

```
<transaction-descriptor>
        <trans-timeout-seconds>180</trans-timeout-seconds>
</transaction-descriptor>
```

Speeding Up Compilation

During EJB compilation and testing, you may notice that the compilation process of the EJB is slow. Luckily, compilation can be enhanced depending on the chosen compiler. By default, EJB compilation uses javac. While this is a good choice for most applications, you may find this to be too slow. In this case, within the BEA WebLogic Console, a different compiler such as Symantic's sj or the open source compiler Jikes, can be specified.

To specify a compiler, follow these steps:

1. Log on to the BEA WebLogic Console.

2. Choose the appropriate portal domain.

3. Choose the EJB in question.

4. Select the EJBC options tab.

5. Modify the Java Compiler property, as shown in Figure 17-2.

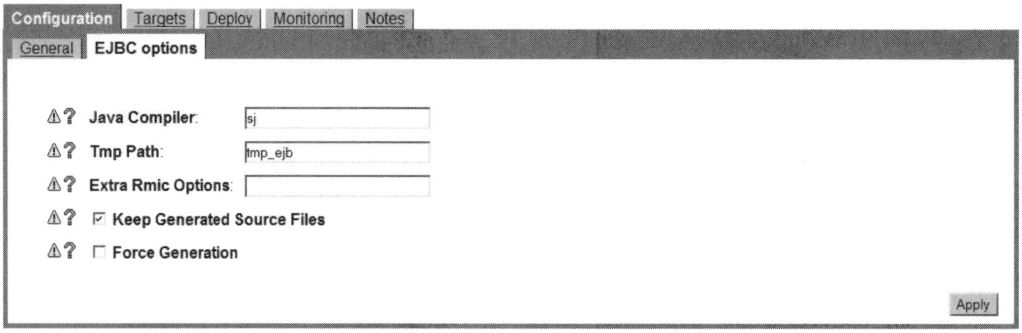

Figure 17-2. EJBC options tab

Java Programming Best Practices

Finally, we explain several general Java best practices that you can use in development, no matter what type of class you are writing.

String Concatenation

It used to be said that developers should never use the "+" operator when concatenating String types—the StringBuffer was recommended instead. However, this statement is not necessarily true. Using the "+" operator or StringBuffer depends on whether the value of the String is known at compile time. If the value is known, then it is safe to use the "+" operator and even recommended. For instance, look at the following code example:

```
String result = "This " + "is " + "a test. ";
```

In the previous code listing, at compile time the value of the Strings to be concatenated are known. Therefore, after compilation, the result turns into this:

```
String result = "This is a test. ";
```

Since the object is resolved at compile time, rather than runtime, like StringBuffer, this methodology is more efficient.

However, consider the next code example:

```
String result = "Some String";
for (int i = 0; i < 100; i++) {
    result += "another String";
}
```

In this case, the String is resolved at runtime and use of the "+" operator is a bad choice. Although StringBuffer is also resolved at runtime, it is able to perform this operation in a much more timely manner. The next code listing demonstrates the use of a StringBuffer instead:

```
StringBuffer result = new StringBuffer("Some String");
for (int i = 0; i < 100; i++) {
    result.append("another String");
}
```

Initialize Objects Properly

Many objects allow you to specify an initial size of an object within the constructor; ArrayList and StringBuffer are good examples. The size specified sets the initial size of the internal data array. For instance, in the case of StringBuffer, if an initial size is not specified, the internal array is 16 characters long. While appending data, if the number of appended characters grows larger than the current size of the internal array, a new array is created internally having twice the size of the current array plus two. Initially the StringBuffer has a 16-character array; after the first increment, the array would be 34 characters long. This sounds great; however, with each increment the StringBuffer must make a costly array copy. For this reason, wherever possible, you should set the initial size of a StringBuffer. This goes for all other objects that give you the ability to set an initial size.

Tighten the Loop

We describe several considerations for loops in this section. Looping leaves a lot of openings for performance issues. You probably already know some of these, but a little iteration won't hurt.

The first issue to consider is using a loop to copy array values. It is common practice to do something like what follows:

```
String[] array1 = {"One", "Two", "Three"};
String[] array2 = new String[3];

for (int i = 0; i < array1.length; i++) {
    array2[i] = array1[i];
}
```

This code sample is common code that is used when copying values from one array to another. However, this code is inefficient and also unnecessary since there is a method for this included in Java. This method is System.arraycopy(), and its use is illustrated in the following code. When copying values between arrays, you should use this method.

```
String[] array1 = {"One", "Two", "Three"};
String[] array2 = new String[3];
    System.arraycopy(array1, 0, array2, 0, array1.length);
```

Another best practice is to avoid any unneccessary instantiation, method calls, or anything else that can be accomplished outside of the loop. At first glance, this may appear as only a slight performance issue, until the number of iterations is considered. Method calls and object instantiation is time consuming, and precious performance can be saved if these actions aren't performed for every single iteration. The following code example shows looping through a result set with a String object being instantiated for every iteration:

```
while (rs.next()) {
    String s = rs.getString("NAME");
    System.out.println(s);
}
```

This loop, although maybe not a major concern, is a performance leak nonetheless. This loop should simply avoid the String instantiation, as follows:

```
while (rs.next()) {
    System.out.println(rs.getString("NAME"));
}
```

Object Objections

Objects are the basis of a Java application and thus a good topic for best practices. This section describes a few methodologies to use and keep in mind when developing objects.

Every developer should be aware of how Java's garbage collection process works. In short, the JVM decides when garbage collection will occur. All you can do is recommend that it occur; whether the JVM acknowledges that recommendation is another story. For this reason, it is necessary that you set object values to null when they are no longer needed. This makes the object eligible for garbage collection.

Use the Proper Scope

Using the proper scope also applies to Java variables. As you should know, in Java, variables can be either local or member variables. The difference is the scope of the variable. Local variables, of course, are only visible locally to a method or branch, while member variables are visible throughout the class. These member, or class, variables should only be used when absolutely necessary. Accessing local variables is quicker than accessing class variables. This also ensures that only the necessary objects are persisted in memory.

Prefer ArrayList

The difference between ArrayList and Vector is a fine line. Both objects appear to be very similar. However, internally there is a great difference. The methods of the Vector object are thread-safe, while those of ArrayList are not. Therefore, Vector should only be used when thread-safety must be guaranteed. Otherwise, the synchronization of the methods produces an unnecessary performance leak.

Once again, when using either ArrayList or Vector, the initial size should be set. This saves valuable array copy time.

Prefer HashMap

Like ArrayList and Vector, HashMap and Hashtable are also very similar objects with the same difference. In this case, Hashtable is the object with synchronized methods, whereas HashMap is not. For this reason, HashMap should be used in all instances unless thread-safety is required.

While using these objects, the initial size can be set within the constructor to improve performance. While with list objects the size refers to the internal array size, in Map objects this initial size is the initial number of buckets the hash table contains. A load factor may also be set for most of the Map objects. The load factor is the maximum capacity of a bucket. Once reaching the load factor, the Map object automatically increases its size by roughly double.

Read What Is Available

When reading input streams and writing to output streams, a lot of developers like to use loops that read/write byte by byte. The following code example shows such a loop. Many other variations of this loop exist, each reading or writing byte by byte.

```
FileInputStream fis = new FileInputStream("C:\\inFile.txt");
FileOutputStream fos = new FileOutputStream("C:\\outFile.txt");
while(true) {
    int b = fis.read();
    if (b == -1) {
        break;
    }
    fos.write(b);
}
fis.close();
fos.close();
```

This is a very time-consuming process that can be avoided by using an array. Both input stream objects and output stream objects give the ability to read/write an array of bytes at a time. The following example enhances the performance of the preceding process:

```
FileInputStream fis = new FileInputStream("C:\\inFile.txt");
FileOutputStream fos = new FileOutputStream("C:\\outFile.txt");
byte[] b = new byte[fis.available()];
fis.read(b);
fos.write(b);
fis.close();
fos.close();
```

Only Catch Exceptions

Try/Catch blocks should not be used for anything other than catching exceptions. Some developers have utilized these exception blocks to control the flow of their programs. This technique is frowned upon and is generally slower than the proper way. The following example demonstrates flow control handled by exception processing:

```
String[] array = {"One", "Two", "Three", "Four"};
int i = 0;
try {
    while(true) {
        System.out.println(array[i]);
        i++;
    }
}
catch (ArrayIndexOutOfBoundsException e) {
//Do Nothing
}
```

This is clearly not a good programming technique. In instances like this, the following code example is clearly the better methodology:

```
String[] array = {"One", "Two", "Three", "Four"};
for (int i = 0; i < array.length; i++) {
    System.out.println(array[i]);
}
```

Of course, there are many tricks of the trade in Java, and technically speaking, the preceding code example is not the most efficient. By comparing the termination condition to zero rather than a variable, greater performance can be achieved. The next example performs slightly better than the preceding one:

```
String[] array = {"Four", "Three", "Two", "One"};
for (int i = array.length - 1; i >= 0 ; i-) {
    System.out.println(array[i]);
}
```

Summary

The necessity for learning and applying best practices is overlooked too often in our industry. With any best practice, the concept is simple. All you need is knowledge of the language and an understanding of what each of your actions will ultimately produce. What is difficult is the continued use of these concepts on a daily basis. Many times we want to sink back into our old habits, due to the extra bit of time it takes to do something right. To quote John Zukowski, noted Java author and developer, "Laziness is not an excuse for poor coding."

Index

About Apress

Apress, located in Berkeley, CA, is a fast-growing, innovative publishing company devoted to meeting the needs of existing and potential programming professionals. Simply put, the "A" in Apress stands for *The Author's Press*™. Apress' unique approach to publishing grew out of conversations between its founders, Gary Cornell and Dan Appleman, authors of numerous best-selling, highly regarded books for programming professionals. In 1998 they set out to create a publishing company that emphasized quality above all else. Gary and Dan's vision has resulted in the publication of over 70 titles by leading software professionals, all of which have *The Expert's Voice*™.

Do You Have What It Takes to Write for Apress?

Apress is rapidly expanding its publishing program. If you can write and you refuse to compromise on the quality of your work, if you believe in doing more than rehashing existing documentation, and if you're looking for opportunities and rewards that go far beyond those offered by traditional publishing houses, we want to hear from you!

Consider these innovations that we offer all of our authors:

- **Top royalties with *no* hidden switch statements**
  Authors typically receive only half of their normal royalty rate on foreign sales. In contrast, Apress' royalty rate remains the same for both foreign and domestic sales.

- **Sharing the wealth**
  Most publishers keep authors on the same pay scale even after costs have been met. At Apress author royalties dramatically increase the more books are sold.

- **Serious treatment of the technical review process**
  Each Apress book is reviewed by a technical expert(s) whose remuneration depends in part on the success of the book since he or she too receives royalties.

Moreover, through a partnership with Springer-Verlag, New York, Inc., one of the world's major publishing houses, Apress has significant venture capital and distribution power behind it. Thus, we have the resources to produce the highest quality books *and* market them aggressively.

If you fit the model of the Apress author who can write a book that provides *What The Professional Needs To Know*™, then please contact us for more information:

editorial@apress.com